TASMANIA'S CONVICTS

Sing! for the hour is come!
Sing! for our happy home,
Our land, is free!
Broken Tasmania's chain;
Wash'd out the hated stain;
Ended the strife and pain!
Blest Jubilee!

Anthem sung in Launceston to celebrate
the end of convict transportation, 1853

TASMANIA'S CONVICTS

HOW FELONS BUILT A FREE SOCIETY

ALISON ALEXANDER

ALLEN&UNWIN

First published in 2010

Allen & Unwin
83 Alexander Street
Crows Nest NSW 2065
Australia
Phone: (61 2) 8425 0100
Fax: (61 2) 9906 2218
Email: info@allenandunwin.com
Web: www.allenandunwin.com

Cataloguing-in-Publication details are available
from the National Library of Australia
www.librariesaustralia.nla.gov.au

ISBN 978 1 74237 205 1

Map by Guy Holt
Set in 11.5/15 pt Adobe Garamond by Post Pre-press Group, Australia
Printed in Australia by McPherson's Printing Group

10 9 8 7 6 5 4 3 2 1

To my children
Jude, Cathy and Ted

CONTENTS

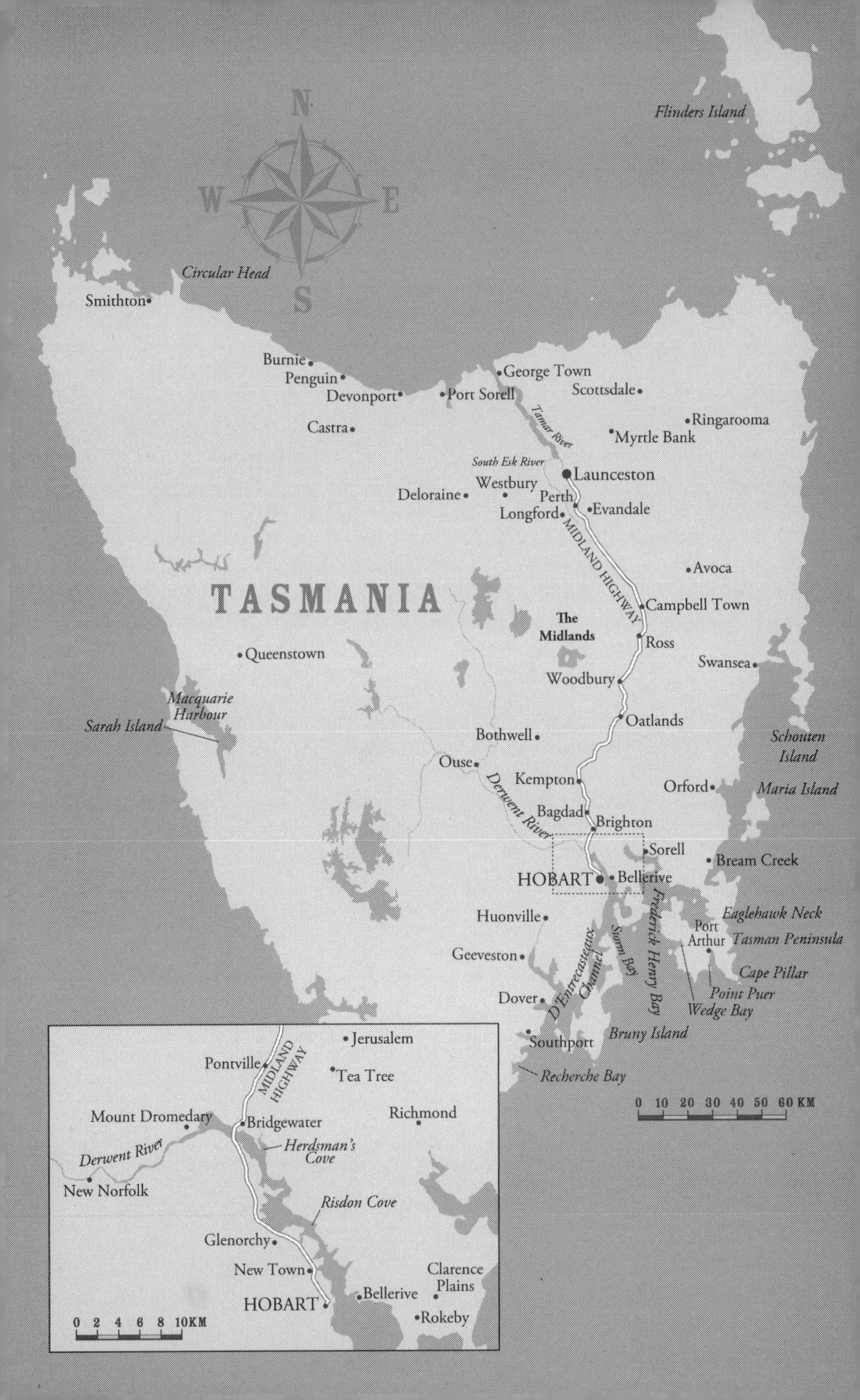
N
W
E
S
Flinders Island
Circular Head
Smithton
Burnie
Penguin
Devonport
Port Sorell
George Town
Scottsdale
Castra
Tamar River
Ringarooma
Myrtle Bank
South Esk River
Launceston
Westbury
Deloraine
Perth
Evandale
Longford
MIDLAND HIGHWAY
Avoca
TASMANIA
Campbell Town
The Midlands
Ross
Queenstown
Swansea
Woodbury
Macquarie Harbour
Sarah Island
Oatlands
Bothwell
Schouten Island
Ouse
Derwent River
Kempton
Orford
Maria Island
Bagdad
Brighton
Sorell
Bream Creek
HOBART
Bellerive
Frederick Henry Bay
Huonville
Eaglehawk Neck
Port Arthur
Tasman Peninsula
Geeveston
D'Entrecasteaux Channel
Storm Bay
Cape Pillar
Dover
Point Puer
Wedge Bay
Bruny Island
Southport
Recherche Bay
0 10 20 30 40 50 60 KM
Jerusalem
MIDLAND HIGHWAY
Pontville
Tea Tree
Mount Dromedary
Bridgewater
Richmond
Derwent River
Herdsman's Cove
New Norfolk
Risdon Cove
Glenorchy
New Town
Clarence Plains
Bellerive
HOBART
Rokeby
0 2 4 6 8 10KM

INTRODUCTION

onvicts: hardened criminals, petty offenders, shiftless tramps, ordinary people? Ancestors to ignore, to defend, to hide, to boast about? A shameful past, or an interesting and novel one? A history to deny, or sensationalise? One that had no effect on the present, or left an indelible stain?

Contrary to what was thought during the transportation period, most of the 162,000 convicts the British sent to Australia were ordinary members of the working class. They were not serious criminals: these were executed. Convicts were mostly petty thieves, at a time when large sections of the working class accepted theft as a reasonable way to eke out scanty earnings in tough times. The bulk of convicts went to New South Wales (80,000 from 1788 to 1840) and Van Diemen's Land (72,500 from 1803 to 1853). Until 1840 they were organised under the assignment system. Most were allocated as labourers to free settlers or the government, so they were living in the general community, doing much the same jobs as they had in Britain. Though some suffered harsh conditions, and imprisonment always means a loss of freedom, for most it was a relatively benign experience which did not alienate them from the rest of society. If they kept out of trouble, once they gained their freedom most could slot back into the community as ordinary citizens.

The tougher probation system was in force from 1840 until transportation to Van Diemen's Land ceased in 1853, and for Western Australia's 9500 convicts from 1850 to 1868. It aimed to train and reform convicts, who lived in large gangs where in fact there was little training or reformation; convicts mostly laboured on the roads for a probationary period, then gained a pass which meant they could work for wages in the community. On the whole they were not alienated either. The convict system did not produce many traumatised ex-prisoners unable to function in the wider society: if it had, Tasmania would not have been able to transform itself so quickly from a convict colony to an ordered, peaceful society.

A relatively small proportion, about 20 per cent, did suffer. They were the ones who committed more offences, and were whipped, sentenced to hard labour in chains and finally, if the offence was bad enough, about 10 per cent were sent to one of the brutal secondary penal stations, Macquarie Harbour or Port Arthur. There they suffered the lash, the ball and chain, the horrors so vividly described later by tourist operators and sensationalised by novelists and filmmakers. Women were not treated so harshly, but their secondary punishment was bad enough, usually hard labour at the washtub in the bleak female factories, which also housed women convicts awaiting assignment, and those who were ill or pregnant.

Once they were freed, half or more of Tasmania's convicts chose to leave the island, most going to Victoria's golden prosperity. Perhaps Victoria contained more Tasmanian ex-convicts than Tasmania itself did. Most ex-convicts settled down to lives of more or less respectable hard work, with many raising families and taking part in community activities. However, their presence gave the convict colonies a dreadful stigma. This came from Britain. Even before the first convict ship sailed, Britain thought its convict colonies were terrible places: a convict colony *had* to be, just because it was a convict colony. Reports from the colonies only strengthened the reputation of the 'hated stain'.

Ex-convicts realised this, and most wanted to escape the stigma and forget their convict past. Most were successful. The community helped them: no one wanted to live in a society where much of the population was known to be criminal, and so those ex-convicts prepared to go along with society's norms—the vast majority—were allowed to pretend they were free immigrants. The only people pointed out as ex-convicts were a marginal group of criminals, tramps and casual labourers—'old lags', mostly single men who had little to lose and no children to inherit the stigma; about 15 per cent of the total. If they were identified as ex-convicts, all others could escape the label. They did so amazingly successfully: by the 1920s many Tasmanians were unaware of their convict heritage. The myth ran that convicts had died single or left the island, and the convict past had no effect on the present.

Apart from the marginal 'old lags', the community united in denying the convict past. The new colonial government's first act, in 1856, was to change the island's name from Van Diemen's Land to Tasmania, and Tasmanians mentioned convicts as little as possible. They rewrote their history, using a special code to refer to anything convict, so outsiders would not realise convicts were still present. To show their respectability, they were well behaved, intensely loyal to Britain, and also patriotic Tasmanians: they were proud of their home, they had nothing to hide! Ex-convicts and their descendants permeated all levels of society, becoming premiers, professors and war heroes, as well as countless farmers, labourers, tradespeople, teachers, nurses, mothers and fathers, indistinguishable from citizens without convict origins.

At the same time, parallel with this denial ran a strong vein of sympathy for convicts. Outsiders had to be hoodwinked, but Tasmanians themselves knew that convicts were ordinary people, not something to be ashamed of. Contrary to the official view of convicts as hardened criminals, the general Tasmanian population believed they had been sent out for trivial offences; people trying to get by in hard times. There was huge interest in books, plays and films about convicts, with audiences definitely on the convicts' side.

After the Second World War, the convict stigma began to fade. Australia was prosperous, and could ignore British opinion—which was forgetting about convicts in any case. The attitudes of the 1960s and 1970s finally broke down the stigma: a rebellious time, anti-government, anti-establishment, when working-class rebellious convicts were seen as heroes. As people began to research their family trees, it became clear that finding a convict was nothing to be embarrassed about. Because of the scarcity of women in convict Van Diemen's Land, only the more prosperous men were likely to attract a marriage partner and have children, and most descendants discovered their convict ancestors were established citizens—tradesmen or farmers, for example—sent out for petty theft, · with any further offences minor or even amusing, such as missing Divine

Service and being found in a pub. Their family histories show convicts as normal citizens, not just during their sentences, but also afterwards, living in the community. The image of convicts has changed accordingly, with academics too broadening their research. More and more convict descendants are coming out of the closet: the prime minister, Kevin Rudd, has convict ancestors. When this was revealed, there was little reaction; it is seen as normal now. As more people researched their family histories, more found the convict ancestors so successfully hidden by past generations. In the early 21st century, a poll found that about 36 per cent of Tasmanians know they have convict ancestors—though, as has been the case since the first Europeans arrived in Van Diemen's Land in 1803, probably about three-quarters of all Tasmanians are descended from convicts.

What effect has this had on the island? Has this convict past left a 'hated stain' on Tasmania? Opinions vary—and there is that other dark stain, the treatment of Aborigines, a viable community of perhaps 5000 people at the time of British settlement in 1803, their way of life destroyed 30 years later. In 1997 I watched a play, *Transylvania* by Richard Bladel, which claimed that the spiritual wounds inflicted by convictism had made Tasmania into 'Australia's psychological sink', with 'a devastating effect on our present'. Growing up in Tasmania, I had seen no evidence of this, and I began to wonder what the effect of convictism had been. Years of occasional research, then three years of concentrated reading, interviewing, lecturing, discussing and writing, resulted in this book.

The convict stain question is very much alive. In 2007 I gave the after-dinner speech at the annual gathering of the Tasmanian Order of Australia Association. It would be hard to find a group of citizens more respected and respectable, all acclaimed for their contribution to the general good. The hundred or so diners were growing mellow by the time they settled back to listen to me talking about convict heritage. I mentioned that half of Tasmania's convicts left the island, most going to Victoria. A spontaneous cheer rang round the room. Someone asked how many people were descended from convicts, and a forest of hands rose, nearly half of those present. Proud of this descent, or at least happy to admit it in respectable company—but glad so many went to Victoria: the question of what Tasmania's convict heritage means is still alive, still contradictory, still causing debate.

1

BIRTH OF A CONVICT COLONY

Embezzlement was Andrew Whitehead's downfall. Originally from Scotland, in 1801 Andrew was working in London as a clerk, and did not include in his master's records a bill for £40—a large sum, about a year's wages. The theft was discovered and Andrew fled, but just as he was about to leave London on a ship bound for New York, he was arrested. Sentenced to transportation for fourteen years, he was sent to join a new expedition to Australia.

Britain had been transporting convicts to Botany Bay since 1788, but had recently discovered that Bass Strait separated the island of Van Diemen's Land from mainland Australia. Afraid that its rival France would seize this strategic area, the British government commissioned Lieutenant-Colonel David Collins to form a settlement there. In April 1803 he left England with two ships carrying 308 male convicts, guards, and a handful of administrators and free settlers. A few convicts and settlers were allowed to bring their wives and children, and among them was the woman Andrew brought with him, who was known as Mrs Mary Whitehead.

Everyone embarked on the ships, the *Ocean* and the *Calcutta*, and at once the moral tone was set for the next twenty years. David Collins took Hannah Power, wife of convict Matthew Power, into his bed; Mary Whitehead had an affair with the commissary; and even the chaplain was said to have a 'thoroughly bad woman' in his cabin. This 'gross immorality in high places' shocked one of the few upright people on board, convict's son John Pascoe Fawkner, who was even more appalled when the whole expedition was held up for two days after Hannah remembered she had left her pet dog behind.

After a six-month voyage rife with storms and dysentery, the expedition landed at Port Phillip at what became the Mornington Peninsula in Victoria. By now Hannah Power and Mary Whitehead were prominent members of the little community, and were godmothers to the first baby born there, with Governor Collins a godfather. Meanwhile, Matthew Power and Andrew Whitehead were members of the Night Watch. Presumably they had little else to do at night.

Collins decided that Port Phillip, with its poor soil and lack of water, was no place for a settlement. In Febuary 1804 he moved the expedition to southern Van Diemen's Land, where the site of Hobart on the River Derwent had an excellent port and plentiful water, not to mention a ramshackle settlement across the river at Risdon Cove. To forestall the French menace, in September 1803 Governor King in Sydney had sent down a small expedition under Lieutenant John Bowen, a gormless young officer who proved helpless in the face of idle convicts and unwilling soldiers. It was all too much and he deserted them, going to Sydney to announce patriotically that he wanted to fight the French in Europe. Collins was horrified to find the little Risdon Cove settlement existing on reduced rations, achieving nothing. He had as little to do with it as he could, and it was soon broken up. He also had as little to do as possible with the original inhabitants, the Aborigines, who themselves tended to avoid the newcomers.

In Hobart there was much to do, to replicate British life on the other side of the world: felling timber, building houses, starting farms to grow food. Convicts were the labour force, working for the government or for the few free settlers who had accompanied the expedition. There were no barracks and convicts had to find their own accommodation, which meant they had to be allowed to earn money, so those employed by the government finished early in the day so they could work on their own account. Rather than criminals set apart, they were part of the general community, workers and servants, in the same way that the working class was in Britain. It was almost as if exile to Van Diemen's Land was punishment enough.

Capable convicts were given responsibilities—there was no one else—and Andrew Whitehead, literate, intelligent and competent, received his freedom in 1807, only six years into his fourteen-year sentence, and was put in charge of the government farm a little way up the river at New Town. He had behaved well, only getting into trouble once—for ill conduct to the commissary, not surprisingly. By this time he was single again. Collins had discovered that Andrew and Mary were not married, and sent Mary to Sydney. This was either breathtaking hypocrisy on Collins' part—he was still enjoying Hannah Power's company—or possibly an arrangement cooked up between him and Andrew, who could well have been tired of his laughable position with his faithless 'wife'.

At New Town, Andrew was a neighbour of the Hayes family—father, mother, daughter and two little granddaughters on their farm. Like many people in early Van Diemen's Land, their respectable appearance hid a chequered past. At their London pub Henry and Mary Hayes had received stolen jewellery, but they were inept criminals. In the bar a servant saw Mary holding a diamond necklace, and her daughter Martha with a pearl necklace and diamond drops. 'Lord, ma'am, what a handsome diamond necklace that is!' the servant exclaimed. Mary failed to buy the girl's silence, and she reported the theft to the police. Mary was sentenced to transportation, and in 1803 sixteen-year-old Martha accompanied her to Sydney. The long voyage through the tropics had a romantic effect on Lieutenant John Bowen and Martha Hayes. When Governor King sent John Bowen to the Derwent, Martha went too.

At the Hayes trial Henry was found not guilty, though it was suggested in court that he was 'as great a sinner as ever lived'. To follow his wife and daughter he volunteered as one of the handful of free settlers who accompanied Collins—which shows what sort of free settlers the government would accept. But they probably took any volunteer; how many people would want to accompany a convict party to a new settlement at the end of the world? Or perhaps they were willing to reunite families (certainly a later policy, on the basis that families were good for the community).

When Henry Hayes arrived with the rest of the Collins expedition at the Derwent, he found—doubtless to his utter amazement—his only daughter, living in the hopeless little settlement at Risdon Cove, seven months' pregnant and with no male partner in sight. However, he soon appeared. When John Bowen had arrived in Sydney, Governor King was furious with him for deserting not only his duty, but his pregnant mistress. He sent him back to the Derwent, and Martha's redoubtable mother with him. They arrived in time for the birth of baby Henrietta, and a second daughter, Charlotte, was the result of John Bowen's return. He set Martha up with land and livestock, but was then recalled to England, and never saw her or the girls again. Martha, still only about twenty, was described as 'the prettiest violet . . . at the Derwent'.

So Andrew Whitehead and Martha Hayes had both moved on from their earlier partners, and in 1811 they married. Andrew, aged 42, was described as an 'elderly man'—which he was, given that the average life expectancy was only about 40. Marriage was a victory for him, for women were in short supply. Far more male convicts than female were transported, particularly at first, and in these early days there were seven men for every woman. Many men could never find a female partner.

It was a strange society, this small population, with only 1460 non-Aborigines in the whole island in 1816. Of the 983 adults, 42 per cent were convicts, and more were ex-convicts. With everyone a recent immigrant, everyone with his or her way to make and a new living to establish, life was precarious; in 1819 a scathing description claimed that there were no regular roads, no industry, little agriculture, and almost all the income came from government spending.[1]

With its overwhelming majority of men, Van Diemen's Land was a tough frontier settlement, whose population enjoyed an enormous amount of drinking, smuggling, adultery, neglected duty, bribery and corruption. Usually in a British community the middle class upheld moral standards. The most respectable person should have been the governor, but of the seven governors in Hobart between 1803 and 1824, all were guilty of at least one (mostly more) of the activities listed above, not to mention incompetence. They were not alone: the surveyor took bribes, the storekeeper forged receipts, the commissary was court-martialled for embezzlement, Edward Lord, the acting governor during 1810, was suspected of smuggling, and so on—far worse than the crimes for which many convicts were transported. Dr Hudspeth, a free immigrant, wrote that theft was so frequent no one took any notice; it was hard to gain information from officials without bribing them; no one's word could be depended on; the clergyman, Knopwood, was a swearer and a drunkard. In a later history, the best the author could say of Van Diemen's Land in this period was that it was 'kindly, but dissolute', while a Quaker missionary was more frank: 'open profligacy and intemperance pervaded all ranks'.[2]

Alexander Laing, a convict, described this life vividly in his memoirs. Once he was chasing a bushranger called Bumpy Jones. His group killed Jones, and then had to cut off his head to prove to the authorities that he was dead. Laing asked a stockkeeper to do the job, offering him a pound of tobacco as payment. 'By Je—s says he I would cut off half a dozen heads for the tobacco.' Laing carried Bumpy Jones' head back to Hobart in a kangaroo-skin bag, and gained part of the reward. Rum was the currency, wrote Laing, and almost everyone 'caught the Derwent fever'—drinking.

For most convicts, conditions were not too hard. They were working in the general community, much as they might have done in Britain; punishments were hard if they ran foul of the law, but only a small percentage did. Many were feisty, showing plenty of what was later termed the 'Vandemonian spirit'. In drunken enthusiasm one man unbuttoned his clothes in front of Government House and turned his 'bare flesh' on it. Unfortunately for him the governor was a good shot, and 'fired at the naked part of the man and actually struck him not mortally but severely'. It was six months before the man could return to work. Another ex-convict sold his wife for a gallon of rum and twenty sheep, even though, the *Hobart Town Gazette* reported, she was in 'no way prepossessing in appearance'. The authorities put both buyer and seller on good behaviour bonds, and presumably the plain wife was forced to return to the husband who had tried to sell her.[3]

Feistiest of all were bushrangers—escaped convicts who took to the bush. They found it hard to support themselves entirely by hunting, and most became thieves, holding up coaches, or descending on settlers' houses and sometimes stealing everything portable inside: food, drink, clothes, guns and ammunition. From 1813 to 1818 the bushranging threat was so severe that some settlers left their farms for fear of them, and many convict workers assisted bushrangers, warning them of the authorities, providing shelter, sharing in the plunder.

Andrew Whitehead was involved in several shady dealings. In 1814 he and another ex-convict, Denis McCarty, planned with a ship's captain to smuggle a huge amount of rum into the colony. Chaplain Robert

Knopwood appears to have been part of the scheme too. The authorities found out and seized the spirits. At once the ship's captain left, taking eight convict absconders with him. The authorities chased him, but he escaped.[4]

Andrew Whitehead and Denis McCarty were sentenced to twelve months' gaol in Sydney, but though McCarty served his time, Whitehead was only put under house arrest. How did he get off so lightly—bribery and corruption? His house arrest sounds pleasant enough, at home with Martha, their baby daughter Mary and the two little Bowen girls. Knopwood often visited, and Andrew did not miss out on the township's main entertainment, horseracing, since the racecourse was on his farm. After one meeting the Whiteheads gave a dinner for a party of gentlemen and ladies, who clearly did not mind that he was technically in disgrace. When Denis McCarty was released from prision in April 1815, the Whiteheads held a celebratory dinner for him.

Clearly, crime and drunkenness were rife, part of everyday life; but so they were in many areas in Britain, and people living in Van Diemen's Land—apart from a few disgruntled newcomers like Dr Hudspeth—tried to describe the colony as an ordinary British community. Government documents depicted an orderly society. The chaplain, Knopwood, kept a diary, which in general describes normal British life, with its church services, social gatherings and so on. No one wanted to admit that the place was anything but a respectable community. People might drink, take bribes, have affairs and so on, but almost all wanted to appear respectable. This gave them, and their children, a place in mainstream society. Only a very few, mostly the disreputable poor, did not try to be included in the mainstream.

There is plenty of evidence that convicts were accepted as ordinary people. Emigrant Samuel Guy opened a shop in New Norfolk, a small settlement 35 kilometres up the Derwent from Hobart. Convicts were in general pickpockets who understood nothing about agriculture, he wrote home, but they were treated well. 'In England there appears something horrid in the idea of Transportation,' he added, but 'believe me, they are far better in circumstances than the poor in England.' Convicts were encouraged, he thought, and 'many of the greatest men in the Colony were formerly convicts'. In his reminiscences, convict's son John Pascoe

Fawkner treated everyone as much the same, convict or not. They all had to establish themselves; they drank, cohabited, stole, shot game, lost crops, married and had children—life was much the same for everyone.[5] In his diary, Robert Knopwood wrote pragmatically of convicts. Most of his 180 mentions of them were factual: they landed from a ship (70 mentions), absconded (38) and were caught (9), and attended church services (13), with other mentions in passing. He saw them as ordinary human beings, not set apart because of their criminality. As a magistrate he examined recaptured absconders, and recorded the conversation as friendly: 'They informd me that on the 2 of May when they were in the wood, they see a large tiger; that the dog they had with them went nearly up to it, and when the tiger see the men which were about 100 yards from it, it went away.' A boatload of prisoners landed: 'A finer set of men never seen.' On 18 March 1825 Knopwood presided at court. 'It being St. Pat.[rick's] the day before not less than 30 prisoners for minor offences and I forgave them as they were Irishmen taken a little too much the day before.'[6]

Many of the people Knopwood named in his diary were ex-convicts, but he did not identify them as such. Instead he described them as farmers, servants, thieves, gardeners, bushrangers or whatever: there was no assumption that a convict would be a thief, and no surprise when one was well behaved. Some convicts were robbers, others were fine men—that was the way it was. Knopwood was friendly not only with the Whiteheads but with other ex-convicts, often dining with them, calling them 'Mr', a sign of social acceptance.

Another opportunity to ignore the convict stigma occurred when in 1807–08, after fifteen years of existence, Sydney's outstation settlement at Norfolk Island was closed, and some 630 of its inhabitants were moved to Van Diemen's Land. Almost all the adults were ex-convicts, but no one ever mentioned this publicly, and the Norfolk Islanders were treated as if they were free settlers, called 'free persons'.[7]

So were the Whiteheads. They lived on the government farm, which Andrew was granted as his own. When Knopwood drew up a list of ladies and gentlemen in the colony, he included Andrew Whitehead, ex-convict; Martha Whitehead, ex-mistress and daughter of a convict; Henrietta and Charlotte Bowen, illegitimate granddaughters of a convict; and ex-convict Maria Lord and her husband Lieutenant Edward Lord, who had become wealthy through shops and farms.[8] So people in the convict group who had money or connections (being Knopwood's friends) could be accepted as gentry.

This was the period when Jane Austen was writing her novels of gentry life in England. She would never have accepted Martha and Andrew Whitehead, with their criminal background and lack of pedigree, as a lady and gentleman; but Van Diemen's Land was not England. Ex-convicts were accepted for what they made of themselves, their background ignored. Even the governor socialised with them. One evening party consisted of Governor Collins, his daughter by his first convict mistress, his present mistress, her ex-convict husband, another ex-convict and Knopwood himself, the chaplain, all drinking spirits together. Most early governors included ex-convicts among their friends, and would ask them to dine at Government House.[9]

In 1817 life changed for the Whiteheads. The government took over their farm to make a road, compensating them with land at Herdsman's Cove, further up the Derwent. Andrew, now well into his forties, had to start again on virgin soil, but in 1819 he owned two horses, 73 cattle and 740 sheep, and employed six workers, five of them convicts. However, tragedy struck: a son lived only two weeks, and soon Martha lost another child when Henrietta, aged nineteen, died suddenly. 'Thus died one of the finest girls on the earth,' Knopwood wrote sadly, and his diary makes it clear that the two Bowen girls were completely accepted as ladies by 'all the first people of distinction' (such as they were). Their convict connections were never mentioned.

The habit of never mentioning convict connections (at least publicly) began early. So did avoiding the word 'convict', 'which is seen by them as opprobrious and highly offensive', as a visitor wrote. They preferred to be called 'prisoners' or 'servants of the crown', and the word convict 'is, by all right-minded persons, carefully avoided'. So right-minded persons were those who considered convicts' preferences in the words they used—a civility that showed surprising consideration for criminals' feelings. Once people arrived in Van Diemen's Land, they quickly changed their terminology. On the trip out to Australia Knopwood always used the term 'convicts' in his diary, but once he was settled in Van Diemen's Land he did so only twice in 29 years, writing instead of 'prisoners'.[10]

And this was in his private diary. Presumably it was even more the case in public speech.

But convicts and ex-convicts still had that criminal past, the dark stain, and did not like being reminded of it. Once in 1809 when Governor Collins was away with his mistress, his deputy Edward Lord suspected a convict worker, Mary Granger, of stealing a glass tumbler. Without holding an inquiry, he put her in the stocks. Furious at this injustice, some other convict women went to Edward Lord's wife Maria, an ex-convict herself. One, Martha Hudson, reminded her of this and pleaded with her for Mary Granger's release, but she refused—and Edward Lord was so furious at the mention of his wife's past that, again without any inquiry, he ordered Martha to be stripped to the waist, tied to a cart's tail and flogged down the street, an appalling punishment. Maria Lord's convict background must never be mentioned.

Early convicts were relatively well treated, allowed much freedom while under sentence and when pardoned given small land grants. Life was not easy for them, but it was not particularly easy for anyone. Most of them stayed on the right side of the law and did reasonably well, ranging from getting by to living comfortably. The shortage of women meant not all could establish a family; of those in the colony in 1811, only half had a female partner and a minority of these had children—altogether, only 19 per cent of all the convicts who had arrived with Collins in the *Calcutta* had descendants in the colony. Andrew and Martha Whitehead were among them. They continued to farm at Herdsman's Cove until Andrew died in 1832, aged over sixty. Four years later Martha astonished everyone by marrying the local police clerk. He was 20, and she was 50—and she outlived him. She died in 1871, aged 84, at the home of her daughter Mary. The local newspaper noted that she was the second-last of the early settlers, but said nothing more about her: no convict relations, affairs with a governor or illegitimate daughters. By 1871 Tasmania was thoroughly respectable.

2

CONVICTS IN BRITAIN AND ON THE HIGH SEAS

'Convicts': the word is often used as if all 72,500 convicts transported to Van Diemen's Land between 1803 and 1853 were much the same, but in fact all had their individual stories. Men and women, old and young, clever and dull, rogues and basically honest, feeble and healthy, skilled and unskilled, gloomy and cheerful, plain and attractive, lucky and unlucky, shrewd and naïve, conformist and rebellious—no two were the same, and it is hard to generalise accurately about them.

So much variety makes it difficult to provide a balanced overview. In his *History of Tasmania* (1852) John West commented that everyone held different opinions about convicts. Englishmen rejoiced that sixteen thousand miles of ocean divided them from such wretches; colonial farmers saw them as labourers; the working immigrant saw them as rivals. 'It is nearly impossible for a stranger to estimate the weight of testimony, so prejudiced throughout, and nearly as impossible for a writer, interested in the issue of its discussion, to preserve unclouded judgment required to arrive at truth . . . no uniform description is a true one.'[1]

The one thing convicts had in common was that they were all sentenced in British-administered courts. Rather more than half had seven-year sentences, a quarter life, the rest mostly from ten to fifteen years. 'Life' rarely meant remaining a convict until death; most lifers gained pardons eventually. For example, in 1827 James Ames arrived with a life sentence for receiving stolen goods, but once in Van Diemen's Land he committed only five minor offences such as stealing a leg of pork, and gained his freedom in 1841.

WHY DID BRITAIN SEND CONVICTS TO AUSTRALIA?

Every society has to work out how to cope with its members who commit crimes. Historically there have been six ways of both punishing them and deterring others, which have usually been authority's aims, rather than rehabilitation. Governments can execute criminals; punish them physically by, for example, whipping them; shame them by putting them in the stocks; fine them; imprison them; or exile them—all preferably while paying as little as possible.

Exiling criminals has a long history. Since the days of Ancient Greece, societies have been exiling those they classify as criminals, and some still do. Exile has advantages. Though tough on prisoners, it is more humane than execution. It is cheap, just sending criminals overseas (as long as they do not cost too much once they arrive). Exiles can be forced to work to earn their keep. And the home society is permanently free of them, since they are far away, while authorities hope that the rest of the population see exile as so dreadful they are deterred from crime. If people are not too concerned about criminals' rights, exiling them can seem an attractive option.

Britain started sending criminals to her American colonies in 1615, but this ended in 1775 when America rebelled against British rule. By then transportation was a major part of British criminal law. Punishment had become increasingly harsh, particularly for crimes against property, even if it was only stealing a loaf of bread—property was sacred, and any theft was serious, no matter how small. With America no longer available as a dumping ground, Britain's gaols were overflowing with criminals: what to do? Humanitarian ideals were slowly developing, and though there were a huge number of capital offences, only the most serious criminals like murderers and large-scale thieves were actually executed, and whipping and the stocks were not widely used. Prisons were expensive to build, many criminals could not pay fines: exile seemed the most practical solution.

Britain looked for another site for its convicted criminals, convicts for short. Various places suggested turned out to be too hot, too unhealthy, too barren or unwilling to accept convicts—with one exception. Captain Cook had recently sailed down the east coast of Australia, and reports described it as an excellent place for a colony. In 1788 the First Fleet arrived at Botany Bay and, as described in Chapter 1, in 1803 British settlement reached Van Diemen's Land.

WHY WERE THERE SO MANY CRIMINALS?

Most convicts were transported for theft—and theft, especially petty theft, is understandably endemic in many societies. Theft is better than starvation, and theft on behalf of your family can seem entirely justifiable. And if goods are just lying about . . . All people are by nature thieves, wrote convict John Mortlock, and all children steal until they are trained out of it.[2]

This is especially so when societies are dislocated or when large sections suffer desperate poverty, and both were the case in late eighteenth-century Britain and onwards. The Industrial Revolution had begun; machines were replacing manual labour in manufacturing, and many country labourers were flocking to the expanding cities to earn a living in the new factories. They could not all find work, and in any case wages were miserably low. There was little help for the poor, with few social services. They relied on themselves, and on their families and friends, who were often just as badly off. Churches, which might have encouraged honesty, had little impact on the working class. Theft was an understandable way to avoid starvation, or make a poverty-stricken life marginally more comfortable. Minor theft— even major theft—was accepted among large sections of the working class as a reasonable way to help yourself and your family, in a society where no one else much was going to assist.

Rudimentary policing systems were utterly inadequate to cope with crime; even today many crimes are unsolved, despite modern technology. Figures are of course unobtainable, but it would seem that most criminals—the vast majority?—got away with it. Convicts were those unlucky enough, or foolish enough, to be caught—like the Hayes family, parading their ill-gotten gains in a hotel bar. Their pub provided them with a living, but they were taking advantage of the lack of police surveillance to try to improve their lives through theft. All these factors—poverty, dislocation, ineffective policing—meant theft was rife. So were other crimes, in a society where violence and alcohol were commonplace. Even the inadequate police could arrest some of the perpetrators, and the result was a large number of people sentenced to transportation to Australia.

WHAT WERE CONVICTS' CRIMES?

If theft is used in its broadest sense of taking items which are not yours, or making money dishonestly (for example, by coining or smuggling), overwhelmingly these convicts had committed some form of theft. Analysis of 5048 records from the assignment period, 1803 to 1840 (when convicts were assigned to the government or free settlers as labourers), showed that 91 per cent of convicts were transported to Van Diemen's Land for theft.[3] Convicts stole from their employers, their lodgings, their families, strangers in the street; from houses, shops, warehouses, sheds and barns; they picked pockets, forged bills, made counterfeit money, smuggled goods from abroad, received stolen goods. The most common items stolen were money, watches, animals (especially sheep), and handkerchiefs and other clothes, but items ranged from a musical snuff box to a few copper coins, and plenty of convicts were sent to Van Diemen's Land for stealing the proverbial loaf of bread or pair of stockings. Some theft was premeditated, but much of it was opportunistic—a pair of shoes from a shop, washing hanging out to dry.

Some theft was really small scale. Thomas Morgan was transported for stealing bacon from a house, Elizabeth Allen for a shawl, Isaiah Cook for taking a countryman's dinner, and there are thousands of similar examples. Some were not particularly heart-warming: George Smith stole a handkerchief from a four-year-old child. Examples of major theft are much rarer, but John Buck was transported for embezzling the enormous sum of £1190, and Eliza Bailey for receiving £2000 of stolen money. 'John Dobson took the Money he escaped away to France,' she told the authorities—some convicts dobbed in their mates. In the 1840s the British government tended to transport people with more serious crimes, so there were slightly fewer convicts with seven-year sentences and fewer really petty thieves, but in the colony these convicts behaved in much the same way as earlier ones. Contemporaries noted little difference and, in any case, these were the convicts who so often moved to Victoria.

In comparing the system with today, many convicts would not be charged at all, many more would be cautioned, or the charge would be dismissed. Only a small minority would be sent to gaol, and the percentage with a sentence of seven years or more would be minuscule. It might include John Buck and Eliza Bailey, but few others.

One form of theft which can appear more understandable than most is poaching—poverty-stricken farm labourers taking rabbits or ducks from a wealthy landowner's domain. (Or organised theft, where these animals were taken on a large scale.) Lord Stafford prosecuted John Adcock for stealing three peacocks and Adcock was transported. He had five previous convictions for poaching and one for assault—not good, but unless you are a large-scale landowner yourself it's hard not to feel that wealthy, established Lord Stafford was unduly vindictive. With poaching seen so sympathetically in later times, especially by those who saw it as a form of class rebellion, the myth grew that many convicts were poachers, but only 1 per cent of the men in my analysis of 5048 Van Diemen's Land convict records were transported for poaching, though 4 per cent had a previous conviction for it. Other terms could have covered poaching, but even so the figure is unlikely to reach 10 per cent.

Over half the convicts, 59 per cent from 1840 to 1853, were transported for a second offence: in the eyes of the authorities, they were habitual criminals. Some were. When Edward Jones arrived in Hobart on a fourteen-year sentence for stealing a watch, he told the clerk that he had two previous sentences for theft. He 'might have been in Gaol on other Charges but cannot recollect'; he had earned his living by robbery from the age of nine. 'It was owing to being away from my father and mother & getting into Bad Comp[an]y', he explained; and he was later found guilty of a long list of offences in Van Diemen's Land. But most convicts with previous offences had only one or two, and these were minor. For example, Margaret Armstrong, transported for picking pockets, had previously been convicted of picking pockets and drunkenness.

Most convicts seemed to accept that they were guilty, but a few claimed that they were innocent. 'I did not steal it I received it from the porter,' said Thomas Bonnor, accused of stealing a parcel. 'I am innocent of the charge,' said Thomas Bryan, accused by a woman and her husband of rape and robbery. 'I am innocent John Townsend & Jas Forster were the men who committed the offence they left before me,' said Samuel Burton. Others made familiar excuses: 'I was drunk when I committed this offence', 'I was out of work', 'distress drove me to do it'.

Others, usually women, described noble motives. 'My sister-in-law committed the offence, but in consequence of her having 2 Children, I took the offence upon myself,' said Martha Bisgrove, accused of stealing money from a gentleman; 'I did not do it I took the Blame on myself to save my Husband,' said Beatrice McBarnett, accused of arson. But naturally people showed themselves in the best light possible, and their explanations should be treated as warily as their gaolers' comments about them. Jerome Savory said he had previously received a heavy fine for 'being on the Wrong side of the Road'. There must have been more to the story than that, but if Savory had been arrested on the wrong side of the road with stolen goods in his pocket, he was not going to say so. Other convicts tried to make themselves sound better by adding impressive information. 'I was wounded at Trafalgar,' said Thomas Bonnor. 'I have never been out of employ—none of my Family have ever been transported or convicted,' said the unusually named Justice Bowles. None of this information made much impression on the judges.

CRIMES OTHER THAN THEFT

The 9 per cent of convicts who were not transported for theft committed a variety of crimes. There were two larger groups among them. In my analysis, 2 per cent of the men were soldiers guilty of military crimes, usually desertion or mutiny. Sentences were harsh. 'I was away above 5 years, I went to the United States, and worked at my trade, and was retaken when I went to see my Wife and Family,' said William Bird, who received a life sentence—but so did Thomas McBrian, absent for only a day. 'Mutiny' could mean trying to take over a ship, but was mostly only disobedience of orders: 'refusing to attend Drill and insubordination to the Commanding officer'. William Shapton, transported for mutiny, claimed that he was only guilty of being 'Drunk and throwing my arms down' ('arms' meaning weapons, not limbs). Military discipline was strict and punishment severe.

The other larger category, also restricted to 2 per cent of men, was political agitation: Irish rebelling against British rule, Englishmen demanding more political freedom, or, more often, men rioting against the new machinery that was taking their living—weavers working with their own looms in their own homes, their livelihoods slashed by competition from machine-made cloth from factories, or agricultural labourers displaced by machinery. Such men were transported for 'rioting' or 'machine-breaking'.

As for the rest—the other 5 per cent or so of convicts committed crimes ranging from abduction, abortion, arson, bigamy, buggery with an animal, incest, manslaughter, murder, perjury, piracy, rape and sodomy to treason. Murder was mostly punished by execution, and murderers sentenced to transportation had extenuating circumstances—like Benjamin Allison, transported for the murder of Eugenia Cripps. 'We had lived together a few months & being so badly off & our friends refusing to do anything for us we were starving & agreed to take Laudanum,' he said. 'We took the same quantity but it did not take effect on me she lived a few hours.' Domestic trouble seemed also to be considered an extenuating circumstance. Sarah Baker told of how when she and her partner were drunk he struck her. She told him that if he struck her again she would blow his brains out, and then hit him on the shoulder with such force that he died. Being the victim of a smear campaign could also save a man from the gallows. Elizabeth Kilsby accused Joseph Walters of unnatural crime with a horse, and he put oil of vitriol in her tea. She survived, and Walters was transported instead of being hanged.

It is hard to see any extenuating circumstance in the case of Thomas Braid, transported for incest and murder. 'Incest with my Sister Mary Morrison, she was tried and sentenced Life. I left her at Edinburgh,' he related. 'I was also indicted for the murder of the child which I had by my Sister 3 months old—the child was found in a canal.' However, the future was happier. 'Has performed the duty of Barber to the convicts with satisfaction throughout the Voyage,' reported the surgeon after Braid's voyage to Hobart. To convicts only—presumably anyone with any choice did not want Thomas near him with a razor.

Rape cases make sad reading, with familiar excuses: 'She was a Common

Woman', 'I had been Drunk with the Girl all the afternoon'. At this time sex with anyone but a human of the opposite gender was a crime, but few convicts were transported for sodomy; most people in this situation were executed. William Bonnill was transported for fourteen years for 'Keeping a Room for unnatural purposes, I was sent out by a fellow servant for some Beer and while I was gone, he and a man, whom he brought with him, were detected in an unnatural situation, they were convicted.' There were a few cases of buggery with an animal; John Blewitt was transported for 'buggering a Female Ass'.

Arson, setting fire to a building or perhaps a haystack, brought little benefit to the person doing it, but was a way of getting revenge on an enemy. Some claimed they were innocent. George Barrett was transported for burning his master's barn, cowhouse and stables. 'I never did it, I never had any . . . cause for it, against my Master,' he said. During the Irish famine in the 1840s a number of women claimed they committed the crime of arson in order to be transported.[4]

THE SYSTEM

Convicts passed through a well-established system before arriving in Australia. After their arrest they were tried in court and, depending on factors such as their crime, previous record, reputation, demeanour in court, and the mood of the judge and jury, they were sentenced to transportation. Similar crimes could receive quite different punishments, with people who stole a loaf of bread sometimes serving a week in prison and sometimes being transported for seven years. John Moody served a twelve-month sentence for manslaughter, but was transported for seven years for picking pockets. Transportation for life was the sentence given to both Thomas Braid for incest and murder, and Thomas Arnold for stealing fowls.

Once sentenced to transportation, women were moved to a prison near the port of departure, and men were mostly sent to the hulks, old ships moored near ports where prisoners lived, working on shore during the day. Some men served their entire sentences on the hulks, a few served them in the new 'enlightened' prisons called penitentiaries, and others were sent to the small colony of Bermuda, and were returned to Britain when their sentences expired.

When a convict transport was ready to sail to Australia, it seems that the authorities in the hulks were asked to make up a boatload of prisoners. Overall, about a third of all those sentenced to transportation were sent to Australia.[5] Criminals' fates seemed dependent to a great extent on chance: whether they were caught in the first place, whether they were sentenced to transportation, where they served their sentences.

Conditions in both prisons and hulks were notoriously terrible, but convicts were fed and cared for, after a fashion. Their basic diet was skilly (porridge), salt meat and bread or biscuit, which sounds dreadful today but was at least regular food. For many this was a luxury. Discipline was strict. Treatment by gaolers was often rough and punishment was severe for breaches of the rules. But for many convicts, life had always been tough. Another factor was separation from friends and family, and all a convict had ever known: heart-wrenching for many, perhaps most, but perhaps bearable for some whose earlier harsh lives were nothing to regret. But all had to cope with being convicts, under coercion, at the mercy of prison guards.

The convict experience ranged from absolutely appalling—torn from friends and family, treated shockingly—to not so bad, for those who had no family, who had been starving, who thought transportation might offer new chances. It is hard to avoid either exaggerating or downplaying the problems and opportunities of transportation: they varied for each convict.

WHO WERE THE CONVICTS?

When convicts arrived in Hobart they were asked about themselves, and though not all were asked the same questions, and presumably not all admitted everything in their past, there is enough information to provide at least minimal figures. Of the sample I analysed, 3 per cent had a previous conviction for vagrancy; comments suggested that 5 per cent of men and 0.5 per cent of women lived by theft; 6.5 per cent had a present or previous conviction involving violence; 1 per cent of women were called prostitutes and 22 per cent admitted to having been 'on the town', which usually meant prostitution. This was a recognised way for a woman to eke out a living.[6]

These figures suggest that the majority of convicts were not vagabonds, habitual thieves, prostitutes or particularly violent people, but instead ordinary working-class men and women. The lack of violence among convicts is particularly notable. At least half had a previous conviction, so were not new to crime; but it was still mostly for minor offences—petty theft, vagrancy, being disorderly or drunk. But some had a string of convictions—like Esther Clark, who had 34 when she was transported in 1839 for stealing money. I estimate that perhaps 10 per cent of convicts had been professional thieves, earning a living by crime; another 15 per cent were casual labourers cum petty thieves, doing what they could to get by; and about 75 per cent were ordinary working-class people who had a job but supplemented their low earnings with petty theft.[7]

Most convicts were just as well equipped to earn a living in Van Diemen's Land as in Britain. When convicts arrived in Hobart they stated their trade. If they were telling the truth, only a tiny minority, about 5 per cent, had jobs they could not use in Van Diemen's Land—mostly factory workers like pearl-button makers, and an errant clergyman who was not likely to be taken back into the fold. The rest—labourers (40 per cent), ploughmen, carpenters, servants, boatmen and so on—could find jobs in the colony. Some men used specialised trades in a more general way; Charles Davis, for example, had been apprenticed to a carriage-lamp maker, but in Hobart set up as a tinsmith. Most women, too, could earn a living in Van Diemen's Land, since the vast majority were domestic servants or were at least familiar with housework.

Nearly all Van Diemen's Land's convicts came from England. In the assignment period, 85 per cent of men did so, with 6 per cent from Scotland, 3 per cent from Ireland, 1 per cent from Wales and the rest from outside Britain. There were more from Ireland in the probation period, 1840–53, when convicts were initially confined to probation gangs in probation stations rather than assigned as labourers.[8] As usual with anything to do with convicts, these figures are not entirely reliable, because many people arrested in England had come from Ireland or Scotland looking for work. Still, Van Diemen's Land was never as Irish and Catholic as New South Wales. Two per cent of male convicts came from Australia, including Van Diemen's Land itself, convicts or free people convicted of crimes, and another 3 per cent came from other parts of the British Empire, from Kabul to Newfoundland, South Africa to Barbados. Some were British soldiers stationed abroad, and others were local inhabitants, such as 'Maria (a Slave)' from Honduras, and Arnoldus Jantjies from the Cape of Good Hope.

The figures for women were different. Hardly any came from outside Britain, though 2 per cent came from Australia, as for men; but many more women than men came from Ireland and Scotland (17 and 15 per cent) and fewer from England (65 per cent), with 1 per cent from Wales. Another difference compared with men is that hardly any women had been previously sentenced to transportation, while 4 per cent of men had, though most had served out their sentences in England or Bermuda.

Convicts' level of education and training varied. The majority were unskilled or semi-skilled labourers, but some were literate, or were skilled tradesmen such as carpenters or blacksmiths. Some had unusual backgrounds: 'I travelled about from Fair to Fair,' said William Quantrill. 'I had a wild Indian, a Girl without arms & a learned Dog.' But even these oddities did not bring enough money for William, his wife and nine children, and he was transported for circulating forged cheques. As noted earlier, almost all women were domestic servants, many with skills in valuable areas such as cooking and sewing. Most Vandemonian convicts were, at least nominally, Church of England (Anglican), with a large minority of Catholics, and a few of other beliefs: Presbyterians, Congregationalists, Baptists, Jews. But many were not influenced by religion at all.

Many convicts had tattoos, gained either in Britain, in the hulks, or in the ship coming out, a good way to while away the time. The tattoos were usually their initials, their families' initials, or standard designs such as an anchor and cable, a mermaid, or the sun, moon and stars. Some had original inscriptions. Joseph Sutcliffe, transported on the ship *Prince Regent*, had a bust of the Prince Regent on his arm, which might have surprised that monarch; William Farrier had 'Fool' inscribed in the centre of his forehead (a cruel joke by the tattooist?); William Langham can have had little spare space, for as well as a man, woman, fish, sun, half-moon, anchor, flowerpot, crucifix, a man with a flag and 'Catch me', he had 'F..k me' on his right arm. Or so ran the convict record.

Family backgrounds varied. About a third of convicts were married or in a few cases widowed, and two-thirds were single. A quarter had children, who were mostly left behind, though some women and a few men brought children with them. The authorities did not seem to consider the destruction of family life that transportation brought; it was unlikely that these families would ever be reunited, and a large number of wives and children were left even more destitute than they had been before their breadwinner's conviction. Convict husbands sometimes said that wives were with their parents, but also that they were 'on the parish'—in workhouses, where food and other comforts were minimal. For example, after John Grant was transported for machine-breaking, his wife Mary had to go to the workhouse, having no other means of support. Not surprisingly, some of these women remarried, despite the fact that their husbands were alive. 'Wife Elizabeth has been Married again, since I have been Transported, I do not know the Mans name received a Letter from my Mother Hannah on the Subject,' explained Emanuel Mellor. The large number of single people was a result of convicts being mainly young; the average age was 26, and for both men and women, 73 per cent were aged between 17 and 30. Some, an unknown number, were in de facto relationships, and many convict men in particular were visited in gaol by women they were living with at the time.

Some convicts had close families, with a number claiming that their spouses were aiming to join them in Van Diemen's Land—a long and difficult trip which would need great commitment by the spouse. Ann Dixon's husband worked his passage on the ship in which she was transported to Van Diemen's Land; 'Husband James Expects to follow me,' said Sarah Cullen of Antrim; 'Wife Margaret at London I expect her here,' said Peter Bourne. James Hevey, who had to leave behind his wife Isabella and two children when he was transported for stealing six silver teaspoons, had tattooed on his arm:

> The ocean may between us Roll and distant tho' we be
> Dearest Should we never meet more I'll Still rememb[er] thee
> Isabella Hevey

But there is more evidence of difficult family life, since the system tended to throw up such material. Some convicts stated that they had no family at all: 'all my relations are dead,' said Samuel Hivall. When

Thomas White and his daughter were transported the authorities noted that Thomas had 'brought up a large Family to stealing & they hope he may not return'. Husbands were transported for assaulting or murdering their wives, and vice versa. 'I shot my Wife in a fit of Jealousy', 'I was going to strike one of the Children she tried to [stop] me & I struck her [with] a plank'.[9] John Naylor said to the authorities: 'I committed this offence [stealing coals] in order to get Transp[orte]d away from my wife.' Convicts stole from family members, with William Branton transported for 'robbing my Grandmother who lives with my Mother of a Gown, Shawl and chemise', which seems particularly callous. Elizabeth Bolton was transported for pawning clothes which did not belong to her. She was 'prosecuted by my Mother, she did it to get rid of me,' she said. Perhaps this was not surprising: Elizabeth had already served a fourteen-day sentence for robbing her mother. Agnes Blair stabbed her father with a knife when she was drunk. She had a previous conviction for fighting with her father, when she had climbed through her mother's window and her father turned her out of the house. 'I went to rob him afterwards.' Some men deserted their families; James Browning had three previous convictions for leaving his wife and five children, but by the time he was transported for embezzlement he described himself as a widower. What happened to his unfortunate children was not stated. Only a minority of convicts had such stories, however, and it is impossible to generalise about convicts' family lives.

A small percentage of convicts were different from the norm. Almost all convicts were working class, but there were a few 'gentlemen', mostly guilty of the white-collar crimes of forgery and embezzlement, and a handful of 'ladies', using 'ladies' in the Jane Austen sense of upper-class women. Most convicts were aged from their late teens to their forties, but there were a few who were very young, from nine upwards, or elderly (by the standards of the day), in their sixties, seventies, even eighties. The oldest was 86.

Stories of youthful convicts make sad reading. James Lynch was only nine when in 1844 he was transported for seven years for stealing toys. It sounds innocent enough—but there were three boxes of them, and it was his third conviction for theft. 'A man named Jas Tucker used to come out with me in the day & send me thieving if I got a good thing he used to say he would give me 2d or 3d,' young James said. Such boys were easy prey for men like Tucker, and others: during the voyage 'a man was seen in his Hammock', reported the surgeon. In Van Diemen's Land James was sent to Point Puer, the reformatory for boy convicts, and later to the Cascades penal station, where laughing in chapel brought him ten days' solitary confinement. He received his free certificate in 1850, but with little experience except stealing and institutional life it is not surprising that he was soon found guilty of more theft, and served another sentence of transportation.

What did the authorities think of the convicts? Early records are scrappy, but from the 1820s records for male convicts included three reports: by the authorities at the gaol where they were first kept; at the hulks; and on the voyage out. The women received two reports, from the gaol and the voyage. Some reports could be unfortunately personal— Thomas Blacks was described as having 'large Ears thin flapping forward like Fishes fins'—but most were more practical.

The gaolers, who often knew the convicts and their circumstances, tended to see them in a poor light: 82 per cent of reports were negative, more so for men (85 per cent) than women (69 per cent). Most convicts were described as 'bad', with bad 'connexions' and former course of life, in the terminology of the day, and only a few were 'good', 'decent' or 'poor but respectable'. It was a different story in the hulks, where the authorities had no prior knowledge of the men and judged them solely on their present behaviour: 89 per cent received a positive report, mostly 'orderly' or 'good'. Similarly, on board ship 84 per cent received a favourable report, though here men scored better than women (86 to 75 per cent). So when they were serving their sentences, convicts behaved reasonably well, obeying the authorities and avoiding further punishments. This suggests that they were not particularly rebellious, especially when there was little chance of success: they tended to be pragmatic, making the best of their situations, going along with the authorities for fear of punishment. An example of an extreme difference between the reports comes in the record of Joseph Shaw, transported for seven years for stealing nails. His gaol record noted that he was a notorious thief with a sullen disposition, the 'terror of the neighbourhood'. The ship's surgeon described him as a 'quiet old man'.

THE TRIP OUT

Early convict trips to Sydney in chartered ships suffered appalling conditions and many deaths, which forced the British government to use naval
vessels to transport convicts. These ships were strictly run. Convicts lived
below decks, herded together, but were brought on deck regularly for exer-
cise. Cleanliness was strictly observed, more for health than other reasons.
Food was adequate.

The trip must have been frightening for the many who had never been
to sea before, and for anyone, a storm would be terrifying. Imagine being
kept below decks with the ship lurching and rolling, little ventilation,
people being seasick, limited fresh water, no washing facilities . . . Voyages
lasted between three and six months, and ships carried from 50 to 399
convicts.[10] Ships landed at few ports and convicts were not allowed ashore.
Usually at sea there was only ocean to be seen. The weather varied from
tropical heat to freezing cold. Discipline remained strict. But convicts were
fed and cared for reasonably well by the standards of the day, sickness
was relatively rare, and they had little work. The few written opinions by
convicts vary. Richard Dillingham found a voyage where there were many
deaths from cholera 'verry unpleasant', but a middle-class Irish convict,
William Dowling, praised a 'hearty meal of "skilly"' on his trip out. He
had to wear convict garb on the ship, and in Hobart he found his own
clothes 'much tighter'.

Each ship had a surgeon-superintendent who was responsible for the
convicts' health, and who sometimes took on other duties, organising
classes in reading and writing, or giving religious instruction. Well-behaved
convicts were given responsible positions such as cook, teacher or boat-
swain. Surgeons reported on the voyage: one would merely say that most
convicts under him were 'orderly', but others wrote a variety of comments,
such as: 'a lazy, indolent, stupid Man, seems to think of nothing but eating, drinking, and smoking', 'a hard working Man, a good Carpenter',
'a restless unsettled character, thoughtless & unstable, but of very good
natural abilities', 'an active well disposed Man, and an excellent Cook', 'a
scampish but not a bad Boy improving'.[11]

Some convicts responded well to religious instruction, and William
Booth, transported for unnatural crime with a mare, was one who saw

the light. The surgeon reported that his behaviour on the voyage was 'uniformly good, useful as a Teacher according to his strength. During his passage from England, has, as far as the circumstances in which he has been placed afforded opportunity, given Scriptural Evidence, that he has turned to God by the Faith of the Gospel.' William was a contrast to Thomas Brown. 'A very bad character', wrote the surgeon, 'having been guilty of much fraud, hypocrysy & Theft & endeavoured to rob others in the Ship . . . [he] concerted measures to effect their escape & to take with him all the property of the Surgeon Superintendent by whom he was employed Binding Books & treated him with the greatest kindness & confidence in consequence of the recommendation of the Revd Mr Price'—who was going to hear all about it, obviously, when the surgeon returned to England.

There were some disastrous voyages. *George III* left England in 1834 with 220 male convicts. Scurvy soon appeared, and by the time the ship sighted the Van Diemen's Land coast, twelve prisoners had died and 60 were ill. As the captain was trying to find a short cut to Hobart up the D'Entrecasteaux Channel on the south-east coast, the ship struck a reef. She began to break up, and for fear of mutiny the convicts were locked up. Shouting to be released, they tried to break out, but soldiers at the top of the hatchway stopped them, and shots were fired. Eventually some did reach the shore, but 127 convicts and only six other people were drowned. Even more convicts died after the *Waterloo*, bound for Hobart, anchored at Table Bay on the south-west coast of South Africa in August 1842. In a storm she lost her anchors, ran on to the shore and was wrecked in the surf. The 219 convicts were only released at the last minute, and 144 died.[12]

Mutiny was another possibility. Soon after the *Somersetshire* left England in 1841, a group of convicts and soldiers formed a plot to seize her, set everyone who would not join them adrift in the ship's boats, and sail to South America and freedom. But the authorities found out, and when the ship put in at Cape Town four soldiers were tried, with one sentenced to death. Nothing happened to the convicts, and the *Somersetshire* proceeded to Hobart as per schedule. So did the *Sarah*, because Christopher Smith, a soldier transported for assaulting a corporal, gave information of a planned mutiny.[13] There were no successful mutinies on convict ships to Australia.

For the times, the death rates were low: some unfortunates were lost in shipwrecks, and 1 per cent of convicts died, mostly of disease, but the vast majority of convicts survived to be landed at Hobart for the next stage of their punishment.

TWO COMFORTING MYTHS

There is widespread belief in two 'facts' about convicts: that many chose to be transported, and many were specially chosen by the British authorities as useful settlers for the new colony. These are comforting beliefs: the convicts wanted to come so were in control of their destinies, they were the pick of the crop.

Some convicts did commit crimes in order to be transported. In 1841 Alice Anderson was transported for stealing £3 from a man's pocket. 'I committed this offence purposely to get transported to my Husband,' she said. Similarly, Christopher Moran said he stole a cow 'to get out to my Father'. John Williams was disappointed when he committed a theft in order to be transported, but was only given a month's imprisonment. He stole two pint pots and finally gained a seven-year sentence. There are other stories of convicts calling out, 'Thank you, your Honour!' when the judge read out the sentence. Apart from the possibility of joining family members already transported, starving people might want the regular rations of the convict system, or think transportation was the easiest way to get to the new colonies, where men were making fortunes—successful convicts' letters home were sometimes published in newspapers, telling of the money they had made. Convicts who said they committed a crime in order to be transported were few, 1 per cent at most; presumably others did not tell the authorities, but the most optimistic total would be only 5 per cent, a small but interesting minority.

Some historians have argued that the authorities did choose suitable convicts for a new country, but I am not convinced. In 1835 several hulk administrators gave evidence in a parliamentary inquiry into gaols. When convicts had to be selected for transportation from among the hundreds on the hulk, they said, the worst behaved and those with longer sentences were transported first, while useful ones like carpenters were kept back. There was some more positive selection, but of convicts well enough to face the voyage rather than those who would be useful in the colony. James

Smith, surgeon-superintendent on the *Moffatt* convict transport in 1842, reported that despite the vigilance of medical officers to keep the unfit from boarding, 'many Prisoners are anxious to get aboard, and to accomplish their purpose effectually conceal their ailments'—two men with tuberculosis among them.[14] If men like Charles Biffon were transported, there can have been little screening for useful workers. Charles was a shepherd, married with nine children. When he was convicted of stealing a horse he was aged 86, rather deaf, and had lost nearly all his teeth. But he was transported to Van Diemen's Land for life. Other workers of questionable usefulness were 40-year-old George Wilson, who had lost an arm when shot by the coastguard while smuggling; John Eyres, who had a wooden leg, his right leg having 'perished by frost'; and Alexsander Szurdurski, a Pole who could not speak English. How did he cope, when no one around him could speak Polish? Such convicts were in a small minority, but the fact that the authorities thought they were suitable for transportation challenges the idea that convicts were specially chosen to be useful colonists.

Transported for theft, Rosanna Keegan claimed to be 44, but admitted to 63, and the ship's surgeon thought she was even older. He would have objected to her coming on board, but she was anxious to be transported on the same ship as her pregnant daughter. He described her as 'an old emaciated creature.' She was becoming more and more debilitated and spent most of the time lying in bed. Again, hardly a useful addition to the colony: what happened to her is not known.

RETURNING FROM TRANSPORTATION

Theft was seen as serious crime, but even worse was any challenge to authority—and a major challenge came from those convicts who returned from Australia when they had not received a free pardon. An unknown number managed to make it back across the globe, and a handful were re-arrested and retransported, with heavy sentences.

It seems harsh, after their great efforts to get back home. Samuel Norster came from Portland in Dorset, and by the mid-1830s he and his wife Jane had four children. Like many locals Samuel did the odd spot of smuggling, and in the early 1830s he served two local sentences for this. Then he and his brother Abraham were found guilty of burglary, and were transported to Van Diemen's Land for life. Abraham died on the voyage, but Samuel survived and was a model convict, behaving well in the hulk and described as 'good very useful' on the voyage.

Samuel was determined to get back home. Good behaviour was the key to promising jobs; he continued to do the right thing, only found guilty of one misdemeanour, and became coxswain of the government boat at George Town on the north coast. One night in 1839 he stowed away on a visiting schooner, among the cattle in the hold. No one knew he was there. After nine days at sea, which must have been hard going among the cattle, the ship reached South Australia. Samuel gained a berth as a seaman on a ship to California, and took another ship for England, probably again working his passage. Finally he reached Dorset and his family.

The reunion was short. Later that year Samuel was dobbed in by 'a countryman', re-arrested and sentenced to transportation for life. Once more he was well behaved, good in gaol and 'very well conducted' on the ship, but in the colony he was sent to Port Arthur in chains. His record ends with the word 'Run' scrawled across the page: Samuel had absconded again. Perhaps this time he reached his home and family without anyone betraying him.

AUSTRALIAN CONVICTS

One per cent of convicts sent to Van Diemen's Land came from other parts of Australia—Fremantle, Adelaide, Port Phillip or, mainly, New South Wales. A mixture of convicts and free migrants, they had been found guilty of transportable crimes in local courts. A few were sentenced in Van Diemen's Land itself.

As usual, most convicts were guilty of theft: John Goff was transported from Sydney for seven years for stealing mutton, and in Hobart, Jane Austen (not the author), who had arrived free, was sentenced to transportation for eighteen months for stealing money. Transported from England for burglary, William Millar was sent to New South Wales, and became a flagellator at a chain gang at Towrang near Goulburn. Flagellators, who performed the sentences of flogging, were scorned by other convicts, and William was no exception. '[I] was driven to abscond by the other prisoners in the Gang they were always at me,' he explained. 'I took to the

Bush . . . while I was out in the Bush I was joined by three others.' They were caught and sent to Van Diemen's Land with life sentences.

In all, a great mixture of men and women were transported to Van Diemen's Land, though they were mostly young adults, mostly transported for minor theft, and mostly reasonably well behaved—or well disciplined—once they began serving their sentences. What happened to them once they arrived on the island?

3

CONVICTS UNDER ASSIGNMENT IN VAN DIEMEN'S LAND

In 1831, at the age of 23, Richard Dillingham was sentenced to transportation for life for housebreaking. While he was waiting to go to 'Van's Die's Land' he sent three letters to his family, thanking them for the parcel they sent him and asking after their health—he had 'nothing perticular' to tell them of his life in the hulks. The authorities described his behaviour there as 'orderly', and on the voyage out 'very good'.

Dillingham arrived in 1832, and four years later reported home that 'I Am Now verry comfortably situated within a mile of Hobart Town . . . In A large market garden.' His job was driving the produce to market in a horse and cart:

As to my Liveing I find it Better than Ever I Expected thank God I want for Nothing In that Respect As for tea And Sugar I almost Could swim in it I am Alowed 2 Pound of Sugar [0.9 kilograms] and ¼ Pound of tea [100 grams] Per week And Plenty of tobacco And Good white Bread And sometimes Beef Sometimes mutton sometimes Pork this I have Every day Plenty of fruit Pudings in the Season of all sorts And I have two suits of Clothes A year And three Pair of Shoes In A year And I want for Nothing but my Liberty but though I Am thus situated It Is Not the Case with all that come As Prisonners It is all owen to A Persons Good Conduct that they Get Good Situations for some through their misconduct Get Into Road Partys and some Into Chain Gangs and Live A miserable Life my kind Love to my Brother James and I hope that my misfortune will be A warning to him . . .

A postscript told his parents that their son was very steady; though liquor was cheap 'he Never gets more than do him Good'. Dillingham was not quite as well behaved as this, for he was mildly punished three times for being drunk, but over eight years this was scarcely riotous. In 1838 he gave his parents a surprising piece of news. 'It is my intention to Get married to a black woman one of the natives of this country and a pretty woman she is I never knew one who pleased me so well.' He sent his best love in particular to 'my poor dear old Grandfather and tel him not to grieve for my account for I am doing much better than many a Laboring man in England, If a man behaves well in this country is sober honest and industrious tho he be a prisoner he is respected by all who know him'.

His startled parents must have replied at once, for only a year later Richard wrote again. First came good news: he had been promised a ticket of leave 'so that I can work for myself and receive wages for my labor'. But 'as to my being married to a black woman I never thought of such a thing it was only my nonsense and my fellow servant who wrote the letter for me had no business to put it in'. The friend even had the cheek to ask Richard's parents to contact his own father and ask him to write: 'Tell him I am Doing much better than ever I expected that I have a good Master and in fact that I never was so well off in my Life.' He was their son's most intimate friend, he wrote, seeing him every morning when he delivered the milk.

In 1840 Dillingham gained his ticket of leave, and in 1843 a conditional pardon—so he served only eleven years of a life sentence. Like many other ex-convicts he went to seek his fortune in Victoria, where he died in 1873 aged 65, apparently never having married.

Richard Dillingham was one of the tens of thousands of convicts and settlers who benefited from the first major method of organising convicts in

Van Diemen's Land: assignment. Until 1824 this was done haphazardly, but the treatment of convicts in both New South Wales and Van Diemen's Land was criticised in Britian as too easygoing, with transportation no deterrent to British criminals. In 1824 George Arthur arrived to reorganise Van Diemen's Land's system. No drinking, mistresses, or neglect of duty here: unlike earlier governors, Arthur was sternly upright and expected others to be so too, sacking incompetent or corrupt officials, and ordering those remaining to either marry the women they lived with, or separate from them.

For convicts, Arthur instituted a graded system of assignment. On arrival, they were assigned to work for settlers or the government. If they behaved well, after a certain time they gained a ticket of leave, which meant they were more or less independent. If they continued to behave well, they gained a conditional pardon, which restricted them to Australia, or a free pardon or free certificate with no restrictions. But if they broke the rules, by being absent without leave, drunk, disobedient—or committing worse offences like theft, assault or murder—they went down the grades, sentenced to flogging, hard labour such as making roads, then, if they committed more serious offences, hard labour in chains, and finally banishment to the dreaded penal stations set up for convicts who committed further offences in Van Diemen's Land: Macquarie Harbour (1822–33), Maria Island (1825–32) and Port Arthur (1830–77) and its outstations such as the Coal Mines at Saltwater River (1834–48). So convicts earned their treatment; their future was up to them. Arthur believed that although some convicts were so evil they could not be reformed—'You cannot make that straight which God hath made crooked'—others committed crimes because of hardship and misery, and could be persuaded to reform by promises of good treatment.[1] Some convicts responded as Arthur hoped, behaving well, passing through the system in minimal time. Others committed multiple crimes, suffered years of punishments and died in the system. The majority gained a pardon in less time than their original sentences, with some punishments along the way.

Assignment benefited almost everybody. The government was spared having to support many convicts, since settlers did this. Settlers gained cheap labour. And for convicts it was the easiest way to be integrated back into the community. They were known to be convicts, true, but most of them lived in ordinary households performing ordinary tasks, instead of being set apart in prison. 'As a means of making men outwardly honest, of converting vagabonds, most useless in one country, into active citizens of another, and thus giving birth to a new and *splendid country*, [assignment] has succeeded to a degree perhaps unparalleled in history,' wrote Charles Darwin after he visited Australia in 1836.[2] Assignment continued in force in Van Diemen's Land until 1840, when it was replaced by the probation system, where convicts began their sentences in government work gangs.

Many convicts were never or seldom punished; of men, three-quarters were never in chain gangs or penal stations.[3] Even when convicts were flogged, they seldom received more than 50 lashes at once, which although severe in itself, was lenient in comparison to punishments administered in the armed forces. Convicts who had been soldiers told of 200 or 300 lashes at one time. 'I have had One Thousand Lashes,' Roderick Flannagan reported after he was sentenced to transportation for life for what the authorities called mutiny and he called stealing from an officer.

Discipline was therefore comparatively mild for most convicts, and they had other advantages. On average their diet was better, with more calories per day, than the working class in Britain; they had more medical care; the government provided shelter. Analysis of convict records shows that convicts had a considerably lower death rate than other groups of people such as soldiers in barracks; it was actually healthier to be a convict than a soldier or indeed a working-class British citizen.[4]

It was not only the system under which convicts served their sentences that influenced their fates. Their backgrounds were also important. Convicts could not bring much out by way of material goods, but they could have other attributes. Skilled convicts such as carpenters and educated convicts such as clerks were valued by convict officials and free settlers, and were mostly treated better than unskilled labourers. They could also more easily earn a living once they were free. Other abilities or gifts could have influence. Attractive people often find life easier than plain ones, and attractive women, especially, could use their looks to advantage. Convicts with good health, the gift of the gab or a natural ability for making the best of a situation were also more likely to succeed. 'Gentlemen'—the few upper-middle-class convicts—were treated better, with most excused from manual labour. And then there was luck, as critics of the assignment system pointed out: some convicts like Richard Dillingham were assigned to kind masters, some to brutes; some ran up against reasonable convict officials, some against tyrants. One aspect that had less effect was the original crime, which was largely ignored in Van Diemen's Land. As one writer pointed out, no one knew convicts' crimes unless they themselves admitted them—which gave them scope to minimise their crime, if necessary, or even make it sound positive, like stealing a loaf of bread to feed a starving infant.[5]

Convicts' fates also depended on their behaviour in the system. Did they obey the rules, or rebel? They could be punished for tiny faults. Robert Gough was found guilty of misconduct for having dirty legs at muster, James Youren for 'rambling about the street', and John Spring for 'making use of improper language in the Watchman's Hut'. Few committed serious crimes; the majority seemed to go along with the system, more or less, aiming to get through it as fast as possible.

As the reformers noted, employers' treatment of convicts varied. They were not authorised to punish convicts themselves but had to take them to a magistrate for sentencing. James Fenton, a farmer near Port Sorell on the north-west coast, had an enlightened attitude. He did not usually punish his men, he wrote, partly because he found this made them worse, and partly because the trip to the distant police station took so long.[6] But another farmer, George Hobler, believed that an occasional flogging encouraged convicts to work hard:

> I have now had sufficient experience of convict servants to be convinced of the impossibility of their being kept in any order without from time to time an example of this nature [flogging] . . . I feed them well . . . and make them . . . more comfortable than honest labourers at home, and in return I will exact a fair proportion of labour, but above all things, subordination and civility. . . . I have now 15 prisoners who do the whole work of the farm without my paying 1s. in wages, but how much looking after they require.
>
> [After a flogging] It is very painful for me to be obliged to flog in this manner, but if I give way to them at all, they at once become my masters.

A study of Arthur's assignment system concluded that about a fifth of convict masters showed a sincere concern for rehabilitating their servants; two-fifths encouraged their servants out of self-interest, so they would work better; another fifth relied on punishment rather than encouragement; and the final fifth were slave-drivers.[7]

As well as the official system, there was an unofficial system among convicts and their overseers—as so often happens in institutions like gaols. Convict clerks could accept bribes to falsify the records, for example shortening a sentence of transportation. Policemen and petty officials could be open to bribes or persuasion. Newspaper editor James Ross described how when he missed one of his workers, Jonathan, another worker explained that Jonathan had 'got into trouble', caught trying to buy goods with a fake coin. He was talking to the constable, who would probably 'make it up for ten shillings'—accept a bribe to clear Jonathan of the charge.[8]

In Van Diemen's Land, Governor Arthur set up a system of informers, who were rewarded for providing information about convicts' illegal activities. This provided plenty of scope for not only convicts but officials to spy, inform, and use the system for their own benefit. The memoirs of convict and bushranger Martin Cash show an active undercurrent of illegal activity, as convicts did the best they could for themselves against both the authorities and other convicts. Trafficking, bribery and theft (selling government goods, stealing from fellow prisoners) were widespread. Arriving at one probation station (probation stations housed probation gangs) late at night, Cash bought two 'fat cakes' and some bread, made by the cook who took part of the prisoners' rations and sold them for his own benefit. At the Jerusalem probation station informers were given a bonus for telling the authorities that some prisoner was about to abscond, or that another had tobacco. In the Hobart gaol, prisoners often stole other prisoners' belongings. These robberies were seldom detected, since discipline was lax. Behaviour in front of a magistrate could affect the convict's fate, wrote Cash, and a witty answer or 'smart repartee' could result in a lesser punishment. So could penitence, a promise never to repeat the crime. Reputation could also have an effect. When Cash had to have leg irons put on, he had nothing to tip the blacksmith with so expected 'something in a verry rough style', but the blacksmith gave him 'the lightest pair I had ever seen', because Cash was seen as a hero for escaping from Port Arthur.[9]

From the authorities' point of view, the skulduggery was all done by convicts. Records, written by the gaolers, tend to show convicts in a poor light, mostly describing their offences. However, they also track the progress of convicts through the system.

About 10 per cent of convicts were never punished for a further offence while serving their original sentence, and a further 25 per cent or so were only punished once or twice, adding up to around 35 per cent who appeared to get through the system fairly easily.[10] Patrick Casey, a 23-year-old labourer, arrived in 1841 with a seven-year sentence. In the colony he was never charged with an offence, and gained his ticket of leave four years later. Hannah Gibb, who began a fourteen-year sentence in 1838, was found guilty of 'making away with the Sum of Sixpence when sent for Flour', and received her pardon in 1850.

A further 30 per cent of all convicts committed the average number of five fairly minor offences. Thomas Armstrong, a baker, arrived in 1823 on a seven-year sentence. He was punished—fined, reprimanded or returned to government—five times, for being drunk and disorderly and abusing his fellow servants, behaving riotously in the hospital and assaulting a man, being absent without leave, and being drunk and breaking windows. He obtained his free certificate eight years after his arrival. Anne Reilly arrived in 1842 with a seven-year sentence and gained her ticket of leave only two years later. She then committed five offences, mostly punished with between one and three months' hard labour, for being out after hours and/or drunk, destroying her master's property and assaulting a constable, and disturbing the peace with indecent language. Anne obtained her free certificate in 1849.

Another group, perhaps 25 per cent of the total, were more rebellious, with more than the average five convictions. William Grant, a weaver, arrived in 1842 on a ten-year sentence. In five years in probation gangs around the island, from Southport in the far south to Westbury in the north, he was charged with 34 offences, ranging from being absent from muster, answering for a fellow prisoner who was absent from muster, and annoying a fellow prisoner, to fighting and—worst of all—absconding or planning to abscond, with offences such as concealing bread and meat (for provisions when he escaped). But at last he emerged from the probation gang and entered employment. Over the next five years he was charged five times with disobedience, being absent, or being found in a brothel. He received his free certificate in 1852. In all his 39 offences William Grant never committed a major crime; he was obviously rebellious rather than criminal, and he never committed an offence serious enough to earn him a sentence to a penal station.

About 10 per cent of convicts were punished for serious offences, though the definition of 'serious' crimes could be different from those of today. In 1846 Michael Lyons, a tinker on a seven-year sentence, was executed after he was found guilty of 'unnatural crime with a Goat'. Other convicts were guilty of murder, rape, violent assault and major theft. Thomas Turner, a brickmaker's wheeler, began his life of crime in Van Diemen's Land in 1824 by being absent from muster, out after hours and insolent. Then he was found in bed in a man's house with two women servants; he 'assaulted and beat' a man; he sheltered two convict absconders; and he committed murder. For this Turner was hanged and 'anatomized', dissected by doctors after his death.

Only a handful of convicts wrote descriptions of their experiences. Naturally they put themselves in the best light: all records have a bias one way or another, but these stories do give the convict version of life in Van Diemen's Land.

Several described how they prospered. Like Richard Dillingham, Henry Tingley was a model convict. Transported in 1835 aged eighteen for stealing a horse, he was never in trouble again; his convict record notes only that he received his ticket of leave in 1843 and a pardon in 1847. On his arrival Tingley was assigned to work for a farmer, and soon he wrote to his parents, sending them his kind love, and telling them he was very comfortable. He was working on a farm at Swansea on the east coast of Van Diemen's Land and he was lucky, for his master treated him well. Tingley's work was the same as at home, he reported; he had plenty to eat and drink, 'thank God for it':

> All a man has got to mind is to keep a still tongue in his head, and do his master's duty, and then he is looked upon as if he were at home; but if he don't he may as well be hung at once, for they would take you to the

magistrates and get 100 of lashes, and then get sent to a place called Port Arthur to work in irons for two or three years, and then he is disliked by everyone.

'This country is far before England in everything, both for work and money,' wrote Tingley. At night after he had finished work he could earn money by hunting kangaroo, 'ducks, or swans, tigers, tiger-cats or native cats . . . I have dogs and a gun of my own'. A fellow prisoner was teaching him to make shoes, which would help him once he was free. 'I am doing a great deal better than ever I was at home, only for the wanting you with me,' he declared, suggesting that his parents emigrate 'as it would be the making of you'. They could get him assigned to them 'and then we should be more comfortable than ever we have been'. Could they send him news from home?

His parents did not emigrate, but Henry established a new family. In 1847, aged 30, he married Barbara Gordon, and they had four children. They moved to Ringarooma in the north-east, and three of the children married and provided Henry and Barbara with grandchildren.

Richard Dillingham and Henry Tingley were able to do well. Perhaps helped by the secure background provided by those loving families, lucky in their good masters, perhaps with a natural ability to accept circumstances and make the best of things, they were typical of convicts who could benefit from the opportunities that Van Diemen's Land provided. But others could not, their stories telling of their inability to settle down, to go through the system, to cope.

Some of those few who came from the upper classes felt they were punished, not just by being transported, but by being lumped in with working-class convicts. Henry Savery, son of a prosperous banker, married with a son, was an unsuccessful businessman. In 1824 he was sentenced to transportation for life, for forging a bill. As a gentleman he was treated well on the ship to Australia, living apart from the other convicts, but once in Hobart this changed.

Savery worked as a clerk in a government office, but was lonely; as a convict he was not admitted to the gentry, and he could not bear to socialise with anyone else. 'Alone . . . —degraded in rank and society—enrolled among burglars, highwaymen, and other criminals, in the one, sweeping, comprehensive term, CONVICT', he was thoroughly depressed when his wife arrived to join him. Savery was about to be arrested for debt, and tried to cut his throat. Mrs Savery, who had enjoyed a close friendship with the attorney-general on the trip out, was appalled by her husband's situation, and, afraid creditors would take what little money she had, went home and never saw her husband again.

Savery was cast into prison for debt, and there he wrote *The Hermit in Van Diemen's Land*, 30 anonymous satirical essays about the colony. Then he was assigned to work for a settler, and wrote *Quintus Servinton*, a novel based on his experiences. It differed from his real situation in several crucial respects; in fiction Mrs Savery's relationship with the attorney-general was pure, she nursed her husband devotedly after his attempted suicide, then went back to Britain to gain him a pardon. Savery ended his novel with his hero also back in England, devoted wife in attendance, grandson at his knee.

In reality, over the next decade Savery leased farms, took to drink, went broke and signed forged bills. Sent to Port Arthur, he died there in 1842 after again trying to commit suicide.

The Hermit showed his anger against the gentry class who would not accept him. An English gentleman arrives to see what a convict colony is like. He expected to find 'a population, who either not having found Old England good enough for them, must themselves be the purest of the pure, or who having been purified of their sins by punishment, must now have repented, and . . . become the most virtuous of the virtuous'. Alas for his hopes! He found many dishonest, argumentative people—but they were Hobart's elite. Convicts were never mentioned, never appear, except in a roundabout way in the sentence quoted above. The word 'convict' was never used, and nor were 'prisoner' or any other euphemism. Of 148 people satirised, only six minor characters had convict connections and these were not mentioned in the book, the information only found in modern annotations. Savery was a convict: his villains were lawyers, businessmen and government officials. Even so, to write a 137-page book about a convict colony without once mentioning convicts is an impressive piece of spin doctoring.

Not all upper-class convicts were shunned socially. Savery sounds a difficult character; other gentleman convicts were accepted by the local gentry. In 1854, when Irish rebel John Martin was about to leave Van Diemen's Land, he published a valedictory letter, thanking people for their kindness. In the letter he wrote of his arrival, five years earlier:

> I never doubted that the colonists (except some of the Irish) would regard me as a wretch to be shunned by all good men. The forms of British law and British opinion had concurred in pronouncing my comrades and myself 'felons' and 'traitors'; . . . Yet I have received hospitable and friendly attentions from almost all the respectable families in whose neighbourhood I have been detained. My acquaintances and friends have been English, Scotch, Welsh, Irish in origin; Protestant and Catholic in religion. From people of all races, sects, parties, and classes in the island I have received kindness, or, at least, civility . . . I so gratefully feel the soothing kindness of my very many friends.

Martin's fellow rebel John Mitchel, a former lawyer, university-educated, son of a Presbyterian minister, was horrified when he was transported, both because of transportation itself and because he, 'a person of education and a gentleman!', had to mix with such appalling criminals. 'I am to spend certain years, then, among the gum-trees in grim solitude' in a land where three-quarters of the population were of convict origin. He decided to hold 'as little intercourse as possible with the people around me' in the 'gardens of hell' that was Van Diemen's Land, where even the capital city, Hobart, had in its coat of arms a kangaroo having its pocket picked (not intentionally, but it does appear so).[11]

Despite his misgivings Mitchel found the island attractive, with a wonderful climate and balmy air. On arrival he was given a ticket of leave and sent to live with John Martin in Bothwell, a farming community some 70 kilometres north of Hobart, and everything was so pleasant that 'in vain I try to torment myself into a state of chronic savage indignation'. The neighbouring gentry treated them as equals, asking them to dinner and lending them horses. The convict class, Mitchel found, 'are strictly tabooed . . . Here, a freeman is a king, and the convict-class is regarded just as the negroes must be in South Carolina . . . which indeed is per-fectly right,' added Mitchel, who as a gentleman, a political prisoner, saw himself as superior to 'real convicts'. 'To show me she is a person of respectability, [his landlady] took an early occasion of informing me that she "came out free"; which, in fact, is the patent of nobility in Van Diemen's Land.' Finally he managed to escape. 'Adieu, then, beauteous island, full of sorrow and gnashing of teeth—Island of fragrant forests, and bright rivers, and fair women!—Island of chains and scourges, and blind, brutal rage and passion!'[12]

Another story was the forerunner to what became seen as the stereotypical convict narrative: an innocent hero ruined by brutal treatment in Van Diemen's Land. It may or may not be true—although the author, 'Henry Easy', was certainly familiar with the system, there is no Henry Easy listed among Van Diemen's Land's convicts—but it is important as a published narrative which influenced British ideas about transportation. A working-class convict, Easy described how he was unjustly arrested in England in 1829 for stealing a watch, and was sentenced to fourteen years' transportation. In Van Diemen's Land he was assigned to brutal Captain Miller at New Norfolk. Easy tried to win him over with hard work, which was a mistake, for when the time came for Easy to claim a ticket of leave, Miller 'tried every act to make me commit a breach of the peace', so the ticket would be delayed and he could retain his worker. Easy tried to keep his temper, but when Miller hit him, 'maddened by the blow and his systematic cruel treatment, and knowing that I was unjustly transported, I struck him'. He was sentenced to 25 lashes:

> The triangle was rigged, and the scourger came with his cat o' nine tails, I was tied up and he soon began his horrid work, he tore away the flesh my mother had kissed so often, scattered the blood my father had reared with so much care. At last fainting and bleeding I was cut loose, and ordered home to my old master. I shall never forget the diabolical grin that sat on his countenance as I almost staggered into the yard. From this time every moment I was threatened by him to be sent to receive another flogging.

One day some cattle got into the garden and trampled the flowers, and Easy knew he would be blamed. He ran away into the bush, but with nothing to eat except berries and raw fish, after six weeks gave himself up. He was sentenced to six months in a chain gang:

Behold me now a chain-gangsman working in chains; the thermometer was often at 120 degree of heat in the sun, which burned ulcers in the back of my neck, my eyes were sore and running, from the intense heat of the sandy place where we were working . . . The labour in the chain-gangs is very severe, and the discipline very strict; the men are flogged for the most trifling offence. Brute law is the order of the day.

In his fourth year Easy was flogged for breaking a wheelbarrow; feeling the sentence unjust he knocked down the overseer, for which he was flogged again. 'I resolved to escape from the hospital into the bush again, to join some of the armed bushrangers, at that time so plentiful in the bush; and as it appeared to me that every man's hand had been against mine, why my hand should be against every man's.'

So he escaped, but was caught by policemen, and shot one in the process. He was about to be tried for this, which he knew would result in his execution, when in 1833 a ship arrived with his free pardon: his prosecutor had admitted that he lied. 'I now stood a free man, after four years of severe and cruel suffering, ruined in body and mind—no not in mind I thank God not in mind.' He returned to England, and published his description of his sufferings in about 1846. There are obviously some exaggerations—it's a rare day in Tasmania when the temperature reaches 120° Fahrenheit (49° Celsius) and Easy would hardly have been set free after shooting a policeman—but the message is that unfair treatment could ruin a convict.

Billy Rowe was another convict who suffered. His voice comes filtered through that of his master, farmer James Fenton of Port Sorell, but it is included because it is one of the few stories of an inarticulate, unskilled convict. Naturally, Fenton described himself positively, but it does seem that like Dillingham and Tingley, Rowe had a good master. He had few other advantages, and Fenton implies that he was not very bright, with an 'evil star' which led him into trouble.

After a second conviction for theft, Rowe was transported for seven years, arriving in Van Diemen's Land in 1832. Still in his teens, he was sent to Point Puer, the reformatory built at Port Arthur for young male convicts, where they were supposedly taught a trade, though Rowe's story shows no evidence of any such training. He was assigned to a settler, but kept getting into trouble, with dozens of lashes and stints in chain gangs and at Port Arthur, for offences such as insolence, drunkenness, absence without leave, idleness and feigning illness. Finally he came to Fenton as an assigned worker. 'I soon discovered I had a strange character to deal with,' wrote Fenton. Rowe hated being watched at work; 'if I stood over him, he would probably throw down his tools and walk away to his hut in a paroxysm of temper'. Fenton did not usually punish his men, and 'I therefore determined to give Billy Rowe his own way as far as possible, for he was an active, good workman when he pleased.' Fenton gave him new clothes, tobacco, respect in asking his opinion about farming, and sympathy, listening to his stories of tyranny. A marvellous change came over him, wrote Fenton. He worked hard and Fenton recommended him for a ticket of leave as trustworthy, hard-working 'and apparently very penitent for his past misdemeanours, which I thought had arisen more from inability to brook coercion than from any innate vice'.

Just when Rowe was about to get his ticket, his 'small reflective powers' meant he agreed to abscond with three of his old mates. They stole a boat and made it to Melbourne, where they posed as free labourers looking for work. Two gained passages on an England-bound ship, but the other two were picked up by the police, and returned to Launceston.

One night Fenton was sitting reading by his fire when there was a gentle knock at the door. Billy Rowe stood there, looking at Fenton with tears in his eyes, crying, 'Master!' Fenton brought him inside, and he threw himself in a chair. 'Oh, master, master,' he sobbed, 'what I would give to be back with you again, but it's too late, too late!' Once he had overcome his emotion, he told Fenton that he and his friend had escaped from custody, and needed provisions. Fenton knew there were heavy penalties for helping convicts escape, but also that the 'poor fellows' faced execution if they were caught. He told Rowe he could not give him food, but would hold the candle while Rowe took it. 'Never, sir, never! I'll take nothing unless you give it to me.' Eventually Fenton persuaded him and he took the food, 'as delicately as possible under the circumstances . . . I have no room to describe the parting scene, which was very pathetic for a bushranger walking off with one's property'. Fenton told Rowe to leave quickly, since he was bound by law to report the theft the next morning. The men escaped by boat but were driven ashore on Flinders Island and captured. Fenton met them by chance at Bridgewater near Hobart, heavily chained, and was not allowed to speak to them. They were sent to Norfolk Island, which had been re-opened as a penal settlement in 1825, but Rowe's convict record provides no further information.

The combination of official records and convicts' stories show that during the assignment period, roughly until 1840 for men (1844 for women), the majority of convicts got through the system reasonably successfully. They were helped by their own capabilities, skills and attitude; good or at least adequate treatment; and an ability to use the system to their advantage, either by good behaviour or street cunning. About one-third suffered: those who were less skilled, less adept at helping themselves, who ran up against tyrannical or unsympathetic officials and employers, or who would not go along with the system. Every convict had his or her own story of course—the female convict voice is notably absent, since there are few letters written by convict women—but overall, it is clear that assignment was a remarkably successful way of integrating convicts back into society. They were not treated like criminals but sent to live in the community more or less as ordinary employees, and freedom, when it came, was more of the same. This was not the primary aim of assignment—which was to save the government money—but it was a fortunate result for many individual convicts and for the Van Diemen's Land community as a whole.

4

CONVICTS AFTER SENTENCE

While they were in the system, convicts were housed and fed by the government; once they left it, they were on their own, having to support themselves. What happened to them? There were three main divisions as far as Van Diemen's Land was concerned: those who never left the system in the first place; those who did but then left the island; and those who stayed.

THOSE WHO NEVER LEGALLY LEFT THE SYSTEM

Not all convicts gained their freedom, for a variety of reasons. Some died while serving their sentences—with the average age of death only about 40, this was to be expected, although the convict age of death was in fact higher than that of the general population in Britain. Convict rations were better than the British working-class diet; convicts received health care, rudimentary though it was; they often worked in the open air, healthier than industrial slums; and while under sentence they had less access to alcohol.[1]

The 6 or 7 per cent who died in Van Diemen's Land while under sentence mostly did so from disease—from John Isaacs, who succumbed to scurvy in Hobart in 1804, to John Bowman, with disease of the heart 62 years later. Others died from a range of causes: 'drowned while crossing the South Esk in a small canoe', 'falling down the shaft at the coal mines', 'died by the visitation of God by dislocating neck through falling from a fence', 'kick from a horse', 'effects of excessive drinking at "The Whalers Return", N[ew] Wharf, Hobart', 'killed by a blow on the head with a stick given by a fellow prisoner', 'mortally wounded by Constables in pursuit of him, as a Bushranger', 'drowned whilst attempting to escape from Tasmans Peninsula'. One woman died on Christmas Day 1852, falling from a coach between Launceston and Deloraine—Christmas then as now was a time for alcoholic celebration.[2] Some committed suicide, others were executed for murder, serious theft or homosexuality. In 1845 Job Harris was sentenced to death for 'Unnatural crime with David Boyd'.

Some convicts who became ill or insane never left government institutions, which at least provided some care. Thomas Blimson arrived in 1826 on a life sentence, which he certainly served: he did not receive a ticket of leave, and died in 1874 in the Launceston Invalid Depot. Charlotte Graham arrived with a seven-year sentence in 1845, received a ticket of leave but no pardon, and died in the New Norfolk Lunatic Asylum in 1892.

Many convicts left illegally, with 'Ran' often scrawled across records. It was relatively easy to escape from assignment and work gangs, and once free, convicts could rely on help from sympathisers, particularly ex-convicts. At the West Tamar near Launceston, the wife of ex-convict William Bond was alone in the house with her baby when at midnight she heard heavy feet tramping round the house. She was terrified. A gruff voice said, 'Don't be afraid, Mrs, we won't hurt you; we only want food; we are starving. Just you shove some vitals outside the door.' She hurried to obey and heard the feet tramp away, but, still terrified, remained awake all night. Her husband returned at dawn and found three men asleep in a shed. He told them to flee, to cross the creek and turn left. He would tell the police he saw them turn right. 'Your grandfather shook these poor, hunted creatures by the hand, and wished them good luck. From time to time he fed and helped in many ways these hunted fugitives,' ran the family story.

It was harder to escape from penal stations, but some did. The Morrisby family, ex-convicts turned hardworking farmers, told descendants how they found a naked man on their property, which lay across Frederick Henry Bay from the Tasman Peninsula. The man asked for clothes, promising that he would leave immediately. Assuming that he had escaped from a penal station on the peninsula and swum across the bay, the Morrisbys gave him warm clothing, and he vanished.

Once convicts escaped from the system, it was easy enough to leave Van Diemen's Land, especially for men with sailing experience—ships were often short of crew. Escaped convicts could bribe a captain to take them, or stow away, like the eight the ship's captain took in Andrew Whitehead's smuggling attempt of 1814. Many captains made 'piles of money' in this way, according to one old hand. Ex-convict John Frost reported that 'it is no very uncommon thing for convicts at Van Diemen's Land to escape to the whalers'—American whaling vessels owed no loyalty to the British, and often helped convicts escape, especially when it brought in extra revenue. John Boultbee, a sailor on a whaler which called at Hobart, described how after they left they picked up two runaway convicts at Bruny Island— 'rascals', wrote Boultbee. John Williams was a cook on a government brig taking prisoners to Port Arthur. It was easy work, he wrote, and since he was paid 'on the sly' in rum which he sold to the convicts, he made money. An American convict asked for help to stow away on an American vessel, and despite the government searchers, he got away.[3]

There were some exciting escapes. In 1828 the *Cyprus* put in at Recherche Bay on the way from Hobart to the penal station at Macquarie Harbour on the rugged west coast of Van Diemen's Land. Led by William Swallow, convicts seized the ship and marooned those who would not join them. Among these was a convict called John Popjoy, who made a coracle and managed to contact a passing ship, so everyone was saved. He was given a free pardon and returned to England. The mutineers sailed to China, where they pretended to be distressed British seamen. Some managed to get back to Britain, but a few were recognised by Popjoy. Several were executed but Popjoy saved Swallow, swearing that the others had forced him to join them. But Swallow had still mutinied, and was sent back to Van Diemen's Land, finally arriving at Macquarie Harbour in 1831, two years after his first aborted trip. He died at Port Arthur of tuberculosis in 1834. A ballad about this temporarily successful absconder was forbidden to be sung, but was still in circulation 130 years later.[4]

Escape was particularly enticing once gold was discovered in Victoria in 1851. Convict John Mortlock reported that gold brought the exodus of nearly all the free men 'and many not free'. Boats taking timber to Victoria would land them in isolated bays, and it was believed that the Tasmanian authorities connived at them leaving, to get rid of them. The police were always open to a bribe, said Mortlock. One man bribed a policeman to take him through the bush to an out-of-the-way port, and accompany him on board a ship. The policeman chatted with him while constables 'went through the form of searching', then everyone shook hands and the police left. Other convicts hid, in casks or large boxes marked 'this side up'. A skipper of a small trading vessel built a sliding panel in the bulkhead and made a hiding place for four people at £5 a head.[5]

With escape apparently easy, why didn't more convicts go? There were disincentives. Punishments for those caught varied from fourteen days' solitary confinement to twelve months' hard labour in chains. Those with seven-year sentences in particular could have thought it easier to serve out their sentences and gain their freedom. For some, such as Richard Dillingham and Henry Tingley, better fed and in easier circumstances than ever before in their lives, there was little incentive. Women found escape more difficult, especially as they could not get jobs as sailors, and there are few stories of women getting away successfully—but perhaps they were more successful in hiding their pasts.

What with dying, absconding or remaining in the system as an invalid or lunatic, about 10 per cent of convicts never left the system officially.[6] But 90 per cent did, about 65,250. What happened to them once they were free?

LEAVING THE CONVICT SYSTEM

Convicts had to apply for the various stages of freedom that enabled them to leave the system. They could gain a ticket of leave when they were half-way through their sentence. They had to report regularly to the police, but otherwise were free to earn their own living. For some, this was enough.

The next step was a conditional pardon, with the most common condition that the convict not return to Britain. If he or she did not want to do this, a conditional pardon was enough. Beyond this was a free certificate, or more rarely a free or absolute pardon. The convict was now legally totally free, and could return to Britain. Early records in particular often did not give such information, but of those convicts whose records did, about 10 per cent died or absconded, another 10 per cent stopped at a ticket of leave, just over 25 per cent gained conditional pardons, and just over 50 per cent gained absolute freedom.[7]

THOSE WHO LEFT VAN DIEMEN'S LAND

Some convicts escaped from Van Diemen's Land while they were still under sentence. Many more left after they were freed. Strong reasons drove them, both pushing them and pulling them.

The pull factor was economic. Though Van Diemen's Land was quite prosperous in the convict period, it has never been wealthy, and there have always been better opportunities on mainland Australia. It is much larger, with a greater population, more industry, more activity. After Victoria was founded in the mid-1830s, Van Diemen's Land labourers went there for the higher wages; by the 1840s, wages in Victoria were double those of Van Diemen's Land. Many ex-convicts left, and even more in the gold rush—in 1852 a third of Van Diemen's Land's population left, in search of quick wealth. Thousands more left in the economic depression of the 1860s and 1870s.[8] Altogether, at least half and perhaps up to 70 per cent of Tasmania's convicts left, mostly for Victoria, which could have been home to more Tasmanian convicts than Tasmania itself.

The push factor was the convict stigma. If convicts stayed in Van Diemen's Land it was hard to escape this, since they were always likely to meet people who had known them as convicts. Their children suffered too. In mainland Australia no one knew them and they had a chance to start afresh. As a visitor wrote, 'the first act of every freed convict would be to hasten from the colony, where the associations are almost exclusively of his evil deeds and punishment'.[9] William Derrincourt described in his memoirs how after he received his ticket of leave he went to Adelaide, where he posed as a new arrival from England—a complete break from his past.

Most convicts went to Victoria, but many went to the other mainland colonies, and to gold rushes in California and New Zealand. Some returned to Britain, though this was harder, because many had only a conditional pardon, and because it was such a long way. But a few turned up there, like Popjoy and Swallow in the *Cyprus* saga. James Backhouse wrote in 1834 that it was commonly said that no more than 1 in 50 convicts— 2 per cent—returned to Britain.[10]

In Victoria, many ex-convicts flourished. One Tasmanian free settler visiting Melbourne was entertained sumptuously by his former convict servant, once a London pickpocket, now living in luxury in a handsome villa with well-kept grounds and a carriage drawn by fine horses.[11] Few did as well as this, but many became tradesmen and farmers, or gained reliable jobs as labourers.

THOSE WHO REMAINED IN VAN DIEMEN'S LAND

Fewer than half the 72,500 convicts who arrived on the island settled there after their release—but that was still between 30,000 and 35,000, in a population which in 1853 was 65,000. Though the reasons to leave were so strong, there were also reasons to stay. Ex-convicts could have found a permanent job or set up a business, or established a network of family and friends they did not want to leave. Perhaps they were ill, elderly or unenterprising, or merely never got round to going. What did these people do in Van Diemen's Land?

There were five broad groups, though they merge into each other, and people could pass from one to another and back again. There is no firm evidence how many ex-convicts were in each group, but I would estimate that of ex-convicts who remained in Van Diemen's Land over the whole transportation period, 1803 to 1853, perhaps 5 per cent remained criminals; 10 per cent survived on the margins of mainstream society; 45 per cent were labourers; and about 30 per cent were in the lower middle class of tradesmen. About 10 per cent were the high achievers, who became wealthy or at least well-to-do, and who joined the middle class.

Some ex-convicts were serious criminals, continuing to murder, rape or commit large-scale theft. For example, George Williams, transported in 1841 for seven years for stealing a knife, gained his freedom six years later but was executed in 1874 for murdering his wife. Of all convicts, 7 per cent of men and 3 per cent of women were tried in a judge's court (which dealt with more serious offences) in Van Diemen's Land.[12] About three-quarters of their crimes were hardly serious: James Webber received two years' hard labour for stealing two shirts. But with half of all ex-convicts leaving the island, the proportion of recidivists among those remaining becomes higher. As noted above, perhaps 5 per cent of ex-convicts, mostly male, continued a criminal career. This is a very low rate of recidivism—in Australia today the rate is about 50 per cent—and supports the case that most convicts were not serious criminals in the first place.

The criminal group merges into the next, a marginal world of ex-convicts who existed by casual labour and petty theft, outside or on the edge of mainstream society. They lived in a world of pubs, brothels and sly grog shops (which sold illicit alcohol, often adulterated), protecting themselves and convict absconders, able to evade the law. Pubs were often rough, holding activities like cock-fighting, dog-fighting and gambling, frequently rigged. The few women in this group often worked as prostitutes.[13]

As James Boyce has described in *Van Diemen's Land*, some ex-convicts lived in the bush, maintaining themselves as best they could: farming a small holding, hunting kangaroo and possums, taking casual work, assisting bushrangers and other law-breakers, sometimes living as vagrants. In the bush the authorities had little power. The authorities suspected that men earning a precarious living in jobs like woodcutting and lime-burning helped bushrangers and escaped convicts, and Edward Curr, a government official, wrote contemptuously of men who did little work but lived on rundown small farms, surrounded by 'disgusting' piles of wool, bones, sheep-skins and manure. Quarters of kangaroo hung from trees, dogs barked, and 'idlers' lounged about. These farmers boasted that they could earn more in one day (presumably by theft) than an industrious man could in a month. All the suspicious locals gathered at their huts, which echoed with boisterous drunken mirth. In the 1840s Bishop Nixon described ex-convicts who 'loved to lead solitary lives, wandering away from towns and settlements, forming little groups in the bush, where they could remain unnoticed and unreproved'.[14]

These people were mostly single male ex-convicts who had not been able, or had not wanted, to establish a more settled life as part of the community. On the gloomy side, they were often in trouble with the authorities for offences like being drunk and disorderly, or petty theft. They could scrape by with their friends until old age, when they either went to the uninviting government institutions, or managed as best they could. But they had the comradeship of their fellows, never had to knuckle down to respectability, and did not care about the convict stigma.

There was some effort to control this group by, for example, making it illegal to hunt kangaroo without a licence[15]—a law which could never be enforced—but it was not pursued with much enthusiasm. This group was too useful to everyone else, the obvious ex-convicts who enabled respectable ex-convicts to hide their past (as will be discussed in Chapter 8). It comprised about 10 per cent of ex-convicts and, with the criminal group, suggests that about 15 per cent of convicts did not join mainstream society.

The third group of ex-convicts were labourers, working in unskilled jobs with low but at least regular pay, often on farms. Others rented small properties, scratching a living by growing crops and running a few sheep and cattle. Their lives were usually hard—though those who were married were often more comfortable—but they had some security. They sometimes turned to petty theft or became vagrants as jobs came and went, but more settled labourers did tend to conform to their neighbours and live respectably. As communities settled down from the 1850s these people did too, sending their children to school, joining in community activities. This group was predominantly male, but included some women, working as domestic servants or wives of labourers.[16]

Tasmania's labourers were almost entirely from the convict group, and whether they minded this being known probably depended on whether they had children to inherit the stigma. Those who did not had little to lose. Those who did, probably did not want to see their children suffer as a result of their own experience. It is difficult to find examples, as contemporary writers were not interested in labourers, but one of the more picturesque was 'Old Watts', presumably an ex-convict as most labourers were, who worked for a farmer at Bagdad, a rural community about 40 kilometres north of Hobart. He lived in the garden in a hut made of wattle sticks, and had a reputation of being the best man with a hoe in the area. In 1885, aged 78, he was still working—he probably had to, to survive. By that stage he had given up drinking, but he was still the best swearer in the district. The newspaper article which described him did not even hint at any ex-convict status.

Though members of this group were often found guilty of misdemeanours like being drunk and disorderly or petty theft, few were charged with anything more serious. The opinion of the time was that as soon as ex-convicts gained any standing in the community, any property or regular pay, they reformed at least to a certain extent, not necessarily from improved morals but because if they misbehaved and were caught they would lose these advantages. This was noted early: Robert Knopwood reported that the term used was 'I will not throw a Chance away.'[17]

The fourth group of ex-convicts comprised those with some skills, education or enterprise who either gained reasonably well-paying jobs above the labourer level, or set up their own businesses as carpenters, blacksmiths, shopkeepers, publicans or farmers. Some women ran businesses such as shops, but most in this group were tradesmen's wives. Early convicts were given small land grants when they were freed, and some became successful farmers. Forty-year-old William Jacobs, a sheep-stealer, farmed his grant at Clarence Plains near Hobart and built himself a four-roomed weatherboard house. He married four times—a great achievement given that there were far more men than women, and that he was an ex-convict with not a great deal of money. He had several children, and died in 1852 at the ripe old age of 90. John Clark, another sheep-stealer, called his Tea Tree land grant 'Rosewood'. He flourished, despite being raided by bushrangers and himself having sheep stolen—he sued the thief, in a reversal of his earlier court case.

In the township of Pontville, 35 kilometres north of Hobart, most businesses were run by ex-convicts. Both blacksmiths, James Undy and James Halley, had been transported, but both married and settled down as hard-working citizens. Thomas Sidney was transported for theft as a tattooed nineteen-year-old and committed various misdemeanours in the colony, but then married and built up a business as a baker. Ex-convict John Davis ran the Castle Inn, the grandest hotel in the district. Such people were not necessarily entirely respectable. In 1841 there was a dramatic occasion when a neighbour, Mrs Burnip, accused Mrs Davis of stealing eight turkeys, and John Davis and his brother-in-law were thrown in gaol. After a dramatic hearing in which Mrs Burnip admitted that the man she lived with was not her husband, the case was dismissed. Still, such disturbances were part of life in the 1830s and 1840s; there were plenty more examples in Pontville, but the community jogged along satisfactorily.

These ex-convicts managed to establish themselves comfortably. They had to work hard, but they became accepted members of their communities. Mostly married, they sent their children to school, helped their neighbours, often went to church, and in later years became the backbone of local football and cricket clubs and other community groups such as friendly societies. This group, the lower middle class in the terminology of the day, was largely made up of ex-convicts, who could have felt proud of their success—beginning as convicts but making reasonably comfortable lives for themselves and their families. Few, if any, mentioned their convict past. This was the largest group of convicts who were married, and many people who are descended from convicts find that their ancestors were from this group.

There was some notice taken of these people, who reflected well on a convict colony. Visitors described how many ex-convicts had become 'sober and industrious members of society'; if they kept off the drink and worked hard, they could do as well as anyone. John Mortlock, a convict who had an extremely positive view of the convict system and its results, used this group as his justification. 'Hundreds of both sexes form connexions [marry or form de facto relationships], live comfortably, and earn an ample maintenance for themselves and children, who, if not expatriated, must, perforce, have continued criminals, or died from want in misery and despair,'[18] he wrote.

The final group—the high achievers—joined society's middle class. The majority of the middle class were not of convict origin, so ex-convicts had to behave extremely respectably to keep their new status. The middle class, mostly prosperous business and professional people, valued education, good manners, respectable behaviour (at least on the surface), community progress and cohesion. Ex-convicts who had made good might be accepted by this group—as long as they said nothing about their background. Members of this group sent their children to private schools, went to church and supported charities and community activities, and (at least outwardly) committed no crimes at all—not for them the scandal of being found drunk and disorderly on a Saturday night. These were the ex-convicts about whom most was written, partly because contemporaries were surprised and pleased to find convicts doing so well, and partly because they were important enough even without their convict past to make their mark.

Benjamin Hyrons, transported for passing counterfeit coins, continued to work in his trade as a shoemaker after his pardon in 1831. He married an innkeeper's daughter and in Launceston ran an inn, opened the town's first theatre and started a coach service that eventually linked all major Tasmanian towns. He also ran a steamer service on the River Tamar. Described as 'civil, obliging, active and industrious', he made a great success of his life, with little outside help—though he did marry four times, so had inside help. He died in 1873, a successful and respected businessman.

Scientific achievement was another way of entering the middle class. After gaining his pardon, Francis Abbott became not just a successful watchmaker but one of Australia's leading amateur astronomers. For 25 years he was responsible for timekeeping and meteorology, working unpaid, and his observatory in Hobart was used to observe comets, transits of Mercury and Venus, and the variable star Eta Carinae. A member of the Royal Society of Tasmania and the Royal Astronomical Society of London, Abbott published many scientific papers; sadly, his controversial theory about Eta Carinae was disputed and only generally accepted after his death.

Art was also a way to success. Thomas Bock helped to procure an abortion for a woman he had seduced, and was transported in 1824. A noted artist, he designed the first Bank of Van Diemen's Land notes, illustrated almanacs, and painted portraits of wealthy patrons, something for which he gained more acclaim at the time than his paintings of Aborigines, for which he is now well known. William Buelow Gould, Charles Costantini, Thomas Wainewright and Knut Bull were also well-known convict artists, and James Blackburn was a successful architect.

Most women who gained acceptance by this group did so through marriage, for it was harder for a woman to succeed in a business on her own. Maria Lord was the island's most prominent ex-convict businesswoman. Originally a convict transported to New South Wales, in 1805 she came to Van Diemen's Land as the mistress of Lieutenant Edward Lord. A naturally shrewd businesswoman, she opened Van Diemen's Land's first shop. It was reported that once when a man urgently wanted a pound of tea for his wife, who was in labour, Maria sold him her last packet at the astronomical cost of six guineas. Through her own eight pregnancies she continued to run various shops for years, always with success, and by 1821

Maria and Edward Lord, now married, owned 35,000 acres, 6000 cattle and 7000 sheep—and most of this success, said a contemporary, was due to Maria, not Edward (although his social standing and connections must have been a help).

Edward often went to Britain to trade goods, and while he was away Maria acted as his agent. But she went too far in independent activity. In 1824 when Edward returned from a trip, he took Charles Rowcroft to court for 'criminal conversation' (an affair) with his wife—though a government clerk, William Parramore, reported that Edward wished to gain 'a divorce from a wife whom he is now ashamed of, because she can't read, and can put herself in the most original passions and curse and swear' [original emphasis]. After Edward Lord won the case he moved permanently to England with the children. In England he in turn enjoyed a prolonged criminal conversation with the children's nurse, who bore him five children. He lost much of his money, which supports the claim that Maria made most of it. Meanwhile Maria opened another shop, which became the best known in Hobart. Two of her sons returned to Van Diemen's Land, though she never saw her other children again.

A handful of ex-convicts did spectacularly well. The most successful arrived early, when a fluid society gave convicts more opportunities, and made a fortune from the land. David Gibson, a 24-year-old illiterate labourer, was transported in 1804 for armed robbery. In Hobart he absconded and received 300 lashes, and was court-martialled for piracy and sentenced to remain a convict for life. It was an unpromising start—but then Gibson became the overseer of Edward Lord's vast landholdings in the north of the island and built up a flock of sheep of his own. He received his pardon in 1813, and six years later a clergyman married him to Elizabeth Nicholls and baptised their two children. That year Gibson received a large land grant on the South Esk River, and he opened an inn on the main road from Hobart to Launceston.

When Governor Macquarie visited Van Diemen's Land in 1821 he stayed in Gibson's inn, and treated him just as he would any prosperous free colonist. The inn was so comfortable, and the dinner of 'beef stakes' so good, and Mr Gibson himself so 'civil and useful', that the party returned there, staying three nights. Macquarie named a site for a local town Perth— 'Mr Gibson who is a native of that town having promised to build a good inn there'—so the town was named after a convict's birthplace. Hard-working and enterprising, David Gibson was an outstandingly successful farmer. By 1839 he owned over 7000 acres, and he and Elizabeth had ten children. Gibson helped establish the Presbyterian church in northern Van Diemen's Land, and when he died in 1858, this former illiterate thief was described as a 'gentleman'.

Thomas Burbury was born into a family of respectable tenant farmers, and in 1832 was sentenced to transportation for life for machine-breaking. In Van Diemen's Land he was working as a shepherd for a farmer at Oatlands in the island's midlands when his wife Mary and their daughter joined him from England. Soon he became a constable, and after catching sheep and cattle thieves, received his freedom. He flourished as a butcher in Oatlands, branched into buying property, and in 1842 a letter in the English *Coventry Herald* reported his progress: he was Chief District Constable, and owned property worth about £6000, a fortune. How demoralising for Englishmen who had led blameless lives, never in trouble, still struggling on a low wage! Thomas was a pillar of the local community, elected to the Oatlands municipal council, a supporter of every local good cause. In 1870 his obituary described him as a highly respected colonist.

WERE CONVICTS BETTER OFF IN VAN DIEMEN'S LAND THAN IN BRITAIN?

In 2007–08 I undertook a survey of 452 contemporary Tasmanians' attitudes to transportation. It showed that many people believe convicts were better off in Van Diemen's Land, where there were more opportunities for them than in Britain—but was this really the case? It is impossible to sum up with accuracy the lives of 72,500 different people, but some factors can be taken into account.

As discussed in Chapter 2, conditions in Britain for the working class were poor, with unemployment, low pay, a low standard of living and no social services except for dreaded workhouses, which sustained life but only just. Almost all convicts came from this class. But as convicts they had dismal experiences: found guilty of a crime, imprisoned, transported across the world and then serving out their time in Van Diemen's Land, separated from their families and friends. The pain of being forced to leave much-loved family and never see them again can't be overestimated, for those who had much-loved family. The whole experience ranged from, at worst, utterly appalling, to at best, challenging.

After this period had passed—what then? Those convicts who joined the lower middle and middle class in Van Diemen's Land were almost certainly better off. Some could have risen similarly in Britain, especially those who had received training in a trade, but they had better chances in Van Diemen's Land, where society was more open, the population was smaller and less established, and there were more opportunities for newcomers.

But the majority of ex-convicts, the marginalised people and labourers who formed about 60 per cent, were not in this position, especially male convicts. Without literacy or training in a trade, they had little chance even in Van Diemen's Land of becoming anything more than poorly paid labourers, as they would have been in Britain. Still, in some ways life was easier for labourers in Van Diemen's Land. The warmer climate made poverty more bearable. Working hours tended to be shorter, and food, especially meat, was cheaper. In Britain, a labourer was lucky to taste meat once a week, but meat was cheap in Van Diemen's Land, and a convict employer measured his convicts' meat as on average three pounds a day—1.3 kilograms. Better diet, a smaller population and lack of industry and slums meant that people were healthier, and life expectancy was higher—about 44 years in 1860, when in Britain life expectancy averaged 41.[19]

But there was a great disadvantage for men: with so few women transported, most male ex-convicts could not gain a female partner. Some might not have wanted to, but probably most did, given the advantages that marriage brought. A much higher percentage of women married than men: of the women transported on the *Australasia*, about 90 per cent married in the colony, but of the men transported on the *Duncan*, only 20 per cent married, generally the young, skilled men with shorter sentences.[20] Figures from two shiploads are not conclusive but do point to a pattern: for the many unskilled older men, and even for younger but less attractive ones, finding a marriage partner was difficult, often impossible.

WOMEN CONVICTS

Female convicts had different advantages and disadvantages from men. There were fewer of them: 12,500 compared with 60,000 males, about five men for every woman. They had to live in a strongly male environment—rough, often drunken, with endemic violence—but there was great demand for them in their traditional roles of wives, domestic servants and prostitutes. On arrival they were almost all assigned to settlers as servants, where, as with men, some were treated well and others badly, with a strong possibility of rape by their masters or other convicts. At times they were imprisoned in the four female factories or houses of correction at Hobart, Launceston, Ross and George Town, when they were awaiting assignment, ill, pregnant or undergoing further punishment. Fewer women than men absconded, but they had another way of escape from the convict system: marriage. The authorities were reasonably enthusiastic about this, believing that marriage made men behave better. Convicts had to gain permission to marry and this was not given lightly, especially in the first years of the sentence, but once a female convict married she was usually assigned to her husband and the authorities took little notice of her, unless she committed an offence.

Almost all commentators at the time saw female convicts as dreadful, worse behaved than men: rowdy, rebellious, disobedient, drunken, and far too free with their sexual favours. As the Reverend H.P. Fry pointed out, once a female lost her virtue (code for sex outside marriage), that was it: 'a felon may grow honest [but] lost female virtue is irretrievable'. Female convicts were 'the most wretched beings you can imagine'.[21] Historians have explained this bad press by pointing out that these women were behaving in much the same way as working-class women in Britain, but writers in Van Diemen's Land, all middle class or gentry, had never been in much contact with such women and their rowdy behaviour. In Van Diemen's Land women convicts were mostly domestic servants and therefore around the house, so these writers had more contact with them than with convict men, who usually worked outside, their drunkenness, rowdiness and so on less visible. At the same time, Victorian expectations for women's behaviour were far higher than for men. While men were allowed their little foibles, women were expected to be quiet, submissive, obedient, sober and sexually chaste, exactly the opposite of the complaints about convict women. Middle-class Victorians had an obsession about chastity, and to writers like Fry the sexuality of convict women, normal to the women themselves, was terrifying.

A woman like Ellen Scott was typical of those who horrified Fry. Arriving in Hobart in 1830 with a life sentence, as a convict she was charged with 48 offences, and in the female factories she was part of the 'Flash Mob'—rebellious, cheeky, trafficking in alcohol and tobacco, sometimes lesbian. 'Flash' was thieves' cant for gaudy, showy, wide-awake, 'knowing'.

In 1833 Ellen was charged with 'indecent behaviour during the performance of divine service by the Revd William Bedford Junr at the Female House of Correction'. This could have meant she raised her skirts and slapped her bare bottom at the clergyman—which could have led to the myth that all the women in the factory bared their bottoms at Bedford during a church service. Flashing (in the modern sense) was a recognised working-class insult, seen before in Van Diemen's Land, and Ellen's story could have been told, retold and exaggerated in pubs and brothels over the next decades until it developed into the myth—there is no contemporary evidence for it at all except Ellen's sentence, and the story of all the women baring their bottoms was not written down until the 1870s, and then by an unreliable source.

Ellen was accused of having an 'unnatural relationship' with another female convict and was punished, again and again, but the Flash Mob was not to be daunted. The women made life hard for the authorities, and from 1839 to 1844 there were at least six major riots in the Hobart and Launceston female factories. Ellen received her final punishment in 1843, thirteen years after her arrival, when she gained six months' hard labour for trafficking in tobacco in the female factory. In 1847 she received a pardon, and vanished from the records. In recent years women like Ellen have been seen as heart-warming examples of convict spirit.

Critical middle-class observers could not accept that immoral, badly behaved women could reform—this was an age where in novels, no woman who had sex outside marriage could have a happy fate. In real life they could. Julia Mullins was the original 'notorious strumpet and a most dangerous girl', as the surgeon on her convict transport wrote. 'The trouble which she gave me is unaccountable. Repeatedly I have been obliged to put her in irons . . .' This from a man who cohabited with another female prisoner during the voyage, and held drinking parties in his cabin for sailors, female convicts and even the ship's captain. Julia, a prostitute, was transported in 1825 aged nineteen for theft. In Van Diemen's Land she was found guilty of 24 offences, mostly being drunk and disorderly, sometimes absent without leave, once drunk and in bed with a policeman. But she gained her ticket of leave in 1836, and shortly afterwards began to live with Peter Hill, with the first of their five children born in 1838. Julia was never again in trouble; she and Peter married in 1848, and settled down as farmers at Campbell Town in the island's midlands, not in the least either notorious or dangerous.

Many female convicts behaved ideally in Van Diemen's Land. In 1834 Sarah Bonner snatched a packet containing five shillings from the pocket of a man in a London street. She was tipsy at the time. Sarah had already served three prison sentences for disorderly conduct, and she was transported for seven years. Not promising—but in Van Diemen's Land she was not charged with any offences at all, and received her certificate of freedom in 1841.

A rare middle-class woman convict was 25-year-old Mary Ann Brown, a London governess, who could teach French, Italian and music—unusual skills for female convicts. Mary Ann was transported for fifteen years for forging an order for the large sum of £470, and arrived in Hobart in 1845. Two years later she bore an illegitimate child, who died aged three months. She committed one minor offence, and married and gained a conditional pardon in 1853, only nine years into her sentence. What happened to her after this is not known.

There were many women like Sarah and Mary Ann who outwardly at least behaved much as the authorities wished, but they were ignored by critics like Fry. Since most women married, and most people, men and women, settled down to a reasonably ordered life after marriage, probably at least three-quarters of female convicts lived a more or less law-abiding existence after they had served their sentences.

FAMILY LIFE

In Britain, with few social services, people relied on family and friends when help was needed. Parents, siblings, uncles and aunts, cousins and neighbours helped in illness, took on apprentices, suggested marriage

partners, lent or gave money, took in orphans, gave advice and so on—
probably also arguing and irritating along the way, but providing a support
network which made life easier. When convicts were transported, in theory
they were torn away from this.

In practice, however, many convicts were transported with a relation
or friend. Of the 200 women convicts who arrived on the *Australasia* in
1849, some 20 per cent were transported with a relation, and a total of
41 per cent with someone who was tried with them—relations, friends,
acquaintances or at least someone from the same area.[22] One boatload is
not enough to generalise, but indicates that there was a reasonable chance
of being transported with a familiar face.

Some families were reunited in the colony. For example, Thomas Field,
transported in 1836 for coining, knew that his wife Sophia with their child
had already been transported to the colony. From 1817 the authorities
paid for the families of well-behaved convicts to join them in Australia.
This was useful as a way to bribe convicts to behave, improve the male
to female ratio in the colonies, and encourage families, for the authorities
believed that family reunions would be 'productive of much moral good'.[23]
Many families did not want to voyage across the world to join a criminal
relation, but some did, and others travelled out under their own steam,
like Mrs Savery and Mary Burbury.

Even if convicts were never reunited with family or friends, the system
seemed almost purpose-built to forge friendships. Convicts had a common
bond—themselves against the authorities—and the long voyage out gave
plenty of opportunities to form new ties. Many of the *Australasia* convicts
remained friends for decades. Twenty-five witnessed each other's marriages, 34 stood as godparents of shipmates' children, and some did both.
Ellen Connor was a witness when Mary Regan married Timothy Shea
in Bothwell in 1852, then stood sponsor to Mary and Timothy's second
child, called Ellen after her. Once in the colony, convicts were together
in barracks or female factories, in gangs, or assigned in private houses.
Again, being grouped together encouraged friendships to form—though
not always, for some convicts treated others badly.

Convicts could also form new family ties. Those who had left a spouse
in Britain were not officially permitted to marry again, but many did. All
the minister needed in the colony was a declaration, not even on oath, that

the convict was single. But if a convict was known to be married, remarriage was impossible unless they could prove the death of their spouse. Settler David Burn noted that convicts used many strategies to appear single; for example, when he was going to Sydney, a convict asked him to post a letter there, addressed to herself. Guessing its contents he opened it, and read a detailed story of how the woman's husband had died in Sydney, leaving her a widow.[24] Some convicts made sure when they arrived that the authorities knew they were single. In Britain William Davis said he was married, but in Hobart when asked his marital status he replied, 'Single, I said I was married I lived with a Woman named Sarah Barnes two year.' Some convicts even carried proof. John Bowtell had also formerly said he was married, but in Hobart replied, 'Widower 1 ch[ild] I have a letter from my master stating that my wife died in Florence. It is signed by him Lt Albert Cunningham.' Had these men changed their stories when they realised they had little chance of seeing former wives and wanted to be able to marry again?

Those convicts who were single or kept spouses a secret and could find a partner were free to marry, and the general opinion was that marriage benefited nearly everyone. 'If matrimony among the convicts were more generally permitted, it would prove most beneficial,' wrote Burn. 'Marriage has, in repeated instances, been the means of taming and reclaiming many.' One settler observed that 'married men in the colony conduct themselves with most propriety, and are the most industrious, sober, and honest'. Those without wives 'to make up for want of domestic comfort drink spirits whenever they can procure them'. 'With a buxom wife I should have been much happier,' wrote convict John Mortlock.[25] Assigned servant William Derrincourt commented that his master's marriage 'added greatly to the comfort of all'.

Through marriage, convicts gained much-needed benefits. For women, it provided financial support and physical protection, otherwise problematic in a strongly masculine society. For men, it provided domestic comforts—not just sex, but home comforts of cooking and housework, and assistance in the family enterprise of farm, shop, pub or trade. For both genders, marriage provided companionship, someone to complain to at the end of the day, and often children, who helped to earn a living, provided a reason to keep going, and could support parents in old age.

Not every marriage provided all these comforts, but on the whole married people were better situated than single. Almost all convicts who succeeded in establishing themselves successfully were married.

But, as discussed earlier, because of the small percentage of women in Van Diemen's Land, many male convicts could not marry. In both 1816 and 1847 as examples, women formed only 30 per cent of adults. This meant virtually all women who wanted to could marry. 'Women are more wanted than any thing,' as one settler wrote home; a shipload who had no skills at all 'could get husbands directly'. (If they wanted them—another settler thought if an emigrant was 'a pious, sensible and amiable girl, I don't think she will very easily find the man of her choice'.)[26]

Mary Smallshaw's career illustrates just how well a convict woman could do through marriage. A Welsh silk throwster—who twisted strands of silk together to form thread—she was transported for theft at the age of 24. Her daughter later described her as a neat and pretty little woman, fond of reading poetry. A year after she arrived in Launceston, Mary married the clerk of the magistrate's court, but he died a few months later. Mary was not alone for long; soon she was living with the magistrate himself, Captain Andrew Barclay. He was 63 and she was 27, but no one seemed to comment on this age difference. In 1820 Mary gave birth to a daughter, and next year Andrew married her. He was described as 'a hard-drinking old sea dog fond of preparing, and presumably drinking, his own wine who had only married Mary to legitimise the child'; but whatever he was like, whatever the reason he married Mary, whatever the age difference, Mary had achieved a great coup for a convict woman by marrying a gentleman, a wealthy man with large estates. They lived comfortably, the daughter married well, and grandchildren were born. Mary died aged 45, her husband following her seven months later.

Not everyone benefited from marriage. In 1831 James Cooper was bound over to keep the peace after being found guilty of assaulting and beating his wife Elizabeth on two consecutive days. It seems a minor punishment compared with transportation for seven years for stealing a shawl, suggesting that the authorities, perhaps the general community, did not see domestic violence as a serious offence. Mary Scott was transported in 1823, and in August 1829 married Edward Sweeney, another convict. He was serving a fourteen-year sentence and had behaved well, in a decade only committing the crime of being absent from Divine Service on Sunday. But in December he murdered Mary. He was executed—but that did Mary no good.

FORCED LABOURERS OR EXASPERATING DOMESTICS?

In 2005 I went to hear a talk entitled 'Mary Morton Allport and her convict servants', expecting to sympathise with the servants—unfortunate women, forced to slave long hours at mind-numbing domestic work which I would have hated. As the talk progressed my sympathies veered round towards Mrs Allport.

In August 1832 free settlers Mary Allport, her husband Joseph and baby son Morton arrived in Hobart. They employed an assigned convict in their home—which consisted of two rooms and the use of a kitchen, so they were all on top of one another. Marion Campbell impressed Mary as being remarkably clean and fond of children, but one day she took Morton to buy vegetables and it was six hours before they were seen again, by which time Marion was tipsy and Mary was beside herself with worry. The third time Marion became tipsy she went to sleep on the kitchen table, and it took three constables to take her away.

Marion lasted two months; Helen McKay lasted eight days. She did little work—she 'seems to consider if she walks about all day at the end of a long broom, it is as much as I can require of her'. Then Mary found her raiding the spirit cupboard. She had to go. Agnes Richardson started off well, but on Christmas morning she was tipsy. The next evening Mary went into labour, and she and Joseph sent Agnes to the watchhouse, since she was still tipsy and they found a rum bottle 'concealed about her person'. Mary engaged a nurse to help with the birth, and though 'a dawdle and a slattern' she had one great advantage—she never got drunk.

In January, Elizabeth Adams became Mary's fourth convict servant in four months. Seventeen days after Elizabeth arrived, Mary invited two of her husband's colleagues to dinner. Elizabeth got tipsy and the meal was a disaster. With only just time to prepare the vegetables she insisted on starting to make an apple pudding, and in the end the guests dined on a tough leg of mutton with no vegetables or pudding at all. Then a pound note was missing and so was Elizabeth, until she was found asleep in a shed in the garden, 'Q.D. of course' (quite drunk), Mary wrote. She and Joseph decided to employ free servants in future, despite the extra cost.

Mary's diary was written from her own point of view, with nothing about what the servants thought. Forced to do long hours of domestic labour, in constant contact with their employers, separated from their families, is it any wonder that many convict servants drank when they could, did as little work as possible, and generally misbehaved according to the expectations of their employers? Assignment was a remarkably successful way of reintegrating prisoners into general society—but it did have its problems.

For every convict story there is a counterfoil. Eliza Williams, a convict working as a trusted servant for the Leake family in the midlands from 1852 to 1856, kept in touch with the family after her pardon, even when she and her husband moved to America. She exchanged letters, called her children after Leake family members, and in 1894 sent them an invitation to her son's wedding in Detroit.

5

CONVICT AND FREE

Isle of beauty! o'er thy favor'd shore
The brightest gifts of Nature's ample store
Are freely scattered . . .

Oh! happy, happy land, to thee 'tis giv'n
To turn the erring from their ways to Heav'n . . .
To win them from the paths which they have trod,
To seek a gracious Saviour and their God.

So wrote 'Frances' in 1833, in a poem entitled 'Van Diemen's Land'. She was almost certainly Frances Gunn, in the coveted position of 'always free' (that is, never a convict), and she was typical of this group in three ways. Firstly, she did not use the dreadful word 'convict', merely mentioning 'the erring'. Secondly, though she seemed to feel superior to these erring people, her own past had its dark side. Her father was a doctor and a gentleman; her husband, an ex-army officer, was a major landholder and magistrate; but her mother had been a convict. This was never mentioned, of course.

The third way Frances was typical was that she led an entirely respectable life. The raucous behaviour which marked Van Diemen's Land's first years had received a jolt. Until about 1820 few free settlers came either to

New South Wales or Van Diemen's Land. Britain was at war with France until 1815, so travel was difficult and men were needed in the armed services. After the war more ships were available and the armed forces discharged most of their men, who had to find work at the same time that Britain was suffering a depression. Suddenly the Australian colonies looked more attractive, with their free grants of land and convict labour. To cash in on this, in the early 1820s three men who had lived in Van Diemen's Land published books to encourage emigrants. They had to challenge a frame of mind in which, as one new arrival wrote, 'emigration of 15,000 miles to a receptacle for convicts was regarded as an almost suicidal adventure'.[1] They did this by ignoring convicts.

The most optimistic chronicler was George Evans, formerly Van Diemen's Land's surveyor-general, distinguished in his term of office for taking bribes. In 140 pages he mentioned convicts only five times, and then positively, stating that farmers had convict labourers, and that convicts had comfortable accommodation. The rest of the book was all about Van Diemen's Land's wonderful climate, 'perhaps the most salubrious of any on the globe', and its scenery, fertility and future prosperity, so encouraging for 'those who are desirous to emigrate to this delightful island', the 'abode of peace, plenty, and rural happiness'. The other two books contained slightly more about convicts, complaining that they were treated too well and became idle and dissipated through alcohol and debauchery, but like Evans the authors mostly described the island's many attractions.[2] If you did not already know Van Diemen's Land was a convict colony, you would not pick it up from these books (or from later books of a similar sort).

As a result of the situation in Britain and encouraging books, from 1820 a stream of British emigrants arrived in Van Diemen's Land. Many were upright, god-fearing citizens, a contrast to the boozers of the past. They started businesses or farms, served as magistrates and encouraged churches. This group provided an alternative to the ramshackle society of earlier years. People who wanted to be thought respectable had to join them, and as this middle class grew, the respectable attitudes of Victorian England gained more and more acceptance. Society developed as a duplicate of Britain's class system, with an elite, an upper middle class, a lower middle class, and the mass of the working class. The first two classes were almost entirely made up of free settlers, but the lower middle class and particularly the working class were dominated by ex-convicts and convicts.

The free settlers were not a homogeneous group. They were divided not only by class, ranging from aristocrat to labourer, but by religion (Anglican, nonconformist and Catholic); education (from university-educated to illiterate); racial origin (mainly English, Scottish and Irish); occupation, with gentlemen such as army officers having nothing to do with those in trade (one man warned his wife not to visit his agent, for 'as a merchant he is not visited by the first class'); wealth (rich and less so); and manners, with one shocked emigrant reporting home that it was not uncommon to hear in 'the first society' dreadful expressions such as 'You are a D–d Scoundrel' and 'You Bug–r go to Hell and be D–d to you'.[3] Some emigrants saw Van Diemen's Land as home, others as a place to make enough money to retire to Britain. They had only two things in common: they weren't convicts, and they hoped to make their fortunes.

Some did. Henry and Sarah Hopkins were a lower-middle-class couple who arrived in Hobart in 1822 as free settlers with four boxes of boots. Henry was an astute businessman, and had training that came in useful in the colony. He opened a shop to sell his boots, but his main interest was wool. In England he had worked in the woollen business, and one day saw wool from Van Diemen's Land lying on the London docks in an unsaleable condition, for the exporter did not know how to present it. Hopkins did, and built up a trade from Van Diemen's Land. In London an agent invested the proceeds in ironmongery, which Hopkins sold in his Hobart shop. In this way he founded not only the Tasmanian wool trade but his own fortune—he was said to double it every nine months—and by 1835 he and his family had moved from their original two-roomed hut to the largest house in Hobart. The Hopkins family could not join the elite, not with the handicaps of both trade and lower-class origins, but they became solid members of the upper middle class, much involved in promoting the Congregational church.

Few free setters had the success of Henry Hopkins. Almost all emigrated, as he did, because they could not succeed in Britain: 'Few emigrate who enjoy prosperity at home,' as an observer commented.[4] This might not be their fault—younger sons, orphans, officers dismissed when the army downsized—but many emigrants were failures in one way or another: unsuccessful businessmen, black sheep paid to leave by their families, people escaping a bad reputation, or one step ahead of the constable. They could not always succeed in Van Diemen's Land either, and many were in a precarious position, socially and financially. But they all had one advantage: they were not convicts.

Educated emigrants provided almost all the information about Van Diemen's Land to their British contemporaries. Like Robert Knopwood, they tried to make the place sound like every other British community of the day, an ordered society with its rule of law, civil service, police force, schools, churches and respectable entertainments. They wrote little about convicts, partly because they were a shameful aspect of the colony, and partly because such authors seldom wrote about the working class (think of the novels of Jane Austen and Charlotte Brontë). 'Knowing how little your fancy is accustomed to follow the transported thieves in their exile . . .', Augustus Prinsep wrote home in 1829. He was one of the few who was interested to see how 'this land of regenerated thieves' was turning out, though in a condescending way. 'The chief amusement to strangers is the constitution of this society . . . founded upon the dregs that have been drained from England,' he wrote, and suggested that everyone in the island would end up misusing their aitches.

Emigrants' attitudes to the penal system varied. Some took convicts for granted. Henry Button recalled that when he landed in Hobart and saw a gang of 40 or so convict men in chains, 'young as I was the sight produced in me a feeling of revulsion, and I was greatly shocked. Alas, I soon became accustomed to the sickening sight.' Many writers ignored the convict group. Sarah Hopkins, the wife of successful entrepreneur Henry, did not mention them in her diary. In 1846 Nehemiah Bartley visited an aunt at Bagdad. The farm hands were convicts, and convict servants were great smashers of crockery, he wrote in his memoirs, but this was his only reference.

Another group of writers admired the convict system, which provided them with cheap labour. As Augustus Prinsep approached Van Diemen's Land, he felt that it seemed like 'some infernal country of torments', so bad was its reputation: 'knowing . . . how gloomy a place the character of such inhabitants makes this country appear,' he wrote home. But like many others he found reality not so grim. 'The convicts I find much better servants than I expected,' one emigrant wrote. These authors thought convicts had better conditions than the labouring class in Britain, since they were well fed and not worked too hard—'Mr Bedford gives his convict servants wine to dinner'. In return, they thought, most convict servants worked as well as those in Britain, and masters had more control over them. William Parramore described his convict servants as more alert than English labourers, and another writer thought they had to have had some intellect to have committed crimes, and were easier to teach than country bumpkins. At Dennistoun near Bothwell the best shepherd at finding lost animals was a former London pickpocket. There were even the arguments that having convicts made the free population behave better, to differentiate themselves, and that helping them was a privilege which enabled you to get to Heaven.[5]

These writers did admit that many convicts stole and got drunk when they had the opportunity. However, added one encouragingly, murder was rare, and with Governor Arthur organising the police better, the colony was more orderly, with less theft and bushranging. Altogether, as William Barnes wrote home, 'We are not in that dread of convicts as you imagine.' Augustus Prinsep made an amusing story of his household. 'If the histories of every house were made public, you would shudder. Even in our small ménage, our cook has committed murder, our footman burglary, and the housemaid bigamy! But these formidable truths are hushed up, or tried to be so.' A third traveller wrote in a similar vein: 'In Van Diemen's Land the highway robber becomes a night watchman; the lost woman [prostitute], the children's governess; the forger becomes a cashier; even the assassin, after purification, turns farmer and labourer; in London he kills his neighbour, in Hobart Town he feeds him.'[6]

Other writers thought the system dreadful. With no character to maintain, convicts were 'desperate in crime', 'void of every good quality'. Obstinate, impertinent, liable to steal, unskilled, assigned workers needed constant watching, which encroached enormously on employers' time. David Burn complained that when he asked the authorities for a ploughman, they sent him a 'tin-japanner'—an industrial worker. Burn failed to 'make him useful' so returned him to the government, and was sent a

London chimney-sweep. No one really understood how to reform convict servants, said George Lloyd, but it was a great topic of conversation in Sorell where he farmed. Lloyd thought treating them as brutes did no good; he agreed with another writer that 'kindness and conciliation will effect wonders even with this abandoned race'. Others thought convicts just took advantage of kind treatment. If a master was generous his convicts imposed on him, wrote a visitor, but if a master was strict, there were a thousand ways convicts could retaliate—ploughs broken, sheep lost and so on. But employers have always complained about servants, and there were just as many complaints about free servants—useless, demanding high pay. Ex-convicts were criticised for combining the worst of both worlds, demanding high wages and being audacious. If reproved, they often told their masters that they were as free as they were.[7] The different points of view were the result of different experiences with convicts, and different attitudes to crime and the lower classes.

Some people did not like the thought of being among convicts: 'there is something extremely unpleasant in the idea of being surrounded by convict servants,' it was 'strange to be in a country of thieves'. Others thought the whole system of transportation was wrong. George Lloyd depicted convicts as 'unfortunates', expatriated from their native land for crimes ranging from murder to stealing bread to sustain life. All received harsh treatment and the 'degrading appellation of a convict'. One settler felt that the convict 'like an ugly nose, spoils the face of the country'. Some writers felt transportation was slavery, morally evil, which meant British character in the colonies became depraved. 'It is impossible to speak or to think [of convicts] without feelings of distress', being surrounded by 'those who have the brand of crime and punishment upon them'. Or, as travel writer Jane Roberts wrote more prosaically, 'gangs of these unfortunate people walk about in chains, which is far from an agreeable sight!'[8]

Writer Caroline Leakey gives the fullest picture of a middle-class person's view. Intelligent, deeply religious, Caroline sailed to Van Diemen's Land in 1847 for her health, and to help a married sister with her young family. She noted what was going on around her, and after she returned to England in 1853 wrote a novel, *The Broad Arrow*, published in London under a pseudonym in 1859. It tells the story of an upper-class convict (as all heroes of convict novels were) battling the forces of darkness—Maida

Gwynnham, accused unjustly of murder after being seduced and betrayed. She feels superior to other convicts, spurns offers of help from lower-class people, converts to Christianity too late to do any good, and ends her days in the dreaded Hobart hospital where her repentant seducer finally arrives, just too late to see her alive. He goes mad. A highly unrealistic picture.

As the heroine, Maida should gain the reader's sympathy. Other convicts do not. Leakey showed that they could do well—two of the convict characters marry and set up a prosperous business—but on the whole she depicted convicts negatively. Too many were dishonest, drunken and not very bright. A nursemaid took Baby out for an airing, and was found hours later drunk in a pub, Baby having cried herself to sleep in a room nearby. A servant wheedled two gowns out of a visitor and swapped them for drink. Next morning there was no breakfast: the cook was drunk, singing coarse songs, trying to fight the master, and the other servant had absconded. Many convicts treated their fellows badly, cheating or abusing them. Women faced special difficulties. The son of one employer tried to seduce Maida, who slapped him. The employer accused her of insolence and improper conduct, and the magistrate sentenced her to a month in the cells. This is unjust, she protested: the magistrate upped the punishment to two months.[9] Leakey's was very much the middle-class view of both convicts and servants, similar to that of Mary Morton Allport—probably with elements of truth, but with no understanding of the pressures on convict women. But whether it was realistic or not, this was the attitude that reached the reading public.

If few writers described convicts, even fewer described how convict and free mixed in the community. Those who did depicted everyone taking for granted the basic distinctions between convict and free, master and servant, but remarkably free-and-easy relations between the groups, probably a continuation of the relations in the first twenty years, which later migrants could not eradicate.

Again, the fullest description of community attitudes comes in *The Broad Arrow*. Convicts might be drunken and unreliable, but their relations with the 'always free' are amazingly friendly. They are seen through the eyes of Bridget, a young Englishwoman visiting family—obviously based on Caroline Leakey herself. She is a more believable character than Maida, and a local review praised the book for its 'fair representation'. Convicts are everywhere in *The Broad Arrow*'s Van Diemen's Land—on the streets, driving cabs, in houses as servants, even in society ('up country several of the most flourishing families are of doubtful origin'). Bridget is advised never to mention convicts in public, lest ex-convicts' feelings be hurt.[10] But convicts, the norm in the community, have little shame about their position. Bridget scolds her young Tasmanian-born cousin for mentioning that someone is a convict. 'Oh! it's nothing being Gover'me't out here, cousin; everybody nearly is—I mean all the poor peoples; *she's* a prisoner,' he says of their neatly dressed servant. '"Yes, ma'am, I'm Government," bobbed the woman, without the slightest tone of self-depreciation.'

Convicts chat with non-convicts in their 'free-and-easy way'. This attitude, the 'unavoidable contact with the mixed and sometimes questionable society', means the free have to accept convicts as people. 'I did not expect that prisoners would so mix with us as they do in every-day life,' says Bridget. There is a gulf between convict and always free, mainly because of their different social class, but at the same time there is remarkably equal social intercourse. Here the convict servant Robert is discussing his marriage with his employers, the Evelyns:

'Which girl do you really want, Robert?' asked his mistress.
  'Well, ma'am, I've sote my mind on Madda . . .'
  'What does Maida herself say?' asked Mr. Evelyn . . .
  'Oh, I haven't said nothin' to her.' . . .
  'I advise you to hear what she says before you think any more of it. I have my doubts on the subject.'
  'Gals is always agreeable to marrying; maybe you'll tell Madda you'll recommend us when we've kept company a bit—she won't go against your wishes.'
  'I'm afraid she will in this instance,' said Mr. Evelyn drily.
  'O darned!'

This free manner of talking is similar to Knopwood's chatty discussion with convicts about tigers (recounted in Chapter 1), and seems fairly typical of relationships in Van Diemen's Land.

Other writers echoed Leakey. In 1830 a visitor noted that a free arrival quickly imbibed from convicts 'such ideas of liberty, equality and independence . . . that he is found to be afterwards completely incapacitated for the situation of a subordinate'.[11] In 1848 surveyor James Calder took a party of convict assistants to the bush, and found John Jones, the overseer, intelligent and authoritative. Like all convicts he was sympathetic to runaways, said Calder, and when the party found four sailors who had jumped ship, Jones asked if he could give them food. Calder knew Jones would give the sailors food anyway, so he replied, 'Go to the devil with you' with a wink. Jones laughed and walked off. 'Disrespectful scoundrel,' wrote Calder with amusement. At Wedge Bay, Calder stayed with the signalman, John Perkins, a convict and former boxer, who was 'very civil and communicative . . . of course I broached no subject about his past life that might in his present condition be distasteful to him'. Of course. In the bush they found the remains of escaped convicts and Perkins, upset, wanted to leave. The work was not finished, but Calder respected Perkins' feelings and let him go.[12]

John Sturzaker, a blacksmith transported for seven years for poaching and stealing a gun, arrived in Van Diemen's Land in 1831. He obtained his free certificate in 1837 and his 'self esteem appeared undented by his convict past', as his descendant Lesley McCoull wrote. In 1843 he was charged with feloniously receiving 52 pairs of stolen blankets. He avoided punishment, claiming the blankets had been given to him by the captain of a vessel, now providentially sailed, in payment for a bad debt. Six days later he was in court again, suing an employer for non-payment of wages, calling himself 'a person of such *unimpeachable* character'. He did not gain his wages, but he comes across as a self-confident man quite able to stand up for himself. So were the convicts one traveller noted in Hobart, annoying and heckling passers-by, 'as impudent a set of rascals as ever existed'.

There were some harsh masters, of course, and some convicts suffered greatly; but even a convict like Henry Easy, who described a brutal master, depicted more personal relations between the two than the cold superiority of a master in Britain. Often writers about colonial Van Diemen's Land contradicted each other, but everyone agreed on convicts' and ex-convicts' attitudes. Confident, impudent, easygoing, disrespectful, unsubdued—all these adjectives indicate that they were not crushed by their situation. No one ever called them humble, obsequious or penitent. The main difference between convict and ex-convict was that, while convicts did not seem to mind their status being known—they could hardly escape it, since the fact that they were prisoners was obvious—once they were free, the majority tried to ignore their convict past.

This confident, cocky attitude was so typical of Van Diemen's Land's convicts that it was known on the Australian mainland as 'Vandemonian'. A Victorian landowner found Vandemonians great 'bouncers'—a Vandemonian entered a room with a swaggering air of great importance, clearly thinking he had no equal, even though he was only a paltry shopkeeper's boy. 'Vandemonians are certainly the most self-important, conceited men I ever had the luck to meet with.' A parliamentarian criticised the behaviour of his opponents, saying it ranged 'from the extreme of vandemonianism to the extreme of namby-pambyism'. South Australians found that Vandemonians were energetic in cutting wood and worked hard (for themselves), but charged high prices. The observant visitor Anthony Trollope noticed that people on mainland Australia used 'Vandemonian' in 'jeering mirth' about all people from the island, convicts or not: Vandemonians had a spirit of their own, said Trollope.[13]

Vandemonians, or 'Vandies' for short, were independent, tough, rowdy, obstreperous, cynical and suspicious of authority, able to come to terms with difficult conditions and battle on in the face of adversity, making the best of often difficult circumstances. You could argue that the Vandemonian spirit was the basis for the Australian national spirit—but evidence is slender, and the claim would irritate mainland Australians. Convicts from New South Wales do not seem to have had the same reputation, possibly because they were less independent and rowdy, but probably because there were fewer New South Wales ex-convicts than Vandemonians in Victoria, which only developed into a thriving community in the period after transportation to New South Wales ended.

The Vandemonian spirit sprang from the circumstances ex-convicts found themselves in. They formed the majority of the population, so were not a despised minority. The crime most convicts were transported for, petty theft, was not seen as a disgrace by the working class—thieves were not particularly ashamed of their crimes. The government had to maintain convicts, who might be punished and treated harshly but would never starve, so it was not a matter of life and death if they did not please a master. There was no need for humility.

The initial twenty-year period where convicts were treated much the same as anyone else in the colony set up a pattern which was later modified but never obliterated. Most convicts were treated quite well, better than labourers in Britain, as many observers commented. All this meant that most were not crushed by the system, but could live within it in a reasonably normal manner.

Pioneer societies with their lack of amenities usually encourage independence and resourcefulness—but not necessarily cynicism and distrust of authority (think of the law-abiding Pilgrim Fathers in America). It was the convict system which did this: it was often unfair, with widely differing punishments for the same crime, and there was a good deal of corruption and arbitrary rule by tin-pot, often unqualified bureaucrats—few first-rate administrators were going to volunteer to serve in a distant, unimportant penal colony. The law was not always strictly enforced, and this led to more cynicism.[14] The lack of women in Van Diemen's Land encouraged a masculine culture, particularly rowdiness and drunkenness; the absence of family encouraged ex-convicts to be obstreperous, to stick up for themselves—no one else was going to. But Vandemonians were still ex-convicts, and carried a stigma that could never really be erased, especially once they were outside the island and not the norm in the population. Perhaps the bravado, the 'bounce', which was part of the spirit was also a cover for the insecurity this stigma brought.

A great question at the time was whether ex-convicts were accepted socially by the upper class. Some free settlers recorded their attitudes. Edward Abbott and his fellow army officers in New South Wales decided to have nothing socially to do with ex-convicts, and Abbott kept to this resolve after he moved to Van Diemen's Land in 1814. At this time few would have agreed with him, but with the rush of upright free settlers in the 1820s he gained allies. In 1821 recent emigrant Janet Ranken told her family that 'the society here is abominable'—they all only wanted to make money 'by hook or by crook'. Edward Lord, gentleman-born and 'worth half a million', was acceptable, but though his ex-convict wife sent her daughter and sister to call on Janet, 'I have never returned the call yet nor shall . . . I shall rather be without the kindnesses Mrs Lord has in her power to show me than visit her'. In 1824 government clerk William Parramore described society's two groups: 'the government party' who were 'friends of good order and government', and the 'liberals', ex-convicts and their friends. Many, even of the government party, 'would not hesitate to associate with an emancipist [a pardoned convict] if his character had been irreproachable since his transportation', said Parramore, but added: 'these characters are very rare and I know of but one'.[15]

A few people were more tolerant. Under the Arthurs, ex-convicts were not invited to Government House, but people with convict connections were not entirely banned. A fuss arose in 1834 when Mrs Arthur invited to a ball a young woman whose grandfather and stepfather had been convicts. Arthur's nephews were so incensed that neither came to the next Government House dinner. Seven years later the secretary of the Bothwell Literary Society wrote to the governor, trying to prevent 'an angry collision' among its members. Some wanted to admit ex-convicts 'who are in all other respects perfectly unobjectionable characters', but others took offence at this, and 'both are preparing for battle'.[16] But Mrs Arthur and some members of the Bothwell Literary Society were in a small minority. Most upper-class free settlers had nothing to do socially with the convict group. Though ex-convicts were not totally barred from joining elite society, most were—in the 1820s Knopwood had only one ex-convict friend, far fewer than in earlier years.

Acceptance by the elite did not matter to most ex-convicts. They came from the working class in Britain, and they would never have expected to attend Government House dinners or meetings of the Bothwell Literary Society. Much more important to them was whether they would be accepted publicly as members of the community, and here the free society had little choice. There were so many ex-convicts that they had to be accepted.

Proof of this is shown by the fact that there was no real name for ex-convicts in Van Diemen's Land, which shows that they were not an identifiable group set apart. In New South Wales pardoned convicts were called emancipists, but this term was seldom used in Van Diemen's Land, which had a much higher percentage of ex-convicts. Nor was 'expiree', as a writer in the anti-transportationist Launceston newspaper, the *Examiner,* stated in 1850: 'There are two terms we detest, emancipist and expiree: every free man is entitled to all the privileges and immunities of a free man, and ought to be known only as a free man.' Generally, when newspapers had to write about ex-convicts they used euphemisms, and elsewhere in the *Examiner* article ex-convicts were called 'all who are now free, but have once been otherwise', 'persons of this class', 'tradesmen' and 'those who have passed through bondage'. Landowner James Ross described a convict shepherd in obscurely delicate terms: in England he had been a smuggler, 'the accidents of which uncertain occupation had finally led to his visit to this colony'.[17]

Free settlers might feel superior to convicts, but they had to accept them in the community, in public if not in private. They could not show superiority, because they would have to give a reason, and this would bring out the dreadful fact that everyone wanted hidden: that convicts and ex-convicts formed so large a part of the community. For everyone's sake, Van Diemen's Land must look like a free community, and nothing about convicts should appear on the surface. In Victorian Britain, appearance was all-important.

There were practical reasons as well. All levels of society, even the elite, became permeated with ex-convicts' families. Especially in the early days when there were far more men than women, even gentry men married convicts or their daughters—they had little choice. William Gunn, chief magistrate in Launceston, was married to a convict's daughter; George Armytage, prominent free settler in Bagdad, also married a neighbouring convict's daughter; Alfred Butler, son of prominent lawyer and landholder Gamaliel Butler, married the daughter of convict Robert Logan—though none of the Butler relations came to the wedding.[18] Even so, they would never, ever hint at the new Mrs Butler's convict past. They wanted no reminder that they were related to a convict's daughter; in the wider community, people wanted no reminder that they shared a community with convicts.

Other areas where ex-convicts and free settlers invariably mixed were religious activity, private education and business. Churches, all struggling to survive in the early decades, welcomed any adherents, especially the less numerous Catholic and nonconformist denominations. Many ex-convicts became pillars of their local churches; if ex-convict David Gibson was prepared to support the Presbyterian church financially, his money was welcome and he himself had to be accepted by the congregation. Schools, too, could not discriminate. Though some private schools in New South

Wales refused to admit convicts' children, this was not the case in less prosperous Van Diemen's Land, where no private school was financially secure and none could afford to reject any pupil. The most exclusive girls' school, Ellinthorpe Hall, accepted daughters of convicts, and Launceston Church Grammar School, founded in 1847 and financially shaky for many decades, accepted all possible pupils. David Gibson's descendants went there, just as convict James Pillinger's grandsons attended the equally 'exclusive' Horton College at Ross.[19] To an even greater degree, ex-convicts were involved in business. A majority of non-convict males were ex-convicts, and they ran many of the colony's shops, pubs, factories, coach services, ferries and so on. Ex-convicts and their families formed at least half the non-convict population, and were so mixed with free settlers in so many areas that discrimination against them was impossible in any way except not asking them to your home.

An advantage to ex-convicts was that there was no physical difference between them and other free people, especially if they were reasonably prosperous and did not look like tramps (people assumed that all tramps were ex-convicts, as indeed most were): no particular racial features to set them apart, no special accent, no identifying mark. This was a great advantage to those who wanted to think of Van Diemen's Land as an ordinary British colony, not one whose population was mostly of criminal stock.

It was a different situation from that in Britain, pointed out John West, minister and historian. There, ex-convicts were few among the large population, and vanished into it. In Van Diemen's Land ex-convicts and convicts were the majority of the population, and people knew who they were, especially if they were at all prosperous—'their prosperity is flagrant,' wrote West.[20] But people kept quiet about it, allowing ex-convicts to blend into the community. Far better for the myth to grow up that everyone not a serving convict was free, had always been free, and that ex-convicts had died or left the colony.

During the 1840s campaign to end the evils of transportation it was said again and again that well-behaved convicts were accepted into the community, not necessarily as social equals but as citizens. 'To the well conducted, the industrious and dutiful man, whatever his former character, the public are indeed disposed to offer every encouragement; and prisoners generally participate in the comparative plenty of the colony,' wrote the *Examiner* in 1843, and in 1845 John West commented that many ex-convicts had 'made atonement by later behaviour', amalgamated with the free population, and obtained the position in the social scale they had before they were charged. 'They have never been taunted with past misfortunes by those more favourably situated,' wrote West. 'Commercial uprightness and moral rectitude have been the only passports requisite to admission into the society of reputable men.' The *Hobart Town Advertiser* wrote that the freed man, when well behaved, could mingle with the free. No questions were asked, and in time his original position was forgotten by others, 'and the consciousness only remained as a stimulus to better behaviour in himself . . . free prisoners were becoming, and become, an orderly race, and fast supplying the deficiency of a tenantry, and a peasantry, in the colony.'[21]

The most thorough description of this process appeared in the *Examiner* on 2 November 1850, when a group was trying to set up an ex-convict association:

> It has hitherto been the boast of this community that the free inhabitants have been a united people: having common objects and identical interest they have gone hand in hand together . . . persons of this class [ex-convicts] may open private schools and pursue any avocation they choose: all the rights of citizens are conferred upon them; and hitherto, except by a few proud and ignorant men of no esteem in society, they have never been reproached. Many of those now appealed to [ex-convicts] have won the confidence and esteem of their neighbours: they have nurtured families; they have been punctual in the discharge of obligations; they have been liberal in sustaining, and forward in promoting social and political reform; they and their descendants are not distinguishable among the mass with whom they freely associate . . . The emancipist has no interest separate from the emigrant or native-born colonist.

So well-behaved ex-convicts could join the respectable community, which in practice involved those who became middle class, the lower middle class, and many of the labourers—about three-quarters of all ex-convicts. They were treated as normal citizens, their past not mentioned by anyone, at least publicly.

An example of the extreme care taken not to ask about the past occurred when the 1847 census was taken. The compilers noted the difference between the numbers of ticket-of-leave holders given by the Convict Department (9012) and the census (5714). The reason was, the compilers explained, that those collecting census information were not allowed to ask respondents about their 'civil condition in life', and probably many ticket-of-leave holders had represented themselves to the census-takers as Free Persons. So government officials were not allowed to ask people their status, but had to accept the version given to them. In the census the Free Persons section was divided into three categories: born in the colony, arrived free, and 'other persons', meaning ex-convicts—the dreadful word was not to be used.[22]

The picture which develops is of a cheerful, reasonably comfortable ex-convict group, who though they mostly found themselves in the lower orders of society, did not particularly mind, since this was only what they expected. Histories depict pleasant, hard-working communities of neighbours who might not always be friends, but who rubbed along pretty well. There was a good deal of drinking, a fair amount of petty crime and some major crime, but most ex-convicts settled down to a humdrum, quite pleasant life. All this group worked together, socialised together and married among themselves. An aristocratic French visitor thought that as ex-convicts found themselves equal and responsible beings in a society composed of 'themselves alone . . . there sprung up a certain energy of well-doing amongst these convicts',.and they worked hard, felt themselves to be men and soon became heads of families.[23]

There were some exceptions to these generalisations. A few ex-convicts did not mind their past being known. They almost all came from the marginal group, those with no status, nothing to lose, and generally, no children to inherit the taint. When an anti-transportation meeting was held in a hotel at Green Ponds in the midlands (later Kempton), a newspaper article described how a group of ex-convicts stood outside commenting on the arrivals. 'Look at that long slender gentleman, the Publican, how would he have become so rich, but for us old lags, when he looked after the Constitution Hill Road Party?' 'Look at the young Bagdad Miller, where would he have been if there had been no lags here.' When no one else appeared, 'Do you think any of these old coveys will come?' 'No, no, harvest and shearing are coming on, and they are full of old lags, and glad to get them.' Here were cheerful ex-convicts who did not mind identifying themselves as 'old lags' to each other—though no names were used in the article, even though the writer was a local who would have known them.[24]

Though in the main ex-convicts were accepted, on the surface at any rate, there was bound to be some friction, especially in an unstable society where everyone had a living to make and few were really secure, either financially or socially. Free servants were often uppity towards convict servants, since they were doing the same job and their status was their only point of superiority. In retaliation, convicts annoyed free servants in any way they could, a visitor reported, and they often said that the only difference between them and free immigrants was that the latter came to Van Diemen's Land for fear of being transported, while 'government people', as they called themselves, had been caught. Convict John Mortlock became a teacher, and said frankly that he particularly enjoyed beating, for 'slight misdemeanours', boys whose parents had not been transported. A few people tried to keep a distance between convict and free: a gentleman was outraged when a gentry wife wrote a letter to a woman whose grandfather had been a convict; a Catholic chaplain did not permit an ex-convict to build a vault over his wife's grave, as he felt a distinction had to be made between the 'meritoriously conducted' and 'those of a different class'.[25]

When tempers were raised, free people could use someone's convict past as abuse. A court case transcript told of how in 1830 an overseer with the Van Diemen's Land Company argued with a convict cook about who owned a knife: 'I asked him if he called me a liar, he said yes, you are a liar, a b[lood]y liar, he said something afterwards, I asked him what it was, he said in reply Bollocks, I then called him a d[amne]d Convict, and again told him it was improper language to use to me.' Sarah Bellian told a New Norfolk court that 'my master's daughter called me a "Government w[hor]e"'. In 1852 the *Hobart Town Advertiser* reported that a man visiting a farm on business heard shouting inside the house. 'You Irish convict bitch, I'll split your head open,' the mistress was yelling at her convict servant. The visitor told the mistress he would report her harsh words to a newspaper, 'just to let people see how many of the unfortunate prisoners (especially women) are treated by persons permitted to have passholders, but who do not know how to behave to them properly.' The mistress said he would not dare—but he did.[26]

In Pontville in 1848 a teacher, Mary Ann Rennie, asked Constable Hodgins why he had withdrawn his children from her school. In a 'raging passion' he told her that it was a blackguard of a school and his were the only respectable children there—the others were blackguard children, children of prisoners. Mrs Rennie complained to the magistrate about Hodgins' libellous remarks, 'quite uncalled for and grossly false'. Hodgins admitted saying there were blackguard children at the school, but nothing else. So he felt he could admit calling children blackguards, but not the offspring of prisoners. Many if not most of the children in Pontville did have ex-convict parents, as everyone must have known, and probably some attended Mrs Rennie's school, but it was not to be mentioned. The magistrate refused to act on Mrs Rennie's complaint—such an outburst must be forgotten as quickly as possible. Ironically, though Hodgins emigrated to the colony as a free man, he had served a prison sentence in Britain and descendants believe the family emigrated to escape the shame—there were obviously all sorts of nuances involved, and many people had something to hide.

Giving these examples of friction makes it seem common, but these are a few examples over 30 years, and the facts that the visitor to the farm bothered to report the story and that Mrs Rennie complained indicate that such incidents were unusual. Some friction between convict and free was to be expected; more surprising was that on the whole the two groups got on reasonably well, their interest in keeping society functioning and in hiding the convict presence from outsiders overcoming their dislike or envy of others.

CONVICTS' POSITION IN NEW SOUTH WALES AND VAN DIEMEN'S LAND

It is generally accepted that there was a much greater division between convict and free in New South Wales than in Van Diemen's Land. Emancipists, as ex-convicts were called, were much more obvious in Sydney: there was a group of wealthy emancipist merchants, and emancipists had a vocal spokesman in William Charles Wentworth, whose mother was a convict. But even in New South Wales, claims historian Michael Sturma, the free–emancipist struggle was for power between different groups of the upper and middle classes. The great mass of emancipists were not involved, and Brian Fletcher describes how they formed their own social groupings, as did ex-convicts in Van Diemen's Land.[27] Van Diemen's Land, however, had few wealthy ex-convict merchants and no spokesman.

In New South Wales, emancipists were clearly seen more as a separate group than as part of the community. The same goes for their children. Convicts' children in New South Wales were often praised as behaving much better—drinking less, working harder—than could have been hoped for, considering their parentage, but there are suggestions that as convicts' children they were looked down on, as never being able to escape the convict stigma, and they were called a derogatory term, 'currency'— 'currency' as opposed to British 'sterling'.[28]

There is little suggestion that convicts' children were looked down on in Van Diemen's Land except, like all the convict group, by the elite. The term 'currency' was seldom used, and there was no other general name for convicts' children. Most writers did not mention them specifically—they were just part of the community, with much the same opportunities as everyone else.

In 1829 a group of seventeen 'Native Born' from the Brighton area, 35 kilometres north of Hobart, addressed a memorial to Governor Arthur—'native born' meant born in the colony, and did not include Aboriginal people. Some were sons of convicts, some the sons of free settlers, but they wrote as one. 'The Native Born, Proprietors of Land and Stock in the Colony . . . descended from Englishmen feel anxious to preserve in this remote part of His Majesty's Dominions the Character habits and Amusements enjoyed by the Mother Country,' they began. They could see that the authorities wished to favour 'native' colonists and 'preserve amongst them the Character of Britons'. By what better means could this be done than by that traditional British sport of horseracing? The memorialists wanted to set up a racecourse. (Arthur refused to allow this notorious haunt of gambling and drunkenness.)[29] These sons of convicts were just as keen to announce their descent from Englishmen and their British Character as any 'always free'.

6

THE TRANSPORTATION DEBATE

Percival Bosworth, a boatman, arrived in Van Diemen's Land in 1844, with a ten-year sentence for theft. Unlike most earlier convicts, he was not assigned to work for a settler. Instead he was sent to a gang to work on the main road between Hobart and Launceston, for by now a new system was in force: probation. At his probation station the aim was for Bosworth to undergo punishment, work for the government and receive training in skills and morals, before gaining a pass (like the old ticket of leave) which meant he could work in the community. He was soon in trouble for getting drunk and being absent; he gained a pass but lost it for absconding; and in 1850 he died in hospital in Hobart. Not all convicts suffered so much under probation, but it was generally harsher than assignment.

The probation system was developed by reformers in England as a response to criticism that assignment was too lenient, too chancy (a minor criminal might suffer with a bad master, and a rogue flourish under a kind one), and had no organised provision for reform. Some reformers disliked transportation altogether, comparing it to slavery, which degraded both convicts and their masters. Dissatisfaction came to a head with the publication of the report of an 1838 parliamentary inquiry into transportation, chaired by William Molesworth, which provided evidence substantiating these claims. In response, the British government stopped transportation to New South Wales in 1840. All convicts were sent to Van Diemen's Land under the probation system, which aimed to return them to the community as skilled and reformed citizens.

But like many well-meaning ideas, probation was not put into practice competently. Nowhere near enough money was spent; far too many convicts—35,000 from 1840 to 1853, far outnumbering free immigrants—were herded into huge probation gangs without adequate instruction in either skills or morals, or even adequate supervision. The small population could not absorb them, the limited labour market could not employ them, since they now had to be paid standard wages, and some convicts had to turn to theft to feed themselves. Many colonists were horrified. They lost their cheap labour. They saw probation gangs as nothing but 'schools of crime', with convicts emerging worse than they went in. Homosexuality occurred; this was a capital offence, dreaded by many as the most degrading of all crimes. Convict administration was criticised as corrupt and severe, rule by terror. Colonists had to pay for police, gaols and much of the probation system, which took up half the revenue, and problems were made worse by general economic depression, which meant difficult times for everyone, with unemployment, bankruptcies and property depreciation.[1]

Convict narratives describe harsh conditions. Life in the gangs was often hard, with brutal overseers and bullying among convicts themselves, and it was difficult to find work afterwards. Overall, hardly anyone liked probation, and at first most colonists would have been happy to return to the assignment system. However, the British government would not revive a system which had been so greatly criticised, so some colonists started to demand the end of all transportation. This possibility had been occasionally discussed for years, and as the free community developed, people assumed that transportation would stop eventually, especially after it ended in New South Wales. But once the problems of probation became obvious, from 1844 a movement grew demanding the end of all transportation and, as the British government showed itself increasingly unsympathetic to colonists' demands unless it agreed with them, self-government as was being granted to New South Wales. The British government stated that Van Diemen's Land could not have self-government because it was a convict colony, so demands for an end to transportation became inextricably mixed with demands for self-government.[2]

At first the anti-transportationists, or 'antis' as they were called, aimed to ask the British government to end transportation gradually and give the island self-government. Public meetings in Hobart in 1845 resulted in petitions with 1750 signatures sent to the Queen and parliament. The antis were incensed when they heard that the local governor, Eardley-Wilmot, told his British superior that most of the 1750 had not read the petitions and would be ready to sign anything.[3]

Gradually leadership of the antis moved to Launceston, under John West. A Congregationalist minister who had migrated from England in 1838 with his family, West established a chapel in Launceston. Earnest, upright, a fine writer and inspiring speaker, with a reputation for integrity which even diehard opponents could not dent, he was described as 'a man of rare intellectual power, genial and warmhearted, who quickly secured admirers who developed into attached and lasting friends'. West was keen to improve the community, especially morally, and helped found a Mechanics' Institute, City Mission, insurance company, cemetery, immigration society and nonconformist high school. He wrote a two-volume *History of Tasmania* (1852), an intelligent, well-researched appraisal, and took part in community life, winning a prize for his vegetable marrow at the Horticultural Society's show. With several colleagues, in 1842 West founded a newspaper, the Launceston *Examiner*, for which he wrote many editorials. At first the *Examiner* showed little interest in convicts and transportation, but as the anti-transportation movement grew West was converted, and came to believe that all transportation was morally wrong.

Most of Van Diemen's Land's many newspapers criticised probation from the colonists' point of view, but the *Examiner* also felt for convicts. Long periods in harsh gangs would drive them to despair rather than reform them, ran an article. Many convicts had committed crimes from 'impetuous passions . . . force of circumstances or temptations', not inherent depravity, and once they had served their sentences they had 'become amalgamated with the free population, and obtained that position in the social scale they had for a time forfeited'. But this was becoming impossible, with opportunities for ex-convicts vanishing as the colony was flooded with prisoners. However, the British government took no notice of complaints. The anti-transportationists saw only one solution: stop transportation.[4]

In 1846 William Denison arrived as governor. He was strongly in favour of transportation, partly because he had to uphold British policy, and also from a genuine belief that convict labour was essential to the colony's prosperity. But opposition to transportation was growing as more disadvantages appeared. Unable to find work with so many passholders on the labour market, many free immigrants and 'useful' ex-convicts were leaving for better opportunities on the Australian mainland, so there was an even higher proportion of convicts and ex-convicts in Van Diemen's Land. The probation gangs were settling into an even worse pattern of laxity, inefficiency and corruption. By now West was in full flight, and in 1847 published his '39 Articles Against Transportation'. The points were not impressive in themselves (to reach 39, some were either repetitive or minor), but the title echoed the Church of England's Thirty-Nine Articles, its foundation doctrine, putting the anti-transportationists among major reform movements. Antis claimed brotherhood with the great moral movements of the day, such as the fight against slavery in America.

In May 1847 another series of public meetings denounced transportation. By this time supporters were repeating the extreme terms used by British critics of transportation in the 1830s: transportation made the colony a sink-hole of crime, a cesspool of filthiness.[5] These were the terms that had helped New South Wales win independence.

Australians who have lived through heated, antagonistic public debates will be familiar with the scenario. Debate builds over an issue, with both sides expecting that as they put their obviously correct case, their opponents will see the light and agree. This does not happen, and debate becomes more heated, more exaggerated, with wilder enthusiasts on both sides making extreme statements. The community becomes polarised, and having made such a strong stance, neither side can compromise. The same occurred with the anti-transportation debate. Both sides used inflammatory language: the anti-transportationists exaggerated the evil effects of convicts, and the opposition press, without an overriding high principle, descended to personal attacks, exaggeration of the antis' activities, and ridiculous statements. One newspaper claimed that the opinion of the London *Times* (at this time possibly the most influential newspaper in the world) was not worth the paper it was written on, and another that the discovery of gold was not likely to affect transportation—when taking felons so near goldmines was a major reason for stopping transportation.[6]

Why did the anti-transportationists exaggerate the evils of convictism, when in the community around them they could see plenty of examples of well-behaved convicts? It was partly because the middle class believed that criminals came from a criminal class who could never really reform (a theory explored more thoroughly in the next chapter). The antis rarely considered the contradiction between this belief and local reality, and John Mitchel's writing provides a good example. A lawyer, son of a Presbyterian minister, Mitchel was transported for joining the Irish rebellion against British rule. Naturally he favoured the antis with their opposition to the British government, and naturally he assumed that all working-class convicts were innate criminals—'perfect fiends'—but he had to admit that the 'horrible convict cut-throats' he employed on his farm had their good points. 'Many of them grow rather decent . . . They are friendly to one another—hospitable to travellers', and behave 'partly like human beings. Yet human they are not.' The whole system was hateful, and the prisoners were debased:

> Many a time, therefore, as I look upon these quiet, well-behaved men reaping, not too arduously, singing, or smoking in the fields . . . — instead of rejoicing in *their* improved conditions and behaviour, I gaze on them with horror, as unclean and inhuman monsters, due long ago to the gallows-tree and oblivion.[7]

The other reason the antis exaggerated was grounded in the colony's tradition of protest. Colonists knew that complaining locally had little effect. Decisions about the colony were made in London, not Hobart, and what mattered was not what locals thought, but what the British government believed—which did not need to have much relation to reality. The British government generally relied on advice from its governor in Hobart, but if his opponents were persuasive enough they could prevail, as happened when assignment ended. Colonists' main weapons were petitions to the British government and lobbying by men on the spot in London, and one of the antis' first actions was to send an agent there. For decades colonists had been exaggerating their woes over one issue or another to

London. The antis believed that transportation was wrong: if to get rid of it they had to exaggerate its evils, the end justified the means.

In 1847 opponents to the antis emerged. The antis believed these opponents were encouraged, even organised and paid, by Governor Denison, whom they themselves viewed as a 'base and unscrupulous tyrant'. West thought that 'in perpetuating the convict curse [Denison] adopted any argument, however false, and tolerated any ally, however abject'. (Denison thought West 'a dirty dog with whom no gentleman would associate . . . a man of some talent, but certainly unscrupulous as to the means he employs to gain his object'.)[8]

The government had three possible groups of supporters: its employees, who had to support its policies or lose their jobs; some major employers, who wanted transportation's labour and could afford the increased cost; and ex-convicts, who could object to terms such as 'sink-hole' and 'cesspit' used to refer to convicts generally. The ex-convicts' first leader was William Carter, a free immigrant and Hobart businessman, who represented a group which seemed to be mainly made up of ex-convicts. Carter spoke against probation at a public meeting in 1845 but then changed his mind, and in 1847 tried to influence an anti-transportation public meeting. The antis had plenty of ammunition to attack him. They accused his group of trying to form class divisions by setting ex-convicts against free settlers, when these sections of the community had always merged in the past; of boasting that it would deny antis a hearing at the meeting, and providing free beer to encourage supporters to attend. This last tactic misfired, for drunken Carter supporters heckled the wrong speakers, and the meeting overwhelmingly supported the antis. Carter spoke, but was burdened with a 'rather peculiar style of oratory', became confused by heckling, and broke down when his every pause was greeted with cheering. The antis' opponents tried the same tactics at public meetings in Launceston, but were even less successful.[9]

Another source of opposition to the antis was the *Guardian; or True Friend of Tasmania,* a newspaper which began publication in 1847. It aimed to 'protect the unfortunate prisoner' and neutralise 'the cankering virulent poison of fell slander, which has been lately so ceaselessly poured forth against our Colony'.[10] Its editor was William Bailey, an Anglican clergyman transported in 1843 for forging a large cheque, and joined in the colony by his wife Mary. His capture of an absconder resulted in a ticket of leave, and in Hobart he joined the Catholic Church and became editor of the *Guardian*, whose owner was another Catholic ex-convict, James Moore.

In May 1847 came news that the British government had decided to halt transportation, but antis feared that the decision might be temporary. It was. Later that year it was announced that the convicts on Norfolk Island, reputed to be the worst of the worst, were to be moved to Van Diemen's Land. At public meetings speaker after speaker decried the move as unjust, with men of hopeless character and horrid vices, the 'quintessence of wickedness', brought to the island. A petition signed by 6000 colonists was sent to Britain, repudiating 'the penal stigma attached to this colony . . . but will they even hear of our petition?' West worried. 'The "odds are still against us".'[11]

The British government was seldom inclined to take colonists' views seriously unless it agreed with them, claiming that by emigrating to a convict colony settlers surrendered the rights they enjoyed as citizens in Britain. But by now even the government admitted that the probation system had its failings, and it was unjust to send all the Empire's convicts to Van Diemen's Land. It tried to find another site, but all other colonies refused to receive them. There was no alternative but Van Diemen's Land, and in 1848 transportation there resumed, though in a modified form, with convicts now called exiles. The antis knew there was little difference.[12]

The antis held more public meetings and sent more petitions, but realised that they had little effect. In November, for example, the tradesmen of Launceston held a crowded public meeting, with three banners inscribed 'The People', 'Let the Ministers Regard Our Rights', and 'Our Children Our Lives and Our Property'. The antis suggested new tactics, such as returning the worst ex-convicts to Britain, using force to protest, or publishing information in Britain about 'the enormities known to exist' (homosexuality) as the only way of rousing British sympathy and indignation. But West was firm: 'moral means only' would be used. He stressed that the antis had nothing against individual convicts, especially well-behaved ones who had always been encouraged by the rest of the community to rejoin it, their past ignored.[13] Though he never wrote down his principles, they are clear from his writing: nothing illegal; no violence; unwavering loyalty to Britain; no criticism of individual convicts, or of convicts already in the colony (though much of convicts generally); and no undue mention of taboo topics like homosexuality.

The antis' next tactic was to form a league of citizens who would pledge not to employ any convicts. The government would be left with thousands of unemployable passholders and its system would break down. The Launceston Anti-Transportation League was formed in February 1849, largely by graziers and by professional men like West. Tradesmen formed a second league, and a third was established in Hobart. Eventually these leagues merged. But the League failed. Not enough people joined it, and some who did still employed convicts, giving their opponents a wonderful opportunity of attacking them as hypocrites.[14]

In early 1850 West described himself as 'sick and sorrowful' at the lack of success. 'Nothing remains but to appeal again and again to the British public', though this had little effect so far. By now some of the earlier arguments against probation had subsided—the economy had recovered from depression, the British government no longer made colonists pay so much for gaols and police—but West remained sure that transportation was morally and socially wrong. No newspaper was pushing for transportation to be retained, but Denison's supporters attacked the antis as insincere, incompetent hypocrites, using 'low abuse and scurrility'; the 'canting morality-mongers and inebriated aspirants after senatorial notoriety' who have 'on every occasion . . . distorted or aggravated facts', and so on. J.D. Balfe, an official in the Convict Department, summarised the anti-anti view: convict labour had made the colony; ex-convicts were not criminals and the crime rate was low; the antis were hypocrites who had got rich by the convict system and now wanted to end it, and who outraged the feelings of convicts and ex-convicts. But he himself exaggerated, saying that ex-convicts—'that expatriated class whose feelings are perpetually outraged by the denunciations of men enriched by the temporary forfeitures of their rights as citizens'—would 'do no dishonour to any country in the world . . . there is nothing doubtful or obscure in the history of this colony'.[15]

Then the antis' fears came true, for in 1850 full transportation to Van Diemen's Land resumed. British attempts to find an alternative site had failed: when the *Neptune* brought a shipload of convicts to Cape Town, the inhabitants formed an Anti-Convict Association and refused to provide amenities for the ship, or cooperate with the government. For five months the *Neptune* sat in the bay, until the British gave up and sent it to Van Diemen's Land, where it arrived in 1850. The convicts were landed easily, the only opposition being a few placards. Similarly, Sydney's population prevented the *Hashemy* from landing convicts there, but they were landed in Hobart without opposition. Western Australia did accept some convicts, but only men in limited numbers.

Why was there no protest in Hobart, when opposition to transportation was so vocal? When the *Neptune* arrived local newspapers did not discuss this question at all, though many admired the Cape inhabitants' stand. There are several possible explanations, and a strong mitigating factor: as soon as the men arrived they were given conditional pardons, ostensibly to make up for their frightful journey. As one newspaper pointed out, they would all make for the opportunities of mainland Australia as soon as they could.[16]

Perhaps the antis feared that they did not have enough numbers, so did not try to oppose the landing physically: that is, they were not as strong as they claimed. Perhaps they were worn down by the struggle: an anti newspaper spoke of people 'demoralised or broken hearted' by their 'utter impotence'. They did not have government support (or at least neutrality), unlike settlers in Sydney and Cape Town. Antis with government jobs would be in trouble if they protested, and respectable middle-class people might not want to. Attending a meeting was one thing, but lining the shore in protest as happened in Sydney could have been quite another.[17] In Hobart the antis' opposition had shown themselves capable of riotous, drunken, even violent behaviour. The antis' leaders faced a nightmare situation where, if they called out their supporters to protest, their opponents could meet them with violence, and the government would blame them. Besides, John West, the overall leader, entirely opposed physical action. Placards and petitions remained the only forms of protest.

This new opposition to the antis had formed earlier in 1850. So far, except for William Carter's brief effort, ex-convicts had been quiet. But it was a fine distinction between calling convicts arriving in Van Diemen's Land moral scum, and including those already there in the accusation.

West admitted that offensive and unjustifiable terms used in the 'warmth of speaking' distressed respectable ex-convicts, and it was hard to keep wilder supporters in check; the *Examiner* sometimes used these expressions itself. Opposition grew, especially in Hobart. In Launceston, with fewer government officials to support transportation and strong nonconformist churches to oppose it, the antis had little opposition. Hobart, the capital city, contained the government and the majority of its employees, who supported transportation or at least could not publicly support the antis; and though both towns had much the same percentage of convicts and ex-convicts, Hobart, twice the size of Launceston, had greater numbers.[18]

In January 1850 a large advertisement in the *Guardian* alerted ex-convicts to an anti-transportation public meeting in Hobart. It told 'men and brethren' that this meeting was going to slander their colony, themselves, their wives and children, by calling them filthy scum, rotten dung. After all they had borne, their wounds were being savagely torn open. Had they not made the colony what it was? They outnumbered their opponents by many thousands and should have a commanding voice. 'Attend the meeting and defend yourselves.' Exactly who wrote this advertisement is not clear.[19]

At the meeting the antis' opponents were vocal. Riotous clamour broke out when wealthy farmer Thomas Gregson said he detested the convict system, and if it continued the colony would be plunged into an abyss of moral depravity. But he had no prejudice against 'any of that class of whom some may be here to-day'; any right-thinking person would be sympathetic to 'the unhappy men among us'. More clamour. When he could, Gregson continued.

'I am aware that it is a very difficult matter to discuss this subject,' he said. 'I know it is one which requires much delicacy, tact, and talent . . . I will not wound the feelings of any man in this assembly . . . [but] to use the word convict or emancipist is to give offence . . . you can't speak of convicts, of emancipists, without touching a cord [sic] that vibrates through the whole Colony!' Gregson claimed he had never offended a prisoner: 'I can bring all my prisoners in my establishment to prove that I never once called them "convicts".' Many of Gregson's words were greeted with hoots, yells, hisses and general clamour. Every respectable emancipist was in favour of cessation, he claimed; one he had talked to—'Name him!' came the shouts. 'If the convict question will not admit of being discussed . . .' More yells. Gregson sat down.

Even more clamour greeted the Reverend T.H. Forster, who stated, rashly, that he was a true friend 'of all virtuous prisoners who have obtained their position by virtuous conduct and honest industry—although there are few, I believe, in the colony!' Deafening yells, loud hisses, and tremendous hootings silenced him.

William Carter spoke for the ex-convicts (no one admitting to being an ex-convict ever did this). He objected to 'lies which disparage this colony, and which have brought down upon Van Diemen's Land its degradation, disgrace and insult (thunders of applause)'. Emancipists had improved their adopted country. Carter wanted 'to remove the stain which, I feel, rests upon this community'. The antis claimed that the brand of convict was indelible to emancipists and their children. But there were many ex-prisoners, said Carter, who were as respected as any immigrant (loud cheers).

The heckling died down as the meeting progressed, and eventually the antis carried their motions, and had their petition read and signed.[20] The *Guardian* continued to champion the case of 'that class of our fellow colonists, who, having emerged from bondage, have shewn themselves by their conduct worthy of the position to which, by habits of industry and unceasing perseverance, they have raised themselves'. Ex-convicts suffered many wrongs, it claimed. They could not be government teachers, magistrates or postmen. Newspapers carried advertisements from those wanting 'always free' employees. 'We deprecate in the strongest terms, any attempt made by any man, be he who he may, to cast the least reflection on those who have been prisoners. If a man is free there ought to be an end of it, and the question ought never be asked, in this Colony, whether a man arrived free or not.'[21]

In August and September 1850 the antis held another wave of public meetings. One in Hobart, with its inevitable inflammatory language—the prisoner population was the curse and ruin of the colony, prisoners were one and all demons incarnate, thieves, robbers and assassins—proved the breaking-point. 'Certain educated emancipists' in Hobart proposed forming a Prisoners' Protection Society, but to avoid 'any expression of feeling relative to caste or class' changed the name to the Tasmanian Union, so all men could join 'without invidious distinction'—evidently people did not want to join a society with 'prisoner' in the title.[22]

Mary Bailey, wife of the *Guardian* editor William Bailey, encouraged the Union:

> Ye who so long in helplessness have borne
> Your vaunting fellow-man's unpitying scorn;
> Whose tears—whose blood have water'd oft the soil
> Where deserts, changed to gardens, own your toil;
> Lift from the dust, once more, your sorrowing eyes—
> The auspicious hour is come—arise, arise!
> . . .
> Beware division—unity is might—
> Dissensions will your fairest prospects blight;
> In moral power proceed—may Heaven your Union bless!
> And grant your virtuous efforts safe and sure success.

Though all the main players in the transportation debate were married, Mary Bailey was the only wife who played a public role in it—and unfortunately for the Union, her good advice was not taken.

The Tasmanian Union's organising committee included several highly respectable men, like Carter and the Catholic priest Therry, as well as several convicts and ex-convicts, such as government clerk James Gray and publican Josiah Hand. But it is mostly difficult to tell which members were convicts, for no one identified them as such, and unless they had unusual names, like Josiah Hand, they are hard to trace. Of the two dozen or so names mentioned in connection with the Union, only Hand, Gray, Judah Solomon and John Davies were certainly ex-convicts. Who was really behind the Union is not clear. It was possibly James Gray, an upper-class law student transported in 1843 for seven years for suborning a witness. A model prisoner, in 1849 he had his conditional pardon and was working as a government clerk, Denison calling him 'a very useful man and one in whom you can confide'—the first governor who had confided in a convict for decades. But Gray was an unlikely leader; he failed to calm heated public meetings, and in his obituary in 1889 the *Mercury* wrote that though he was genial, benevolent and on the side of struggling settlers, with a long political career, 'many viewed lightly his political convictions'. Other suggested leaders were James Moore, the owner of the *Guardian*, and unnamed magistrates and constables—or Denison himself, working through these people.[23]

The Union's stated aims, strangely, did not include defending ex-convicts. Instead, it aimed to elect 'good' men to the Legislative Council, the governor's advisory council recently made partly elected, and rebut slander about the colony with statistics. An address called on possible members to unite, for 'we' had vastly superior numbers. Eleven branches were planned, and several were set up.[24]

The anti press attacked the Union strongly. The monstrous fact was true: 'persons who had been subject to penal laws' were marshalling their forces. Were they trying to make the stigma indelible? If a respectable man of this class kept quiet about it, that was fine; but if he ignored this 'civic disguise' and openly said he was an ex-convict, it was disgusting folly. Men might remain in oblivion of the past, yet they chose to make it public, creating the very scandal they hoped to cure. 'It is they who proclaim what no one takes an interest in.' The Union ignored the difference between respectable ex-convicts and 'hoary sinners who began life as they mean to end it. They are shunned, not because they *were* offenders, but because they *are* scoundrels.' The *Examiner* was more moderate. An ex-convict was only known as such if he admitted it, but the Union wanted to bring this division into the open, to have people labelled as convicts forever, to introduce discord and class division, to perpetuate what law and custom had made temporary. This was folly, and would bring disgrace to the whole community, for people in England did not discriminate, but saw everyone as contaminated by the convict stain.[25]

Newspaper attacks were the least of the Union's problems. Its support was already waning, for a number of reasons. It was obviously exaggerating: not all convicts were honest and respectable. It was hard to defend a group of people when none would admit to the status being defended, and whose leaders would not be named. There was truth in the argument that the Union's activities would perpetuate division by bringing the issue into the open. Most ex-convicts did not join, with claims that many respectable ones did not because they preferred to keep their past hidden; it seems that only men from the marginal group, 15 per cent of ex-convicts, would openly support the Union. Their rowdy behaviour deterred respectable people. The leaders misbehaved in some unspecified way, and disagreed with each other. Transportation was another problem: so many people opposed it that the Union did not want to defend it, but since the Union defended convicts it could scarcely oppose it. The *Guardian* at first opposed the British government exporting more convicts to 'infest these shores' because they competed for work with ex-convicts already in the colony; but later it tried to ignore the topic. Since transportation was the major question of the day, this was not a successful move. But it was typical of the Union: it did not really stand for anything, just opposed the antis.[26]

In February 1851 the Tasmanian Union held another crowded public meeting. Who converted this colony into a garden? asked one speaker. Who transformed comparative wilderness into a rich, luxurious and smiling country? The colony owed all its culture and improvement to the prisoner population (loud cheering). 'Where is there a man in this Colony who has not erred in some way or other?' But this was the Union's swansong. A public meeting in March attracted only eight people—the excuse that the Ethiopian Serenaders were performing that night was childish, thundered the *Guardian*, and it urged members to put petty differences aside.[27] Lack of leadership and support, internal differences, an unclear role and rowdy behaviour led to the Union's end.

Meanwhile, the antis' prospects were improving. In mid-1850 West was still gloomy, and the *Examiner* listed reasons why people refused to sign the Anti-Transportation League's petitions: they thought they were useless; they thought people in the League continued to employ convicts so were hypocritical; they didn't care one way or the other; they were about to leave the colony so weren't bothered; they didn't want to interfere in politics; they were government employees so they couldn't sign; they never signed anything. Then West tried another tack: appeal to mainland colonies for support. This had been suggested before, but by 1850 these colonies were more receptive. Large numbers of convicts and ex-convicts were leaving Van Diemen's Land for the opportunities of the mainland; naturally they were seen as responsible for all crime, and alarm grew. West organised a conference in Melbourne in 1851.[28]

On his Melbourne steamer was an upper-class British visitor, Colonel

Godfrey Mundy, an enthusiast for transportation or, as he described it, 'the privilege of shooting so much moral rubbish upon other and distant premises'. He was shocked when at Launceston a government official inquired into the history of every passenger, even his own, to ensure no convict was escaping, and horrified that some fellow passengers were ex-convicts: 'it seemed monstrous that they should be permitted to jostle gentlemen of character on equal terms'. He found West and his fellow delegate 'truly excellent men', but so keen to win him to their cause that he hid from them. They certainly did not convert him:

> It seems rather a hard case that old Mrs Mother-Country may not stuff her naughty children into a corner to punish and keep them out of further trouble, and to make them, as she hopes, good boys for the future. But so it is—England is not to be allowed to keep the little out-of-the-way useless island of Van Diemen's Land as a general penitentiary.[29]

If this attitude was typical of the British governing class, no wonder the antis had such a battle.

The conference in Melbourne was a huge success. West was an inspiring orator, and the meeting formed the Australasian League, dedicated to abolishing transportation from all Australia and ridding the country of the convict stigma. The discovery of gold in New South Wales in May 1851 stimulated more support—gold would attract even more ex-convicts—and soon the League had branches in New South Wales, Victoria, South Australia and New Zealand as well as Van Diemen's Land, and a board in London. From now on, editorials in the *Examiner* were confident. Union was strength; success was sure. In Launceston the largest public meeting ever—with women present, for the first time—inaugurated the Australasian League. Its banner was unfurled: a true-blue background for a just cause, a white border for purity, a Union Jack to show it was no banner of rebellion, and the five stars of the Southern Cross as an emblem of the members' new home, showing that the league looked to heaven for success (not, as opponents claimed, a reflection of the flag of the rebellious United States). The meeting sang 'God Save the Queen' to show its loyalty, and speakers announced that the League was giving transportation its death blow, with a force no government would dare despise.[30]

At the same time that the Australasian League was growing, Victoria became independent, and Van Diemen's Land was given a partly elected Legislative Council, with a reasonably wide franchise—Governor Denison made sure that many ex-convict men could vote. Despite this, the antis swept the polls, winning fifteen out of sixteen seats. The British noticed this, as well as the formation of the Tasmanian Union, with the alarming possibilities of mob violence and a convict takeover, especially coming soon after the 1848 revolutions in Europe with their terrifying scenes of public revolt overturning governments. One English article about the Union was so 'severe' that the *Examiner* cut out the worst passages before reprinting it. In the parts left, the article claimed that 'English felonry' in Van Diemen's Land aspired to alarming domination, and the island would become a republic of thieves.[31]

Also alarming was the behaviour of a group in Launceston during the elections. Outside an antis' dinner, they broke windows and waved the French tricolour, the flag of rebellion. On nomination day a similar group attacked the antis' speakers, the ringleader shouting: 'You b[lood]y old lags, go it—hit the b[astard]s. We've all been convicted that's supporting you—and, thank God, some of us have been two or three times convicted.' This has been quoted as an amusing example of convict spirit, but it would have been far from amusing at the time, with its threats of violence. The group tried to intimidate speakers, but Richard Dry (leading anti, son of a convict) addressed the ringleader with: 'Why, you're a perfect cur. Why do you incite the fellows to fight? You're a big fellow—why don't you go down amongst them yourself, and try it?' This deflated the group. A few rotten eggs were thrown (by whom is not clear) and the men dispersed.[32]

This type of action was frightening to people in both Britain and Van Diemen's Land. Convict John Mitchel wrote home:

> The policy on which the governor and his party rely is almost too base and diabolical for belief. It is to represent the anti-transportation movement as a thing hostile to the prisoner-population and their descendants, instead of being, as it is, the first step towards gradual obliteration of the social distinctions (which must for ever subsist while the country is an actual jail), and the amalgamation, within a generation or two, of all the people; so would the stream of this colonial life begin to run clear . . .

till men might safely forget the abominable fountain from whence the current flowed at first.

Sir William Denison, conscientiously working for his 'Government', and for his gaoler-salary (poor devil!) is trying, through every agency at his command, to get up a convict *esprit du corps*: for this purpose, veritable Government mobs of convicts, organised by convict officials, have actually begun to threaten the peace of Hobart Town . . . They are taught to call themselves 'the people', to speak of themselves as a 'class of society', and when duly excited by drink and nonsense exaggerating the natural brutality of their manners, and emboldened by the idea that they are 'Government-men', and under the special protection of his Excellency, these fellows are not a little dangerous to honest people.

Surely, it is no wonder that the decent, free colonists should desire to be rid of the system which breeds this misrule.[33]

Meanwhile, no mainland colonies wanted Vandemonian ex-convicts, who were seen as 'robbers and murderers'. Those with free pardons could not be barred, but New South Wales and South Australia passed laws controlling the entry of those with conditional pardons. The British government disallowed the laws, as infringing the royal prerogative: holders of conditional pardons were mostly free to go anywhere in Australia. California passed laws against ex-convicts too, but here the British government had no power of veto. They proved to have no power in Victoria either.

After Victoria was settled in the mid-1830s many people from Van Diemen's Land went there to enjoy its high wages and freedom from the past. Perhaps 25,000, even 35,000, convicts and ex-convicts were among them. Goldfields attract crime, and naturally people believed crimes were committed by the obvious criminals in their midst, ex-convicts. A politician was horrified to find that almost all criminals in the Melbourne gaol were Vandemonian convicts and ex-convicts. In late 1852 he introduced a Convicts Prevention Bill to prohibit from entry those with only conditional pardons (roughly a third of ex-convicts). The Victorian government passed it enthusiastically.[34]

Everyone in Van Diemen's Land expressed anger, and protest meetings were held. The Launceston meeting, run by the antis, passed off peacefully, but it was a different story in Hobart, where both groups, the antis and their opponents, advertised meetings. The opponents asked supporters to sign a petition asking the Queen to disallow the *Convicts Prevention Act*, which they described as a disgraceful insult. 'Will they try to keep you in chains and fetters?' thundered speakers. The audience booed and hissed a member of the Australasian League, though he tried to say that they were all fighting for the same thing, the future prosperity of Van Diemen's Land with no class distinctions. But the audience, presumably much the same as at Tasmanian Union meetings, believed the League was behind the Act: 'It's all the League's fault! Don't hear them! Turn them out!'[35]

The League held a public meeting the next evening to put forward its own petition, which asked the Queen to disallow the *Convicts Prevention Act*, stop transportation, give most convicts a free pardon, and encourage free emigration—that is, using anger at the Act to promote the League's own aims. This infuriated their opponents. When the doors were opened for the meeting, they stormed in and took over. Many had been drinking, and some had weapons such as handkerchiefs containing lead—and some, claimed the *Examiner*, were under orders from officials of the Convict Department. 'Yellow jackets to the Point!' was the call—'yellow jackets' referring to the convict uniform. Any League speaker was silenced by shouting, hooting, groans, hisses, the ringing of bells and banging of cymbals. Richard Dry could not take the chair, though former Tasmanian Union members James Gray and Isaac Reeves pleaded for calm. In the end the League representatives left.

The *Guardian* was proud. 'The People have triumphed!' it trumpeted. The uproar, 'the most hideous noises', had never been equalled. A fellow newspaper claimed that 'the people, sore oppressed by a tyrannical and grasping oligarchy, have arisen in their might', and denied that anything untoward had happened except a little rough speaking. The anti press was horrified by the 'frenzied passions, brutal violence, coarse and filthy jests, frantic gestures and grating yells', a 'cataract of filth and brimstone', by a band of 'low, disgusting and brutal ruffians ... drunken rabble', intimidating its opposition by force, not argument; 'a triumph of ignorance over knowledge, of clamour over reason, of malice over good-will, of violence over order'—'red republican'. West commented that it was good to have 'the mongrel disease', the threat of anarchy and social revolution, out in the open, for the British government to observe.[36]

London ordered the Victorian governor to repeal the *Convicts Prevention Act*, and there was a huge furore in Melbourne. The threat was worse than cholera, shouted one speaker at a public meeting, and John Pascoe Fawkner, himself an ex-convict, thundered that a century would not wash from the national character the stain produced by convicts. The governor refused to repeal the Act, and the Victorian parliament passed a stronger one. London caved in, and convicts discovered in Victoria continued to be returned to Tasmania as late as 1867.

In Hobart feelings were so heated that the community could not even unite for the annual regatta, with the antis holding one and their opponents another. When in 1853 Launceston and Hobart citizens elected their first municipal councils, feelings ran high. In Hobart the ex-convict group canvassed actively for votes, and, the antis claimed, intimidated not just voters but possible candidates, so that it was hard to find antis to stand for office. In Launceston the League won six out of the seven seats, but in Hobart League supporters were apathetic, or intimidated, and their opponents won six seats. 'The people again triumphant!!!' crowed the *Guardian*. One of the six men appears to have been a convict, and another the son of a convict. The six were not successful as councillors; the municipality made few concrete achievements and they gradually resigned. The Leaguers in Launceston were more successful, constructing a modern water supply.[37]

Meanwhile, in Britain opposition to transportation was growing. It was scarcely punishment to transport criminals so near the goldfields; the antis' campaign convinced many, especially once the *Times* supported them; the violent behaviour of the antis' opponents alarmed them; penal reformers argued against transportation; and with the government starting to build more prisons in Britain, it was becoming cheaper to house convicts there. In December 1852 the British government ended transportation to Van Diemen's Land (though it continued to Western Australia until 1868).

The news arrived in the autumn of 1853, and the League and its followers asked Denison to announce a public holiday on 10 August, said to be the 50th anniversary of the colony's foundation by Lieutenant John Bowen. (He actually landed in September.) Denison refused, so the League itself organised a massive celebration for what was now called Jubilee Day. Meanwhile, the *St Vincent* landed the last load of 201 male convicts on 26 May 1853.[38]

On Jubilee Day, claimed the *Examiner*, Launceston was 'all alive', crowded with people in holiday attire. There were church services, a procession, gifts for children, bonfires, fireworks, blazing tar barrels and a huge gathering which listened to triumphant speeches and sang the stirring Jubilee Anthem, to the tune of 'God Save the Queen':

> Sing! for the hour is come!
> Sing! for our happy home,
> Our land, is free!
> Broken Tasmania's chain;
> Wash'd out the hated stain;
> Ended the strife and pain!
> Blest Jubilee!

In Hobart government employees were told not to be seen out of their offices on Jubilee Day, and the Hobart council, consisting mainly of recently elected Tasmanian Union supporters, refused to take part, claiming that the celebrations would be looked on as an expression of triumph, not conciliation. They were wrong. Thanks to astute planning the celebrations were conciliatory, with even the pro-government newspaper describing similar events to Launceston's, including a lavish afternoon tea for children. As well as sandwiches, cakes, tarts, ginger beer and lemonade they all received a piece of the enormous Jubilee Cake, almost 5 metres across, so large that the bakery where it was made had to be partially demolished to get it out. It stood on a stand surmounted by the Union Jack and a banner depicting a kangaroo. Thousands attended the events, more than ever seen together before. Hobart also had its Jubilee Anthem, which looked forward to 'Tasmania's unstained future'.

Similar celebrations were held in towns around the island. Oatlands people chased a pig, Sorell had children's games, Bellerive residents enjoyed boat races, and in the evening Ross looked very pretty, with candles lit in people's windows. Several people commented that there was no ill-feeling or party spirit; 'the humbler classes [code for ex-convicts] evidently made up their minds to enjoy a time of harmony and good fellowship'.[39]

It seems that most people joined in the celebrations, enjoying the cake, roast lamb, ale, fireworks and the rest of it. The League planned the day well. Having the celebrations on another anniversary meant they were not merely the League triumphing and could be given the neutral title of Jubilee; they were free and lavish; fireworks would attract almost everybody and most parents would let their children go to an afternoon tea, so a good attendance was certain; given the circumstances, the festivities were not unduly politicised. The unity of the celebrations was a good basis for the future. And though the League had described convicts as moral scum during the transportation debate, as soon as it had won, such offensive words were no longer used, and did not appear anywhere on 10 August. The 'unstained future' was as close as it came. The theory that all convicts came from a criminal class was also forgotten, or at least never mentioned.

The celebrations marked the end of the League. It had achieved its aim, so there was no more need for it. It faded, and so did its opposition; the *Guardian* moved to discussing immigration, the police, and whether music should be allowed in pubs. The division provoked by the transportation debate disappeared, for several reasons: the League's conciliatory policy; the departure of many ex-convicts for the Victorian gold rush; Governor Denison's promotion to Sydney; and the fact that division was in no one's interest. Not even James Gray, the most likely ex-convict leader, wanted a convict voice heard anymore: he settled down to a comfortable middle-class life as a senior public servant and later as a politician. Once transportation ended the island's population was more or less united—and one strong strand of this was a determination to get rid of the convict stain.

Which was stronger, the anti-transportation cause or its opponents? Most people at the time and since thought the antis had more supporters. The overwhelming victory at the 1851 Legislative Council elections indicated that most men who could vote supported the antis; the municipal elections showed support in Launceston and an equivocal position in Hobart, where the antis did not put up a fight. The *Guardian* publicly and Denison privately admitted that the majority of colonists opposed transportation— though some colonists were not interested either way.[40]

The antis had three advantages: they remained united under a strong leader in John West; they had a strong and inspirational moral platform; and they promoted self-government, which was popular. Their opponents were disunited, with a variety of motives, and some of their violent tactics alienated others. They had few positive policies, mostly merely opposing the antis, never a satisfactory basis for a political stance. They did want to end the convict stigma, but this was difficult to argue in public since it meant admitting that it existed. I conclude that by the late 1840s the probation system had produced so many disadvantages for Van Diemen's Land, and there were so many other arguments against transportation, that a majority of people wanted it to end. This majority must have included a large number of ex-convicts.

In the few years when it could be heard in Van Diemen's Land, the ex-convict voice showed bursts of energy but no staying power. Only the stimulus of extremely offensive criticism made a small minority of ex-convicts join together and speak out publicly, and their main point was resentment of this criticism. They never used statistics to rebut the Anti-Transportation League, or tried to gain permission to be, for example, postmen. They elected members to the Hobart Council, but these achieved little. The great majority of ex-convicts did not join the Union.

So even when ex-convicts could feel justified resentment, most did not voice it. Even if it only meant attending a public meeting and shouting out insults at their enemies, which many people enjoy, most ex-convicts did not join in. And no ex-convict was willing to come out in the open and admit this status. No one was named as a convict or ex-convict, by either side (except James Gray who in the first and last case of this type, sued a newspaper for calling him a 'convict clerk'. He lost his case, the court stating that he had been less than candid with them in trying to avoid acknowledging that he had been a convict). The outcome of the transportation debate nullifies any suggestion that only middle-class convicts or the free upper classes wanted to hide the convict stain. The Tasmanian Union story shows that almost everyone did.

What ex-convicts disliked most was being reminded of their convict past. Their fellow citizens realised this, had realised it from the beginning of settlement. Once the League and its criticism vanished, there was little mention of anyone having a convict past, indeed of the island itself having a penal history. But as many speakers claimed during the debate, a stigma did rest on the community, had done so from the beginning, and it proved pretty well indelible for a century and more.

7

THE CONVICT STIGMA

Born in London in 1824, Charles Davis was apprenticed to his father, a carriage-lamp maker. At sixteen, Charles served three months in gaol for robbing a till. The next year he was caught stealing silk handkerchiefs. Now seen by the authorities as a habitual offender, he was transported for ten years, arriving in Van Diemen's Land in 1842.

Little is known about Charles' years as a convict since later his record vanished, but he did commit three offences 'of a trifling nature', perhaps being out after hours. He was never again in trouble with the law. In 1847, aged 23, he received his ticket of leave. He and another ticket-of-leaver, John Semple, set up in Hobart as tinsmiths. The following year Charles married Emma Hurst, daughter of a convict. They had two children, attended the Congregational Church and were a decent, respectable family, who themselves employed convict workers—mainly women, domestic servants to help Emma. Sadly, in 1852 their daughter died of diarrhoea, an all-too-common fate for babies at the time.

Charles tried his luck at the goldfields, but by 1854 he was back in Hobart. Davis & Semple grew, branching into gasfitting. Charles joined the Independent Order of Rechabites, total abstainers, and his name was on the electoral roll for Tasmania's first parliament in 1856. Meanwhile, Emma gave birth to six more children, though the family suffered another death when a son fell from a loft. Emma herself died of heart disease in 1865, aged 36.

That year the firm moved into importing and retailing as well as manufacturing, and advertised a huge range of wares, from farm equipment like ploughs to the most modern appliances such as sewing machines. Two years later Davis split from Semple. Their later histories show who had possessed the business brain: Semple disappeared, while Charles Davis built up a major Tasmanian business, manufacturing a wide range of items, and selling them as well as imports in one of Hobart's largest department stores, with branches round the island. He kept a firm hand on the reins until he was 87, when he turned the business into a limited company.

Charles Davis was as active in family life as in business. He remarried, but his second, third and fourth wives also died; in all he married five times, fathering twelve children. His last wife had no convict connections, showing his higher social standing. Widely admired as a worthy and upright citizen, he was generous to good causes, notably the Young Men's Christian Association, which provided boys with alternatives to getting into mischief.

In 1914 Charles Davis died, aged 90. Newspapers printed handsome obituaries, praising his flourishing business and his generosity. His funeral was enormous. The hearse, 'beautifully draped in purple and black', was followed by a long procession. At the cemetery '86 sorrowing employees' lined the path to the grave, then formed a circle around it as the body of Charles Davis was lowered amid 40 floral tributes to its final resting place.

As with many another respectable ex-convict, Charles Davis's past was never mentioned, not by himself and not publicly by his descendants for over a century. By 1899, when articles started to be written about him, the story went that he worked in his father's business until he emigrated to Van Diemen's Land in 1842 and started work for himself in 1847. This story continued to be repeated, for example in a longer biography written in the 1940s, and it was not publicly admitted that Charles Davis had been a convict until the 1990s.

A British friend asked me, 'Why was there all this fuss about convict descent in Tasmania? In Britain people don't worry about such things.

A friend of mine talks openly about her grandfather who served a prison term.'[1]

In most societies people would not be so embarrassed about admitting that a great-great-grandfather had served a gaol sentence for stealing hand-kerchiefs. But in most societies the stigma on ex-criminals is different. It is not so much a blanket stigma, but depends on the nature of the crime—worse for murder, less for petty theft—and the behaviour of the criminal afterwards. Good behaviour can go a long way towards eliminating it. And the stigma fades over later generations. In Tasmania, the stigma was on all convicts, no matter what their crime and behaviour—for the loaf-of-bread thief who never broke the law again, just as much as the rapist who contin-ued his criminal habits until he ended on the scaffold. For over a century the stigma remained on all descendants, no matter how many generations removed. At a wider level, it rested on the whole community. Why?

There usually is a stigma on those who have been found guilty of a crime, and at the time of transportation to Australia it was particularly strong, encouraged by the contemporary belief about criminals. From the Middle Ages onwards many people in Britain believed that most crime was committed by a criminal class, people who refused to earn an honest living, and instead supported themselves by crime. It was seen as a choice: you could be honest or dishonest, and criminals chose their path in life, preying on the rest of society. They passed on their evil ways to their chil-dren, so crime became almost hereditary. This theory developed in the late eighteenth century and reached its peak in the 1850s, when Henry Mayhew described London's criminal class from first-hand evidence. Its best-known appearance in fiction was in Charles Dickens' *Oliver Twist* (1838) in which wicked Fagin does no honest toil but makes his living by picking pockets, and teaches this to a gang of children. They all live out-side the community, distinct from the norm. (Fagin was said to be based on Ikey Solomon, a convict transported to Van Diemen's Land.)

This theory saw criminals as 'the other', opposed to everyone else, who lived by honest toil. Criminals could hardly seem worse. It did not really matter whether their crime was slight or serious—as members of the crim-inal class they were capable of anything, beyond redemption. Convicts, being criminals, were seen as members of this class, dyed-in-the-wool vil-lains. Even enlightened thinkers who wanted a more rational system, with criminals treated appropriately for their crime and helped to reform, saw them as choosing crime of their own free will.[2]

Modern historians agree that some people did live by crime, but that they were few. Convict records concur. Only a few convicts, 5 per cent of men and 0.5 per cent of women, were noted as living by crime; for example, his gaolers described James Butler as an 'idle character supported himself by picking pockets'. There were probably others who escaped having this written on their records, but the total was unlikely to reach 10 per cent. Far more common were those with one or two previous convictions and a job—'I have always got my living by Work,' said George Beard in 1834—and a study of crime in one English district from 1835 to 1860 indicates that most people prosecuted for offences were normally employed. In Van Diemen's Land, the great majority of ex-convicts settled down to a life of 'honest labour' rather than crime, suggesting that this was what they were used to; the low level of serious crime suggests they had not been members of a professional criminal class.[3] But some members of the criminal class did continue their activities, and landowner James Ross reported that one of his assigned servants told him, without any shame, that burglary was 'the trade in which he had been trained'. He looked on it as a business from which he was taking an enforced break, and would take up again as soon as he could.

The fact that some people did live by crime and examples like James Butler and Ross's servant could be cited was proof enough to many people that the criminal class theory was correct. Naturally they wanted to believe it, since it was more comforting to think of these outsiders preying on the community and most of the population honest, than a situation where a large part of the working class were capable of theft. John Mitchel, a gentleman convict, took it for granted that other convicts came from a criminal class, that 'their training [in crime] has made them subterhuman'. James Backhouse, a Quaker missionary who spent two years inspecting Van Diemen's Land in the early 1830s, thought many, though not all, convicts were criminals by profession, having 'belonged to a society of thieves in London', or 'trained in vice from infancy'.[4] Convicts were seen as appalling, innate criminals.

Contrary to this opinion, even convicts who really were from the criminal class could settle down as ordinary citizens. The MacWilliams family—father, mother Jean and five daughters—lived in Glasgow, where the father said he was a weaver and the womenfolk ran an ale-house, an excellent cover for illegal activities. Apart from the sale of drinks and perhaps some weaving, there is no evidence that any members of the MacWilliams family ever earned money honestly. Instead they lived by theft and receiving stolen goods. They were often in trouble with the law, sometimes dobbed in by each other: in 1820 a daughter gave evidence to police which resulted in the arrest of sixteen people, including her father, mother and a sister. The police had no problem finding her father—he was already in gaol.

In 1821 Jean MacWilliams was transported to Van Diemen's Land, and three of her daughters followed her, all for passing forged notes: Margaret, Mary and Dorothy. When asked why they committed their crimes, two stated they 'wished to get out to our mother', a respectable, heartwarming sentiment—as long as people did not know the mother. Gaol reports described them as depraved, their former course of life 'bad'. Dorothy had a tattoo, Mary a large scar, and both had been in prison before.

Sometimes convicts acted as 'experts' expected, and sometimes they did not. In Van Diemen's Land the four MacWilliams women, members of the dreaded criminal class, extremely unpromising settlers, behaved admirably. None was punished for any offence, and all soon married, despite two already having husbands. They quickly obtained their freedom, though conjugal bliss was limited, mainly owing to the high mortality rates of the day. Aged only 22, Mary died the year after her wedding, perhaps in childbirth. Jean died in 1833. Dorothy married Robert Blinkworth, the son of two convicts who were by now respectable farmers. A baby Blinkworth who died aged one day could have been Dorothy and Robert's child. Then Robert died, and in 1836 Dorothy married again. Margaret married George Scrimger and they had a son. Two MacWilliams sons came free to the colony, and they and George Scrimger junior carried on the line.

The convict stigma was strengthened when the morality of the Victorian era came to the fore from the 1820s. It stressed respectability above all things: honesty, uprightness, decency, chastity. At the same time, the influence of organised religion grew, and it too emphasised the importance of honesty and upright living. No longer was it winked at for men to have mistresses, or government officers to take bribes—some still did, of course, but now in strict secrecy. Illegitimacy was a source of shame. Clothes covered the human body, male and female, from neck to toe. If legs were unmentionable, crime was beyond the pale. The convict heritage appeared even worse in the Victorian period than it had been before.

The stigma against convicts was present in much the same form in all three convict colonies: New South Wales, which received convicts from 1788 to 1840; Van Diemen's Land, 1803 to 1853; and Western Australia, 1850 to 1868. This was despite the different situations for ex-convicts in the three colonies. New South Wales was more central for trade, had much more land for grazing and natural resources, and could support a far larger population that Van Diemen's Land. As Brian Fletcher and John Hirst point out, ex-convicts blended in to the New South Wales population as farmers and labourers. Middle-class free settlers did not accept them socially, but they had no other disadvantages. This was similar to Van Diemen's Land, but a major difference was that Sydney's advantages for trade saw the rise of a class of wealthy ex-convict merchants. They were shunned socially by wealthy free settlers, and this brought into the open a division between free and convict which was not so apparent in Van Diemen's Land. A vocal group defended themselves, led by William Charles Wentworth, a convict's son through his mother but an upper-class gentleman through his father. This made the 'always free' more vehement in their opposition to the rights of ex-convicts. 'At Sydney there is a decided division into friends and enemies of the emancipists,' wrote William Parramore in 1824, 'but here [in Van Diemen's Land] there is not that decided distinction.' In 1836 Charles Darwin much preferred Hobart to Sydney partly because of its aspect and climate, but also because of its more agreeable society, 'free from contamination by rich convicts, and the dissensions consequent on the existence of two classes of wealthy residents'.[5] In Van Diemen's Land no leader encouraged ex-convicts, and there were not enough wealthy ones to form a class, so they did not defend themselves publicly as happened in New South Wales.

But in New South Wales passions were not so much roused by the question of ending transportation; once it was raised the British government gave in easily. They still had Van Diemen's Land as their convict receptacle, and by now New South Wales was a large, prosperous colony, which could rebel against British rule, as the American colonies had done—a nightmare possibility for the British government.

New South Wales also had a smaller percentage of convicts in its population. It received much the same number of convicts as Van Diemen's Land but far more free immigrants, since it was larger and wealthier. In 1840 when transportation to New South Wales ended its population was 119,000, almost double Van Diemen's Land's 63,000 in 1853. There was more free immigration in the 1840s, and by 1846 only about 20 per cent of New South Wales' adult males were of convict origin—against 75 per cent in Van Diemen's Land.[6] Even after transportation ended to Van Diemen's Land, with little immigration the percentage of ex-convicts and their children remained much higher than in New South Wales.

Western Australia had a different history again. Founded in 1829 as a free settlement, the small colony struggled for decades, largely because of a lack of labour and capital. Mainly to gain British government expenditure, landowners asked for convicts, male only, and between 1850 and 1868, some 9718 arrived—a fraction of the number in the eastern colonies, but a substantial part of Western Australia's white population, over half the adult males in 1859, and the backbone of the labour force.

Ex-convicts in Western Australia had an even harder battle to achieve acceptance in the community than in the eastern colonies. With its convicts arriving later than in the eastern colonies, Victorian morality had taken a stronger hold, and convicts were viewed with greater contempt. About half left the colony at the expiration of their sentences, as in Tasmania. The four or five thousand that remained were a smaller percentage of the total population than in Tasmania, and with no convict women to marry, they were on their own. There was a bitterness between convict and free, and those ex-convicts who wanted acceptance faced an endless battle to achieve respectability. As well, Western Australia did not have a native-born white majority until well into the twentieth century, unlike the other colonies, and the largely British-born population was even less accepting of the convict past than the other colonies. Convictism was utterly taboo. A 'kind of general amnesia' took over, and the convict past was never mentioned, helped by the fact that people tended to connect convicts with New South Wales and Tasmania, not Western Australia—whose population did all they could to encourage such an idea.[7]

But though the stigma was so severe in Western Australia, it was also strong in the other two colonies. In all three, despite their different histories, there was a stigma on convicts from the beginning; and more than that, on the whole society. So the stigma did not come only from within colonial society, from non-convicts towards convicts, but from outside the colonies as well. How did this happen? The answer must be a factor common to all three convict colonies, and one stands out: all three were settled by the British.

Think of the reputation public housing suburbs have today among people from more affluent areas: the perception is that they are riddled with drug addiction, violence, theft and other crime. The reputation comes partly from reports in newspapers, and partly from rumour and supposition: a public housing suburb must be dreadful. Everyone living there is tarred with the same brush by outsiders, whatever they are like in reality. But these suburbs do not have convicted criminals making up half their population, as Van Diemen's Land did. To envisage what the British thought of their convict colonies, take the reputation of a public housing suburb and double it, perhaps treble it.

Since 1718, Britain had been sending convicts to its American colonies, and many Americans hated this, not just because criminals were brought into their communities, but because of the bad reputation this created. They detested 'the false and bitter reproach, so commonly thrown upon us, that we are the descendants of convicts'. 'Emptying their jails into our settlements is an insult and contempt, the cruellest that ever one people offered to another,' wrote Benjamin Franklin, and the Virginian legislature thought transportation brought 'great danger and disrepute' to the colony. Some colonial governments tried fruitlessly to ban transportation.

The new United States of America refused to accept British convicts, and blotted out its convict past. Its advantages were that its convicts had been sold as labourers, so there was no machinery of administration and no buildings, nothing visible left as a reminder; and after 1783 its ties with Britain fell away, and Americans could ignore British opinion. British convicts were rarely mentioned as part of America's history. So successfully did Americans obliterate their penal past that until recently the country's convicts were little studied or even acknowledged. Only now are books and articles starting to be written. 'I'm reasonably well read in American history and [the convict past] was a surprise to me,' wrote Andrew Jampoler, an American maritime historian, in 2008. 'Here our history re slavery gets all the attention, and [the convict past] is pretty much in the shadow.'

After 1788 Britain sent its convicts to Australia instead, and its disdain for its new penal colonies began even before the First Fleet arrived at Botany Bay. As soon as settlement was suggested English cartoonists began sending it up, with jokes about how uncouth it would be—because a convict colony by its very nature had to be either ridiculous or dreadful. Witty ballads circulated, and while the First Fleet was still at anchor in Portsmouth, *Botany Bay*, 'a high-spirited burletta', was being performed in a London theatre. When news arrived that a celebrated pickpocket had been made a policeman in Sydney, there were even more jokes.[8] Just what we expected! How deliciously humorous!

Once settlements existed, they were treated with contempt. David Collins, judge advocate at Sydney and later governor of Van Diemen's Land, said the British attached odium to everyone who went to Botany Bay, even a free officer like himself. Cunningham, a naval surgeon, reported that when he mentioned in England that he came from New South Wales, people would find some excuse to move away from him, and would even check their pockets. New South Wales was the only place in the world 'which you are ashamed to confess having visited'. Intending emigrants faced scorn, embarrassment, and entreaties not to go to such a terrible place.[9]

The jokes continued. 'Do you wish to go to *Hell* or *Botany bay*? Sir', an 1829 cartoon ran. A ticket clerk is questioning a group of odd-looking travellers. They answer, 'I wonts to go to Bottamybay', and 'I should like to see the *Naughty Place* better than any thing'. When New South Wales requested self-government there were howls of amusement in Britain: 'A precious tale the sage Australia weaves—A House of Commons for a Den of Thieves!' Australians were called 'the most rascally and villainous population . . . on the surface of the globe'; 'New South Wales is a sink of wickedness, in which the majority of convicts of both sexes become infinitely more depraved than at the period of their arrival . . . no man who has his choice would select it . . . for his dwelling place.'[10] The main positive information was about convicts who made good, but for the middle class this only made the place worse, for the usual British class structure was turned on its head.

Many authors had a motive for making the convict colonies seem terrible places. Travellers expected to be appalled, and descriptions of horrors helped their books sell. 'What, indeed, but desert can be imagined the home of the convict to be?' asked Hordern Melville. In Britain, wrote H. Butler Stoney, 'Van Diemen's Land bears a very bad name, on account of its having been for many years a penal settlement: its very name is associated with chains and crime.' Mrs Favell Lee Mortimer never visited Van Diemen's Land, but in her travel book for children wrote: 'This island is as cool as Great Britain; yet it is not a pleasant land to live in; for it is filled with convicts.'[11]

'Of Australia I have ever felt the utmost abhorrence,' wrote convict John Mitchel, before he had set foot on the continent:

> It was always a matter of wonder to me that free emigrants with their families . . . went voluntarily to settle in a penal colony and adopt it for their country. To live among natural unsophisticated savages, though it were in Labrador or the Sahara, would be tolerable; but to dwell and rear one's children amongst savages who are outcasts of civilisation, savages *de*-civilised—savages uniting more than the brutality of Timbuctoo with all the loathsome corruptions of London, is a nauseous and horrid idea.[12]

When ex-convicts like Mitchel returned to Britain and published their stories, they provided more detail of the frightfulness of the colonies—ex-convicts nearly always portrayed their sentences as dreadful, their suffering as hideous (as they sometimes had been). Mostly political prisoners, transported for rebelling against British rule in Ireland and Canada, or protesting against the political or industrial situation in England, they saw themselves as innocent and were outraged by their treatment. The Canadian Exiles, transported for rebellion, found Van Diemen's Land barbaric and inhumane, with hard manual labour, inadequate clothing and shelter, poor food and brutal treatment, much worse than slavery in America. 'All laws lose their force in Van Diemen's Land, bribery and corruption attending poor justice at every turn as her favourite handmaidens. The manners of the people are gross and sensual; they are composed of pardoned convicts, blacklegs, gamblers and libertines, and many are entirely destitute of morals and common decency.'[13]

In their accounts of their sufferings some ex-convicts included terrible details, notably John Frost, who in *The Horrors of Convict Life* claimed that 'never . . . has society existed in so depraved a state as I have witnessed in the penal colonies'. Most convicts were not originally as bad as people supposed, he wrote, but their treatment drove them to desperation: starvation, the hardest labour any man could endure, flogging, cruelty, injustice, corruption and worse, sodomy and homosexual rape. As a clerk at Port Arthur, Frost was horrorstruck by the cruelties he saw, and described them in public lectures in London. Women were not admitted to the lecture in which he described a man held down and raped.

Such books and lectures mainly influenced the middle classes; the working class relied on stories of ex-convicts making good and ballads, which were widely published and sung. They uniformly gave the convict colonies a bad press, depicting them as cruel places of torment. Most were about Botany Bay, a name with a good ring and easy beat, but several described Van Diemen's Land. One ballad, 'Beware Young Men', told 'all you wild and wicked youths' of the terrible hardships of convicts in Van Diemen's Land. After the voyage out, convicts went ashore 'all shackled hand to hand', and saw their fellow sufferers chained to harrows or ploughs, in bare feet, the supervisor standing over them with a cane, ready to beat them. The ballad ended in beseeching young men and maidens to give away their wicked ways, or else they would spend their days 'upon Vandemons shore'.[14] No matter that these ballads were inaccurate, that this one was an adaptation of an earlier American transportation ballad: for much of the British public, ballads were the main source of information about the colonies—and it was all negative.

Other claims that transportation debased the whole community came from reformers, either those who wanted first to abolish assignment, then all transportation; or others who aimed to deter wrongdoers by threatening them with the horrors of transportation. In the 1830s Archbishop Whatley of Dublin, who had never been to Australia, published several works describing the convict system as producing crime and immorality, including homosexuality.[15] William Ullathorne served as Vicar-General in New South Wales and visited Van Diemen's Land and Norfolk Island. In 1837 he published *The Catholic Mission in Australia*, which painted the blackest possible picture of the convict colonies:

> Fifty thousand souls are festering in bondage . . . We have taken a vast portion of God's earth, and have made it a cess-pool; we have taken the oceans, which, with their wonders, gird the globe, and have made them the channels of a sink; we have poured down scum upon scum, and dregs upon dregs, of the offscourings of mankind, and, as these harden and become consistent together, we are building up with them a nation of crime, to be, unless something be speedily done, a curse and a plague, and a by-word to all the people of the earth.[16]

To Ullathorne all convicts were degraded; if they were not when they were convicted, they became so through association with those who already were. Convicts were slaves. Floggings were sickening: there was a graphic description. The numerical disparity between the sexes led to 'indescribable evils'. Drunkenness was widespread, crime was rife. And 'there is another class of crimes, too frightful even for the imagination of other lands . . . crimes which are notorious—crimes that, dare I describe them, would make your blood to freeze, and your hair to rise erect in horror upon the pale flesh. Let them be enfolded in eternal darkness.' Presumably Ullathorne meant homosexuality, but he used 'crimes' in the plural: as often happened when authors discussed vice, Ullathorne used opaque language and the exact meaning cannot be ascertained. At the end the aim of his book appears: a plea for funds so more priests could fight such degradation.[17]

In response to the reformers, in 1838 the British government set up a parliamentary inquiry into transportation, chaired by William Molesworth, already a staunch opponent. He linked transportation with slavery, using much the same language as anti-slavery crusaders. Evidence in the Molesworth Inquiry came from people in Britain with experience of Australia who had their own agendas, and the inquiry concluded that the assignment system failed utterly to reform convicts. It was slavery, 'inefficient, cruel, and demoralizing', and the colonies to which it had given birth were depraved and vicious because of it, with many free settlers 'low and abandoned characters'. In Australia there existed 'a state of morality worse than that of any other community in the world'. Molesworth barely mentioned homosexuality, only stating briefly that the high disproportion of men to women encouraged unnatural crime. He made it clear that by 'depravity' he meant not only homosexuality but a range of activities including rape, murder, bestiality, drunkenness, the corruption of young children by convict servants, and anything involving violence. Molesworth's report was widely read.

So Molesworth damned not just the convict system but all Australians, encouraging the British to view the colonies as 'the most depraved communities in the universe', their inhabitants, even the free, as 'reprobates of the most abandoned stamp', as Van Diemen's Land author David Burn wrote.[18] The result of the Molesworth Inquiry, as noted in the previous chapter, was that transportation to New South Wales was stopped, and in Van Diemen's Land the probation system was introduced, with its aims of reform.

With this almost uniformly bad press, it is not surprising that the British opinion of the convict colonies remained negative. Visitors proved this: in Van Diemen's Land, they showed 'a sort of morbid dread of every man whom they met, with a tendency to walk about with loaded pistols in their pockets'. Colonel Godfrey Mundy arrived in Sydney in 1846. Much had been written and spoken, he reported, about the 'hideous depravity' of the local population. He was rowed ashore by prisoners, and 'expected to see these men chained like galley-slaves to their oars'; that night, he listened to music among a crowd of men who, 'according to the habit of newcomers, I fully believed to be convicts and their spawn, intent one and all on exercising a right of search into the stranger's pockets'.[19]

Colonists who visited Britain reported a cold reception. An old colonist (code for non-convict) visiting Britain was asked by a landlord not to tell anyone he came from Van Diemen's Land 'or I shall be ruined'. A butler resigned at once on hearing that his employers came from the island, and other servants said the family came from India. Katherine Turton, visiting London, reported that her aunt did not want to see any other members of the family. 'I rather think she would rathe[r] there were no such people, as she considers V.D.L. as [a] penal abode,' wrote Katherine.

The aunt hinted that it was better not to talk of Van Diemen's Land. 'Why not?' Katherine retorted. ''Tis quite as agreeable a country as any . . . I have no idea of letting people run down a country they know nothing about,' she wrote back to Van Diemen's Land.[20]

As the Molesworth report described, one reason for convict colonies gaining such a bad press was that they were associated with 'unnatural crime'. 'Natural' crimes like theft were seen as, if not praiseworthy, at least understandable reactions by villains to their circumstances. But 'unnatural' crimes broke rules held sacred at the time. They included cannibalism, homosexuality and bestiality. Stories were widely told of cannibalism and homosexuality in the convict colonies. Examples of bestiality existed— in 1837 James Miller was sent to Port Arthur for two years of 'severe discipline' for 'having had certain carnal & venereal intercourse with a Cow'—but they were not made public.

Tales of cannibalism had been told for thousands of years, and surfaced again when European explorers in the Renaissance discovered new countries and could tell stories of savages eating each other. There were few such stories from Australia, but one was not only told but true. In 1822 eight men, including Alexander Pearce, escaped from the penal settlement at Macquarie Harbour; either two or three turned back, but the rest tried to penetrate dense, inhospitable bush and reach settlements in the east. As they ran out of food, they killed and ate each other one by one. In the end only two men were left, but eventually one fell asleep and Pearce managed to kill and eat him. When he reached settled areas he was caught and returned to Macquarie Harbour. He escaped once more and another convict was rash enough to go with him; he too was eaten. Pearce, now notorious, confessed his crimes and was hanged in 1824. His story was widely told; for example, soon after arriving in 1837 the governor's wife, Jane Franklin, passed the story to her sister back home in England. So Van Diemen's Land (but not New South Wales) became notorious for cannibalism—notorious enough for veiled comments to need no further explanation. A London newspaper reported the arrival of the Anglican Bishop of Tasmania in the colony and added, 'it is earnestly to be wished that the next accounts may not bring word that he has been eaten up'.[21]

Australia was even more notorious for another 'unnatural crime': the capital offence of homosexuality. It certainly occurred in the colonies, especially in probation gangs, where large numbers of men lived together. When it was discovered, the authorities were horrified—but not too horrified.

In 1835 Ephraim Folley was transported for stealing lead. The ship's surgeon's report ran: 'An unnatural young Monster, punished [with] 42 lashes (well laid on) over the bare buttocks with a cat [o'nine tails] for frequent intercourse with William Franklin.' William Franklin, also described as 'an unnatural Monster', gained 60 lashes, and in Van Diemen's Land had to sleep alone in a cell for a year, though not in chains. He was punished for no more offences and gained his pardon in 1841; Ephraim ran foul of the law several more times but he too eventually gained his pardon. These men, found guilty of homosexual acts, were punished, but not extremely severely: exactly how was homosexuality regarded?

Homosexuality was a capital crime, and some authorities reacted hysterically. When 23-year-old convict John Demer was found guilty of 'Buggery' in 1843, he was sentenced to death. This was commuted to transportation for life, and his sentence ran: 'To be transp[orte]d for Life & to be sent to Port Arthur & kept at hard labour and not permitted to join any of the gangs & to take his meals separate & to sleep in an apartment separate from every person & at all times to be kept so as to be under the immediate observation of the officers of the establishment.'

Other authorities played down homosexuality, perhaps because they did not regard it as a serious crime, or because its acknowledged presence would reflect badly on them. Probation stations, where hundreds of men lived communally, increased the likelihood of homosexual behaviour, and intermittent reports of it came to a head in 1846, when several convict officials complained that it was rife but underreported by government orders, so that no one could tell it was happening, especially the British authorities. James Purslowe claimed that homosexual practices were common at two probation stations he had served at, but if a man was accused of this crime it was punished as 'misconduct', on orders from the Convict Department. Another junior officer, Thomas Lafarelle, was so appalled at the department ignoring homosexuality that he wrote a 62-page letter to the British government, describing how the local authorities had been 'screening the crime of Sodomy and other delinquencies among probation men', and giving examples of this widespread activity.

There are problems for the historian with this topic, quite apart from the difficulty of understanding the nineteenth-century mindset that labelled homosexuality a 'disgusting' capital crime. References were so vague that it is not always clear exactly what is being discussed: 'vice' could include many activities, and it is not safe to assume that a coy reference necessarily means homosexuality. John Sinclair, transported for theft, was reported by the surgeon on his ship to be 'bad', and a private report of his disposition and character was to be sent to Governor Arthur. Was this a cover for homosexuality? No, in fact: claiming to be a butcher, Sinclair had been given a prized job, but it turned out that he was no such thing. He had tricked the authorities—a serious offence.

There was discussion in the Van Diemen's Land and British press about the extent of homosexuality in Van Diemen's Land, with much exaggeration. One story of men removing the boards which separated their beds so they could be together was enough—for people who saw homosexuality as abhorrent, any such activity was terrible. Others, however, said that such stories were exaggerated and that there was no more homosexuality in Van Diemen's Land than in other similar societies.[22]

All this was useful and/or interesting to two groups of writers in Britain. Some travel writers described not only homosexuality but female sexuality and floggings in a lascivious way that approached pornography, and could boost sales.[23] Reformers like Whatley and Ullathorne used homosexuality as an example of the horrors of convict colonies, though only one among the many horrors there.

During the anti-transportation debate in Van Diemen's Land from 1846 to 1852 both sides accused each other of adding to the stigma on the colony. Both accepted that it was there already. In his first editorial in 1842 the anti-transportation campaigner John West described Van Diemen's Land as 'a penal colony; in the eyes of Britain debased in its character and degraded in its destiny', and in the mid-1840s all newspapers wrote of 'the penal stigma attached to this colony', 'the lasting stigma of a penal colony'. West pointed out that this applied not just to convicts, but everyone.[24]

The antis' opponents accused them of fixing a stigma on Van Diemen's Land by discussing 'the disgusting subject', accusing the *Examiner* of writing about homosexuality every fortnight. This was not true: the *Examiner* and other anti newspapers in fact seldom mentioned homosexuality, and a reading of the *Examiner* from 1843 to 1853 shows very little written on the topic. The antis defended themselves by stating that convictism had always made the character of the island odious, especially since the writings of Whatley and Ullathorne. The island's name would not be redeemed until transportation ceased.[25]

The antis in turn accused their opposition of increasing the stigma on the colony by reporting unfavourably on the island: it had been 'stigmatised at home as no country ever was—most unjustly and falsely. There was no statement, no device, no expedient, which had not been resorted to to blind the eyes of the home authorities.' The antis also pointed out that the activities of ex-convict groups like the Tasmanian Union involving drink, weapons, force, assault on its enemies and undemocratic methods alarmed the British with the spectre of mob rule, lynch law and convict revolt, and made the island's reputation worse.[26]

How true were all these accusations? Probably the activities of both sides increased or at least publicised the stigma to some extent: but it was already so well established, so much encouraged by previous writers such as Whatley, Ullathorne, the Molesworth Committee and the various ex-convict narratives, that more information in the late 1840s made little difference. As far as the British government was concerned it had heard complaints of homosexuality in the colonies for years, and probably the most alarming revelation was the threat of convict revolt.

Historian Babette Smith claims that the antis' complaints of homosexuality were mainly responsible for the convict stigma, but further research shows little evidence of this. Both sides accepted that the stigma existed at the start of the debate. When the Western Australian colonists asked for convicts in 1850, they insisted that all must be male, so cannot have feared homosexuality unduly—which they surely would have, had fear of homosexuality caused the stigma. It is sometimes claimed that because of the anti-transportationists' accusations, homosexuality became 'inextricably mixed' with Tasmania and instilled an enduring sense of shame, which culminated in enduring homophobia; Tasmania was the last Australian state to decriminalise homosexuality.[27] There is no evidence for this, either of more homophobia than anywhere else in the later nineteenth century, or that the late decriminalisation can be linked with the convict system. Tasmania was a smaller, less sophisticated society than other states, and its later decriminalisation of homosexuality can be seen as part of this picture.

Many factors contributed to the convict stigma, but I suggest that it originated in British contempt for the convict colonies and was strengthened by reports from them, making the British see Australia as even more inferior than ordinary colonies. America shared this stigma when it received convicts, but once it was independent it could ignore Britain's scorn. Not so the Australian colonies, which retained strong ties with Britain. They remained under British rule and influence, with local independence but with British governors and a British Queen, part of the British Empire. Almost everyone in the colonies had been born in Britain, or had parents born there. More emigrants from Britain arrived each year. Colonists read books from Britain, received letters from Britain; their newspapers reported British news in detail. Even the pro-convict working-class *Guardian* regularly reported such news as: 'Her Majesty, the royal children and Prince Albert were in the enjoyment of good health. Her Majesty was again in an "interesting" way.' Australians' social and cultural practices were based on those of Britain. Visitors noted that all colonials in British colonies, not just Australians, were obsessed with their colony's image, especially with what the British thought of them; and this was reasonable, because as colonies their future was tied up with Britain.[28] So British opinion was important—and Britain thought badly of its Australian colonies, because they were or had been penal colonies. British contempt turned the stigma from disapproval of those of convict descent into contempt for the whole place, the full-blown 'hated stain'.

The sort of thing Australians had to put up with from condescending British visitors is captured in letters home by Charles and Ellen Kean, actors who toured Victoria and New South Wales in 1864. They later toured Tasmania; their letters home are not extant, but probably shared much the same attitude. Soon after the Keans' arrival in Sydney they reported an amusing convict anecdote. A native-born Australian servant refused to accompany a family back to England. 'Oh Mam I could not think of going to England, that's the country where all the convicts came from.' How quaint! (This popular story, probably apocryphal, was long lived; David Burn told it in Van Diemen's Land as long before as 1842.)

The Keans found Victoria rowdy, but New South Wales worse, common and vulgar. 'There are many descendants of convicts, but "*Oh! no we never mention this.*"' The wife of the 'very vulgar' premier was descended from 'a *notorious convict*'. An inn had a 'fat clean little old Landlady' and someone asked, '*I wonder what she was sent out for*'. It turned out, wrote Ellen Kean, that she 'had come out forty years ago at *the expense of the government*. It is a queer place Mary. There is a man here named Bill Nash, a desperate ruffian who even now cannot keep his hands from picking and stealing . . . worth his *hundred thousand a year*. The fortunes here are enormous but very much in the possession of convict families or *old hands* as they are called.'

After a few weeks Ellen wrote:

I have been out all day seeing my friends descendants of people *sent out* and very nice people some of them are. There is something very sad in it to me. *They* cannot help it and I cannot help thinking of *what they came out* for all the time. *You must not talk of this for they are marrying into most respectable families and you do not know whom you may offend* . . . Nearly all the rich people here are of this class.

This is for your private eye Mary. Sydney is a lovely place and the people are very hospitable but I should not like to live surrounded entirely by such people . . . I have to smile at a great deal I see and hear.

Charles had similar opinions: 'As a general rule the people here [in Melbourne] are a very second and third rate lot and their antecedents are no hindrance to their advancement . . . Many are the sons of convicts. The Mayor for instance and some have been convicts themselves.'

The Keans hated the way Australia's middle class were non-gentry people with working-class antecedents. They lacked education and polish, they misquoted Latin, they thought Richard II was a son of Richard I—'it is scarcely to be credited'. The convict stain made everything so much worse. The Keans could never forget the colony's convict history, could not leave it behind. 'I cannot help thinking of *what they came out* for all the time.' 'I have to smile at a great deal I see and hear.'[29] With the British always remembering the convict past and smiling condescendingly, no wonder Australians were defensive.

The stigma was given a boost, if one was needed, when the most famous fictional convict appeared: Magwitch, in Charles Dickens' *Great Expectations* (1861). The book opens with a terrifying scene in a misty, gloomy churchyard, where the hero, young Pip, meets

> a fearful man, all in coarse grey, with a great iron on his leg. A man with no hat, and with broken shoes, and with an old rag tied round his head. A man who had been soaked in water, and smothered in mud, and lamed by stones, and cut by flints, and stung by nettles, and torn by briars; who limped and shivered, and glared and growled; and whose teeth chattered in his head as he seized me by the chin.

There is even a hint of cannibalism, with the ruffian admiring Pip's fat cheeks: 'Darn Me if I couldn't eat 'em.' Magwitch is a convict, escaped from Australia, who forces Pip to bring him food and help him keep out of the clutches of the law. Out of gratitude to the boy, after Magwitch has made his fortune he pays for Pip to be brought up as a gentleman, but despite this generosity, when the adult Pip meets him 'the abhorrence in which I held the man, the dread I had of him, the repugnance with which I shrank from him, could not have been exceeded if he had been some terrible beast'.[30]

OTHER CONVICT COLONIES

It is difficult to compare the stigma on Australia with that on other convict colonies, because nowhere else was quite the same. Between 1415 and 1954, six countries sent convicts to their colonies: Portugal, Spain, Holland, France, Russia and Britain.[31] In most cases convicts did not become part of a civil society after they were released, so the question of a stigma did not arise. Many colonies were tiny, and did not really have a civil society. Tropical colonies had such high death rates that the question of what happened to convicts after they arrived hardly mattered—in France, transportation was known as the 'bloodless guillotine'. Some countries like

Spain and Holland exiled only a handful of convicts. Some brought them home after their terms expired.

There were only two other places where large numbers of ex-convicts merged with the local population. One was Britain's American colonies, which received 50,000 convicts from 1718 until 1775. These convicts were few in a large population, into which they vanished after their release, and there was no visible physical reminder of their presence, such as buildings.

The other convict site was Siberia. Russia sent over a million convicts there from 1649. In many ways this system resembled Australia's. Most convicts were petty criminals, but about 1 per cent were political exiles. Many more men were transported than women. Siberian convicts developed some traits similar to those in Australia, notably mateship. Convicts with useful skills tended to fare better. Some convicts were set up as farmers, others were employed in towns, and families could join them; this milder punishment was called *ssylka*. The more dreaded *katorga*, which about one in seven suffered, involved forced labour in mines or convict prisons, and was even worse than life in Australia's penal settlements. The penal settlements gave Siberia and Australia dreadful reputations, with Siberia known as 'the cesspool of the tsars'.

There were major differences. New South Wales and Van Diemen's Land were founded as convict colonies and convicts dominated the population; in Siberia they were always a minority. Australia received about 162,000 convicts in 80 years: Siberia received seven times as many over three centuries. Australian convicts were generally better treated, retaining rights as citizens under the rule of law, even if it was sometimes arbitrarily applied. Russian convicts had fewer rights.[32]

In 1890 Anton Chekhov studied the prison system in Sakhalin, an island to the east of mainland Siberia. He found that those convicts under the *ssylka* regime

> walked the streets freely, without chains and without guards; you meet them in groups and singly every step of the way. They are everywhere, in the streets and in the houses. They serve as drivers, watchmen, chefs, cooks and nursemaids. I was not accustomed to seeing so many convicts, and at first their proximity was disturbing and perplexing . . . Soon I became accustomed to this. Everyone becomes accustomed to it.

Chekhov was told that these 'unfortunates' were better treated in Siberia than they would have been in Russia, that men fared much better when they were married but women formed only 10 per cent of the population; that if convicts obeyed the rules, they could live in reasonable comfort. But penal servitude, *katorga*, was absolutely appalling, with terrible conditions. It sounds similar to the Australian convict colonies, with one major difference: Sakhalin, cold and barren, had hardly any civil society but was almost entirely a penal settlement.[33] There is no evidence as to how the convict inhabitants of Siberia tried to escape any stigma; like convicts in America, their situation was different enough from those in Australia to make comparison difficult.

8

INITIAL EFFORTS TO DEFEAT
THE CONVICT STIGMA

In 1853 transportation to Van Diemen's Land ended, and three years later the colony received self-government, and was free to try to transform itself into a new non-convict paradise. 'Van Diemen's Land had passed away with many of its evil associations, and in its place there had arisen Tasmania, a fairer and more prosperous land, bright with promise,' wrote devoted patriot Charles Walch. But how were its inhabitants going to show that the island was 'one of the most delightful countries in the world', an entirely different place from Van Diemen's Land?[1] How could they beat the convict stigma?

New South Wales was succeeding, at least outwardly. Since transportation there ended in 1840, visitors reported that 'the painful class distinctions and old feelings of rancour between the free and the freed' were gradually dying, and that many Australians did not care about convictism either way. (Or claimed they did not.) Efforts to hide the convict past were helped by large numbers of free immigrants; by 1846, the convict group formed less than a fifth of the population.[2] The 'hated stain' did continue—the dread of being thought a convict descendant, the defensiveness of the whole population when convicts were mentioned. But by the later 1840s, only a few years after transportation ceased, the colony could claim to be putting its past behind it, at least on the surface—and in the Victorian age, appearances were all-important.

Could Van Diemen's Land do the same? It was a major task. When New South Wales emerged from transportation it was larger and more prosperous than Van Diemen's Land, with far more free immigrants. Van Diemen's Land had been much more reliant on the convict system, its history, wrote one visitor, 'simply the history of a convict establishment'.[3]

Tasmanian attitudes were complex. What were they afraid of? Not of ex-convicts themselves: most were living quietly in the community, no threat to anyone. Not of a high crime rate or any other effect on society, since clearly this was not happening. No: what Tasmanians were afraid of was that outsiders might think badly of them because of their convict past. There was some stigma on ex-convicts in the community because they had been found guilty of offences; but overwhelming this was the stigma imposed from outside, from Britain. This was what made Tasmanians ashamed: that the British thought they were so crude and criminal. Responses to the stigma were designed to convince outsiders that Tasmania had left the past behind. They were not nearly as ashamed of the convict system or of individual convicts as of their reputation. So when the local government was trying to attract free immigrants with cheap fares, it accepted those sponsored by local people, even if they were ex-convicts. If it had really been ashamed of convicts, their relations would not have been acceptable; but the government, and all Tasmanians, knew that convicts were mostly ordinary people, that people they sponsored would also be ordinary people. But to outsiders they could be called 'free immigrants', nothing to do with convicts. Again, it was the appearance, to the British in particular, which was important.

In hindsight it might have been better to brazen it out, to say that Tasmania was a fine place despite its convicts; but it would have been hard to be brazen in the face of British condescension and ridicule, and no one seemed to consider this option. Instead, everyone seemed to agree that the only way to defeat the stigma was to show that Tasmania had nothing to do with convicts. In the two decades from 1853, they tried a variety of methods, by instinctive reaction rather than a methodical plan. Some of these methods were contradictory, but in the desperate attempt to white-wash the past, contradictions, falsifications, exaggerations, even outright lies did not matter.

At least Tasmanians were now united in this. Despite the divisions caused by the transportation debate, once it ended everyone worked together to deny the past. Some historians have assumed that this was an upper-class or middle-class activity, that the working class, mostly of convict origin, were proud of and stood up for their heritage. Evidence does not support this belief. The upper and middle class were certainly more vocal, as they were on every issue; they were the ones with the education and self-confidence to write letters to newspapers, to stand for parliament, to enter public life. The working-class voice was scarcely heard. But the huge crowds turning out for patriotic occasions show that the whole community wanted to be seen as respectable and law-abiding, nothing to do with convicts. Working-class families 'forgot' their convict past in the same way middle-class ones did. For 40 years no voice was ever raised against the policy of denial. A handful of ex-convicts admitted to the past, even gloried in it, but they were few, almost always marginalised men with nothing to lose. Tasmania was divided into different classes in the usual British way and there were plenty of issues on which the community divided along class lines, such as conditions of work, but on the convict past they were largely united.

As we have seen, the policy of ignoring, even denying, the convict presence had already begun, despite the difficulty of overlooking convicts while they were being transported in their tens of thousands. After 1853, Tasmanians totally embraced this policy, and over the next two decades made huge efforts to implement it.

One immediate strategy was to change the island's name. 'Van Diemen's Land has never been a name of happy omen'; it was 'tainted with the sound of gaol and harsh with the crack of the gaoler's whip'; it 'ever brings a conscious blush of shame'. Fortunately there was an attractive alternative—Tasmania, named after the island's European discoverer. First used in 1808 in an atlas, from the 1820s its popularity grew. Many ships, clubs, newspapers and books adopted it, such as Godwin's *Emigrants Guide to Van Diemen's Land, more properly called Tasmania* (1823) and the Tasmanian Turf Club (1826). Not only the elite favoured the term; by the 1840s it was in widespread use by, for example, the ex-convict Tasmanian Union.

As soon as the colony obtained self-government, parliament organised the change, and even before the new name was ratified, an American visitor headed a letter, 'Hobart Town (no longer Van Diemen's Land)'.[4] There was no opposition; no one at all stood up for Van Diemen's Land.

This change might seem cosmetic, but people at the time believed, or hoped, that it would 'efface the possibility of the very memory' of the convict colony. Visitors were quickly told not to refer to the island as Van Diemen's Land, and in his *History of Tasmania* published in 1884 James Fenton took great pains to avoid the term. He spoke of the auspicious change from 'the name given by the old Dutch navigator—so expressive of crime and wretchedness' to 'the more euphonious one of Tasmania'.[5]

Not only did people avoid the name Van Diemen's Land, they continued to avoid the word 'convict', or even any word that too clearly meant convict, like 'prisoner'. Many quotations show the verbal gymnastics people went through to obscure their language: 'any of that class of whom some may be here to-day', 'that gloomy phase of colonial life, which, thank God, is become a matter of tradition and history', people 'of doubtful origin' and so on. In his *History*, James Fenton gladly moved on from the period 'when the fair island of Tasmania was bowed down under the weight of a monstrous system which raised its giant arm in antagonism to the progressive efforts of spirited colonists'. The *Mercury* excelled at these euphemisms: 'although it was at one time our misfortune to be subjected to a different regime to that which now obtains here', for example. It was a careful balancing act, because the reader still had to understand what was meant. Locals must have become experienced at deciphering the code, which they could understand but which obscured the truth from outsiders. If they were referred to at all, ex-convicts were called 'old lags' or 'old hands', more friendly terms which avoided words like convict or prisoner. 'Old lag' did mean ex-convict, but 'old hand' was ambiguous. It could also mean someone who had been in the country for a long time, or an experienced person. So in 1850 a newspaper referred to something 'which no old hand, either master or man, can remember', and in 1917 to the Scottsdale football team containing 'lads and old hands'.[6] This was a useful term, as outsiders could be ignorant of its local meaning.

No histories of Tasmania were written in the twenty years after the end of the convict system—no one wanted to write about the past for fear of what they would have to admit—but even those who wrote private memoirs avoided mention of convicts. Hugh Hull and Sarah Walker emigrated as children with their families in about 1820, and in old age wrote lengthy reminiscences. Each hinted at the convict presence only once, Hull reporting that 'a number of prisoner servants' cleared the farm, and Walker describing a man as 'sent out'. Even more reserved was John Pascoe Fawkner, with reason: both he and his father had been convicts. In 1866, prosperous and prominent in Melbourne, he wrote his memoirs. There was no mention whatever of his convict connections, or of Van Diemen's Land being a convict colony. Some people were 'prisoners', but this was said only in passing—you could exchange 'prisoner' for, say, 'carpenter' without changing the sense. Fawkner implied that his family were free settlers, and the only time he used the word 'convict' it seems to refer to people from Sydney. He admitted that Van Diemen's Land was 'outrageously wild', full of thieves and drunks, but he was not going to admit that it was a convict colony.[7]

Not only were convicts in general never mentioned, it was absolutely not acceptable to indicate that anyone had convict connections. Obituaries, news reports, court reports were all silent. Embarrassing questions were not asked. In 1859 a letter in the *Mercury* complained that drunkenness was more prevalent in Tasmania than elsewhere: '*why* this is so, I will not pause to enquire'. Certainly not. In 1873 the government asked Brighton Council for a list of all ex-convicts found by the police to have committed further crimes. Councillors refused, 'as the questions that would have to be put by the Justices sitting on the trials, would be highly objectionable and offensive'—so the question 'were you a convict' to someone convicted of a crime was 'highly objectionable and offensive'.[8] The extravagant language shows how seriously this was felt. Some records did identify convict pasts, such as court and police documents, but they were only for official use and never made public.

Conflicting with this way of dealing with the stigma, but with the same broad aim, was the occasional reluctant mention of convicts to try to defend Tasmania's reputation. One claim was that most had gone: 'The great majority left the country as soon as their sentences expired and there are surprisingly few left', a visitor was told in 1867. It was true that many had gone—half or more, as shown earlier. Writer after writer emphasised this, and Charles Walch even claimed that the authorities connived at it, so that 'we got rid of our worst criminals' to Victoria.[9]

John West claimed that the remaining convicts left almost no trace behind. 'Thousands have died in chains; thousands and tens of thousands perished by strong drink.' Their children were few, 'partly by the effects of vice [syphilis], and in part by the impracticability of marriage [due to the scarcity of women]: they melt from the earth, and pass away like a mournful dream'. Like many statements made by anti-transportationists, this claim was based on truth but exaggerated. At the same time, in an example of the contradictions of the time, West claimed that convicts' descendants had reformed. 'The swarms of children rushing from a village school participate the blood of men, some of whom were once a terror to society, or of women who were its reproach. In the lists of religious societies, commercial companies, jurors, magistrates, will be found traces of their lineage.'[10] But convicts' children were rarely mentioned; people did not want to suggest to outsiders that they existed.

No one, not even the most ardent patriot, could claim that all convicts had left Tasmania; instead their impact had to be minimised. A popular tactic was to identify some ex-convicts so that the mass could escape the stigma. As Michael Sturma commented about New South Wales, once transportation ended, only respectable behaviour was socially acceptable: attending church, sending children to school, looking neat and clean, no bribery and corruption, no adultery, no being drunk in public. But people 'can be considered as moral and respectable only if there are others regarded as immoral and disreputable . . . The more successful they are in stigmatising others as immoral, the greater their chances of being themselves regarded as law-abiding and respectable.' In the fluid societies of the colonies—not just in Australia but all British colonies—where people had much more liberty to reinvent themselves than in Britain, respectability was a major weapon.[11]

Fortunately for those wanting to be seen as respectable—which from 1853 onwards was the vast majority of the population—there was a disreputable ex-convict group ideal for the purpose: the perhaps 15 per cent of ex-convicts who refused to behave in an acceptable manner, usually single men who kept on drinking, committing petty thefts and living on the edge of the general community. Those visitors whose main interest was seeing how a convict colony was faring as a free society, and who went on to write books about Tasmania for the world to read, were encouraged to see ex-convicts only as members of this group. Even more, they were encouraged to see these men not as dangerous criminals, but as harmless, pathetic, even amusing and quaint.

Here the 'convict look' theory came in handy. This held that you could tell a criminal by his (never her) appearance. In 1851 Henry Mayhew described London's criminal class as having high cheekbones, protruding jaws and 'the deep-sunk and half-averted eye which are so characteristic of natural dishonesty and cunning'. In 1876 the criminologist Lombroso developed this theory. Many criminals were throwbacks to an earlier form of species on the evolutionary scale, he wrote. Their distinctive physique included low foreheads, prominent jaws and cheekbones, protruding ears, and long hairy arms, like apes.[12] No writer mentioned a convict look in Van Diemen's Land before the 1850s, but the idea then took off, since it suited society nicely: as with the criminal class theory, it made convicts 'the other', set apart from non-convict citizens, who looked normal.

Almost all visitors who wrote books about Tasmania claimed that they could tell ex-convicts by their look. In 1868 Prince Alfred toured the island, and his chaplain wrote an official history of the trip. Thirty pages describe balls, receptions, decorated arches over roads, cheering and general excitement, all very loyal and respectable—until they came to Perth, just south of Launceston. A large crowd cheered as the royal party drove under an arch erected by the Perth Working Men's Benefit Society, but then they passed an inn, where a mob of men, 'with unmistakable convict faces, many of them drunk, added their quota to the general greeting, and called out, "We made the roads for the Government!"' 'And we have no doubt they did,' commented the author. When the Marquis de Beauvoir and another aristocratic young Frenchman landed on the quay in Launceston in 1866, 'we fancied we saw some dark, fierce faces, which seemed branded with their too illustrious origin'. They were so appalled they discussed returning to Melbourne. It was easy to recognise ex-convicts, said Henry Nesfield: 'old men who hang round stables in pubs are often redolent of government discipline, their hangdog cringing look, prison gait, close-shaven cheeks, all tell of the convict gang'.[13]

People who have been through trauma can look different; a soldier in the British Army after the Second World War recalled that Germans returned from prison camps in Russia often had a withdrawn, defeated look, and some convicts, especially those who had been at penal stations like Port Arthur, could well have had a similar appearance. This could account for the 'hangdog cringing' looks. Other parts of the criminal look could come from being old and poor, weather-beaten, not able to afford—or not caring about—neat clothes, washing, haircuts. Years of heavy drinking would not have helped people's appearance, and if they lost their teeth their cheeks would appear sunken. This was tough on the poor, who could easily have the 'criminal look', but made things easier for anyone who could afford to look neat and tidy, and therefore non-convict. Most people with a job could avoid the convict look. Conditions for working men were better than in England, as James Boyce has documented in *Van Diemen's Land*. Food was cheaper, pay was higher; the working class had enough food, clothing and shelter, and could educate their children.

As instructed by their hosts, most writers saw convicts only in the marginal group of tramps or casual labourers. One visitor, David Kennedy, asked an old man, 'Have you been here long?' 'I'm a ten-yearer,' replied the man, who told him how he had been transported for theft leaving his fiancée behind, suffered terribly and was now blind, but was reasonably happy as he and his dog got a meal a day. 'This poor waif of humanity,' noted Kennedy. Traveller Henry Nesfield gave the only recorded example of a prosperous ex-convict who admitted his past, when he asked the landlord in a country pub about convicts. 'Some of our biggest nobs could tell you about that,' said the landlord. 'I'm a lifer.' Nesfield said politely that in those days men were sent out for next to nothing. 'So they were, so they were, young man,' said the landlord. 'But mind you' (with a confidential wink) 'I wasn't sent out for nothing.' Nesfield commented pompously that such 'old lags . . . have an honest pride in their antecedents that is most refreshing and novel'.[14]

A few other writers described ex-convicts who had become respectable, though in general terms, never mentioning names. Kennedy noted that many had become well-to-do shopkeepers and hotel owners—you had to guess which they were. 'The community is largely permeated with this element, and they are a distinct class from persons of more spotless pedigree, a strong but imperceptible barrier. I saw faces of unmistakable convict stamp, but most old hands are now decent members of society, their children grown up respectably, and the general motto seems to be "Forget the past"'.[15] So the barrier might be strong (though this was a rare comment) but at least it was imperceptible.

In 1862 Frederick Jobson noted that many old hands had gone to the gold rush, and others had drunk themselves to death, so the convict class was barely a quarter of the population. But 'enough remain to constitute a formidable class . . . and the visitor has to be careful not to make too close enquiry'. 'In Tasmania it is not safe to ask a stranger *why* he left home—you can ask *where* he left from,' wrote another visitor.[16] Convict questions could only be asked about the marginal group.

Some visitors thought efforts to live down the past were failing. The Marquis de Beauvoir felt that the presence of the convict element, 'left too long flourishing', led to Tasmania's restricted suffrage, narrow ideas, exaggerated feelings of caste, and backwardness in business. Others thought Tasmania would take years to escape the stigma; it was only beginning to recover 'from the poison so long administered', it would need a century or more 'to purge or even partially to purify the social atmosphere of the infectious vapour with which it is impregnated', it had not escaped 'its former blight'. Anthony Trollope thought the attempt was doomed: it could never have been hoped, he thought, that the small population of Tasmania could swallow so many criminals without becoming noted for its convict element. By 1872, the traveller did not hear much in New South Wales about convicts—transportation there had ceased 30 years earlier—but in Tasmania the convict system was 'recent, fresh, and ever-present'. However, Trollope wrote elsewhere in his book that the convict flavour was quickly passing away, and Tasmania would throw off 'the disease' like New South Wales had. Most writers were similarly encouraging. Considering its antecedents, said Kennedy, Tasmania was a 'wonderfully decent and orderly colony'. Some noticed a change as soon as transportation stopped: as early as 1855 an American visitor wrote home, 'I have no reason to speak in anything but praiseworthy terms of what a short time since was the great Prison House for British criminals.'[17]

A few brave colonists challenged the convict stigma by joking about it. A visitor was told a story about a man at a party who kept his hat on inside the house—not socially acceptable. A young lady said 'Mr So-and-so has probably heard a very bad account of this colony, but I think you might venture to assure him that he might leave his hat in the hall with perfect safety!'[18] But jokes were rare: the topic was too touchy, jokes too close to the bone.

With ex-convicts publicly seen as confined to the small marginal group, everyone else had to be accepted as non-convict, even if their behaviour was questionable. This is seen in the career of John Davies. It was simply impossible to admit to outsiders that the owner of Hobart's major newspaper had been a convict.

Born in London in 1813 into a Jewish family, as a clerk John Davies committed fraud, and was transported to Van Diemen's Land in 1831—following his father, sentenced for the same crime. John Davies' behaviour under sentence is unknown, since his record was later removed, but in 1832 he was allowed to join his father in Sydney. As a policeman then journalist he was often in trouble for his fiery temper and reputation for violence. He was also bumptious, and never managed to lose his 'low-class unpleasantly grating accent'.

So far this is hardly a story of success, but in 1850 Davies brought his family to Hobart, and took over the *Guardian*, the newspaper which championed convicts, and turned it into the *Mercury*. He ran the Theatre Royal and was a captain of a volunteer rifle company. But, still pugnacious, he featured in a number of court cases—taking a headmaster to court for beating his son, fighting a servant's charge of non-payment of wages, defending himself against a charge of assault on Samuel Prout Hill, a journalist. Hill announced publicly that he had resigned from the rifle company because its captain 'made us a laughing stock in the community by giving us wrong orders on the march . . . as long as these commissions are issued indiscriminately, without reference to men's birth, education, and former position in life, the whole Volunteer Movement must inevitably be turned into ridicule'. 'Former position in life': code for 'convict'.

Davies beat up Hill, and when Hill was well enough to appear in court, Davies was tried. The judge thought Hill's published letter provided 'grievous provocation of the extremest character', but that in seriously injuring Hill, Davies had gone too far—a lenient attitude which showed how much sympathy even a judge had when a convict's past was brought up. After serving three weeks in prison, Davies stood for parliament, and despite his convict past, prison sentence and violent reputation he was elected (he did own a newspaper). Elected four times in all, he supported the welfare of the working class and Tasmania's prosperity, and he was at the height of his career when he died in 1872. His sons attended exclusive schools and had distinguished parliamentary careers, and his descendants continued to own the *Mercury* for over a century.

When Davies died, his convict past was not of course mentioned: but neither did the *Mercury*, his own newspaper, provide an obituary. Even by those well versed in the code, it would have been too difficult to write, since his convict past was so well known. A few years later, however, his son wrote an expurgated version of his father's biography, and family members were told this, according to descendent Margaret Davies.

Tasmania's change from a British prison to a free, self-governing community brought upheaval. Suddenly the machinery of colonial administration, the bureaucracy and even more importantly the British money that had so greatly assisted the local economy, vanished. Meanwhile, thousands of Tasmanians were leaving for the mainland, which offered not only gold, but land and jobs. For a brief period the Tasmanian economy benefited from the gold rush, providing Victoria's thousands with food, timber and other staples; but then Victoria developed its own industries, and from the late 1850s Tasmania suffered an economic slump.

Despite upheaval and depression, Tasmania progressed in many ways. With the end of transportation and the departure of so many of those single men prone to drinking, gambling and so on, Tasmania quickly became more sober and orderly, even though the convict group still dominated the population. In 1853 they formed about 51,000 of the island's 65,000 inhabitants: 77 per cent. Though many ex-convicts went to the goldfields, in 1857 some 60 per cent of adult males were convicts or ex-convicts, and ten years later they still formed a third of all adult males. Their descendants formed a large part of the remainder of the population. Between two-thirds and three-quarters of the Tasmanian population came from the convict group. This percentage continued, possibly even increased, since

Tasmania had few immigrants to bring in new blood, and intermarriage meant more convict descendants.

Although so many people belonged to the convict group, the high levels of petty crime, drunkenness and violence of the convict years fell dramatically. In 1853 the district of Brighton had eighteen policemen; ten years later, with much the same number of people, the decrease in crime meant only four were needed. In the decade 1860–70 the number of pubs in Clarence fell by more than half, from ten to four, while the number of schools and churches doubled (four to eight, two to five respectively). In 1862 Alexander Laing returned to Sorell after sixteen years away. He noticed 'a very great improvement amongst the inhabitants'. In the early days life had been a saga of drunkenness, quarrels, fighting, robbery and murder, but now Laing found 'very sober, industrious people [who] live upon very amicable terms'. There were no drunken scenes, crime had almost vanished, and people could leave their houses unlocked and their washing on the line without fear of theft. The odd stray drunk was the only reminder of the old days. Overall, crime figures showed a steady decline.[19]

This rapid improvement came despite economic recession in the 1860s and 1870s, and a general malaise, which observers of the day thought was due to the end of the convict system. People were used to depending on the British government's money and cheap labour, and its withdrawal resulted in listlessness and apathy.[20] This sounds as if the malaise was generally in the employer class, the main people met by chroniclers; workers, small farmers and tradesmen, mostly ex-convicts who had not benefited from British money or labour, did not miss these so much and were settling down to hard-working, more or less respectable and more or less prosperous lives.

An aid to increasing respectability was the higher proportion of women. In 1841 there were 41,000 men in Van Diemen's Land; in 1852, when many left for the mainland, there were 25,000; ten years later, 20,000. The percentage of women rose, jumping almost overnight from 47 for every 100 men in 1851, to 65 the following year. In some age groups there were even more women than men, and the story ran that at the height of the gold rush exodus, if a male stranger over the age of ten appeared in a Hobart street, half a dozen windows would be thrown open and the cry would be passed on, 'A man! A man!' In the nineteenth century it was received wisdom that women were better behaved than men, that they tamed men, making them bring their pay home to feed their families instead of spending it at the pub. Tasmanian life in the 1850s and 1860s seemed to bear this theory out. Respectability was also encouraged by the need to show you were not a convict: convicts were rough and lawless, so respectable behaviour demonstrated non-convict status.[21] By 1870 Tasmania was respectable, on the way to becoming, as its inhabitants desired, a model British community.

One way of defeating the stigma might have been to boast about this new respectability, but it would have meant saying why it was such a great thing, so on the whole it was avoided—though Tasmania's low crime rates were praised in the London *Times* in 1870. It was safer to praise Tasmania's other advantages, to prove what a wonderful place the island was. Strong feelings of patriotism encouraged this. As early as 1824 it was noted that 'there is already a degree of nationality in Van Diemen's Land', and in 1831 an emigrant commented about the generation born on the island: 'It is extraordinary the passionate love they have for the country of their birth.' In 1842 David Burn wrote that 'in no bosom does the love of country burn more intensely than in that of the native-born Tasmanian'—'in no bosom', presumably comparing the island with the rest of the world. In *The Broad Arrow* Caroline Leakey has a locally born lad glorying 'in being a genuine "gum tree", and not a stupid British oak'.[22] This applied to children of both convict and free: no writer noted that patriotism belonged particularly to either group.

This sentiment appalled well-born (if irritable) gentleman and public servant George Boyes:

> The people of this Colony very much resemble Americans in their presumption, Arrogance—Impudence and Conceit. They believe they are the most remarkable men on the Globe and that their little Island 'whips all creation'. They are radicals of the worst kind and their Children are brought up in the belief that all Governments are bad that they are deprived of their rights and that they are ground and oppressed by the Mother Country and mocked by the Officers sent out from England to rule them.[23]

Charles Walch, who certainly believed the island whipped all creation, went so far as to call Tasmania Paradise:

> All hail, Tasmania! O had I the power
> Of grand old Milton, e'en for one short hour,
> Then would I raise my voice in glorious song,
> And sing with rapture, and the notes prolong,
> Till the whole world, to earth's remotest bound,
> Should cry exulting—Paradise is found![24]

Patriotic citizens tried various ways of improving Tasmania: a prosperous and respectable colony could have nothing to do with convicts. Businessmen like Henry Hopkins would put money into almost any project which seemed likely to produce economic development: gas lighting, railways, exporting guano from Bass Strait islands, mining coal on Schouten Island off the east coast, finding gold. Others set up improving institutions such as temperance societies and the first working men's club in Australia, to curb drink and provide alternatives to pubs; ragged schools to educate, feed and clothe the children of the poor; charitable societies to help and improve the deserving poor. But these societies received little help from the general community, since people knew that they mostly helped convicts and their offspring, and either did not want to have anything to do with convicts, or thought they had brought their fates on themselves.

Free immigrants were encouraged, in order to outnumber convicts and swamp the convict group, and governments offered cheap passages. As before, information for prospective immigrants did not mention convicts. *Information Regarding the Colony of Van Diemen's Land*, published in 1853, even had the cheek to report that 'from the commencement of the Colony, [it] has been resorted to by free Settlers of unquestionable respectability'— and failed to mention anyone else. In 1859 Hugh Hull wrote a book to encourage emigrants, providing '*reliable* information about Tasmania, the GARDEN OF THE SOUTH'. It contained plenty of information, all positive, about Tasmania's climate, agriculture, postal arrangements and so on—but only four lines about its 2580 current prisoners, and nothing at all about past ones.[25] Few immigrants arrived, for the mainland colonies were far more prosperous and enticing, and Tasmania's reputation in Britain still too daunting.

Another way of distancing the community from the convict stigma was by being ultra-English, which presumed an English past, not a Tasmanian one (ironic, considering that most convicts were English). In Caroline Leakey's novel a visitor is warned never to use the term 'colonial' to describe anything but produce—colonists like to be praised as 'English'. The relationship with England was complex, however; John West ruled that 'a community little more than half a century old cannot be entitled to denounce Englishmen as foreigners, or to complain that strangers usurp the rights of the country-born'.[26] For him to state this, the locals must have been denouncing Englishmen as foreigners, like the boy who did not want to be a 'stupid British oak'.

Englishmen in Tasmania might irritate; Englishmen in England were the focus of loyalty. Tasmanians were almost English-mad, wanting to be thought like the English, wrote Trollope. Even for a relatively minor occasion like the Prince of Wales' marriage in 1863, 'all Hobart was aglow with gas-and-candle illuminations, fireworks, flags, and green branches'. When Queen Victoria's son Alfred toured the island in 1868, the colony wallowed in loyalty—a third of the entire population of the Brighton district turned out in pouring rain to see him drive past—and when two months later Alfred was nearly assassinated, Hobart held Tasmania's largest meeting to that date to demonstrate colonists' sympathy, horror and loyalty.[27] This was a much bigger meeting even than those held in the heyday of the disputes about transportation, showing what colonists thought important. Such large gatherings meant that not just the upper classes were involved, but the wider population.

Tasmanians supported the Empire's causes enthusiastically. The Crimean War was fought in the 1850s in distant Russia, with no Tasmanians involved, but when British communities were asked to subscribe to a fund to aid soldiers' widows and orphans, Tasmanians donated the most per capita, ten times as much as in Britain itself, 'a subscription *unparalleled in the British dominions*', as colonist Hugh Hull wrote proudly. Queen Victoria was so impressed that 'she directed that *Her high sense* of [Tasmanians'] *liberality*, cordial sympathy, and loyalty, should be conveyed'.[28] Such donations were much more than Tasmanians gave to local charities.

Tasmanians participated enthusiastically in exhibitions in London, to show how civilised they were. They contributed far more than other colonies to the Great Exhibition of 1851, though exhibits were haphazard, ranging from the tanned skin of a thylacine to jars of pickled vegetables. At the next exhibition in 1861, Tasmania tried to convey an image of stability and progress, notably with a 100-foot (30-metre) high wooden tower made of various timbers, to display its raw materials.[29] This was a considerable enterprise, especially as the colony was sinking further into depression. It showed what the government thought important: trade, but also making a positive impression in Britain.

Occasionally, despite efforts to ignore the convict past, it pushed its way into the public domain. Fear of convicts still under sentence (now all at Port Arthur) appeared in 1863 when all but 21 British soldiers in Tasmania were sent to fight the Maori in New Zealand. Tasmanians were without defences against the convict hordes! Uproar broke out, and parliament passed a law which sentenced convicts to death if they even attempted to assault an officer. Britain disallowed this 'barbaric' edict.[30]

That year the *Mercury* revealed that Britain did not know how to cope with her criminals. A ticket-of-leave scheme had failed; in Australia pardoned prisoners could leave their past behind, but in Britain they were sucked back into it, wrote the *Mercury*, and suggested reviving transportation, to provide labour in an economic slump. Many citizens wrote letters to the editor. Some argued that transportation would revive the economy: 'We have the name of a convict colony without any of its benefits,' wrote 'A Tradesman'. But most disagreed: 'the work of healing, which ten years or more has effected in the old sore, would be immediately undone, and the old class distinctions and bitter feelings' between bond and free would be revived. Tasmania would suffer 'social deterioration, moral pollution, national infamy, and a world's scorn'. Marriages between descendants of the two classes would be embittered, friendships rent asunder.[31] These writers clearly thought divisions had been decreasing, only a decade after transportation ceased.

The following year a Victorian court fined a ship's captain £5 for bringing an ex-convict from Tasmania. There was excitement in Melbourne, and the *Mercury* was scathing. Was this the first, or last, ex-convict in Melbourne? Where did Melbourne people come from? If a man had served his time, he should be treated the same as anyone else. Tasmanians resented Victorians' attitude; proud of not having been a convict colony, they 'never lose an opportunity of pointing the finger of derision at this colony for its having been made the depot of England's criminals'.[32]

The *Mercury* was much quieter when Caroline Leakey's novel *The Broad Arrow* was published in London in 1859. Its depiction of life in convict-era Hobart in the late 1840s was positively reviewed in England: 'a breadth and vitality . . . perfectly true . . . throws light on the vexed and difficult social question of secondary punishment . . .'

But few Tasmanians wanted any light thrown on this vexed question. *Walch's Literary Intelligencer*, the only local literary journal, noted the novel's publication and advertised an edition 'specially got up for Tasmania' at half price. 'No work has ever been issued from the English press in which Tasmanian scenes and Tasmanian doings (as they were) are so graphically depicted,' ran the *Intelligencer*. The next month a long review appeared, with the reviewer rather wary:

> The task of reviewing this book is one of some difficulty and delicacy. It deals with that gloomy phase of colonial life, which, thank God, is become a matter of tradition and history, rather than of present experience and observation. Our complete redemption, however, from by-gone evils is a work of time and the scars of political and social conflict are yet too fresh to bear the rough touch of an ungentle hand . . .
>
> That in the main it is a fair representation of a past phase . . . there can, we think, be no reasonable doubt . . . we have read it with mixed pleasure and satisfaction.

Others gained no pleasure from the novel. Newspapers did not mention it. People did not rush to buy it. In 1861 it was remaindered, and most libraries did not stock it.[33]

Despite Tasmanians' efforts to show their community as happy and united, there had to be some tensions with convict and free living together, as Henry Reynolds demonstrated in his article, 'That Hated Stain'. To a certain extent, the ruling elite tried to keep the working class, who were presumed to be ex-convicts, in their place: some landowners tried to stop them taking up farms, the franchise was more restricted in Tasmania than in other colonies (in 1869, only 42 per cent of adult males could vote for the lower house, and a mere 10 per cent for the upper house) and the *Master and Servant Act* of 1856 was severe, with employers able to arrest servants and hold them for up to a week without trial. On the other hand, the government was more or less forced into a paternal role, providing care for the hundreds of aged, ill, poor or insane ex-convicts who, on a labourer's wage and without family, could not make provision for old age. Almost despite itself, it set up the most comprehensive welfare system in Australia, with orphanages, hospitals, asylums and old-age homes.[34]

There are very few stories of conflict between convict and free, or of convicts being identified. In about 1869 there was some upset in parliament, probably when a member accused another of being a convict, or the son of a convict. It was referred to only in 1894, not noted in the press of the day. In the 1860s a man gained a temporary job as a butcher. His employer introduced him to the other workers: 'Jim's a convict, so's George, Bill's another damned convict,' he said, in front of the men.[35] It is hard to know how often such distinctions were made, but clearly it happened sometimes. The reactions of Jim, George and Bill were not noted—but jobs were scarce in the 1860s, so they probably had to put up with it.

However, the community as a whole accepted ex-convicts for what they could make of themselves, enabling them to live down their past if they wanted to, and recognising people's abilities by electing them to responsible positions. The pro-convict group elected to the Hobart Council in 1853 made poor use of their power, and this was the last time such a group stood, but individual ex-convicts and their children had more success. One ex-convict (John Davies), eight sons of convicts and one son-in-law were elected to parliament between 1856 and 1870, and one son, Richard Dry, became premier. Several descendants of convicts became magistrates, and other ex-convicts and convict relations were elected to municipal councils. In three municipalities I have studied, Glenorchy, Clarence and Brighton, about a quarter of all councillors came from the convict group. Outstanding in Brighton was William Gunn, major landholder, councillor for 42 years from 1863 to 1905 and warden for 33—yet he was descended from a convict. (This might already have been forgotten at the time of Gunn's election, for his female convict ancestor arrived with the First Fleet 80 years earlier.) Abraham Barrett, mayor of Launceston, was also of convict descent. Many more ex-convicts were successful businessmen and tradesmen.[36]

An illustration of how convict and free mixed comes from Henry Hopkins's household. An assigned convict called Screwby stayed on with the family after his pardon, becoming a trusted servant. Devoted to his master, Screwby lived in a room over the stables, and he would take Hopkins's young granddaughter Grace for rides out to Glenorchy to visit his old friend, former bushranger Martin Cash. The two ex-convicts would talk over past times, while Grace listened avidly. Clearly Henry Hopkins saw no possible danger for her in these visits.[37]

Existing beside the public policy of denial was an undercurrent of sympathy for convicts, a wish to remember them. Not everything possible was done to remove evidence of their existence, such as convict buildings. Over the years some disappeared, but though people occasionally suggested that they be demolished to remove the convict stain, if they were dismantled it was for their stone or their sites, for new buildings. With no money to waste, other convict buildings were renamed and used for other purposes, such as girls' homes or refuges for fallen women. Outsiders would never know their background. Several visitors observed that as the economy slumped in the 1860s and 1870s there was nostalgia for the lost days of plenty, when British money had poured in. A former governor told an English audience that many women lamented the end of their excellent convict servants, while their husbands deplored the end of the 'good old times' of convict labour.[38]

Convict stories, ballads and other traditions continued into the twentieth century, so they must have been carried on through this period, but the most noticeable evidence of sympathy towards convicts was the reaction in 1864 when American actor Joseph Jefferson put on a season of plays in Hobart. On his last night he performed *The Ticket-of-Leave Man*. Set entirely in England, it showed the problems of Bob, a discharged prisoner. In London Queen Victoria had been among the audience; with this example, the Hobart performance was patronised by the governor and his wife.[39]

Newspapers commented only briefly on the play, stating that it drew a large audience, with the dress circle 'a perfect galaxy of beauty and fashion'—which sounds most respectable. These reports did not mention the rest of the audience, but in his memoirs Jefferson reported that Tasmania retained a 'strong flavour of the convict element' among its lower classes, and there was excitement when the play was announced. On the evening he performed it:

> The faces in the pit were a study. Men with low foreheads and small, peering, ferret-looking eyes, some with flat noses, and square, cruel jaws, and sinister expressions,—leering, low, and cunning,—all wearing a sullen, dogged look, as though they would tear the benches from the pit and gut the theater of its scenery if one of their kind was held up to public scorn.

When Jefferson appeared as an ex-convict, with sunken eyes and a shaved head,

> There was a painful stillness in the house. The whole pit seemed to lean forward and strain their eager eyes upon the scene; . . . there were little murmurs of recognition and shakings of the head . . . deep-drawn sighs for the sufferings that Bob had gone through, and little smothered laughs at some of the old, well-remembered inconveniences of prison life; but then, Bob was a hero, and their sympathies were caught by the nobleness of his character and his innocence of crime, as though each one of these villains recognised how persecuted he and Bob had been.

The ex-convicts' enthusiasm increased as the play progressed. When Bob was ill-treated they howled their indignation, and when he ended the play unscathed 'they cheered to the very echo'. Outside the theatre, some old lags looked on Jefferson as a friend, poking him in the ribs and winking at him. 'Rather irksome,' he commented. No wonder the newspapers were silent about the enthusiasm shown by the audience. Note that it was not just ex-convicts who attended the play: there was the governor, as well as all that 'beauty and fashion' from the upper classes, who either joined in support for the convict hero or remained quiet. Jefferson might have been exaggerating a reaction he expected to see, but even so there was clearly a good deal of interest in the play, and sympathy for the convict hero from a wide cross-section of society.

Why was there so much interest in *The Ticket-of-Leave Man* and so little in *The Broad Arrow*? *The Ticket-of-Leave Man* had a convict hero but did not mention Tasmania, and was written from the convict's point of view. *The Broad Arrow* mentioned Tasmania all too much, was written from an upper-class, non-convict point of view, had an upper-class convict heroine it is hard to like, and depicted convicts negatively. No wonder those who flocked to see *The Ticket-of-Leave Man* did not buy *The Broad Arrow*, which reminded Tasmanians all too vividly of why the British scorned them.

The difference is notable: general sympathy with convicts was fine, specific mentions of Van Diemen's Land were not. Though there was interest in convicts, it was an undercurrent, not mentioned in the press, and it could happily co-exist with the collective public desire to ignore the past.

9

FORGETTING THE PAST

Tasmanians as a community tried a variety of methods, both overt and instinctive, to repudiate the convict stain. As described in Chapter 8, they banded together to defend themselves against outsiders. Within that community, also, individuals tried to hide their past, for no matter how much the community was united against the stain, there was some stigma on individual ex-convicts and their families. But this was not said publicly; the general population supported people trying to hide their past—most of the general population were in a similar situation anyway—because if hardly anybody was known to be a convict, everyone could see that Tasmania had nothing to do with them anymore. Everyone would be distanced from the convict stigma.

As noted earlier, a few convicts, living on society's fringes, were happy about their convict past being known. Even so, there are very few stories about ex-convicts admitting their position. There were the drunken loafers who heckled Prince Alfred's procession in Perth in 1868; the occasional ex-convict who admitted the fact to visitors who told the stories in their books; and one prosperous one, the midlands innkeeper who told Henry Nesfield he was a lifer. Some Tasmanian children later described how they enjoyed talking to old men about convict days, and people assumed many other elderly men were ex-convicts, but there is no evidence that they themselves admitted it.

At the other end of the social spectrum, a handful of families could not escape the stain. Their convict ancestor had been well known for his or her success in life—which, ironically, became a handicap for later generations. Charles Davis the successful merchant, and David Gibson and Thomas Burbury the successful graziers, were so famous as convicts who prospered that their descendants could not hide their past. But these families were a tiny minority, perhaps ten in total.

The rest, the 85 to 90 per cent who wanted to, and could, hide the past, were remarkably successful. The evidence for this is that by the 1920s the overwhelming majority of people descended from convicts did not know about this history, and nor did anyone else. Almost everybody managed to hide it. They had major advantages to help them. All colonies, where so many people were immigrants, were flexible places where people could more easily reinvent themselves than back in Britain where their families and their history were known.[1] Transportation left no identifying mark—no concentration camp tattoo and no brand, unlike deserters among soldiers who were branded 'D'—so there was nothing physical to show that people had been convicts. The small percentage whose backs had been marked by the lash could keep their shirts on. To avoid recognition, ex-convicts could move away from the area where they had served their sentences.

The most common way to escape the stigma was to invent a new past which had nothing to do with transportation. Some enterprising people paved the way by giving a false name when they were arrested, back in Britain. Most seem to have been convicted under their real names, because they were arrested in the community where they lived, they were known to the police, or they did not think of changing their names. Only a handful are known to have given an alias—though perhaps others kept the secret. Some could not. In 1837 John White was transported for stealing fowls and rabbits, on the same ship as his father—who was transported in the name of John Brown. Other names were obviously pseudonyms: a machine-breaker, a political protester, gave his name to the authorities as Worthy Mann. Some people already had aliases, which were often noted on their convict records; 'James Brown alias William Stratford' is one such entry. Women often had maiden and married surnames, but the authorities were skilled at making notes regarding the use of both aliases and married names, so they were of limited value for people who wanted to change their identity—though presumably some managed to keep aliases secret.

A few convicts, usually middle class, gave false names so their families could escape the shame of having a convict relative. 'Frederick Thomas' was transported to Sydney for swindling, and sent inland as a shepherd. He tried to escape several times, but eventually he was pardoned and worked in Sydney as a clerk. Then he was arrested for stealing money, and transported to Van Diemen's Land. 'I am not here in my real name I have never divulged it & do not wish to do so now,' he related. 'My Father is a Gent[lema]n of Fortune, I committed the Crime I am now here for the purpose of getting money to make my Escape.' He was sent to Port Arthur, where he was punished with hard labour in chains for a string of offences such as having tobacco in his possession—but he still did not divulge his real name. Perhaps Frederick Thomas and Worthy Mann were hoping to return to Britain and take up their old lives again under their real names.

But the great majority of convicts served their terms and were freed under their own names. They had to earn a living, to establish themselves in the new country, and most wanted to do this under a new persona, as 'always free' people, which meant passing themselves off as free immigrants. This was not particularly difficult, since free immigrants were not recorded in nearly as much detail as convicts. No proof was needed by the general community.

The 50 per cent or perhaps more of all ex-convicts who left Tasmania did so partly because economic prospects were better on mainland Australia, but also so they could leave their convict past behind and start afresh in a place where they were far less likely to be recognised as ex-convicts. They could easily change their life stories to omit their convict years. Victoria, South Australia and Queensland were proud of their convict-free status, and no one there wanted to point out any inhabitants as ex-convicts, which would taint the whole community. If ex-convicts lived respectably in these colonies and never mentioned their background, they had little to fear. When he escaped to Adelaide, convict William Derrincourt said he had just arrived from England as a free immigrant. Samuel and Anastasia Withers, both convicts, married in Van Diemen's Land and moved to Victoria. They told their children and presumably their neighbours that they had married in Britain and emigrated to Victoria in 1853. They dug for gold and kept a pub at Bendigo, and stories were passed down through the family of how Anastasia was so highly trusted by the miners that she looked after gold for them, hanging it in little bags under her voluminous skirts; and how she and two other miners' wives made the famous blue and white flag for the Eureka Stockade, using a petticoat for the stars. The family, eventually with nine children, bought land, built a house, planted an orchard and ran a store, all most respectably. Only research by their descendents in the 1990s discovered their convict past. If a couple like the Withers behaved respectably, told a respectable story of their past and never mentioned Tasmania, then there was no reason for anyone to link them with convicts.

Similarly, two Irish convicts, Matthew McGann and Johanna Regan, married in Hobart in 1853, had two children, and then moved to New South Wales. The birth certificates of two subsequent children stated that the parents married in Dublin in 1848, while one of the Tasmanian-born children informed the authorities when he married that he was born in New South Wales, and his obituary reported that he was born at sea. A similar story was discovered by historian Noel McLachlan, who was brought up to believe himself a third-generation Victorian of respectable immigrant stock; instead he found that at least two of his great-great-grandparents were Vandemonian ex-convicts.

Historian Lyndall Ryan's great-great-grandfather, John Cronin, came from Cork, leaving his family there when he was transported for ten years in 1850 for stealing a cow. He was so well behaved that he soon became a constable; his one offence was sleeping while on duty, for which he was reprimanded. In 1853 he gained his conditional pardon, and later that year went to Victoria, calling himself John Glass. Meanwhile his first wife was struggling, and in 1855 their daughter Hannah emigrated to Australia to look for her father. She spent years searching, and in the late 1860s married and moved to Sydney, where she hired a solicitor who eventually found her father, living quite near her and with a second family. He refused to have anything to do with her, which shocked her deeply but was a great relief to her respectable husband, a German immigrant carpenter, who would never let the family mention the word convict. His and Hannah's great-granddaughter Lyndall grew up knowing nothing about all this, but when she was in her twenties—old enough to cope?—her aunt told her the family secret.

There were hundreds, even thousands, of similar stories of ex-convicts leaving Tasmania for a new life in Victoria, other mainland colonies, New Zealand, even as far away as America. Benjamin Shadbolt, transported to Van Diemen's Land in 1846 for burglary, gained his pardon and in 1859 migrated to New Zealand, where he became a respected sawmiller, farmer, shopkeeper, publican and local politician. Either he or his children kept quiet about his convict origins, which later descendants knew nothing about until research brought the hidden story to light.

Most people tried to make their new life story fit reality as much as possible, just changing the convict details and perhaps the date they arrived in Australia, but at least one ex-convict decided that if he was going to make up a new past, it would be a good one. John Dow, alias John Colquhoun, alias John James Colquhoun, was transported for seven years for obtaining goods under a false name, and arrived in Van Diemen's Land in 1826. He received his freedom in the early 1830s. Calling himself Lord Lascelles, the eldest son and heir of the Earl of Harewood, Dow attended St David's Church and tried to sell some poems to the *Hobart Town Courier*. The *Courier* described him as a 'little prim gentleman, of rather an eccentric, poetic appearance'.

The so-called Lascelles fared better in New South Wales. Taking advantage of the many British government enquiries into the colonies, he claimed he had been commissioned by the Secretary of State to look into the proper treatment of convicts, and went about with a briefcase taking down statements from prisoners. As a peer, he was welcomed by colonial society, though not by everyone. In 1833 the little prim gentleman eloped with Lilias Dickson, daughter of a well-to-do Sydney family, and after her family found and reclaimed her, Lascelles had the cheek to try to recover her through the Supreme Court. He was listed in the judge's notebook as 'calling himself Edward Lord Viscount Lacelles, eldest son of Earl Harewood'—so someone suspected his story. These events were reported in England, and the Earl of Harewood declared that the person calling himself Lord Lascelles was 'a rank imposter'.

In 1835 Lascelles was tried for signing the name Edward Lascelles to a cheque. He defended himself well, with an aristocratic air, but Van

Diemen's Land witnesses proved he was John Dow, and he was sent back to Van Diemen's Land to serve a second term, for life this time. The *Courier* decided that he was insane, possessed with the idea that he really was Lord Lascelles. On arrival in Hobart, the prisoner John Dow alias Luttrell told the authorities that he was the son of the Earl of Harewood, and named his seven aristocratic brothers and sisters. He received his ticket of leave in 1843, and which of his five aliases he then lived under is not known.

Other ex-convicts remained in Tasmania, but told a version of their past in which convicts were not mentioned. Alexander Laing wrote his memoirs in 1867, telling his family that he had signed up for seven years with the Gordon Highlanders and received his honourable discharge in 1813. Then he 'engaged with a gentleman in Edinburgh to go out with him to Van Diemen's Land as his gardener and overseer'. He worked for various employers in the Sorell district, and in 1820 became chief constable. He retired in 1838, worked in various places, and in 1862 settled in Sorell.

His true story was different. Born in Scotland in 1792, Laing did enlist with the Gordon Highlanders, but in 1813 was found guilty of theft and transported to New South Wales. Two years later he arrived in Van Diemen's Land. He worked as an assigned servant in the Sorell district, and though he was a constable in the 1820s he was still under sentence, certainly not chief constable. He was employed as a constable and gaoler in various areas, married twice, fathered twelve children, and composed musical pieces for the piano. In his memoirs he told only of activities creditable to himself, and manufactured the rest, based vaguely on reality.

Another ex-convict who hid her origins was Rosina Davis, a London servant who told her prosecutor that the £20 worth of jewellery, silk and clothes found in her possession was a present from her young man. A pity that the patterns matched those of goods which had been stolen. A theft worth more than £2 was a capital offence, but nineteen-year-old Rosina was convicted only of stealing goods worth just under £2, and arrived in Hobart in 1823. Her record notes only one offence, another theft. In August 1826 she married James Luckman, an ex-convict who ran a pub, and their first child was born the next month. The family prospered, eventually owning a number of properties, and Rosina and James sent their sons to elite private schools.

In keeping with her new middle-class status, Rosina reinvented her biography. She obtained a small red leather-bound Bible and wrote inside the name she had chosen, the aristocratic-sounding 'Rosina Augusta DeBoone', with the date 'May 6, 1820'. Underneath she wrote: 'James Luckman and Rosina Augusta DeBoone married 14 of August 1825 at St Davids Church Hobart Town Van Deimens [sic] Land'—making the first child's birthdate a respectable year after his parents' marriage. The Luckmans' children often used the names Augusta and DeBoone among their offspring, implying that they accepted their mother's impressive new name. Did they realise that the Bible Rosina dated 1820 was printed in 1827? Apparently not, and in later years many family members did not know of the Luckmans' convict background, until research revealed it in the 1990s.

Like John Cronin, some ex-convicts changed their names. James Freeman, a coachman, was transported for life in 1825 for stealing a mare. As a convict in Van Diemen's Land he behaved well, and in 1832 was a gaol attendant. The next year he married Mary Bowyer, a free immigrant with a job as a servant. The Freemans had ten children, and James worked as a gardener. He received his free pardon in 1839. This is a fairly typical story of a successful ex-convict—but, unusually, James and Mary Freeman changed their name to James and Mary Prince. Their descendant Leonie Mickleborough could find no reason for this other than to avoid the convict stain; there were no Princes in either family tree. All their children except one son also changed their names to Prince. What sort of discussions took place around the Freeman/Prince table can only be imagined, with most family members changing their surname but one son sticking to the original.

Many new life stories can be seen in obituaries in local newspapers. Dozens if not hundreds of convicts made good, became pillars of their local communities, and had long and admiring obituaries published after they died. These never mention the convict past, but tell the refashioned story. After his involvement with the pro-convict Tasmanian Union, James Gray had a career in the public service and then politics. When he died in 1889 his obituary told how he 'arrived in the colony about half a century ago, and in 1848 he accepted a clerkship in the Civil Service'. In 1912 the *North West Post* wrote an obituary of Mrs Thomas O'Donnell. Born in Galway, she arrived at Forth in the island's north-west in 1852, settled on a farm with her husband and eight children, and had lived in the district ever since. All very respectable—but she had actually arrived at the Forth as an assigned servant, having come to Van Diemen's Land as a convict in 1849. James McHugh was transported in 1848 for sheep-stealing. Once freed he married another Irish ex-convict, Mary Judge, and they farmed at Riana, south of Penguin. When James died aged 93, the *Advocate* wrote a glowing obituary, describing him as one of the early pioneers of the district. He was born in Ireland in 1822 'and 18 years later came to Tasmania . . . The late James McHugh was well known and highly respected throughout the Latrobe district, a man of honor, whose word was his bond, and with a heart filled with true Irish hospitality.'

It was easier for women than men to hide their convict past, for from the Tasmanian Union onwards, virtually everyone who wrote anything about convicts assumed they had all been male. An added advantage was that on marriage women changed their names, so Mary Smith, ex-convict, became Mrs John Brown, wife of John Brown. As a wife, a woman gained respect, because this was the role society expected her to fill. If she became a wife and mother, cooking and cleaning for her family and raising her children—the role the great majority of women had no option but to take—Mrs John Brown could not possibly be a dissolute ex-convict. While few men were named as ex-convicts, almost no women were.

While much of the forgetting happened in the first generation with the convicts themselves making up new life stories, sometimes it was later generations who did not pass on the knowledge. In his memoir *In Sunshine and in Shadow*, writer Martin Flanagan documented the 'forgetting' in his family. Thomas Flanagan, an Irish farm labourer, arrived in Van Diemen's Land in 1849 as a convict, transported for stealing meal and a small sum of money during the Irish famine. It was his first and last offence, commented Martin. Thomas worked for grazier William Archer, who helped him bring out his wife and eight children. Thomas became Archer's tenant farmer, and was still alive when Martin's grandfather was a boy—but Martin's father Arch, born in 1923, was never told about the convict origins. 'Dad's family either chose to forget its convict forebear and his family or forgot to remember; either way, within two generations they were gone to such an extent it was as if they had never been there at all.'

Martin's maternal grandfather's family, the O'Learys, were not convicts, and 'having nothing to hide, were even mildly rebellious'. But his maternal grandmother, Kathleen Green, was descended from Eddie Green, an Irish 'White Boy', rural rebels who fought the evictions by landlords of tenants who could not pay their rents. Eddie was one of four who broke into a home from which a local family had been evicted, assaulting the new inhabitants. He was transported and, unlike Thomas Flanagan, committed many more offences in Van Diemen's Land; he too eventually gained his pardon, and settled down on a farm near Sorell.

On her deathbed, aged 99, Kathleen admitted that she knew Eddie had been a convict, and had met him when she was a child. He was a rough old man, she said. But she had told her children that Eddie was 'a sergeant in the British Army who had journeyed on to the more southern colonies with his governess wife after a spell in India! In fact his wife was a barely literate convict's daughter,' wrote Martin.

Another way to hide the past was vagueness, and researchers have noticed that convicts' children were often vague about details on parents' death certificates, showing either that they were not told family histories or did not want to repeat them. But some were more forceful, and the convict records of three men who had become prominent disappeared, removed from the volumes. Indents of prominent ex-convicts Henry Propsting (father of a premier), John Davies (newspaper proprietor and politician) and Charles Davis (businessman) somehow vanished.[2] The story of 'Mr Propsting's Page' became part of public service folklore, as Geoffrey Stilwell told Christopher Koch in the 1960s:

> W.B. Propsting came from a highly successful Hobart merchant family, and had gone to South Australia as a schoolteacher. He had become engaged to the daughter of a prominent citizen, who did not feel that a teacher was from a background socially important enough to make him a suitable match for his daughter; whereupon, Mr Propsting returned to Hobart to verify details of his respectable ancestry. But his attention was drawn by a friend to one of the convict registers then in the charge of the Supreme Court; Mr Propsting asked to see it, was left to examine it,

and discovered to his horror his ancestor Henry Propsting: transported for stealing a goose. Mr Propsting departed; and when he'd gone, it was discovered that his ancestor's torn-out page had gone with him.[3]

So William Propsting, born in 1861 when his father was 51, had not known that his father was a convict. (Or so he said.) When he became premier he certainly did not mention it. How many people did know such facts? It is sometimes said that 'everybody knew' who were the convict families, yet of course this cannot be true. What it means is that some people knew that some other people were ex-convicts or their descendants, for no one can have known everybody, and even by the 1850s it appears that people like Alexander Laing and Rosina Davis had their new stories accepted. But no one said publicly that anyone was descended from a convict, and it was not done to ask people embarrassing questions.

There was private talk, naturally. There is no description of this to date in Tasmania, but Paul Hasluck wrote that in Western Australia:

> There was a sort of code among the old free settlers . . . that they never gossiped about those who had come from convict stock. Although they knew many who had been 'lagged', they kept the confidence to themselves. They knew but never told a stranger what they knew. They might pass a name to their own sons. Even among ourselves the old free settlers used a euphemism when referring to such a person. 'He didn't pay his own passage', or 'His father didn't have to raise the fare'.[4]

Occasionally such things were written down in Tasmania, but in private. In 1876 John Whitehead wrote to a friend with a shocking story. John Foster, a wealthy midlands grazier, had married an ex-convict, Ann Dinham—a prostitute, transported for ten years, married with two children, reported Whitehead. When Foster was ill she became his nurse, and after the suspicious death of her husband he married her. Whitehead was appalled. 'If you have not made the acquaintance of Mrs John Foster, *don't* if you have, *drop it*', he urged his friend. What appalled him most—prostitution, convict status or possible murder—he did not specify. Perhaps this sort of talk, identifying people as convicts, was quite common among friends, but it never made the public arena.

One place where people's ex-convict status was sometimes noted was various government and municipal records—though never in so many words. Instead, the ship the ex-convict had been transported on was written beside the name, or initials such as 'F.S.' (free by servitude) or 'F.C.' (free to colony)—in code, so only those in the know understood. In the 1890s the Brighton police still noted the names of people's convict ships, in which they might have arrived half a century earlier. In 1892 an 89-year-old ex-convict was sentenced to eight days in gaol for being idle and disorderly, found in a shed, unable to give a good account of himself. A 78-year-old former convict received two months in gaol for stealing two loaves of bread from a farmer's house.[5] Why did the police note the name of these men's ships, establishing that they were ex-convicts? A bureaucratic hangover from convict days? Mere curiosity? Such information was never gathered together and published, so there was no administrative need for it.

Convict records sometimes noted ex-convicts' later history. On arrival in Australia, each convict was allocated an entry in a register which recorded his or her sentence, offences and date of freedom. If the ex-convict again came under government notice, more information was added: subsequent offences, execution, or entry into a government institution such as a lunatic asylum, and death there. This is understandable, for officials might have wanted to know how many convicted criminals were ex-convicts—ex-convicts in institutions were sometimes paid for by the British government. It is also understandable, just, that when clerks noted those ex-convicts who claimed the old age pension in 1909, over half a century after transportation ended, someone might have been interested in such a statistic.

But clerks sometimes wrote information about ex-convicts who had nothing further to do with the system. William Buck arrived in 1843 and gained his free certificate in 1857. Half a century later, a clerk wrote on his record that in 1901 he died at his residence, 'Clarence Reach' near Rokeby on Hobart's eastern shore. A home dignified by a name, a respectable farmer—why did the clerk note this fact? Someone also noted that Charles Naish, transported in 1835 and gaining a conditional pardon in 1843, died in South Melbourne in 1900 aged 84, some 57 years later and in a different colony, and that Ann Foster née Dinham died in England in 1882. How did they know? There must have been gossip, people must have talked. One can envisage a clerk coming to work and saying to a colleague, 'I heard old Charles Naish died—wasn't he sent out?' 'I'll check', and sure enough, there was Naish's record, so the clerk added this new piece of information, not as part of the government system but as an interesting fact. None of this was made public; as far as is known, no one but the clerks, and the occasional visitor like William Propsting, ever saw the records.

William Hartnell was transported in 1824 for receiving stolen goods, and was in trouble for being out after hours, disobedience, stealing, and cruelty to a bullock, knocking off one of its horns with a blow, and threatening another convict with a knife if he told. Eventually he received his pardon, and went on to marry and settle down. On his record one of these anonymous clerks wrote: 'father of the Hon W Hartnoll'. William junior was educated at the prestigious Launceston Church Grammar School, established a firm of stock and station agents, owned his own grazing property, and sat not only in the Tasmanian parliament but in 1902 in the new federal parliament. Certainly he would not have wanted his convict parentage made public—but some clerk not only knew but noted it down.

The clerks also remembered John Hornsby, a teenage thief transported from the slums of London in 1851. He became a policeman, but disgraced himself by running away when bushrangers approached. Nine months' hard labour in chains resulted, and assaulting a man and stealing ten shillings brought another two years. By the end of it Hornsby was once more a policeman, and gained his free certificate in 1855. After this troubled start, he settled down much more happily. In 1858 he married Sarah Turner and they had ten children. Hornsby tried farming, then worked for the Education Department. The ex-convict who at eighteen could 'read & write a little' wielded a pungent pen as a drama critic, wrote articles for newspapers, and in 1895 published *Old Time Echoes of Tasmania*, memoirs of his time in the police. Though he sympathised with convicts, he did not even hint that he had been one himself, and nor did his death notice and obituary. This described how Hornsby came of good old English stock, emigrated to Tasmania aged fifteen, and joined the police force aged nineteen. A 'genial, companionable man', he had a successful career, dying aged 73 of a painful disease which he bore with Christian fortitude.

All extremely respectable—but on his convict record is scrawled, 'Died at Hobart 28 April 1903'. Someone remembered after 50 years.

Despite these private rememberings, in the second half of the nineteenth century the forgetting process was in general well underway, with some people able to hide their past, others remembered by only a few people. It is impossible to say what the percentages were. Did a quarter, half, three-quarters of convict families manage to hide the stain? What is certain is that over the decades, more and more managed it, and knowledge of the convict past diminished. Someone, possibly the convict, possibly the convict's child or grandchild, did not tell the next generation, and, amazingly, no one else told this generation either—no aggrieved neighbour, no teasing classmate at school, no *in vino veritas* in the local pub. With the stigma so entrenched, a convict past was thrilling gossip to pass on, but enough people managed to ignore the temptation. This astonishing feat shows how much the whole community wanted to hide the disreputable past: people would prefer to shield the entire community than spread enticing gossip. Perhaps the gossip about who had been sent out was only among friends, only of the same generation. Other people did not want to know. The silence continued. Christine Walch, born in Hobart in 1893, recalled that you never asked people about their background, for fear of what they might have to admit.

The amazing result of the forgetting process was that by the 1920s and 1930s, the general population did not know that anyone, or hardly anyone, was descended from convicts—even though most of them were themselves. Interviews that I conducted in 1997 with twenty Tasmanians who grew up in the 1920s and 1930s were startlingly unanimous. They said that they rarely thought of convicts at all; they were never discussed and few people knew that anyone was descended from them. Born in 1918, Lindsay Whitham recalled that he heard very little talk about convicts, though there was the feeling that they were 'something to be swept under the carpet'. No one owned up to having a convict ancestor, and both he and his sister Marie said they had no idea at all as they were growing up that anyone was descended from convicts.

Others made similar comments. 'When I was growing up, we didn't hear a great deal about convicts,' said former premier Eric Reece. 'I can't recall that the convict system was ever mentioned', 'no one ever talked about convicts', were typical comments. Some knew that a few people were descended from convicts, but 'of course they shooshed it up'; 'You'd get short shrift if you asked them about it'; 'it was very improper for any-one to mention it'. 'The notion was widespread that "You were what you were", that who your ancestors were didn't matter.' There was a great scan-dal, one woman recalled, when 'at a dance in the midlands, the Camerons came dressed as convicts, and it was thought they were making a mock of people like the Gibsons who were descended from convicts. They were never forgiven'[6]—not just by the Gibsons, but by everyone at the dance. The whole community realised, had realised from the start, that it had to hide the fact that most of it was descended from convicts, to save every-body from the stigma.

This situation continued. It was an outstandingly successful example of a community united to achieve an end: ignorance of convict inheritance.

10

FOR THE TERM OF HIS NATURAL LIFE

In 1870 efforts to defeat the convict stigma received what appeared to be a huge setback, with the appearance of the major convict novel, *For the Term of His Natural Life*.

Despite—and because of—the shame, Tasmania's convict past provided potential. Such a dramatic and different history was full of opportunities, for tourists and for novelists. They started to show their interest in about 1870, and have been showing it ever since.

The few tourists to Tasmania in the 1850s and 1860s were officially told little about the island's convict past. As a guidebook published in London in 1863 ran: 'It is not our purpose to enter into the tedious and somewhat painful history of the early colony, which enjoyed a notorious name as a penal settlement.' But by the late 1860s tourism was beginning to develop, and the *Guide to Excursionists from the Mainland to Tasmania*, published in 1869, took a different path. The author was a Victorian, Henry Thomas, who lacked Tasmanians' sensitivity towards the convict system, and thought tourists would be interested in it. He gave them a sensational description of Port Arthur, and pointed out where they could see the ruins of probation camps. He sympathised with 'poor prisoners' for their sufferings, but described the remaining convicts at Port Arthur as 'the most incarnate villains on earth'.

Did Thomas receive angry letters from Tasmanians? In later editions of his guidebook he toned down his convict material, and included a brief history of the island, which in true Tasmanian style scarcely mentioned convicts. As well:

> A very short visit amongst Tasmanians will do much to disabuse the mind from the absurd prejudices which exist with many, who cannot forget . . . the antecedents of the colony. The people are proverbially hospitable, and there is an entire absence of anything likely to recall the fearful ordeal through which the colony has passed.

Thomas had become as good at avoiding the dreadful c–word as any Tasmanian.

Perhaps to rebut Thomas, perhaps to cash in on the growing tourist industry, in 1871 the Tasmanian firm of J. Walch & Sons printed their own guidebook, written by well-known local author Louisa Meredith. No convict ruins or sympathy here; Meredith gave the least possible prominence to convicts.[1] As well as taming their own writers, Tasmanians had managed to tame Henry Thomas. They did not succeed with Marcus Clarke.

Born in England in 1846, Marcus Clarke emigrated to Victoria aged seventeen and became a journalist with the Melbourne *Argus*. Ambitious, a talented writer, he was inspired by Victor Hugo's *Les Miserables* to write a great convict novel—so from the start his novel was going to be miserable, with convicts ground down by the brutal ruling classes. The *Argus* commissioned him to produce a series of articles about Tasmania's convict system, and early in 1870 he visited the island to research both the articles and the novel.

Clarke went to Port Arthur, which was still a working prison. The registrar showed him old records, and recalled that Clarke insisted on seeing only those of the most notorious criminals. He was appalled by Port Arthur: 'there seemed to me to hang over the whole place a sort of horrible gloom, as though the sunlight had been withdrawn from it'. The gloom did not stop him working fast. His novel, *His Natural Life*, began publication as a serial in March 1870, and the last instalment of its 370,000 words came out in June 1872. The shorter book version, later and ever since known as *For the Term of His Natural Life*, was published in 1874.[2]

For anybody who does not enjoy long-winded Victorian novels, *His Natural Life* is hard going. How it became so popular is a mystery, with its long-drawn-out narrative, endless descriptions, improbable coincidences, and the certainty that nothing good is ever going to happen to the hero— unless it was because people enjoyed reading of unrelenting misery and gloom, of torture, floggings, cannibalism, rape and brutality. Yet this was and probably remains the best-selling novel about Tasmania, still in print 140 years later.

From the start the cards are stacked against Richard Devine, a gentle- man hero. Nobly taking the blame for a murder he did not commit, he is transported to Van Diemen's Land as Rufus Dawes. On his ship are Mau- rice Frere, a brutal officer; bumbling Colonel Vickers; another convict, John Rex, who resembles Rufus; and Colonel Vickers' wife and daughter, golden-haired and blue-eyed Sylvia. John plans mutiny, but Rufus betrays the plot. The mutineers denounce him.

Everyone ends up at the Macquarie Harbour penal settlement, where conditions are frightful, and Rufus is brutally punished again and again, unjustly of course. The settlement is abandoned, but on leaving John Rex and his convict friends seize the ship and maroon Maurice, Mrs Vickers and Sylvia. Rufus saves them but Maurice claims credit. No one can chal- lenge him, since Mrs Vickers has died and Sylvia has lost her memory. Both Maurice and Rufus are in love with her. Rufus is sent to Port Arthur on a trumped-up charge. Everything there is terrible, and even worse is Point Puer, the boys' prison, where young lads of twelve commit suicide by jumping off a rock rather than continue living in such cruel conditions. Adult convicts, too, commit suicide rather than live. They draw lots: one kills another and is then hung for murder, so both can quit their hopeless lives. There is a homosexual rape. Meanwhile John Rex reaches England, but is sent back to Van Diemen's Land. At Port Arthur he realises that Rufus is the heir to the Devine fortune.

Years pass. Sylvia marries Maurice but is not happy with her brutal husband. John Rex escapes again; he reaches Sydney, but his companions are lost in the Vandemonian bush, and murder and eat each other. In

England John claims to be Richard Devine (he turns out to have been Richard's half-brother), but unjustly gained riches can't bring happiness in a Victorian novel: he dies of a heart attack. Meanwhile Rufus is sent to appalling Norfolk Island. Under Maurice as commandant, he suffers floggings and torture on the rack. The system has finally degraded him, until he is saved by a flower plucked by Sylvia's fair hand. On a ship with Rufus, Sylvia realises that he saved her and she loves him, uttering the immortal words, 'Good Mr Dawes'. The ship sinks and, finally clasped together, they drown.

For the Term of His Natural Life shows the convict system as monstrous and cruel, degrading everyone who comes in contact with it. The more kindly assignment or probation systems are barely mentioned, and the novel implies that all convicts were sent to penal stations, flogged and chained and worked inhumanely. No one's sentence ever ends. No convict except Rufus shows any positive characteristic: they are all brutal and vile, living in filth and despair, betraying, raping, murdering and eating each other. The free population is not much better: weak, hypocritical, drunken or rough, or at best, like Sylvia, victims. No one in Van Diemen's Land is happy. It is a place of utter misery.

This is a gross distortion of the convict system. Like another famous novel which exposed a cruel system, Harriet Beecher Stowe's *Uncle Tom's Cabin*, it takes as the norm the experience of a small minority—in this case the most notorious of the 10 per cent of convicts who were sent to penal stations like Macquarie Harbour and Port Arthur. It picks out transportation's most dramatic events over 50 years, making them look like the norm. A few convicts did seize a ship, sail to South America, return to England, be recognised, and end up back in Van Diemen's Land. There was an example of cannibalism among escaped convicts. There were dreadful punishments, and stories about convicts committing suicide to escape. Convicts were flogged and had to work hard. Injustices did occur. But boys did not commit suicide at Point Puer, most convicts were not flogged, only a small percentage suffered in penal stations, and only a small percentage worked in chains—whereas Rufus seemed to be in chains almost the entire time.

Clarke briefly described Van Diemen's Land society, again treating the worst stories as general truth:

Of the social condition of these people at this time it is impossible to speak without astonishment . . . The profligacy of the settlers was notorious. Drunkenness was a prevailing vice. Even children were to be seen in the streets intoxicated . . . All that the vilest and most bestial of human creatures could invent and practice was in this unhappy country invented and practised without restraint and without shame.[3]

Outside Tasmania *His Natural Life* received positive reviews: with its 'frightful realism' it provided authentic information with the 'unmistakable stamp of reality', 'all the solemn ghastliness of truth'.[4] After its success in Melbourne, it was published in London and New York. But at least one Tasmanian was unhappy. S.H. Wintle, amateur geologist and prominent Hobart citizen, accused Clarke through a letter to the *Mercury* of painting Tasmania as 'a Pandemonium of horrors, crime and suffering', raking the vaults of the past for things far better forgotten. Clarke's novel was offensive to Tasmanians, 'and even inimical to the interests of the colony'. And Clarke was unreliable—Wintle had had a geological controversy with him. Clarke replied the book was 'founded on *fact*'. His aim was not to attack Tasmania, but to expose 'the infamies and horrors of a gigantic and cruel legislative blunder'.

Wintle retorted that the book might be based on evidence, but Clarke should not have used this evidence. 'The most absurd notions exist in England respecting the moral tone of society in this colony, and which Mr Clarke's book is well calculated to increase and intensify . . . let the "Dead past, bury its dead".'[5] Wintle claimed that all Tasmanian readers of *His Natural Life* agreed with him, but none wrote to the *Mercury* in his support. Had they not read the serial, did they think it best ignored, too degrading to write about? Did they actually enjoy it? Their absence of support is more significant than Wintle's letters, which only represented the views of one man, who already disliked Clarke.

Wintle was correct in one particular: the picture of the convict system painted in *His Natural Life* does not seem to have been accepted in Tasmania, where writings about the convict system generally had a more gentle view, and more sympathy towards convicts. In 1874 the convict system had only ended twenty years earlier, and almost all people over 30 could remember it. They knew, and could tell younger people, that only a tiny minority suffered as Rufus Dawes had done, that most convicts had a less brutal experience.

How much does a novel influence people? Did middle-class English people reading Dickens believe that conditions were so appalling for the poor? Did Americans reading *Uncle Tom's Cabin* believe the same about their slaves? Some did, and these novels were influential in changing public opinion, but other readers, those who did not want to change their opinions, saw these novels as fantasy, propaganda or merely stories which had nothing to do with reality. Tasmanian readers of *His Natural Life* were not convinced, but many outsiders were, and Tasmanians became even more defensive about the past, if possible.

Whether viewed as fact or fiction, *His Natural Life* was extremely successful, then and since. In 1914 a poll found it to be the most popular Australian novel, but it was also widely read as soon as it was published, not just on the Australian mainland but in Tasmania itself. In 1886 the *Mercury* said there was no need to summarise the plot, since everyone knew it, and there was much speculation about the basis for its characters. Many people thought Rufus Dawes was based on Captain Melville, a well-known absconder, and when James Choppee, known as 'Cheesy', died in 1894, the press noted that a character in *His Natural Life* was supposed to have been based on him.[6]

Port Arthur, where the most dramatic action occurred, came to be the main site associated with *His Natural Life*. Established in 1830 as a place of secondary punishment for convicts who committed serious offences in Van Diemen's Land, from the start it was both criticised as harsh and praised as well run. After transportation ended in 1853, it housed convicts still serving out their sentences. Descriptions dried up in the early 1850s as interest waned, in keeping with the general Tasmanian attitude of ignoring the convict system. Interest revived from 1869, with Port Arthur described in not only Henry Thomas' guidebook but the *Mercury*, whose reporter was not the last to praise the site's beauty, but regret that such a pretty spot should have had 'such a sad use'. In 1872 Anthony Trollope felt that over the past 60 years no spot on the globe—the entire globe—had seen more suffering than Port Arthur. The prisoners were about to be moved to Hobart, and after that, prophesied Trollope, the buildings would fall into dust, as little notice would be taken of the place.[7]

Trollope was wrong. By the time Port Arthur closed in September 1877, *His Natural Life* had been published. The authorities renamed the place Carnarvon, to remove its convict associations, but this was a failure. That December, a boat brought tourists to the site. They have been visiting ever since.

Many tourists were inspired to come to Tasmania by reading *His Natural Life*, and the first book by such a visitor appeared in 1880: William Senior's *Travel and Trout in the Antipodes*. Senior found Port Arthur so awe-inspiring that it 'oppresses you into silence', with its walls 'raised with the blood of convicts'. He believed that 'the execrable doings described with such painfully vivid power by Marcus Clarke . . . are founded on facts . . . Such dreadful scenes, one wonders that the very stones do not cry out.' The whole of his visit to Tasmania was coloured by *His Natural Life*; he asked questions about it constantly and decided that much in Tasmania was gloomy and depressed.[8] It seems a strange focus for a book entitled *Travel and Trout*.

Senior's approach was typical of writers influenced by *His Natural Life*. They visited convict sites: 'of course the principal interest in Tasmania centres in its old convict history'; 'I wanted to see convict places, ancient prisoners, convict jailers, places where victims were driven mad'; 'One feels a thrill of horror as the entrance to Port Arthur is pointed out'. Guides, mostly former convicts, told them the ghastly tales of brutality they wanted to hear. 'There was proof of the most horrid stories, such as the marks of blood from the floggings on the ceiling of the chapel.' Having read *His Natural Life*, they saw all convict experience through its lens, and they knew it was all true: hadn't many Tasmanians (that is, tourist operators) assured them it was, and couldn't they see the blood on the chapel ceiling which proved it all? Even guidebooks published in Tasmania gave in, though clearly unwillingly. In 1890 Garnet Walch, Tasmanian born and bred, wrote a *Guide to Tasmania*. Everyone who had read *His Natural Life* wanted to see Port Arthur, he acknowledged. Its disagreeable associations were better relegated to the past: its old-time horrors, where once reigned darkness and despair—the clank of chains, curses of brutalised, lash-driven, hopeless men—'enough!'[9]

Soon, not only Port Arthur was being seen by tourists in this light, but also all Tasmania, 'a land of hell, the whole place seemed to reek of abominations and cruelties'; 'the curse still hangs over the country'. Convictism was 'darker, more loathsome, more hellish' than either 'Negro or Russian slavery'. 'Every hundred yards of the main road between Hobart and Launceston cost a man's life.' A visitor heard that while this road was being made, 21 prisoners had once been hanged together before breakfast. In short,

> the shadow of the nameless wickedness and agony of those times and its embalmment in that prince of novels, Marcus Clarke's 'The term of his natural life' hang like a pall over Hobart, over Tasmania, and indeed, I think, over its people and paralyse its progress.

These tourists equated Tasmania with convicts. One writer said just about everything in Tasmania was about convicts: 'Lovely land of pathetic, tragic, and historic memories!'[10] The convict stigma could not be eradicated. Clarke had set his novel in convict times, and had not said that Tasmania would never lose the curse. However, readers of *His Natural Life* decided that the convict system had been so unjust, so appalling, so cruel, that the whole island had become tainted forever. Tasmania could never leave its convict past behind.

Such publicity was a wonderful boost to the tourist industry. As one guidebook wrote, 'No one who has read Marcus Clarke's powerful romance, "His Natural Life"—and what Australian worthy of the name has not?— but would like to see for himself.' Tasmania had beautiful scenery, but so did other Australian tourist sites; only Tasmania had such interesting and well-preserved mementoes of the dreadful convict days. Tasmanians did not complain too loudly when the convict past was brought into the open to attract tourists. Perhaps the 1850s and 1860s had been so miserable economically that anything that offered development was acceptable. At least the convict story, as tourist operators presented it, stopped in 1853—well in the past, nothing to do with the present.[11]

It helped that both the major sites, Port Arthur and Macquarie Harbour, were remote, far from the centres of population. Tourists visited no other sites—not the many convict buildings in Hobart or on beautiful Maria Island, a former penal station on the eastern sea route from the mainland to Hobart. These places weren't in *His Natural Life*, so they weren't inspiring. The book's influence can be seen in the activities of a group of visitors on Sarah Island in Macquarie Harbour in the early 1890s. After exploring the ruins, at night they sat round a roaring fire and did what they believed every visitor to the island for the past twenty years had done: read passages aloud from *His Natural Life*, imagining 'the horrors of the past, when the place was peopled with desperate criminals and their brutal gaolers, and the swish of the lash was an all too frequent sound'.[12]

Locals were not such keen visitors as outsiders, and many Tasmanians were pleased when in 1895 and 1898 two fires swept through Port Arthur, but tourists were not deterred, for the buildings now looked more romantic. Hotels and steamer services developed, and despite the odd debate about pulling down the buildings they remained, and in 1914 were repaired.[13] By then convict tourism was well established.

Information for these tourists was strictly rationed. Guidebooks were coy about convict history. Most did not mention it except in their sections on the Tasman Peninsula—and some did not say much even then, explaining how to get to Port Arthur but not what to do there. They preferred to discuss topics that did not have to include the words 'convict' or 'penal', such as the line of fierce dogs that had guarded Eaglehawk Neck. Their purpose was to deter convicts from escaping across the narrow isthmus, but this was not always explained to tourists. A few guidebooks mentioned convicts elsewhere, where they had built roads or eaten each other,[14] but this was rare.

There was another convict attraction: the prison hulk *Success*. It briefly housed convict exiles in Melbourne in the 1850s, and was on show there from 1891, complete with convict clothes, leg irons, wax figures of the Kelly gang and a detailed history. The *Success* came to Hobart in 1894, with no objections made by Hobartians.[15] Of course not: it had nothing to do with Van Diemen's Land, but showed that other colonies had convicts—and Victoria too, after Victorians had been so quick to point out Tasmania's criminal antecedents. No wonder thousands of Tasmanians flocked to it.

Meanwhile, no one could flock to anything that showed the experiences of the bulk of convicts, under the assignment and probation systems. They had lived in the community, wearing ordinary clothes, and there was little if anything connected with them for tourists to look at. They had no dramatic novels written about them, either. The tourist version of the convict experience concentrated on the 10 per cent who suffered the horrors of the penal settlements, who had more dramatic stories, and who left relics behind for tourists to see.

Marcus Clarke was not the only one to write about convicts. Others did— but they were ex-convicts, telling their stories presumably for profit, since they did not claim any other motive. None had anything like Clarke's success in informing public opinion about the convict system.

The first, as we have seen, was Henry Savery, whose *Quintus Servinton* was published in Hobart in 1830. Its influence is doubtful; few copies sold, no one in the nineteenth century mentioned reading it, and in any case the hero's ghastly Van Diemen's Land experiences are only covered near the end of the book. In the 1840s and 1850s a number of convicts published books in Britain and North America about their experiences. They were mostly political prisoners, vindicating themselves as innocent despite frightful treatment and oppression by the British. Such accounts are seldom if ever mentioned as having been read in Tasmania, though they were more widely read overseas.

Another narrative appeared in 1864: John Mortlock's *Experiences of a Convict*. A 'gentleman' prisoner, Mortlock was transported to Van Diemen's Land via Norfolk Island for attacking his uncle who he believed was cheating him out of his inheritance. Mortlock returned illegally to England, but was recognised and transported again to Western Australia. Once finally free he went back again to England, and in 1864–65 published his memoirs. Fewer than a thousand copies were printed, but at least one made its way to Hobart, and an article in the *Tasmanian Morning Herald* was positive:

We presume that there are few citizens of Hobart Town to whom the writer of this book . . . is unknown. And in fact, throughout the colony, from Cape Pillar to Circular Head his familiar round and smiling face . . . was always welcomed, and his company eagerly sought. Poor fellow, he was very eccentric, but in the highest degree honourable, and always cheerful. Every one knew that he had been a convict, but none respected him the less on that account . . . —he was a real genuine good fellow,—so simple and temperate in his habits and tastes;—so respectable in his demeanour;—so interesting in his conversation; that wherever he went he was always a welcome guest—from some of the highest in Tasmanian society—to those amongst whom his fortunes frequently cast him of the lowest.

Mortlock was liked by all, his experiences as a convict were mild, and he gave a pleasant, even jolly, view of the system, and of Van Diemen's Land and its people. Another reason for the *Herald's* positive review was that its editor was about to publish Mortlock's memoir in instalments. All was well at first, but when he was about to land in Van Diemen's Land, the instalments ceased abruptly.[16] Had the hard word been put on the editor? As far as is known, no one else took any notice of Mortlock's memoir, which was almost unknown until it was republished in 1965. It is unique among convict autobiographies in its positive description of the system.

Those convicts who published their stories in Australia had more influence locally, but they were few. Not many convicts wanted to write their experiences, were literate enough, or could afford a ghostwriter. However, some did appear. At some stage William Derrincourt's autobiography was published in the Sydney *Evening News*, and 'many years' later, in 1889, as a book in New York. Born in 1819, Derrincourt claimed he was transported for innocently selling goods which turned out to have been stolen. In Van Diemen's Land he was flogged, sent to Port Arthur, 'crushed down, worked like a beast of burden, and oppressed more than human nature could endure'. After he received his ticket of leave, his masters ranged from brutal to kindly.

Two convict autobiographies did become reasonably well known. In 1870 J. Walch & Sons of Hobart published *Martin Cash, the Bushranger of Van Diemen's Land*. The introduction stated that the book was written at the request of 'a number of old and influential colonists'. Cash said he aimed to present a faithful picture of former times, and show the evils that arose from the 'undue severity of prison discipline', which turned convicts, that 'unfortunate class', into brutes. Born in 1810 in Ireland, a wild youth, Cash related how he shot a man he saw dallying with his girlfriend and was transported for seven years, arriving in Sydney in 1828. (His convict record says he was transported for housebreaking.) Cash was always in trouble, of course through no fault of his own—the cattle he helped brand turned out to be stolen, and so on. He gained his freedom but, in trouble again, escaped to Van Diemen's Land in 1837. There he took on casual jobs but kept getting into strife, and was sentenced to seven years' transportation for theft. He ran away and was caught several times, but ended up in Port Arthur, the worst place of all, especially because of its villainous sub-overseers, convicts themselves, who treated the men brutally.

Cash escaped, but surrendered after five days with no food. The escapade turned him into a hero among the other convicts. He escaped again with two companions, Jones and Kavanagh, and they lived as bushrangers for eighteen months in the Brighton area north of Hobart, robbing houses of food, clothes and ammunition, carousing with friends, retreating to a fortress on top of Mount Dromedary near Brighton when the chase got too hot, then going out to rob again. But, said Cash, they never offered unnecessary violence, and never harmed a woman; they never drank much, or stole unnecessarily; there was no swearing, though sometimes characters said 'D–n' or 'the d–l'; and they were fair, for example not robbing a magistrate who acted leniently to them. They were brave and daring, with clever escapes and witty ripostes. Most other people, officials, settlers and convicts, were flawed in some way—rough, cowardly, dishonest, stealing from each other, informing the authorities. Cash portrayed some good people among both convicts and officials, but he himself was the main hero, intelligent and humorous. Normal people, for Cash, were convicts; it was the officials and wealthy settlers who were the outsiders. And so it must have been for convicts, the majority of the population.

Finally the three bushrangers were captured. Jones was hanged, having used violence when Cash was not there to restrain him, but Kavanagh and Cash were sent to Norfolk Island. An exemplary convict, Cash was eventually freed and returned to Tasmania, where he ended his days on his farm at Glenorchy on Hobart's northern outskirts, 'enjoying the goodwill of all'. His book is a sanitised view of the convict system—little drinking, convicts' worst swearing being 'Damn'?—but it is plausibly written, and gives a remarkably cheerful version of a convict's life.

Martin Cash, the Bushranger of Van Diemen's Land was compiled with the help of a ghostwriter, James Lester Burke, himself an ex-convict. A modern scholar, Buck Emberg, thinks the book is largely in Cash's words, with Burke's few generalising interpolations easy to recognise. The 1870 edition did not sell well, just as *The Broad Arrow* had not sold well. But *For the Term of His Natural Life* created interest in books about convicts, and Walch's put out a second edition in 1880, cut by 30,000 words. This sold much better, as did two later editions.

Perhaps cashing in on this success, in 1893 the Launceston *Examiner* published *A Burglar's Life, or The Stirring Adventures of the Great English Burglar, Mark Jeffrey: A thrilling history of the dark days of convictism in Australia*. Also ghostwritten by Burke, it sold well, going into a fifth edition. Jeffrey portrayed himself as wilful and self-confident, well meaning but unable to control his temper. Like Cash and Savery, he was always in trouble. In England he was an itinerant worker then a burglar, which paid much better, but in 1850 he was sentenced to fifteen years' transportation. He served two miserable years on Norfolk Island, and arrived in Port Arthur in 1852. There, discipline was less severe and in 1855 he gained his pass so he could find work in the community. But he could not stay out of trouble, and was in and out of Port Arthur. In 1872 he killed a man in a drunken fight and received a life sentence. Jeffrey became something of a legend and various people, even the governor, tried to help him, but could make no progress due to his violent temper. Jeffrey was finally released in 1890. He lived in the Launceston Invalid Depot and earned a little money peddling goods.

Looking back, he felt humiliated. 'Instinctively, I am not a criminal; and, moreover, I firmly express my consciousness of having done no intentional wrong to anybody during my forced confinement. I have always striven to act fair and square to those who treated me as a *man*, and the majority of evil deeds recorded in this book should be charged against those who acted towards me as if . . . I was some untamed wild beast.' So he had always been right; it was the others who had been wrong.

Of the convict narratives, Cash and Jeffrey had the most impact on Tasmanian public opinion. Both presented the convict system as oppressive and unfair, with the convict the hero. Yet the picture was not black and white; there were rascally convicts and good administrators, and both books humanised the system. Instead of Clarke's absolute hell on earth, with characters so monstrous as to be scarcely recognisable as human beings, they had reasonably ordinary characters. The penal stations were hideous, but much of the narrative took place outside them, in a more or less ordinary society. And in both accounts the convict was the norm, and the convict hero is reasonable and likeable, his woes due to bad luck. These books challenged much of Clarke's picture of the convict system, but were not nearly as influential in shaping public opinion.

Why was *His Natural Life* so much more successful? It is more dramatic, it has a love interest, and there are all those gruesome and/or titillating descriptions of brutality, flogging, cannibalism, homosexual rape and the rest of it. Nineteenth-century readers did not mind wordy novels—they were used to them. Many enjoyed sensationalism and exaggeration, rather than the ordinary life of Cash and Jeffrey. Their books were published only in Tasmania, which limited sales—and perhaps even there they were too close to home, too realistic. *His Natural Life* appealed more to public taste, and provided its audience, especially outside Tasmania, with what they wanted to read about convicts.

The major effect of *His Natural Life* and the other convict narratives, as far as this book is concerned, was that they brought convict past out into the open. Because of *His Natural Life* in particular, tourists came to Tasmania and spent money, so the convict past they wanted to see had to be allowed to exist. And people read these books, so knew about the system and learnt to sympathise with convict heroes. These books, as well as family stories told among some convict descendants, encouraged a more positive opinion of convicts than the official version. They bolstered the undercurrent of interest in convicts which kept going even in the repressive atmosphere of the 1850s and 1860s.

But there were negative aspects, particularly in *His Natural Life*. Its convicts were criminals, forever tainted by their convict status, however undeserved, so they could never live normally within the community. It committed the crime of telling outsiders about Tasmania's convict past, just the sort of publicity which invigorated the stigma and fuelled Tasmanians' desire to play down the convict system, to pretend that modern Tasmanians had nothing to do with it.

The young John Bowen. No portrait was painted of Martha.
Tasmanian Museum and Art Gallery

The small town of Hobart in the 1830s, surrounded by bush with convict transports in the bay. By Louis Auguste de Sainson. Allport Library and Museum of Fine Arts, TAHO

A small cottage, animals in the street: life was tough for everyone in early Van Diemen's Land, convict or free. There is no way of telling the status of the man in the jacket. Painted in 1806. National Library of Australia

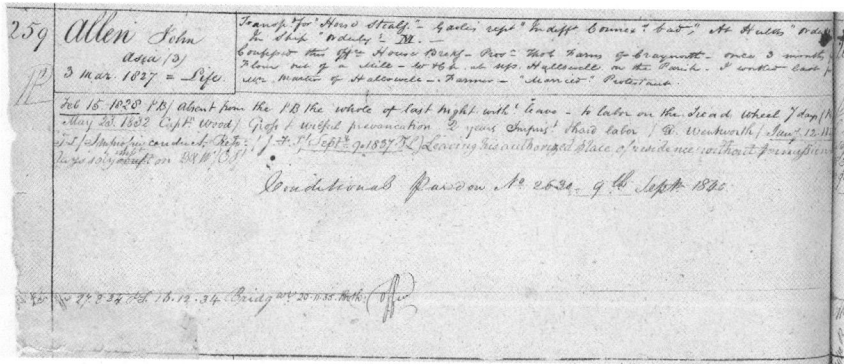

John Allen's convict record shows that on 3 March 1827 he was sentenced to transportation for life for horse stealing. He behaved indifferently in gaol and was noted as having bad 'connexions' (family and friends), but was 'orderly' in both the hulks and on the voyage to Van Diemen's Land on the *Asia*. On arriving in Hobart he told the authorities that he had been transported for housebreaking. He had been in prison once before for stealing flour out of a mill, and left a wife and six children at Upper Hallswell 'on the parish'—supported by local poor relief. 'I worked last for Mr Martin of Hallswell –. Farmer', he added. He was a Protestant.

In Van Diemen's Land being absent from the prisoners' barracks for a night earned John seven days on the treadwheel, and 'Gross & wilful prevarication' to his employer, Captain Wood, led to two years' imprisonment with hard labour. After gaining his ticket of leave, he was reprimanded for 'Improper conduct' and served some days in solitary confinement on bread and water for 'leaving his authorized place of residence without permission'. He received his conditional pardon in 1840, but did not bother to gain a free certificate. With four offences in thirteen years, John was a fairly typical convict. CON 31/1/1 no 259, Archives Office of Tasmania, TAHO

A French visitor's painting of a group of convicts, guarded by a soldier: mournful but civilised, rather than the uncouth rogues seen by the British. Painted in the 1830s. Allport Library and Museum of Fine Arts, TAHO

'A young artist after labour with the pencil invigorating his fundamentals and enjoying the wit of the Convict Servants in their hut': a rare depiction of convicts as ordinary people, laughing and enjoying life, by artist John Glover, about 1835. National Library of Australia

Convicts found guilty of further crime had a more sobering experience. Soldiers guard a chain gang in Hobart; the convicts wear chains round their wrists and ankles, and carry spades and picks for their work. Archives Office of Tasmania, TAHO

An even worse experience was being flogged, seen in this graphic sketch from the 1850s by James Scott. National Library of Australia

Convicts working the tramway at Port Arthur, using their muscle power to propel visitors through the bush. They were used instead of animals as beasts of burden. Painted by Colonel Godfrey Mundy in 1852. Archives Office of Tasmania, TAHO

The worst-behaved convicts were sent to the dreaded Port Arthur, with its hard manual labour and harsh discipline. Archives Office of Tasmania, TAHO

John Funt, still a convict in the 1870s, at Port Arthur. Archives Office of Tasmania, TAHO

Ex-convict Bill Thompson, now a free man, dressed in his Port Arthur convict outfit in the 1870s. He does not seem to be enjoying reliving the past. Allport Library and Museum of Fine Arts, TAHO

An unidentified convict at Port Arthur in the 1870s—the stereotype of the 'criminal look'. Archives Office of Tasmania, TAHO

Poor, old but not defeated, still able to hold their heads high (apart from the one in the centre): elderly inmates of the Launceston Invalid Depot, almost certainly ex-convicts. Allport Library and Museum of Fine Arts, TAHO

Thomas Jefferies and John Perry, on trial for robbery. In these sketches from around 1826, ex-convict artist Thomas Bock does not depict them as desperate rogues, but as mild, even ordinary, men. Allport Library and Museum of Fine Arts, TAHO

Two images of convict bushranger Martin Cash: a sketch while he was being tried—the artist seeing him as romantic, an antipodean Lord Byron—and a photograph when he was a far-from-romantic single elderly farmer with tie askew, button missing and untidy hair. The eyes are the same. Archives Office of Tasmania, TAHO

Francis Abbott, watchmaker, was transported in 1844 for obtaining two watches under false pretences. After gaining his ticket of leave in 1849, he set up a watchmaking business in Hobart and also became a leading astronomer. His family joined him, and in 1858 they were photographed: son Alfred, wife Mary, Francis holding astronomer's equipment, daughter Maria and son Francis, a thoroughly respectable and prosperous middle-class family, less than a decade after Francis had gained the first stage of freedom. Tasmanian Museum and Art Gallery

Outwardly indistinguishable from the ex-convict Abbotts, Henry Hopkins's family prepares for an outing in their carriage in 1858. Henry holds a wriggling granddaughter, and the impressive coachman holds the reins. The man to the right could be either a son-in-law or ex-convict servant Screwby, while a woman, unmoved by the exciting new process of photography, reads a newspaper on the verandah. University of Sydney Archives

Even more prosperous: Charles Davis, in shining top hat, leaving his large business establishment to go home for dinner in 1907. His son and heir Charlie is about to join his father in the carriage, while a groom holds the horse's head. Allport Library and Museum of Fine Arts, TAHO

Turbulent but successful ex-convict John Davies, member of parliament and owner of the influential Hobart *Mercury.* Allport Library and Museum of Fine Arts, TAHO

Ex-convict William Cripps and his wife Eliza (who arrived free), photographed in 1881. Their flourishing bakery enabled them to afford good-quality clothing, with a fashionable dress for Eliza. The bakery still exists. Archives Office of Tasmania, TAHO

Through marriage, ex-convict Mary Smallshaw joined the upper classes, as wife of wealthy pastoralist and gentleman Andrew Barclay. Andrew, Mary, their daughter and pet dog provide a happy family scene. Sketched by John Glover (n.d.). Tasmanian Museum and Art Gallery

Ex-convict Eliza Wheeler in old age with her daughter, dressed in their wonderful best for the photographer. This photograph, taken in the late nineteenth century, was provided by Eliza's great-granddaughter Frances Burgess.

In 1847 Mary Wilson was transported for stealing a coat, and in Van Diemen's Land her long record of convictions for offences such as using indecent language, drunkenness and larceny continued until 1884, when she and her husband Charles Nye were admitted to the New Town Invalid Depot. Mary died there in 1891, aged 83, and was buried in a pauper's grave. Queen Victoria Museum and Art Gallery

The photograph is entitled 'Mrs Gifford', and she has done her best with a new cap and lace collar, but on the back someone has written 'Sarah Ann Hunt, convicted Central Criminal Court, London, Augt. 22, 1842. 14 years'. Allport Library and Museum of Fine Arts, TAHO

A traditional gravestone hides a murky past: Jane was transported for theft with violence, and later committed bigamy and possibly murder. When William appeared, she refused to live with him. Their family united them in death.
Catherine Alexander

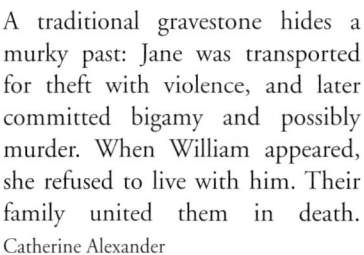

Descendants of convict and free mix in this private school in 1898, and it is impossible to tell the difference. James Pillinger, convict descendant, is third from left, second row from the top. W.L. Crowther Library, TAHO

Tasmanians were particularly loyal to Britain, perhaps in order to distance themselves from the disreputable past. In 1868 Hobart citizens welcomed Queen Victoria's son Alfred with an elaborate display of arches, flags and other decorations. Archives Office of Tasmania, TAHO

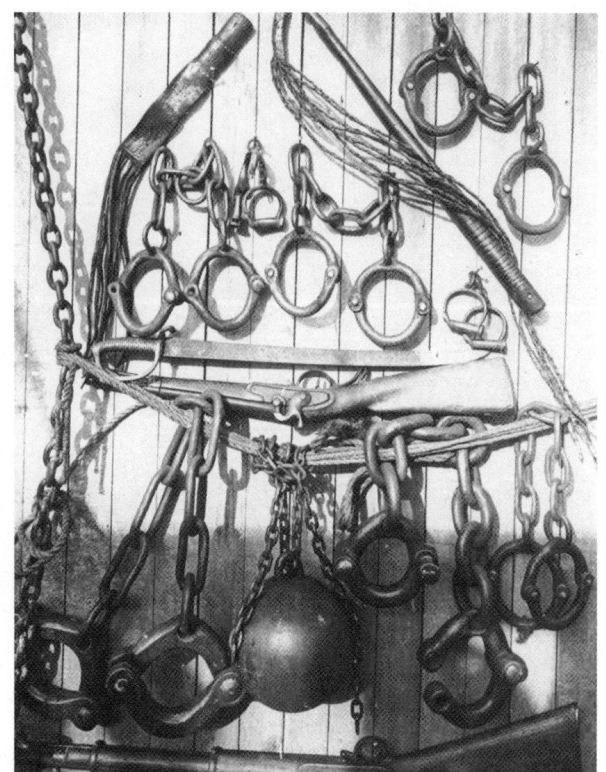

Convict tourism centred on the brutalities of Port Arthur, with leg irons, whips and balls and chain: Beattie's museum display, Hobart, 1890s. There was nothing to show for the many more convicts who were not punished by these harsh instruments. Tasmanian Museum and Art Gallery

Convict descendant Lewis McGee, VC, with his wife Eileen and baby daughter Nada, before his heroic death on the Western Front in the First World War. This photograph was provided by family member Patricia Rubenach.

John Earle, the first Labor premier of Tasmania (1909, 1914–16) and son of a convict. Archives Office of Tasmania

Convict descendant Clive Lord, curator of the Tasmanian Museum and Art Gallery and secretary of the Royal Society, photographing a kestrel in 1920. Tasmanian Museum and Art Gallery

Amy Rowntree, distinguished educator and granddaughter of a convict, as a young teacher at the piano with a class of children in 1916. Tasmanian Parliamentary Papers, 1916, TAHO

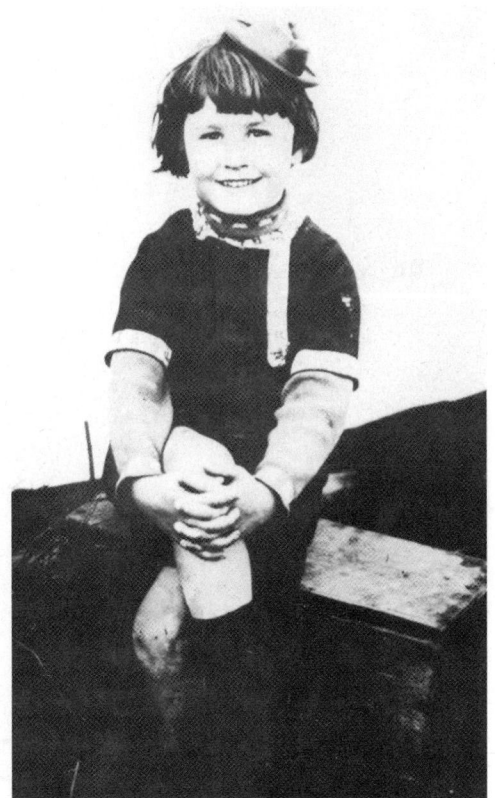

No trace of the 'convict look' in young convict descendant Errol Flynn in 1913, with his trademark grin even at the age of four in his birthplace, Hobart. World fame as a film star lies in the future. University of Tasmania Library

For the Term of His Natural Life depicted convicts as brutally treated. Lashed on by vicious overseers, they strain at the plough in the 1927 film version. Archives Office of Tasmania, TAHO

Pathetic boy convicts with the sympathetic heroine, before they commit suicide . . .
Archives Office of Tasmania, TAHO

Depicting convicts in 1953: filming an advertisement to lure to tourists to Tasmania. Dressed as a Port Arthur convict, the actor is yelling, 'For hell's sake, stop!' as a second actor applies the lash. Dick Wordley, *Tasmanian Adventure*, p. 78

Convict descendant and the first locally born governor of Tasmania, Sir Stanley Burbury (centre), opening the Narryna Folk Museum in 1957. W.L. Crowther Library, TAHO

The convict past lives on: re-enactment by members of the Female Factory Research Group, Cascades Female Factory, in 2006. *From left:* Leonie Mickleborough, Joyce Purtscher, Chris Woods, Dianne Snowden, Trudy Cowley and Jenny Croxton.

11

THE ONE FORBIDDEN SUBJECT

James Pillinger was part of a gang of teenage boys from the Bristol slums who stole a silver watch. Transported to New South Wales in 1792, he was moved to Norfolk Island, where after his release he owned a small farm. He married Elizabeth Wood, whose mother was transported for stealing two pairs of stockings. When in 1807–08 the government closed the Norfolk Island settlement and moved the population to Van Diemen's Land, the emigrants included the Pillinger family. They were given a 76-acre land grant at Clarence Plains, and by 1819 they and their seven children kept 50 sheep and grew wheat, beans and potatoes. James and Elizabeth have hundreds if not thousands of descendants in Australia today.

Their son James junior, born in the colony and so 'always free', gained a larger land grant at Woodbury. His grave can be seen beside the highway, inside a white picket fence—on the spot where he dismounted from his horse and first stood on his own land. Known for his great strength, he worked hard and built up a sizeable property. In 1836 he married Sophia Peters, whose father had been transported for stealing ten silver cups. By 1880 the Pillingers owned 11,217 sheep, the eighteenth largest flock on the island. They were most respectable, pillars of the local church: Sophia used to go round the local township of Tunbridge with bags of sweets to lure children to Sunday School. Their sons attended the exclusive (or at any rate expensive) Horton College at Ross.

James and Sophia's son Alfred, born in 1839, joined the family grazing enterprise and became warden of the Oatlands municipality. In 1886 he married Georgina Nichols, from a prominent 'always free' farming family at Castra in the north-west. By then Alfred was the local member of parliament. Though no orator, he was respected for his shrewd judgement, sincerity and good temper, and as Minister for Lands and Works he was generous in creating jobs for the unemployed and supporting those in distress, especially the aged. Perhaps this showed pro-convict sympathies?

In 1889 Pillinger's department advertised that the convict buildings at Port Arthur would be sold for demolition. A deputation urged that the buildings be kept, to encourage tourists and retain history, but Pillinger told them that most people wanted the buildings removed. Personally,

> He considered [the buildings] monuments of disgrace to the British Government. If there was anything good about them then there might be some reason for preserving them, but when he thought of the cruelty and misery that had been practised and experienced there, he had not the slightest sympathy for those who wished them to remain.[1]

For the Term of His Natural Life might have brought the convict past into the open; exploiting the convict past might bring tourist money; but for Tasmanians like Alfred Pillinger, typical of the majority in that he had convict ancestors, the past was best forgotten. Note that Alfred avoided sensitive words, and the buildings disgraced the British government, not Tasmania.

Despite *His Natural Life*, like Alfred Pillinger the great mass of Tasmanians continued to publicly ignore or deny the convict past, with great success. They continued the subterfuges of the 1850s and 1860s. Convicts were never mentioned, as far as was humanly possible. In 1899 the magnificent two-volume *Cyclopedia of Tasmania* was published as 'An Epitome of Progress', describing positively everything that had happened in Tasmania. It contained articles about each town, each industry and many colonists, written by the people concerned. Naturally they did not mention anything discreditable, and the only biography of an ex-convict, Charles Davis, merely claimed that he started his business in 1847. Carnarvon (formerly Port Arthur), with its church, post office, hotel, law courts and pretty scenery, was 'yearly becoming a greater resort for tourists', but the uninformed reader might wonder what they expected to do there, for the description includes nothing especially worth seeing, and certainly no mention of convicts. The *Cyclopedia* concentrated on the prosperous present and marvellous future. Federation of the Australian colonies was likely, and

> although by far the smallest, yet, with her unbounded wealth in minerals, her large agricultural and pastoral industries, and last, but not least, her unequalled climate and unrivalled scenery, it may be fairly predicted that the brightest star in the future great Southern Commonwealth will be TASMANIA.[2]

The historical section in the *Cyclopedia* used an ingenious invention also seen in tourist guides. Potted histories of Tasmania described early explorers, a safe topic, then Bowen arriving with some prisoners. That was fine, since Bowen played no further role in Tasmania's history. Prisoners were often not mentioned again. Collins arrived—possibly a brief mention of prisoners—and then it was all achievements, sealing, wool, railways and mining. The end of transportation sometimes featured, but not what it implied, and there was nothing to link it with the earlier mentions. It was not clear that Van Diemen's Land was a convict colony at all.[3]

Tucked away at the end of the *Cyclopedia* was a section called 'Curious Facts of Old Colonial Days', by historian James Bonwick. It described churches, governors and so on—and then came the sub-heading 'State of morals in the early days'. These were dreadful, with theft, depravity, adultery and 'the brutal sensuality of men of crime'. Bonwick wrote openly about convicts, in the next sections as well: 'Strong Drink in Van Diemen's Land' (plentiful) and 'Female Prisoners in Van Diemen's Land' (immoral and disorderly). How did this get past the unofficial censors? Perhaps they did not realise the article was there: it was hidden away and would have taken some time to find, especially since there was no index. It was an anomaly, and most other histories ran along the lines of the rest of the *Cyclopedia*. One concluded: 'What a remarkable history, and one of which people of the State may justly be proud!'[4]

School history lessons took much the same line. At first only British history was taught: in Marjorie Butler's school exams in 1892, History was a list of English kings, and Tasmania appeared only in General Knowledge: 'By whom was Tasmania discovered?' and 'Why was Hobart so called?', safe non-convict questions. Then public examinations were established, junior (age fifteen) and senior (matriculation). Tasmanian history was introduced for juniors in 1908. The textbook, Samuel Lovell's *The Centenary of Tasmania*, did not use the word 'convict', and only mentioned prisoners the usual three times: Bowen and Collins both arrived with prisoners, and transportation, 'that is, sending prisoners to Van Diemen's Land', was stopped. The people then 'put away the old, ugly name of Van Diemen's Land, and took the sweeter one of TASMANIA'. Now, wrote Lovell, a wilderness had become 'the dear home of a civilised people'. (Lovell would never have admitted that he himself, esteemed Inspector of Schools, had a convict ancestor.) Senior pupils studied Australian history, and their textbook admitted that New South Wales and Tasmania were convict settlements, saying that many convicts were 'the most depraved and hardened villains to be met with in the history of crime', though others became 'decent, orderly farmers'. But Hobart's Head Teachers asked that the History syllabus include less Australian history and more European, to remove 'insular prejudice and the notion of the isolation of English history from World History'. Was this code for 'not teaching Australian history which includes convicts'? Tasmanian history was dropped, and Australian history moved to the junior exam, with an innocuous textbook.[5]

In 1918 the new textbook was Ernest Scott's *Short History of Australia*, which described the convict system, with convicts seen as both inefficient workers, a jumble of thieves, cut-throats and swindlers; and as useful and dependable citizens. It is doubtful if much of this reached students. Nearly all questions in examination papers for the 1920s were about English history, and the few Australian questions were about safe topics like Federation, or general knowledge, for example: 'Who are:– David Lloyd George, De Valera, Lenin, Sir Walter Lee, E.A. McDonald, Gandhi, President Harding, Marconi?' (Strange to see Lee, the conservative Tasmanian premier, beside communist Lenin.)[6]

Convicts were virtually ignored in the celebrations of Tasmania's centenary in 1904, the *Mercury*'s historical article describing how early settlers transformed the foul into the fair, and despite crime and 'unutterable immorality' established a peaceful and honourable society. The uninformed reader, mystified by so many works at this time, might have wondered where the foul, the crime and immorality came from, for they were not explained. Tourist guidebooks kept convict information to a minimum. For example, *The Tasmanian Motorists' Comprehensive Road Guide* of 1916 called Carnarvon (Port Arthur) 'a little Eden' but did not mention convicts. Only an advertisement let the cat out of the bag: the Hotel Arthur welcomed visitors to 'Australia's only bone fide Convict Ruins'.[7]

Some towns which had housed convicts at probation or penal stations were renamed. Jerusalem became Colebrook, and as the Tasman Peninsula was opened up to settlement, former penal stations were given Aboriginal names. The Cascades became Koonya; Impression Bay, Premaydena; Wedge Bay, Nubeena; and Norfolk Bay, Taranna. Aborigines were thought to have vanished and were seen as picturesque, no threat to Tasmanians' self-image, but convicts were disgraceful. Euphemisms continued. The Bridgewater causeway over the Derwent River was built when 'the Government had a large amount of labour at command available for such purposes'. The Main Road north from Hobart was 'made in the good old days by the gentlemen who had the doubtful pleasure of being the guests of the Government'. The Ship Hotel in Hobart was a 'favourite resort in its time of a race of old Colonists who are fast dying out'.[8]

If convicts had to be mentioned, a new twist was to describe convict days as in the long distant past rather than a mere thirty or so years earlier: 'days happily long passed away', 'ancient history', 'the far bygone days when this beautiful island was used as a penal settlement', 'a state of society that has now passed away almost as completely as the Dark Ages'—and the Dark Ages had been a thousand years earlier.[9]

The convention continued of only acknowledging as ex-convicts that marginal group who did not mind being outed, who had nothing to lose. By the 1870s many ex-convicts were elderly and ill, and many who had no family to care for them were herded into bleak government institutions, homes for the aged, government hospitals and the lunatic asylum. The peak year was 1879, when they housed 897 people, almost all ex-convicts, as was well known. They were separated from the rest of the community, they were no threat, and they were dying out with no descendants. They could be acknowledged as ex-convicts: 'When the last of these decrepit old men dies, the last vestige of the old penal settlement will disappear', was the hopeful prophecy.[10]

Also acknowledged as ex-convicts were the 'old lags' who remained in the community as tramps or casual labourers. In the 1880s John Skemp's father was among the settlers clearing small farms at Myrtle Bank, as Skemp described in his memoirs, published in 1952. The farmers were mostly illiterate, narrow-minded, rough and ready, but 'self-reliant and indomitable', making a living by growing what they could and splitting palings. They were the elite, said Skemp, for there was a lower social class—old lags. 'Some had made good, but others had been demoralized by the treatment and among them were habitual criminals and criminal lunatics. They were often drunken and degraded, frequently thieves, and generally regarded with disfavour by their fellow-settlers.'

Old lags were often known only by nicknames. Bandy Jimmy gained this name from his gait, to distinguish him from Primrose Jimmy and Jimmy the Rat. Bandy Jimmy lived in a hut on a small block of land, and apart from getting drunk occasionally, was fairly trustworthy. He made a living by doing a bit of paling-splitting and shepherding.

Nell Stewart was 'an old she-devil, hard as nails and completely amoral'. When she and her husband earned a bit of money from splitting palings, they invited other old lags for a spree. 'This was a regular carousal, and since their language was as foul as their manners, it was no more edifying to hear than to see.' They would be sprawled around a keg of beer, riotously and raucously drunk. Nell once staggered to the pub for more beer, but abused the publican, who threw her out. She fell in the gutter and went to sleep, despite rain and later frost. In the morning she roused up, shook herself, and walked off down the road, apparently none the worse. These old lags had no children, and existed on the fringe of the community, apart from everyone else—Skemp did not mention them going to church, playing sport or socialising with the rest of the district.[11]

It is hard to see much difference between the old lags like Bandy Jimmy and the 'elite', who were also illiterate, drunk and uncouth, and probably in many cases ex-convicts themselves, or convicts' children. But they did not want it known, they were trying to live it down, were part of mainstream society, and so no one said anything about their forebears. The old lags were different; they were not trying to live respectably and did not care. It was acceptable to admit they were ex-convicts, and they were harmless, even amusing. Admitting their presence shielded more respectable ex-convicts. Skemp's 'some had made good' was never expanded, names were never listed.

People viewed these visible old lags in various ways. Growing up in the Brighton district, ten-year-old John Halloran was thrilled when an old lag said to him, 'I'll pull my shirt up and show you how some of us were flogged at Port Arthur.' John saw the scars, so bad, he told his sons, that the convict carried them to his grave. Other people saw ex-convicts as workmen. Many labourers were 'old hands', wrote farmer Charles Furlong in the 1870s. They worked for a spell, then went to town to 'knock it off'—drink until their money was spent—and returned home with only the shirt and pants they started out in. Edward Braddon, who migrated to the north-west coast in 1878, mentioned convicts only once in his many letters home. 'These relics of a by-gone epoch . . . must remain under suspicion to the end of their days—an end that for most of them cannot be far off.' He thought some injustice had been done to convicts; the best worker he had was 'one of this pariah sect'. In 1878 John Whitehead, a farmer, wrote to a friend about employing labour for the harvest: 'the old hands have mostly disappeared, you seldom see one now'.[12] By the 1890s there were hardly any left.

Some people wanted a more active role taken in denying the past, such as closing notorious Port Arthur, still used as a prison. 'The very name, in fact, was enough. It was a name reeking with associations anything but pleasant.' They succeeded in 1877, and some like Alfred Pillinger wished to destroy the buildings, but these were important for the tourist industry and were never demolished. There were still possible problems. Leslie Maddock, born in 1908, was visiting Port Arthur with his family in about 1918 when he stopped to look at a convict record book on display. 'Here's someone called Maddock,' he said, and was quickly dragged away by an elder sister.

Convict records were sensitive, because of the names they contained. Many of those in New South Wales vanished. In Tasmania there was consternation in 1879 when it was reported that old police records had been put up for sale at a Hobart auction mart. Worse, in Melbourne, records of Port Arthur were published, with the names of 'people sent out' and particulars about them. This was 'a bitter, cruel thing to do', said the *Tasmanian Mail*. 'There are many people in the colonies whose lives have been blameless, and against whom nothing can be said except that their parents have been sent out. To revive the old, sad stories may do much harm, and can do no good.' When it was reported that a few records had been accidentally burned some Tasmanians rejoiced, and when Joseph Lyons, Minister for Education, not descended from convicts himself, found convict records in a store he recommended that they be burnt, because Tasmanians should not remind themselves of their past.[13]

The Commissioner of Police asked for all convict records to be delivered to his office, whether for safe-keeping or privacy is not clear, and though 'Decency' wrote to the *Tasmanian News* demanding that the records be destroyed, since they contained the names of peoples' ancestors,[14] they were retained. They could only be read by those in the know, but few were interested.

The most likely critic of the denial of convicts was the left-wing newspaper the *Clipper*, which enjoyed implying that the landed gentry were all descended from convicts, and saw the villains of the past as not convicts but their gaolers and the upper classes generally. It implied that only the upper classes were ashamed of the convict stain—the only source to do this—but still, it never stated its own position, never explained why it poked fun, never named a convict descendant. That would have been going too far. And even the *Clipper* wanted to defeat the convict stigma:

> Tassy's had enough disgraces
> (Nations reap what nations sow),
> But we mean to shift all traces
> Of the Smudge of Long Ago.

When the *Clipper* did imply that someone had been a convict he was a member of the marginal group, and even the *Clipper* did not use the dreadful word. So it described the hundredth birthday of 'Chummy' Newton, sent out aged seventeen, in and out of trouble for years, finally becoming a shepherd and retiring at 97. He loved to reminisce about troubles on Norfolk Island, and capturing a cannibal escapee, said the *Clipper*.[15] But this is the only example found of such a story.

There was still the odd mention of tension between bond and free. Earlier the free population had despised convicts, wrote one visitor, and though these distinctions had gone, the feelings associated with them were not so easily eradicated. 'Even now the descendants of convicts are sometimes secretly looked down on, and a great many have, on that account, left the island.' Mr Reibey of Launceston—now prosperous, but descended from convicts, though this was not divulged—told a visitor that 'many families, now highly respected, cannot escape from this bar sinister on their escutcheon'.[16] These two pieces of information, however, are not conclusive. Just because Reibey saw convict descent as a 'bar sinister' did not mean that everyone did (he might have been ultra-sensitive); and even if some non-convicts despised convicts' descendants, they did it 'secretly'. On the surface at least, Tasmania was a contented British colony like any other.

In the twentieth century new methods of attacking the stigma appeared. Several New South Wales writers—though not Tasmanian, the figures would have been too difficult to manipulate—claimed that there were few descendants of convicts left. In 1913 historian Frederick Watson calculated that with the high percentage of male convicts, the many women who were prostitutes and therefore infertile, and the many free settlers then and since, it was no more possible to see traces of convicts in Australians than to see traces of Anglo-Saxons in the English. Two decades later, P.R. Stephenson calculated that in 1855 Australia's population was 800,000. Of the 150,000 convicts, many had returned to England and few had children, since there were so few female convicts. Convicts were only one in twenty in 1855, and with the tremendous influx of free immigrants this figure was zero by 1900. Very few Australians were descended from 'the dolorous English convicts, poor miserable creatures', and there was no need to whitewash the convict past. Few went quite so far, and a journalist who wrote historical articles for the Sydney *Truth* advised a colleague to call convicts 'early settlers' or 'pioneers'.[17]

Another method of denying the past that did spread to Tasmania began in New South Wales in the late nineteenth century as an alternative foundation story: Australia had been formed not by convicts, but by sturdy pioneers. These could include convicts, as the *Truth* journalist related, but everyone assumed at least outwardly that pioneers were all upright free settlers. They bravely battled the bush, fire, drought and all sorts of other hardships to found our glorious nation. Western Australia and South Australia really had been founded by free settlers, Victoria could pretend it was (ignoring the fact that many of its early colonists were convicts from Van Diemen's Land), so could Queensland, and New South Wales and Tasmania joined in the chorus. Pioneers were a much more acceptable basis for the new nation than convicts. They were extolled in stories, poems, journals like the *Bulletin*, and early Australian films, such as *The Squatter's Daughter* and *The Bushman's Bride*.

Pioneer worship came to Tasmania in the early twentieth century. John West had foreshadowed it in his 1852 history, but after him no one said much about who established Tasmania, for fear of the answer. However, in its centenary edition in 1904, the *Tasmanian Mail* listed those historical items 'we would gladly forget'—petty quarrels, immoral governors, the brutal convict system and the treatment of the Aborigines—and moved happily to more positive history. Pioneers subdued nature, demanded that transportation cease, and made substantial progress. By the 1920s pioneers were presented as the state's real founders. Roy Bridges and G.B. Lancaster, both descended from non-convict pioneer families, wrote historical novels with these families as the heroes, though convicts appeared and were seen sympathetically. Leslie Norman wrote a history of Tasmania for tourists and stated, straight out, that 'the author seeks to gloss over three things generally associated with Tasmania's early history: the days when a few English subjects were sent here for their country's good; the bushranging days; and certain racial troubles such as generally occur where the white races have supplanted the natives' (now, ironically, major topics for Tasmanian historians). Note the 'few' convicts—though of course Norman did not use the word. His story was almost entirely about the progress made by free settlers.[18]

The ultimate in pioneer worship was the Pioneer Memorial Highway, a plan to line the Hobart–Launceston road, all 123 miles (200 kilometres) of it, with trees in honour of the pioneers. More than 6000 were planted. Pioneer-worshippers sometimes commented that Tasmania owed more to pioneers than to convicts. 'A frequent theme of oratory on special occasions is the debt which the people of the present generation in Tasmania owe to the pioneers,' opined the *Mercury* in 1936; but unfortunately 'the attention of the community, and of the world, is directed almost entirely towards the remains of the convict system, which has the smallest possible connection with the history of the real development of the State.' George Porter, an Englishman who published a travel book about Tasmania in 1934, agreed: 'Serious historians do not attach much weight to the early convict era of the island's history as an influence in the development of the modern State of Tasmania.' Which serious historians did he mean? None had actually claimed this. Porter was not one, since he went on to write a chapter about convicts. But, he said, modern Tasmanians gazed on convict ruins in the same spirit as the English gazed on their ancient dungeons and pillories, as reminders of the barbarism of a century ago. And Tasmanians were asserting themselves, said Porter, amused by a map of the world upside down, with Tasmania at the top and England at the bottom.[19]

As in earlier decades, Tasmanians remained keen to demonstrate their loyalty to the British Empire, to show that the uncouth convict past had no effect. At Queen Victoria's Golden Jubilee celebrations in 1887, Hobart's houses and public buildings were decorated with hundreds of Chinese lanterns and gas illuminations. An enormous procession marched to the Domain, where 25,000 people gathered to watch 4000 schoolchildren sing the national anthem and hear guns roar a salute. Hobart's population was only 27,000, so just about every Hobartian who was physically able, as well as many country folk, must have been among the 29,000 people on the Domain. There was similar support for the Empire on every imperial occasion: the South African War, the Coronation, and particularly for the visit by the Duke and Duchess of York in 1901. Tasmanians were consumed with enthusiasm and loyalty, as they had been for the royal visit of

1868—but just over thirty years later there were no convict faces in the crowds, no drunken heckling.[20]

As Tasmanian patriotism grew, the earlier desire to appear 'English' faded. Pride in Tasmania developed, building on the earlier patriotism. Several stories show people born in the mid-nineteenth century as proud of their country. In 1881 Henry and Sarah Hopkins's granddaughters Grace and Minnie Clarke visited relations in New Zealand. 'Grace who is most aggressively patriotic always tries to make people believe that H[obart] is second only to London,' Minnie wrote home. In 1889 another young woman, Mary Walker, went to study art in England, and her brother James advised her not to let the haughty English or Germans lord it over the freeborn Tasmanian. 'As the Americans used to say, "This is going to be a big country—Yes, Sir!"' Mary scarcely needed the advice, and her letters home show a comfortable pride in her country, in her case Australia rather than Tasmania. The rough crowd at the Lord Mayor's procession was 'very different from anything one sees in Australia', English girls were as 'slangey' as any in the colonies, and she clearly identified herself as Australian. 'I am not English said I. No what are you then? Australian. And you don't call yourself English? Oh no of course not.' Children were sometimes baptised with patriotic names: Tasman for boys, occasionally Tasmania or Tassie for girls.[21]

The depression of the 1860s and 1870s lifted in the 1880s. Mining started on the west coast; wool prices rose; fruit-growing, timber-cutting and secondary industries developed; transport improved with railways, steamships, and from the 1900s, motor traffic. In 1901 Tasmania became part of federated Australia, and commonwealth subsidies cushioned its economic life. While Tasmania never became wealthy, it was more prosperous than before.

It was also more comfortable, like most of the rest of Australia. Crime rates continued to fall: in 1890 the government statistician was pleased to report that in some categories Tasmania had a lower crime rate than the mainland colonies and Britain. Forces encouraging respectability were increasing. In 1867 the thirteen-year-old son of two ex-convicts told a court that he could neither read nor write and had never been to church, chapel or school, but twenty years later education was compulsory, outlawing such isolation. Schools taught children not just reading and writing, but other lessons: cleanliness, tidiness, obedience, polite manners, loyalty to the British Empire. Churches developed, as did self-improvement groups, friendly societies and the temperance movement. Drunkenness decreased: the average consumption of spirits fell by two-thirds, from 2 gallons (9 litres) a head in 1857, to 0.70 (3 litres) in 1889, when it was 1.17 gallons (5.3 litres) in eastern Australia generally. Sport, especially cricket and football, was widely played, with every small township having teams. This provided more healthy activity for young men than the pub—or, perhaps, as well as the pub. There was still a good deal of drinking and rowdy behaviour, but overall Tasmania was a peaceful, orderly community, similar to other British communities around the world. So peaceful was it that in 1884 the ruling class was brave enough to widen the franchise, so that a majority of adult men could vote. Liberals felt that this would 'banish all degrading associations of the past' and removed the 'badge of inferiority from the working class'.[22] The code again: the badge of inferiority came from the convict past.

Challenging the theory that convicts were responsible for the boisterous, independent Australian national character, the working class of the colony with the highest proportion of convicts was quieter than others. Trade unions took longer to gain ground and were not radical. No one was radical; the island tended to be conservative, traditional, pro-English—unlike the Australian stereotype. This was not necessarily the result of the convict system. Tasmania was small, isolated, unimportant, not wealthy, with many of its brightest young people emigrating to greener pastures. Such places are rarely radical. Tasmania had twenty years of depression from the mid-1850s and only moderate prosperity afterwards, and it is hard to tell how much of its character was produced by the convict system, and how much by being a remote backwater.

With the lack of crime, the respectability, the patriotism and so on, by the 1880s travel books often commented that Tasmania had left its convict days behind. 'Practically there is nothing to remind one that he lives in a land that was once a penal settlement'; convicts 'have left little or no trace behind them, for, in all the world, there is not a better class of people to be found than in Tasmania'; 'to the present generation there is little to indicate

the old regime . . . the town itself [Hobart] has been swept clean, or almost
clean, of the evidences of convict days.' In 1891 one visitor wrote that the
exodus of so many convicts, and immigration of free colonists, had almost
completely obliterated the convict taint, and it was impossible to detect
any difference between Tasmania and other districts in religion and morality. Where so many years ago oppression, misery, cruelty and vice used to
reign, wrote another, there were now only signs of industry, prosperity and
happiness: 'Thank God the "good old days" are gone.'[23]

But though there were claims that the convict past was dead, anyone rash
enough to mention it received a furious, exaggerated response. In 1878 the
Tasmanian Mail was annoyed by an article by 'Tasma', 'Holiday Impres-
sions of Tasmania', which appeared in the *Australasian*. It was pretentious,
patronising, asking visitors to look out of the train at the sites of old convict stations, and claiming that a ghost story hung about the streets of
Hobart, thundered the *Mail*. How dare this person say such things! Didn't
most towns have ghost stories?

Fourteen years later 'Tasma' was again in hot water. By now it was
well known that she was Jessie Couvreur, a Tasmanian-born novelist living in Europe, 'rather a feather in our cap' as the *Tasmanian Mail* wrote,
but Tasmanians would have to reconsider her worth. In a lecture to the
Royal Belgian Geographical Society she had discussed the drawbacks of
Tasmania's early experiences, and her life in a penal settlement. Then she
'tried to be positive', but the harm had been done—she had talked of
chain gangs and bushrangers. What a pity she could not have confined her
remarks to 'what is pleasant in our history!' The *Mail* seized on any negative comment, however small, and ignored praise, however much, and also
the way Tasma described the island in her books—'the Arcadian island of
Tasmania', that 'earthly paradise'[24]—let alone her flattering pseudonym. It
is the mark of the extremely touchy, incapable of coping with the slightest
criticism.

In 1886 the British prime minister, W.E. Gladstone, referred to Tasmania's convict past. How dare he! The Anglican Bishop of Tasmania
wrote sternly to him and Gladstone duly apologised. There was similar
resentment in 1902 when reports arrived that during the installation in

England of the new Bishop of Tasmania, a preacher said that when Bishop Nixon went there in 1842 and the island was cursed by a convict penal system, it was a common saying that there was no God in Van Diemen's Land, and this could still be the case. In fact it turned out that the preacher had upheld Nixon's work, but the suggestion of 'Tasmania Libelled', as letters on the topic were headed, was enough. The Tasmanian premier cabled the Tasmanian agent-general in London: 'Use utmost endeavour to deny emphatically gross misrepresentation', and five citizens wrote to the *Mercury*. 'Southern Cross' said these shameful statements made any Tasmanian burn with indignation. 'The reference to convictism can, with more justice, be applied to the State of New South Wales than to this State . . . [we should] let the motherland know that the taking away of the character and fair fame of this isle are untrue, and that we protest, and resent them.'[25]

Other writers tried to explain away the statement, not very successfully, and Edward Innes, who had arrived in 1842, wrote a long letter saying how godly Tasmania had been then, with churches of all denominations full, devoted clergy, and generous citizens who helped others. At the probation station where Innes worked, most convicts were 'tractable, well-behaved men, transported for trifling offences. Many, no doubt, valued the religious privileges they were afforded, profited by them, and became afterwards useful and valuable members of society.' The irreverent *Clipper* made fun of Innes' letter, joking that 'the quaint Tasmanians who are falling over each other in their spluttering assertions of what godly place this Tassy was in the good old convict days [one letter!] are a joy to all reasonable observers. Some day a fossil will rise to prove that the convict settlement was really and by intention a missionary enterprise for the promotion of peace and goodwill in this wilderness.'[26]

Another point of view came from 'B.D.T.', who wrote that if there was a saying that there was no God in Tasmania, it probably originated with the convicts, 'whose sufferings, if the knowledge we have of them be correct, warranted it—the infamy of which the island makes such strenuous efforts to bury, as it buried the dust of her former inhabitants [Aborigines], and to sweep off, as she swept them off, the face of this fair island'.[27] This was one of the few times convicts and Aborigines were linked as fellow sufferers from British settlement.

During the South African War the British government suggested sending Boer prisoners of war to Tasmania to be guarded, and the Tasmanian cabinet did not object, but the new Australian government did. When the story broke, newspapers expressed gratitude to the new federation for saving them from 'a revival of the convict curse'—though the *Examiner*, so often a voice of reason, thought the prisoners would benefit from seeing a prosperous, contented British community.

Tempers could be roused if people thought they were being accused of having convict blood. There was a dreadful scene in parliament in 1894, when hot-headed Crosby Gilmore interpreted a comment by Allan McDonald as implying that he was sent out to the colony. Gilmore walked over to McDonald and asked him to apologise, or be thrashed. McDonald refused, so Gilmore struck him in the face. Gilmore was suspended for the rest of the sitting—though not the rest of the session. 'The fracas caused a painful feeling in the House, being the first of the kind for twenty-five years,' ran a report, in a mainland newspaper—Tasmanian ones were silent.[28]

There was good reason for this sensitivity: Britain—the Mother Country, Home—continued to hold a poor opinion of Australia, partly because it thought all colonies were by nature second-rate, but especially because of the convict past. The *Times* was frank: 'Distance, the taint of a penal origin, and the dullness of pastoral occupations, seemed to condemn the Australian colonies to remain long far in the rear, and England scarcely wished to see herself reflected in communities so ill-fated and so rude.' The Melbourne *Age* quoted this with horror. 'Englishmen think of the colonials as an inferior race,' remarked a French visitor to New South Wales in 1883, 'but the Australians believe themselves every bit as good,' he added. Australia's appearance in Oscar Wilde's play *Lady Windermere's Fan* was typical of the British attitude. The Duchess of Berwick is encouraging her daughter to marry a rich Australian. Money from Australia is fine, but the place itself is not. When the suitor proposes taking his bride to Australia the Duchess is indignant: 'To Australia! Oh, don't mention that dreadful vulgar place.'[29]

In 1892 the Empire's poet, Rudyard Kipling, wrote a sentimental poem entitled 'The Song of the Cities', with every major city of the Empire addressing the Mother Country. Each verse includes what Kipling saw as the city's salient features, not always flatteringly—Cape Town was 'snatched and battered', Auckland was lonely, Melbourne 'loud-voiced and reckless'. Hobart's stanza ran:

> Man's love first found me; man's hate made me Hell;
>> For my babes' sake I cleansed those infamies.
> Earnest for leave to live and labour well,
>> God flung me peace and ease.

Exactly what Kipling meant by 'Man's love first found me' is not clear, and really he need not have brought up Hell and infamies, but at least they had been cleansed, and he talked of 'peace and ease'. It was much the same with Sydney:

> Greeting! My birth-stain have I turned to good;
>> Forcing strong wills perverse to steadfastness:
> The first flush of the tropics in my blood,
>> And at my feet Success!

'The Song of the Cities' was certainly not among the poems Tasmanian schoolchildren were taught.

In 1899 a new young governor of New South Wales landed in Western Australia on his way east, and conveyed a message to colonists through a journalist, in which he quoted the line, 'Greeting! My birth-stain have I turned to good.' He meant to flatter, but did not succeed. The *Bulletin*'s editor was affronted. 'What on earth,' he asked, 'could ever have induced the young gentleman to thus "put his foot in it" by leading off with so direct a reference to the One Forbidden Subject, to the fact that the N.S.W. community is a pumpkin, a large and succulent pumpkin grown on a particularly nasty dung-heap.' Other newspapers were silent, but people were not: everyone was talking about it, wrote a university lecturer to a friend. 'The conversation might start with the North Pole: but before long it would make its way to this unfortunate message.' There was similar affront in 1879 when a visiting English cricketer called the crowd at the Sydney Cricket Ground 'sons of convicts'. A riot broke out.[30]

This defensive reaction persisted. In 1888 New South Wales held its centenary celebrations, and as in Tasmania the authorities tried to avoid any mention of convicts. But this was a larger colony, and in the *Bulletin* it had a radical journal which enjoyed attacking the establishment. It met a suggestion that the colony be renamed Australia with alternative suggestions: Convictoria, Injailia. Cartoons showed New South Wales chained to the image of a convict, and a settler declaiming, 'For heaven's sake, hide our past!' But the *Bulletin* did not defend convicts as much as attack Britain for sending them to Australia, talking of the festering vileness of England cast ashore to putrefy on the coasts of New South Wales, beginning a reign of slavery and loathsomeness and moral leprosy. It could have been Bishop Ullathorne writing.

Travellers commented that the convict nerve was still raw. In 1894 Frenchman Léon Blouët said Australians were not interested in ancestors: 'Like the rest of the human race, they have ancestors, but some of them would prefer to have none.' The topic was not to be touched on in New South Wales and Tasmania, he warned. This continued to be true—and not just in these two colonies. 'We know how our sensibilities have quivered under the stupid ignorance of our countrymen at home in thinking of us, and in sometimes saying and writing of us, that we are the descendants of convicts,' wrote a Victorian parliamentarian.

The British view continued into the twentieth century. In the 1930s the English still viewed Australians as 'Spawn of convicts', a 'land of convicts, cricketers and kangaroos'. A young woman from Sydney studying at the Royal College of Music reported that she was often greeted by 'Here come the clanking chains!' and a boy at school in England had similar stories. Winston Churchill nursed a prejudice against Australians, saying they came of bad stock.[31] This story could be apocryphal (a primary source is elusive) but has often been repeated as credible and unsurprising, showing the attitude people associated with the British.

In 1938 Edith Emery, an Austrian doctor and ardent socialist shocked at the Nazis' treatment of Jewish friends, accepted a job in Tasmania. 'I knew very little about Australia and nothing whatsoever about Tasmania—only that it was an island south of the Australian continent,' she wrote. On the ship out she met her first Australians, who were strongly patriotic but also attached to Britain, which they called 'Home'. But they hadn't enjoyed everything about their visit there: the harping on the Australian accent upset some so much they were reluctant to open their mouths, and others had it rubbed in that they were descended from convicts, 'one young man blushing to the lobes of his ears when telling me so that I had the impression that it was probably true—but so what?' Edith might think this, but she too found that convict ancestry was not to be mentioned among Australians.[32]

It was not only the British who were contemptuous of Tasmanians for their convict heritage. In 1944 the Commonwealth Labor government held a referendum over increasing government power. Various heavies came to Tasmania to campaign, and a letter in the *Mercury* accused the secretary of the New South Wales Federated Clerks' Union of describing Tasmania's Legislative Council as 'convict born'. 'I wish visitors would not cast slurs on Tasmania because we had a penal settlement once,' wrote W. Hewer of New Town. 'Tasmania will not vote "Yes" on the referendum. Insults will not make her do it.' Playing on people's dislike of such slurs, the Tasmanian Constitutional League placed a large advertisement in the *Mercury* on the day before the referendum:

WHO ARE THESE MAINLAND 'YES' MEN THAT CALL US
'CONVICT BORN'
. . . insults decent Tasmanians and dignified Tasmanian institutions
such as the Legislative Assembly [sic] by calling them 'convicts' . . .
Tasmania is today a paradise compared to any other Australian state . . .
BE LOYAL TO TASMANIA
VOTE NO

Almost two-thirds of Tasmanians did vote No, though how many were influenced by this advertisement is not known.[33]

The other slur from the mainland occurred when the prime minister, Robert Menzies, was addressing a crowd in Launceston. The story goes that when someone heckled him, he retorted, 'I haven't come here to talk to the sons of convicts!' No date is ever given for this story—perhaps it was apocryphal, though Menzies was known for his quick replies and forceful way with hecklers.

Though the sensitivity continued, the campaign to deny the past was succeeding. Blouët noted Australians' sensitivity about the past, but when he visited Tasmania he saw not so much a sensitive society as a dull one. 'How is it possible that a land so privileged by nature comes to be inhabited by such an uninteresting population? I never saw any people more peaceful, more ordinary, more bourgeois, more provincial, more behind the times.'[34] Tasmania was boring—what a triumph! Instead of viewing it as exotic and different because of the convict past, a Frenchman saw it as just like anywhere else in the British Empire, provincial and uninteresting. British visitors were still likely to link Tasmania to its penal past, but it was a major victory in defeating the stigma.

A noble Austrian visitor was too polite to describe anyone as uninteresting, but did comment on 'this imaginary stain':

> Considering morals, the population in Tasmania is very strict, something that one would not surmise from a people that in part descends from former convicts. Perhaps the noble striving to remove this imaginary stain by excellent behaviour is so much more intense because the other inhabitants do harbour a certain prejudice against them. However this prejudice is vanishing more and more . . .
>
> But enough of these memories from a dark time, which are now material for stories in the nursery, let us return to the present, happy circumstances in Tasmania.[35]

By the early twentieth century, the Blouët attitude was widespread. 'Nice people these Tasmanians, but naturally on the dull side as it's all so out of the way,' wrote Edward, Prince of Wales, to his lover during his 1920 tour. A major advantage was that ex-convicts were dying out: perhaps the last was Catherine Keane, who died aged 93 in 1925.[36] Finally, Tasmania was convict-free, after 122 years.

By the 1920s people could ignore the convict past, not just out of shame, but because they thought it was unimportant. Novels could describe both Australia generally and Tasmania in particular as places that had nothing to do with convicts:

> This romantic island, with its great wild beauty of dense tangled bush, cornflower-blue hills, lofty mountains lifting bold undaunted crags into azure skies; . . . this island with its many moods, sometimes silent,

brooding, reflecting, profound; at others smiling, dazzling, laughing; some days tender, exquisitely yielding; on others, convulsed with passion, impetuous, ungoverned; but always beautiful, always alluring in its bewildering waywardness!

This marvellous place is Tasmania, as described by Marie Bjelke Petersen in her 1917 romantic novel *The Captive Singer*. A Danish migrant who fell in love with Tasmania, Marie depicted it as a place of catharsis, where fugitives from decadent Europe could find peace, love, truth, God and the real meaning of life. The sole mention of the past in Bjelke Petersen's six novels about Tasmania comes obliquely, when a criminal is called a 'black-shooter'.[37]

So in 1917 a novel could be published—and sell well, 100,000 copies—which presented Tasmania in this extremely positive way, with no mention whatsoever of its convict origins. And no one questioned this; the many reviews never mentioned the past, or expressed surprise that Tasmania should be written about without reference to it. Had Tasmania finally left its convict past behind?

Hiding the stain, forgetting the past, and all those school lessons that did not even suggest that the convict past had anything to do with the present, all had their effect. In 1997 I interviewed a number of Tasmanians who grew up in the 1920s and 1930s. Besides seldom knowing that anyone was descended from convicts, they believed that convicts had nothing to do with present-day Tasmania: 'It never meant a thing to me'; 'People didn't feel that it impinged on their lives or affected them much'; 'We didn't worry about it much. We just got on with our ordinary lives.' And on the rare occasions convicts were talked about, it did not seem to have anything to do with contemporary life: 'there was nothing to link us to it'; 'I was not aware of convicts being part of the fabric of society'; 'There was no feeling of a dark past'; 'There was no effect, no dark stain'; 'There was no dark or horrid feeling of shame'; Port Arthur was 'just a pretty place to have a picnic'. 'We were never made to feel ashamed that it had happened. We did hear stories of exciting escapes, a bit like highwaymen. That was part of history, and they were exciting stories told with gusto, not shame.' These people believed that convicts had benefited by coming to Tasmania: 'Many people were bettered by coming here; life in England was so awful'; 'a lot of the convicts were better off out here than in London'; 'The convicts had such an opportunity of a better life, they could jump outside their class'; 'Of course some stole to get out here'.[38]

What this unanimous evidence implies is that by the 1920s and 1930s, children were being brought up rarely knowing that anyone was descended from convicts, and not knowing anything much about the convict system, which was seldom mentioned. If it was, it was as distant history, nothing to do with the present. Seventy years of denial had produced a population that did not connect the convict past with present life. The policy of amnesia had worked.

But the convict stigma was still lurking, though in the background now, rather than the foreground as in the 1850s and 1860s. Efforts to ignore it continued, but reminders would crop up. For example, in 1927 the English governor opened a girls' school fair by telling the pupils: 'I want all the young people of Tasmania never to hide the fact that they are Tasmanians, but to be proud of the fact that they were born in this wonderful garden isle.' Even the suggestion that people hide their Tasmanian origin was close to the bone: was there muttering among affronted parents? In 1933 the Hobart Walking Club visited Port Arthur, and an article describing the trip concluded: 'Much could be written of these old relics of Tasmania's early history, but, perhaps, it is better that a veil be drawn over a past that is far from creditable to our race.'[39]

Pioneer worship, fear of the convict stigma, silence and snobbery about the discreditable past, all were gloriously sent up in 1939 by two writers, Miles Franklin and Dymphna Cusack, in their novel *Pioneers on Parade*. In 1938 Sydney celebrated 150 years of European settlement with a Sesquicentenary, whose organising committee determined to ignore convicts. There was protest, on the grounds that convicts were part of the colony's history. Poet Mary Gilmore was particularly condemnatory:

> Shame on the mouth
> That would deny
> The knotted hands
> That set us high.

The committee ignored these complaints.

This was a goldmine for Franklin and Cusack. Their heroine, beautiful Primrose Brankston, dabbles in university studies; her mother Audrey is a social climber, who wants a knighthood for her husband George, grazier turned banker. Fifth-rate English nobles, there for the perks, include Lord Cravenburn and his sex-mad daughter Lucy. To gain clout with the Society for Purer Australian History, Audrey invites to Sydney the stereotype pioneer, sunburnt, hard-working Aunt Lucy, who has run her country property since her husband's death. She arrives with her grandson, upright William. The superficial revels roll on. Lucy junior tries to seduce William, but he holds women sacred and will not touch her. In desperation she asks him to marry her. Everyone is delighted—the family property is valuable—but all collapses when the Brankstons find out from the Society for Purer Australian History that they are descended from convicts. One stole a currant bun and was arrested by Cravenburn ancestors, who are actually related, on the wrong side of the blanket.

The news is 'a dreadful blow to William. "You don't mean a—a convict?" He could hardly say the dreadful word.' His uncle George thought it was true—'It accounts for lots of things that I could never understand about the family. Whenever I asked any of my great-uncles they would not pursue it.' 'You mean they knew and kept it dark, and it has to come out and ruin everything for me now?' asks William.

Primrose, too, is appalled by 'this crushing discovery . . . the bottom [had] fallen out of life overnight'. Her mother wants to keep quiet about it—'Everyone else does'—but honest William tells Lord Cravenburn, who refuses to allow his daughter to marry into such a family. His adulterous wife, happy to see her daughter settle in distant Australia where she cannot show up her mother's age, makes him relent, but Aunt Lucy baulks: her grandson to marry into a family whose ancestors treated so badly a girl who only stole a currant bun? But all is resolved. William and Lucy marry (though the authors, both single, assume this will not last). George realises what is important in life, refuses a knighthood and returns to the land; Audrey goes off to England with Lady Cravenburn to indulge in snobbery; and Primrose spurns marriage and decides to study hard so she can help the underprivileged. She determines to be proud of her convict ancestry, to learn how to make currant buns and 'stuff them down the throats of everyone who calls on me', have a seal made with a broad arrow 'and swank it on my letters'.[40]

Most of *Pioneers on Parade* describes what was going on at the time: the hideous shame of convict ancestry, the desperate attempts to keep it hidden. No one actually did take pride in it, but here the book was describing not reality, but the authors' ideal. Few agreed with them.

The picture Franklin and Cusack painted of aristocratic British visitors might be thought exaggerated, but it was kind compared with reality. As a young woman Hermione, Countess of Ranfurly, accompanied the official party as a secretary, and recalled in her memoirs how on his first night in Australia the Lord Privy Seal, honouring the colony with his presence, terrified her by 'plunging, naked, through my mosquito net'. He pursued many other women in like fashion, but only when he was seen in a nightclub 'clutching a pair of knickers from which its owner had only just escaped' was he sent home in disgrace.[41] Australians, from despised convict stock, must have loved repeating this story about the antics of the supposedly superior British aristocrat.

12

'A THING OF WHICH WE MAY WELL FEEL PROUD'

In public people might deny that the convict past had existed, or at least had anything to do with modern Tasmania; but in private there was a strong undercurrent of sympathy with convicts—as long as no one was identified as a descendant, the past was kept separate from the present, and the outside world knew nothing about it. The sympathy is not surprising. In the 1850s, as noted earlier, convicts and their families formed about three-quarters of the population. With little immigration and much intermarriage, the proportion remained fairly constant over the next century. In 1880, some 86 per cent of Tasmanians were native born, a much higher percentage that any other Australian colony. The large majority were children, grandchildren, even by now great-grandchildren of convicts. This was rarely even hinted at, though there was the occasional mention. In 1900 'Decency' wrote to the *Tasmanian News* complaining that the Commissioner of Police was collecting convict records. These, said Decency, 'are full of the names of people (oppressors and oppressed, tyrants and victims), who were the ancestors of the bulk of the Tasmanians of to-day'.[1] So Decency thought convicts were oppressed victims, the ancestors of most Tasmanians, and apparently no one contradicted this.

As Decency implied, there were tens of thousands of convicts and their descendants among all groups in society. The pattern of the 1850s and 1860s continued, with all except those on the margins of society accepted as ordinary citizens. The rising standard of living gave those from the working class more opportunities, especially as the government education system developed from the 1880s. Convict descendants starred in sport, sat on municipal councils and parliament, worked in charities, played a role in every aspect of Tasmanian life. Many were prominent. James 'Philosopher' Smith made the first important mineral discoveries; William Piguenit was the first well-known Tasmanian-born artist; J.W. Israel was chief clerk in the Audit Department in 1880 and later Commonwealth Auditor-General; A.J. Taylor was Hobart's librarian. The fact that they were convicts' children and grandchildren was never acknowledged.

Many politicians were descendants of convicts, and two ex-convicts sat in parliament, John Davies and James Gray, both former Tasmanian Union members. Early premiers included convict descendants Thomas Reibey and William Propsting, and with the advent of the Labor Party in power from 1909, about half Tasmania's premiers have been of convict descent—Labor parliamentarians generally came from the working class. John Earle arrived as a convict in 1832; his son John was the state's first Labor premier. Albert Ogilvie (Labor premier, 1934–39) was the son of a Hobart publican, himself the son of ex-convicts. Ogilvie qualified in Law and built up a successful practice before his election to parliament. John Blyth Hayes, Liberal premier in 1922–23, was the great-grandson of a convict. But, of course, these premiers' convict descent was never publicly mentioned, and possibly the men themselves did not know.

Convict descent was also never mentioned in connection with acclaimed heroes: First World War servicemen. Ten thousand or more convict descendants were among the 15,485 Tasmanians who enlisted to fight in the First World War, and at least four were among the eleven who were awarded the Empire's highest decoration, the Victoria Cross. (Some others could have been; with surnames like Brown it is hard to tell.)

Convict James McGee arrived in 1830, and his grandson Lewis McGee, an engine-driver, enlisted from Avoca in 1916, leaving a wife and daughter in Tasmania. He travelled to France with the 40th Battalion, and his Victoria Cross came for conspicuous bravery in action at Ypres in October 1917. During the attack Sergeant McGee led his platoon 'with great dash against all obstacles under heavy fire'. The Company was held up by an enemy machine gun firing from a pill-box, and McGee rushed forward by himself, shot the machine-gunners with his revolver and captured the strong point. 'Throughout the whole operation, his bravery and coolness stood out as a splendid example to everybody.' He was later killed in action. So was Alfred Gaby, grandson of convict Robert Whiteway, born in 1892 in Ringarooma, awarded the Victoria Cross for 'conspicuous bravery and dash in attack'. Stan McDougall, grandson of convicts, won his Victoria Cross for conspicuous gallantry when, virtually single-handedly, he took two enemy machine guns, killed their crews and routed an enemy attack. 'He is absolutely fearless and his contempt of danger is amazing,' read his citation. Stan survived the war.

The most highly decorated man in the entire British Army and the most highly decorated Australian ever, Harry Murray, was the great-grandson of two convicts. The family had no idea of the convict background; the story ran that the first Murray was a free settler, and Harry's mother was proud to marry into the family. A timber-cutter who enlisted as a private, Harry Murray rose to become Lieutenant-Colonel Murray VC, CMG, DSO and Bar, DCM, Croix de Guerre. Famous throughout the AIF as 'Mad Harry' for his fearlessness and his ferocity in hand-to-hand fighting, Murray was also a skilled tactician who planned attacks meticulously and trained his men with great care, trying to avoid casualties.

Perhaps bravery was to be expected, part of the Vandemonian spirit, but academic brilliance was not. John Dunbabin, a farm labourer, arrived as a convict in 1830, and was assigned to a merchant who had a farm at Bream Creek. John married another convict, Anne Eccles, and they lived on the farm with their six children. They later acquired the property and prospered, buying much more land. Their grandson Robert won a scholarship to study at Oxford and was Professor of Classics at the University of Tasmania from 1917 to 1939, and Vice-Chancellor of the University in 1933. Who would have dared to prophesy that a convict's grandson would lecture in Ancient Greek and head the state's highest educational institution? Contemporary students had no idea of Dunbabin's convict background.

Amy Rowntree, born in Hobart in 1885, was also a convict's grandchild. She became a teacher, and was chosen to study in Sydney the new field of infant teaching and develop it in Tasmania. In 1919 she was appointed Inspector of Infant Schools—Tasmania's first female inspector of schools. She was extremely successful in her job, and as an articulate public speaker, promoted the ideals of early childhood education. She also wrote historical works, was prominent in intellectual organisations and was awarded the Order of the British Empire. Who would have thought . . .

In one case people might not have been so surprised, but apparently no one did think of convicts in relation to the most famous Tasmanian of all—dashing film star Errol Flynn. Born in Hobart in 1909, Errol left behind all sorts of stories of wild youthful behaviour when he left Tasmania, first for Sydney and then for Hollywood. He claimed that an ancestor was a *Bounty* mutineer, but a recent researcher has discovered that Errol was descended through his mother from William Madden, sentenced to seven years' transportation for stealing a hat and shirt.

Though many families managed to hide their convict origins, a few kept the knowledge alive. This was often—naturally—in a sanitised version, with the convict ancestor the hero, the crime understandable, even glamorous. In Lorraine Wootton's family, some branches did not know about their convict ancestor, and others were told that he shot a rabbit which disappeared through the fence of the local 'bigwig's' estate. The ancestor tried to retrieve it and was caught by the gamekeeper. 'It was the only way he could provide for his family, etc.', wrote Lorraine. In fact he had been transported for stealing two bottles.

In 1942 businessman Frank Bond asked his aunt Sarah for the family history, and she wrote him a long account. Her father, William, told her that he had been a clerk, and 'borrowed' money from his firm to tide him over till payday. This was discovered, and he was transported. His own father told him never to darken his doors again. The convict ship was a floating hell with men of all ages and crimes herded together. Sarah assured her nephew that many wealthy families like the Gibsons, Thirkells and the *Mercury* Davies were also descended from convicts. One convict was transported simply for taking a loaf of bread from a baker's cart and giving it to a starving woman, 'intending of course to pay the owner on his return'— of course, just as William aimed to return the money he 'borrowed'.

In Van Diemen's Land 'the ship was unloaded of her human cargo'. Some men were put in cells only fit to house wild beasts, like the cells Sarah had seen at Port Arthur. Her father was made 'Time Keeper Clerk' and 'got to know most of the men's grievances', helping them as best he could, and writing letters for them. The officers were often devils incarnate who took pleasure in inflicting suffering, and the convicts murdered one particularly brutal specimen. The harsh treatment converted ordinary, intelligent men into maniacs. 'But why dwell upon these inhuman incidents?'

When William gained his ticket of leave he set up as a shoemaker, and met a pretty English maidservant, 'a vision of charming womanhood . . . in that garden of thorns and briars'. At first she was not interested in William, but a friend advised him to persevere, 'even if it is a disgrace for a young lady to marry a man sent out here under suspicious circumstances'. Eventually they married, prospered, though with ups and downs, and reared a large family.

Another embroidered story came from Mary Wilson. Transported for stealing a coat, she had to leave four children in London when she was sent to Van Diemen's Land in 1848. There she had a long list of convictions, such as 'Being in her Masters Stable on a bed with the Groom'. The magistrate gave her six months, and she flared out, 'You will have no better luck and you will have a widow's curse.' He gave her three more months. In 1854 Mary married Charles Nye, sentenced for stealing a shirt and gown and with punishments in Van Diemen's Land for idleness, insolence, smoking, assault and failing to assist a policeman who was drowning. How they made a living once they were free is not clear, but Mary's convictions for indecent language, larceny, absence without leave and assault continued until 1884, 36 years after she arrived. For example, in 1869 she was charged with stealing £37, and hitting a man on the head with pieces of crockery while an accomplice beat him with a whip. In 1884 Mary and Charles were admitted to the Invalid Depot; Mary died there in 1891, aged 83, and was buried in a pauper's grave.

Mary was one of the few convict women to have her photograph taken, and on the back was written information she told about herself. She said she was the wife of a farm labourer who was transported for stealing an egg. She herself committed a trifling offence to join him, though she could not find him in the colony. Her brother was in demand to teach boxing to royalty, and his pupils included George III. Apart from the fact that she and her husband were both convicts, this is all a fable.

Minimising the original crime, damning convict officials and the system, seeing convicts as the heroes, using euphemisms like 'sent out', remembering that many respectable families were descended from convicts—such stories presented convicts in an entirely sympathetic light.

A few people did argue that the convict past should be acknowledged, for two reasons. One was to encourage tourism, as described in Chapter 10, and this was generally accepted, as long as it was confined to distant Port Arthur. The other was as history. Any serious historian had to grapple with the convict system, since it dominated settlement for 50 years, and four historians wrote about it, with greater or less enthusiasm.

The only full-length history written between 1852 (West) and well into the twentieth century was James Fenton's *History of Tasmania* (1884). Fenton emigrated to Van Diemen's Land as a young free settler in 1834, and became a wealthy farmer. He said frankly that he aimed to describe the island's 'rise and progress'. He had to discuss convicts, but mentioned them as little as possible, and mostly described heroic, or at least energetic and interesting, ones—idealistic political prisoners, dramatic bushrangers—and the noble fight against transportation. The convict system itself occupies a scant 2 per cent of the book, and Fenton was sure its effect stopped when transportation did: 'these dregs of convictism, however, soon died out'.[2] None of the heroic convicts had any children in the colony to be identified, and as with the old lags, by acknowledging that they were convicts, the great bulk of the convicts were ignored, and the reader gained a reasonably positive view of convicts and their impact.

Forty years after Fenton arrived, another teenage emigrant was John Beattie, whose family farmed at New Norfolk. 'Those were the days when my soul got soaked in the lore of Port Arthur, all our working men being "old hands", and the romance of their experiences fascinated me.' Beattie publicised the more dramatic aspects of the convict system, possibly because he relied largely on tourists for his revenue. From 1882 a noted photographer, he enjoyed taking images of relics of the convict past, especially Port Arthur. He opened a museum, sold thousands of photographs, gave illustrated lectures on historical topics, and published books of photographs with accompanying text. He tried to be accurate and to avoid sensationalism; but his subject matter was controversial, and in his lantern-slide lecture on Port Arthur he described the hardships—the solitary cells, underground cells, floggings and heavy leg-irons. His museum and talks were well patronised and his books sold well. Some people appreciated his frankness, others did not, as the left-wing *Clipper* claimed:

> Beattie has lots of historically interesting material, and uses it to advantage. Rather pleasing to note that he did not shirk the black spots in our history, but was fair all round, though his denunciations of the treatment of the 'free' press in Governor Arthur's time, the tyranny of certain jailers, the woes of the poor devils who in the jail yard 'went up at eight and came down at nine' [i.e. were flogged], and the inhuman annihilation of the aborigines, were evidently unpalatable to some lingering remnants of the old regime, who gnashed their gums in the semi-darkness of the Town Hall.[3]

Also interested in convicts was James Bonwick, a teacher who emigrated from England to Van Diemen's Land in 1841. After he moved to the mainland in 1850 he became engrossed by Australia's history, writing over 60 books. Some were about Tasmania's history, including its convict past. He also transcribed records from British archives for various Australian governments, including Tasmania's. Some people were not enthusiastic, thinking this 'valueless matter' could cause distress, and the government would not allow even the Royal Society to read it. Bonwick was more interested in Aborigines than convicts, but they were there, acknowledged, though without much sympathy—Bonwick saw them as disreputable criminals, as also seen in his earlier-cited article, 'Curious Facts of Old Colonial Days' in the *Cyclopedia of Tasmania*. His transcription work was the foundation for *Historical Records of Australia*, published by the New South Wales and Commonwealth governments from 1913 and providing many records of first settlement. This was a brave decision, for though the records were written by the authorities and convicts' names were omitted, their presence was obvious.[4]

Bonwick's transcriptions were widely used by James Backhouse Walker, who was born in Hobart in 1841, the son of Quaker free settlers. He became a lawyer and was among a group of liberal thinkers who strove to improve Tasmania with working men's clubs, public libraries, rational religion and improved education. Walker had little time for hidebound conservatives, often grumbling about them in letters to his sister Mary. An enthusiastic member of the Royal Society of Tasmania, Walker began to research Tasmania's history, presenting his first paper in 1889. 'I had a crowded room last night and lots of compliments,' he wrote to Mary. 'People professed themselves greatly interested, but how much was civility it is hard to tell. The doings of convicts & soldiers set down in the bush of a new country gets monotonous, even with blacks thrown in.'

When the papers were published, Walker added an introduction which was, he told his sister,

> principally aimed at Sir Lambert [Dobson, a judge] & those other don-keys who would wipe out all our past history, because it is not particularly heroic. I maintain that the fact of our having been able to get rid of the bad origin, & to stand today as a community as well behaved and as con-tented as any people in the world, is a thing of which we may well feel proud. I always maintain that there is no place on the face of the earth where people generally & all round are as comfortably off & as free from anxiety & want—besides enjoying all the freedom they want—as here in Tasmania.[5]

Walker did not make these views public; his introduction was much milder. Some thought Tasmania's early history better left unwritten: 'They would, if they could, sweep away all records of what they call the dark ages of the colony, and would have Tasmanians bury the past in silence and oblivion.' But now historians were interested in the development of communities, and an Australian community was 'springing into a vigor-ous growth . . . and is showing itself to be inspired by ideas of national life by no means sordid or ignoble'. To understand how to progress, 'we can-not afford to ignore our history'. This was true of Tasmania, 'uneventful, trivial, and even painful as much of her history may be. The story of the settlement on these shores of a handful of Englishmen, and the develop-ment of that handful, during a period of something less than ninety years, into a happy and prosperous people of 150,000 souls, ought to have an interest to every Tasmanian.' That the earlier history was 'not of a character to be dwelt on with pleasure' was regrettable, but 'we, as a community, are no more responsible for it than a man is responsible for the circumstances of his birth'. It was good to be born noble, but even better for a man born in ignoble surroundings to succeed despite this.

But even Walker shied away from the word 'convict', and his ideals are not particularly evident in his work. He said little about convicts, mostly writing about exploration and the activities of administrative leaders, in the usual style. Like Bonwick, he seemed more sympathetic to Aborigines than convicts. And unlike his lively letters, his papers were heavy, even boring, and their impact seems limited.[6] Even these four historians, the most enthusiastic about convicts, did little for them in print, showing them in a negative or at best neutral light. But at least they gave convicts a place in Tasmania's history.

Many Tasmanians already thought convicts had a place in their history, though they seldom talked about it. During the convict period, almost all commentators took it for granted that convicts were serious criminals who deserved their punishment. Afterwards, the view started to appear that they were victims of a harsh system, normal people transported for trivial offences like petty theft or poaching, 'which you regard with lingering pity'. In 1861, giving evidence to an enquiry, James Youl said that convicts had mainly been sent out for political offences and poaching: 'there was always a very large body of convicts who prided themselves that they were not thieves and rogues'. A decade later Anthony Trollope noted a tendency to downplay convicts' crimes in both New South Wales and Tasmania. An ex-governor of Tasmania told an English audience that many convicts had been sent out for trivial offences, and were able-bodied and industrious labourers. One visitor wrote: 'We now know many wretched convicts were innocent, or their only offence would now get a fine or a short prison term', and visitor Mark Twain echoed this view: convicts were heavily punished for trifling offences, and though some were 'very bad' most were probably no worse than the average person in England. A few people suggested convicts were guilty of trivial offences but had been brutalised by the system, but generally the view was growing that convicts had committed only trivial offences and were ordinary people, to be seen with sympathy.

These ideas fitted in well with a new theory of crime which became popular in the later nineteenth century: that it was a result of environment, poor living conditions, rather than a depraved nature or a hereditary tendency. There were also suggestions that convicts had not been so unhappy in Van Diemen's Land, and for decades the occasional controversy would result in letters to the press claiming that, for example, 'these people were all as happy as in those rough times the working people could expect to be'. Some writers did not even think convicts suffered much, opining that their lodgings were comfortable, they had plenty of liberty, and 'it is said that the convicts had a very good time of it'. Had not Imperial Rome been founded by thieves?[7]

James Fenton might have minimised the convict impact in his history of Tasmania, but he gave another picture in his reminiscences, published in 1891. His assigned servants were 'quiet, manly, good-tempered, hard-working', he recalled. One insisted on working hard, sometimes till midnight, to earn extra so he could bring out his old father. He did this, bought a farm, married, and became highly respected as a good honest farmer, wrote Fenton:

> While that man was in my service I often contrasted his noble disposition and faithful conduct with his degradation as a prisoner of the Crown . . . and I grieved over the cruelty and injustice of the criminal laws, which prescribed transportation beyond the seas as the punishment for trivial offences that would now carry with them a sentence of a week or so in gaol . . . Extreme poverty in England and Ireland often compelled the peasants to pilfer in order to save their families from starvation, and these men made excellent servants.[8]

In 1895 the ex-convict policeman John Hornsby published *Old Time Echoes* under a pseudonym, 'The Vet'. He described vividly how dreadful the convict system was. His sympathy was with the convicts: 'great injustice prevailed here unchecked for many years; but it is gone, buried with the actors'. Many convicts became 'good and prosperous citizens', said Hornsby.[9] Such attitudes humanised convicts, making them more like ordinary people than the distinct criminal class of mid-nineteenth-century theory. And once the 'trivial offenders' theory appeared, it took root quickly, a far more comforting belief about people's forebears than the criminal class theory.

Much the same attitude was seen in New South Wales, with politicians claiming that convicts were sent out for trivial offences on which 'we can afford to look very lightly now'. Many had done no more than take 'a lolly out of an old lady's lolly shop'. These views were not based on research, but on a growing tradition, which perhaps stemmed from families' stories. A more authoritative view came from J.F. Watson, librarian and archivist, responsible for the monumental *Historical Records of Australia* series and so one of the few familiar with early records. In 1913 he suggested that convicts on the First Fleet were guilty of only relatively minor offences.[10]

A 1921 address by Arnold Wood, Professor of History at Sydney University, was therefore not entirely novel. His research convinced him that convicts were more sinned against than sinning, and he told a meeting of the Royal Australian Historical Society that convicts were 'the most important founders of New South Wales'. Even if they were not entirely moral, nor was the British royal family. Convicts were transported because they 'disturbed the comfort of aristocrats', by protesting in favour of a decent living wage, by poaching to feed their families, or by being Catholic and therefore 'undesirable'—conduct which 'according to modern opinions', wrote Wood, 'was not bad, but good'. Those who were thieves mostly stole small items. Wood saw the main guilt as lying with the ruling classes who were responsible for 'an unfair social and judicial system'. However, he tended to contradict himself, and wrote elsewhere that for many convicts, 'thieving was not only a habit, but also a skilled and fascinating trade', describing them as 'a disorderly mob of indolent, stupid and vicious people'.

In New South Wales, wrote Wood, convicts behaved 'remarkably well', with each generation rising to greater worth, culminating at Gallipoli and in Flanders where 'the Australian-born proved themselves to be among the greatest and noblest souls who have ever grown among the British race'. Not everyone agreed with Wood, as he himself acknowledged in a postscript to his article. 'So no good people remained in England after the convicts left!' was one reaction, and the Royal Australian Historical Society was so scandalised that it published no more articles on convicts for twenty years. General opinion agreed with Wood, though probably because of a growing tradition rather than his arguments. In 1930 another historian, Keith Hancock, wrote that 'the popular imagination has created the legend of a typical convict "sent out for snaring a rabbit".' My 1997 survey of Tasmanians who were children at the time came up with similar comments, such as, 'In many cases the convicts were guilty of minor offences and became good citizens afterwards.'[11]

Almost all Australian writers were adopting the trivial offence theory, but there were some diehards. In his *Short History of Australia* (1916), Ernest Scott stated that though some convicts were not inherently bad, 'the mass were rascals and ruffians'. Scott would have agreed with the muckraking Melbourne newspaper *Truth* on hardly anything else, but they had the same views on convicts. In 1915 *Truth* published a series of 40 anonymous articles about convict Van Diemen's Land, then produced them as a book, *The History of Tasmania*. The author said he used authentic official records to provide 'a reliable record of the dark deeds of the old convict days in Tasmania, which are now, happily, for ever over and done with'.[12] The book consists of sensational stories painting convicts as murderers, ruffians and rapists, linked by historical narrative. Dramatic headings include 'Convict Cuts Boy's Throat in Court', and in the triumphal ending Tasmania, a beautiful woman, radiant with the smile of Hope, steps forward over the dead ashes of the past towards a happier destiny. But a cheap paperback from the notorious *Truth*, dotted with advertisements for Foster's Lager and Restoring Lost Manhood, was not likely to be taken seriously. Nor was *Inhumanity: Historical tales of the old convict days*, by 'The Captain'—the more sensational books were usually anonymous. No other writer from the period mentions having read them and they appear to have had little impact.

In general, then, people were viewing convicts positively. Convicts were talked about privately—and always sympathetically. Angus Bethune grew up in a grazing family at Ouse. His nurse had lived next door to ex-bushranger Martin Cash, and told young Angus that he was 'quite a nice fellow'. Warren Reid's grandfather had also known Cash, and told young Warren that Cash 'always had a twinkle in his eye'. One story shows private sympathy from a government official. In 1887 Frank Belstead, the Secretary of Mines, told James Walker about an old ticket-of-leave man, an industrious fellow who kept his family decently, but did not realise that he was meant to report to the authorities every six months. Presumably he had been living like this for years, but an assiduous (or nosy) official found out. The old man was charged with absconding, and the magistrate gave him six months in gaol 'for being alive'. Belstead and others, shocked at the injustice, supported his family. 'Belstead said it was the most cruel thing he remembered.'[13] But even so, Belstead only helped privately, and made no official protest—he could, for example, have told the premier and asked for action, but this might have led to publicity.

Sympathy for convicts was also shown in attitudes to books, plays and films about them, with good sales for books from the publication of *His Natural Life* onwards, and huge audiences for plays and films—not just from the working class, but from all levels of society. And this interest was seen as 'natural', even by the conservative *Mercury*. As discussed in Chapter 8, in 1864 the play *The Ticket-of-Leave Man* was performed to a large and sympathetic audience, which included not just working-class people but the elite. Then there was the support for *For the Term of His Natural Life*. One person objected publicly to it but no one else did, and it sold extremely well and was read with great interest. Convict Thomas Flanagan's grandson could hardly do more than sign his own name, but he worked his way doggedly through the long, wordy, complicated novel.[14]

In 1886 a stage version of *For the Term of His Natural Life* was performed in Hobart. 'Naturally,' said the *Mercury*, the performance excited public interest, for the novel 'has been read perhaps with greater interest in Tasmania than elsewhere, because of its local associations.' There was apprehension that it would glorify 'melancholy facts best sunk in oblivion', but the *Mercury* reported nothing to worry about, for there was no 'undue pandering to morbid craving for sensational excitement'. Besides, 'it is now in the long long ago', and there was nothing except the fact that it was set in the same place to connect the Tasmania of today with the play. (An amazing claim only 30 years after the system ended!) The story was so well known, concluded the *Mercury*, that there was no need to retell it—the novel had had more readers than all other Australian stories put together. The stage version departed from the book in that it had a happy ending, with Rufus and Sylvia united, still alive.

The play performed to packed houses—it seemed as if 'all Hobart and its environs' wanted to see it, even though it lasted for nearly four hours and many in the audience had to stand. 'No play ever produced in Hobart has caused more interest or drawn together a more varied audience', and it was estimated that in its first six performances a total of 9000 people saw the play, though the theatre had seating for under 1000. The *Mercury* had only one criticism, that the backdrop depicting Mount Wellington had too many peaks. The audience was enthusiastic, cheering the heroes and groaning at the villains, clearly on the convicts' side. 'Every scene and incident according with popular approval was applauded to the echo, while villainy, as depicted, aroused vigorous demonstrations of antipathy . . . actors who play repulsive parts have to submit nightly to a very torrid execration.' These repulsive parts were those of British officials. There were no letters in the *Mercury* disapproving of the play, in fact no letters about it at all.

The actor portraying the villain, officer Maurice Frere, recorded that he had talked to old lags to get his appearance right, and when he entered the stage 'something between a growl and a roar' rose from the pit, culminating in 'shrieks of rage and hatred' so loud that the actors could not be heard. He came slowly to the footlights, looking carefully over the audience, which quietened. He took off his wig, to a universal sigh, and told the audience the play would start again. This worked, and the play continued.[15] Who were in the audience? By now the youngest ex-convicts would have been in their fifties, but there were still many of them and it seems as if many attended. But the *Mercury* said 'all Hobart' was there, a varied audience, so the play appealed to a cross-section of the community.

Three years later the play was staged again, having been successful in Brisbane and Sydney. Once more it attracted large audiences—and on one night, in the interval, prizes won at the Lindisfarne Regatta were presented, showing how much the play was accepted by the general community. Shortly afterwards the fate of the buildings at Port Arthur was debated, and in arguing that they should be saved, James Walker commented that *His Natural Life* was produced night after night without any ill-feeling in the community.[16] *The Ticket-of-Leave Man* was performed again in 1885, tolerably successfully according to the *Mercury*, but it was plays based on *His Natural Life* which excited real interest, set as they were in Tasmania itself.

But things could go too far. In 1891 a third version of *His Natural Life* was put on at the Theatre Royal, which was 'packed from floor to ceiling', according to the management, with hundreds turned away. They still felt the need to advertise the play, so their chain gang paraded through the streets, with a 'constable' in charge. 'A deputation of indignant citizens waited on the Premier and made a strong representation against the spectacle,' reported the *Mercury*:

> The deputation was sprung upon the Premier unawares, and apparently he misunderstood the somewhat excited language of the members, for he queried, 'What can the gaol authorities mean by such conduct?' When it was explained that the gang was a clever advertising dodge, the Premier fairly roared with laughter at his own misapprehension, and the comical situation, and promised that he would see what could be done to prevent the feelings of the deputation being ruffled . . . [Meanwhile] the 'chain gang' had dropped into a hotel to have something to cheer them up, and the next news of them was that the Superintendent of Police had marched them into the police station where their fetters were knocked off and real gaol ones threatened in substitution if the parade was continued. The gang thereafter disappeared, and probably it will be just as well if they do not show out again in the streets of Hobart.[17]

Convicts in the theatre were all very well, but convicts on the streets were too close to the bone. The article was headed 'AN UNWELCOME REMINISCENCE'—and carefully did not explain why the reminiscence was unwelcome. But the premier (Philip Fysh, a liberal with no convict blood) did laugh, and the article was written not in outrage, but in a jovial vein.

In the 1900s came a new excitement: films. Australians began to make feature films in 1906 with *The Story of the Kelly Gang*, and over the next eight years the industry flourished, mainly in Sydney. By 1914, some 130 films had been made. Australian themes were popular, and fourteen of the films—a significant but not huge number—were convict melodramas, though two were set entirely in Britain (one was a film of the play *The Ticket-of-Leave Man*). Of the twelve set in Australia, five took place in Van Diemen's Land, two of them based on *His Natural Life*. The plots usually depicted an innocent hero or heroine transported to Australia, suffering horribly before either dying, or being reunited with a lover. *The Lady Outlaw* described the fictional life of Dorothy, who followed her transported lover to Van Diemen's Land and ended up as a bushranger. This film screened quietly in Melbourne, but won a far more positive response when it opened in Hobart. The two other films about Van Diemen's Land were *Assigned to His Wife* and *The Assigned Servant,* which was received in Hobart by 'a crowded and enthusiastic audience'.

By far the best known of these early films was *For the Term of His Natural Life* (1908). Based on the stage version of the novel, it was short (a fifth as long as the 1927 version). No expense was spared, cameramen and crew travelling to Port Arthur for filming—other films set in Tasmania were actually shot around Sydney. The film was very successful, running for an extraordinary eight weeks in Sydney. It was shown in Hobart in December 1909, and was the first film reviewed locally. 'As Marcus did Tassy the honour of making it famous,' wrote the *Clipper* irreverently, 'no doubt Shingleville will turn out in force to see Sylvia say "Good Mr Dawes", and all the ancient history of the ancestry of the landed gentry in Tasmania.' The film, shown at the Theatre Royal, thrilled large houses. 'The gentle British process of making a man into a hyena was portrayed very disloyally, but no one noticed that part.' There were no negative comments, no complaints, but the usual large audiences.[18] So the audiences for these films about convicts were large; whether they were mixed socially is not known. Possibly the middle class did not go to gaudy new entertainments like films.

It was a different story in 1926, by which time films were part of mainstream life. An American company proposed filming *His Natural Life*. Many Australians preferred British influence to American, or wanted to censor unwholesome films, and there were three prongs of protest: that Americans should not be allowed to film an Australian book; that the film would glorify crime and present gruesome and unwholesome scenes (the book contained cannibalism and homosexuality); and that it was undesirable to rake up the convict past.

There was some protest in mainland Australia, mainly for the first two reasons, though Labor opinion tended to welcome the film as telling the truth about nineteenth-century oppression. Most protest came from Tasmania, where the novel was set. A leader was Clive Lord, great-great-grandson of a convict, curator of the Tasmanian Museum and Art Gallery and secretary of the Royal Society of Tasmania, which resolved, though narrowly, to protest against the film. So did the *Mercury*, owned by convict descendants. 'Had we the power, we would sweep away every relic of those bad old times whether in stone, in paper, in film or anything else capable of perpetuating memories far better forgotten . . . It is utterly unjust to rivet upon Tasmanians the stigma of degeneration from convictism—biologically and politically and sociologically unjust. Yet who can doubt that this outrageous lie will be soon broadcast through the world if this film is made?'

A dozen or so letters supported the *Mercury*'s view. Their authors did not want the convict past, 'a time we should be only too glad to forget' and which was not Tasmania's fault, dragged up again, by Americans, for the sake of filthy lucre. The book had been distressing enough, and the film would be worse. 'To our everlasting credit real Tasmanians have overwhelmingly blotted out the stigma produced by the convict system'; 'We have lived down the notoriety of "Van Diemen's Land", and we do not want to do that work again'. Several writers, though stressing that they themselves were not descended from convicts, said that many convicts had been innocent or transported for trivial offences and in Tasmania lived respectably, and their descendants could well be proud of them.[19]

Clive Lord sent the British prime minister a letter of protest, probably on the suggestion of a former governor of Tasmania who was the prime minister's friend. The governor added a covering note:

Mr Clive Lord I knew extremely well . . . He is also descended from a *convict*. Of this he informed me *himself* and it is only when one knows people very well that they tell one of this sort of thing . . .

Some years ago there was a very dreadful, ghastly book published, I think in Australia, by an Author named 'Marcus Clarke' called '*For the term of his Natural Life*'? I read it years ago when, as a young man, I globetrotted in Australia. But I forbad anyone in Government House, as far as I could, to *touch* the Book. It is a 'Pot-pourri' of horrible incidents in various convict Settlements . . . [a] Mosaic of Ghastly Horrors. The incidents may be true individually, but certainly not as a whole. But granted that such incidents are of interest historically, to bring them up in a 'Film' *to be reproduced all over the World* tears the heart-strings of thousands and thousands of our fellow-citizens of the Empire in Australia, who are very *sensitive* on this subject and who *do not deserve* such treatment, as, out of a bad beginning, they are working up a most progressive, right-thinking and Patriotic British Race.[20]

Others welcomed the film: it would bring business and show Tasmania to the world, while all nations had grim episodes in their past. Opponents were merely 'those neurotic persons who are ashamed of the truth and to whom history is an anathema'. Some *Mercury* letter-writers welcomed the film, saying that viewers would realise that the convict days were past history, as they did with films of Ancient Rome. The *Examiner* (not owned by convict descendants) thought the good name of Tasmania was not in danger. Films depicted America as a 'jazzing, bootlegging, woman-degrading nation', yet Americans did not worry, so why should Tasmanians? There were no letters of protest in the *Examiner*, and general protest was not strong enough to make governments act.[21] Filming went ahead—some actually in Tasmania.

The excitement of the filming of the most expensive picture yet made in Australia, and the arrival of glamorous American film stars, seemed to quieten protest. Detailed progress reports appeared in all newspapers (even the *Mercury*). Work started at Port Arthur the day the film crew arrived, and the *Weekly Courier* reporter was thrilled by the rugged activities: convicts had to wade through muddy rivers, and Rufus Dawes was drenched to the skin by eight waves with the director crying, 'Look desperate!' until the scene was filmed just so. Historian J.W. Beattie, who did well from advising the film crew, praised their enthusiasm for detail; they had gone to great trouble to ensure even the uniforms and boots were correct, and glass montages filled out Port Arthur's ruins to their original shape. Crowds came to watch the filming, and the Americans noted their ambivalence; some bewailed the harm *His Natural Life* might do, but others hustled the tourists to see Port Arthur and convict relic displays. Some lucky locals actually took part in the film as convicts, though they had to work in a field as a 'human plough' (not actually in the book but described by Beattie). Old residents of Port Arthur gave the producer 'much-appreciated assistance', and local dogs formed the Eaglehawk Neck canine chain. The Port Arthur hotel, where the visitors stayed, made a killing.

Filming lasted three weeks. The crew then visited Launceston and did some token filming—they really were trying to please the locals, since Launceston did not feature in the book—and finished the rest around Sydney. Like the play, the film had Rufus and Sylvia still alive at the end, floating on wreckage. The censor had his way, the producers agreeing to modify 'the man-eating business', taking out a caption which read 'It tastes like pork', and promising not to show anything gruesome. They more or less kept this promise, and tried hard to win Australian hearts with a gushing introduction:[22]

> Today Australia is a great and prosperous country whose rapid progress leads on to a greater destiny rich with tremendous promise.
>
> Yet its history has been similar to that of other great countries when brave men with noble ideas have struggled with life's social problems in a rugged and mighty land.
>
> And this great drama of a hundred years ago is purely a work of fiction.

Tasmanians of the 1850s could hardly have used more obscure wording to imply convictism.

His Natural Life was released in June 1927. In Australia it was a huge commercial success, especially in Tasmania. The governor graced the opening session, and in Hobart all three daily sessions were full, even those in the immense city hall. Schoolchildren were admitted for a nominal fee; the authorities must have thought the film was good for them. Audiences were held spellbound, it was reported, and the film attracted 'unbounded applause' and 'the most eulogistic comments'. Even the *Mercury* reviewer came round, finding the film 'intensely gripping', glad that 'genuine long-faced English-looking people' played relevant parts, only annoyed that the incorrect term 'Hobart' was used instead of 'Hobart Town'. There were just three dissenting voices. One had not actually seen the film, another was an earlier objector repeating his stance, and the *Mercury*'s editor remained opposed, seeing the film as propaganda for the communists. We know, ran an editorial, that convicts who behaved well could gain their liberty and marry, while worse characters were kept in prison and had no opportunity of marrying and leaving descendants. And we know that crime is not hereditary but a mental defect created by circumstances. But 'why be so hideously cruel to the unoffending people of a whole State to compel them to be on the defensive to resist libellous propaganda?'[23]

The Launceston *Examiner* was calmer. The 'much-discussed and long-awaited' film was packing the Princess Theatre, and it dispelled the fears that had been voiced. The film toured the state; Lindsay Whitham remembered that it filled the Geeveston Town Hall for the Saturday night flicks. With little Tasmanian history taught in schools, he thought most people's ideas of the convict system came from the film. Eric Reece, however, thought it was just an adventure film, which 'made no impression about our convict heritage'.[24]

All over the island crowds flocked to see the film. Joseph Lyons thought people should see it if only to take in how much society had advanced since convict days, and Edmund Dwyer-Gray, another Labor politician, said a chance acquaintance had recently declared himself to be the child of one who had drawn a plough—so the film produced stories of two people who admitted convict descent (the other being Clive Lord), though not publicly. With the crowds of viewers, and voices raised in support of admitting the convict past, the episode showed that many Tasmanians were feeling more at ease with this, though there were plenty who still tried to hide it. But they need not have been afraid of the world's opinion, for the film was barely shown in America and not at all in Britain. The arrival of 'talkies' in 1928 meant all silent films became old fashioned.

Why was there protest against filming *His Natural Life* in 1926, when there had been only one voice raised when the book appeared in 1871, and no complaints at all about the play in 1886 and 1889, and films in 1908 and 1911? Films were more prominent by 1926—but the play had been prominent. Was it the threat of world-wide circulation that caused the stir? Was it the personal feelings of convict-descendants Lord and the *Mercury*'s owners—was it far enough after the end of transportation for them to feel able to protest publicly?

In any case, only a few people objected to *His Natural Life*; they were far outnumbered by those who flocked to see it, who avidly read every detail about it in newspapers. Some were still sensitive, but the majority did not seem to mind the past being brought up. While no one openly claimed descent from a convict—the British attitude remained and this would have been going too far—the general feeling towards convicts was one of acceptance and sympathy.

13

PAVING THE WAY

By the end of the Second World War, the tradition of denying Tasmania's convict past was beginning to break down. Some people were starting to talk openly about convicts, as the causes of the convict stigma were fading. Crime was now seen as created by poverty rather than innate tendencies, environment not heredity, nurture not nature. It was widely believed that convicts had been petty offenders transported for trivial crimes like stealing a loaf of bread. So they were seen not as terrible criminals, but as people trying to get by in difficult times as anyone might have done. The division into convict and free had vanished, since few people were aware of being descended from a convict. If they did, they kept quiet about it. Many adults in the 1960s had grown up in the 1920s and 1930s, when convicts were not much discussed. If convicts were not talked about, if no one was descended from them, there was nothing to be ashamed of.

Perhaps most importantly, the British attitude to Australia was changing. In the nineteenth and early twentieth centuries contempt for both convicts and colonies dominated, but after the Second World War Britain was recovering from devastation while Australia was booming. Admiration, even envy, developed. Many British people emigrated to Australia for the higher living standard, higher salaries, better opportunities, sun and sport and outdoor life.

Australian attitudes to Britain were also changing, as Australia became more successful and self-confident, especially after Britain's inability to defend the Empire in the Second World War. From the 1930s onwards Australians enjoyed many triumphs: the Invincibles, Bradman's cricket team, who swept all before them; victorious Phar Lap; tennis champions like Ken Rosewall and Frank Sedgman; Jack Brabham in motor racing; Australia's victories not only in the Melbourne Olympic Games, but in hosting the games successfully. There were cultural stars like diva Joan Sutherland, ballet dancer Robert Helpmann, film star Errol Flynn. Australians felt that their country was as good as any other if not better, and could ignore British snobbery. The British, especially the upper classes, did tend to see Australians as crude and vulgar, but by the 1960s Australians could laugh at this, with the popular film *The Adventures of Barry McKenzie* (1972) sending up the British idea of Australians. Convicts were largely forgotten, and many people who migrated to Tasmania in the decades after the Second World War had little idea of the island's convict past. Migrants made the population much more diverse, with a growing percentage who did not see the convict past as a dark stain, some not even aware it had ever existed. Many people of convict descent were among the high achievers—Lew Hoad, international tennis champion; Eric Reece, premier of Tasmania in the 1950s; Sir Stanley Burbury, distinguished lawyer, in 1973 chosen as the first Australian-born Governor of Tasmania—though no one mentioned convict ancestors.

The British still showed some lingering contempt for Australia because of the convict stain. My aunt Jill visited England in 1953 and remembers the odd person 'slinging off at us about being convicts. I didn't care. It didn't worry me,' she added; she was more irritated by being called 'colonial', which happened far more often. In the early 1970s a friend remembers Cambridge academics making laughing, patronising references, but young Australians visiting Britain did not cringe like those before the war. After I finished my university Arts course I went to England for two years, in 1971–72. No one ever mentioned convicts to me—I would have been astounded if they had, having hardly ever thought about them, and certainly never in connection with the Tasmania of my childhood. Young Australians like myself were inclined to scoff at the English for their antiquated class system, their lack of friendliness, their boringness and dreadful flat beer. The class system was shocking. I worked as a nanny, and one day the cleaner, recounting some foible of our employers, remarked sadly, 'And they're supposed to set us an example.' 'No, they aren't!' I cried, and gave her a passionate lecture on equality, while she looked blankly at me. These English, tied to an obsolete past—they had no idea.

The feeling among the young Australians I met in Britain was that it was fine to visit, but Australia was a much better place to live. More irritating than any possible comment about convicts was the way some English people thought Australians were rough and coarse, and like many others I always called myself Tasmanian rather than Australian to avoid being stereotyped as a drunken lout—ironically, considering Tasmania's convict past. Martin Flanagan was another young Tasmanian who had little time for British attitudes. As a young man he went to England and worked at Brent Borough Council, where 'no-one gave a fuck, busy as they were selling items of council property to second-hand dealers and using the council trucks to do what was known in the trade as privates'[1]—just as their great-great-uncles had been doing when they were caught and transported to Van Diemen's Land.

As shame in the past faded, interest in Australian history exploded from the 1940s, with academic texts, general works and popular novels appearing. The Second World War gave Australian nationalism a boost, and the confident post-war nation had a new interest in what had made Australia. For the first time, convicts were brought into mainstream history. But academics tended to take a negative view of convicts, probably mainly because their research focused on analysing official convict records.

Convict records were written by the authorities and included the convict's crime and sentence, reports from the gaol, hulk and ship, then a list of offences in Australia, ending, usually, with a pardon; they mainly recorded convicts' negative behaviour. Praiseworthy deeds were rarely reported. For example, Jane Hadden won her freedom by warning her master that bushrangers were approaching the house, but this was not written on her convict record. A typical record was for Thomas Dibble, sentenced to transportation for life in 1832 for 'Felony'. His gaol report ran, 'Conv[icte]d before Ch[aracter]r &c bad'. He was orderly in the hulk, but was punished on board ship, the surgeon describing him as 'Worthless fellow'. In Hobart he told the authorities that he had been transported for 'St[ealin]g the tire of a Wheel'. He had previously served two short prison terms for stealing rabbits and vagrancy.

As with convicts in general, there are two ways of looking at Thomas Dibble. He had two former convictions, he was a vagrant, his character '&c' (meaning his reputation, family and friends) were 'bad', the surgeon thought him worthless. Not promising. But on the other hand, the items he stole were small (a tyre and rabbits), he did not use violence, his vagrancy might have been due merely to bad luck, and he was orderly in the hulk. An ordinary person caught up in hard times? Later historians tended to stress the positive; in the 1950s and 1960s they stressed the negative. Like so many others, they saw convicts as one homogeneous group, and reduced them all to a stereotype. Manning Clark, Lloyd Robson and A.G.L. Shaw concluded from the records that most convicts were professional criminals, outcasts of society, ne'er-do-wells from city slums, urban thieves with 'little to recommend them'. A decade or more later Humphrey McQueen had a different view, describing convicts as petty bourgeois, keen to advantage themselves, with little group solidarity; for a socialist historian like McQueen this was the worst criticism possible.[2]

In 1958 Russel Ward published a bombshell, *The Australian Legend*. He claimed that convicts' values were the basis of the Australian national character. 'We Australians often display a certain queasiness in recalling our founding fathers,' he wrote. 'Even to-day many prefer not to remember that for nearly the first half-century of its existence White Australia was, primarily, an extensive gaol.' Most historians preferred to think that gold-rush immigrants swamped convicts. Ward argued that the distinctive Australian ethos—the masculinity described by writers like Henry Lawson, laconic, pragmatic, anti-authoritarian, supporting mates—came from convicts, which made the convict experience central to the national sense of self.[3] This was a far more favourable view of convicts, more in keeping with the tradition that had grown up—convicts were ordinary people, if rather rough and ready. When I studied Australian history at the University of Tasmania in 1968, *The Australian Legend* was the main text, and to our inspiring left-wing lecturer, Malcolm MacRae, Ward's laconic, anti-authoritarian convicts were the heroes, the oppressive British government and capitalist squatters the villains. Even so, Malcolm did not tell us that he himself was descended from a convict—though he might not yet have known.

Increased interest in Australian history appeared in other areas. In 1951 the Tasmanian Historical Research Association was formed. It held lectures and published articles and books; a third of its first four years' papers were about convicts, seen very much from the academic viewpoint.

Convicts appeared elsewhere in a positive or at least neutral light, for example in *The Crimes of the First Fleet Convicts* (1970)—which was greeted with some protest by descendants. Enthusiasts collected convict ballads, now known only by older people who had learnt them in their youth. Presumably after about 1920 the ballads were displaced by popular music on the radio. The first volume of the *Australian Dictionary of Biography*, published in 1966, identified many people as convicts or children of convicts, including Francis Greenway in New South Wales, and Tasmanians Richard Dry, Thomas Burbury and David Gibson. (The only convict whose origin was hidden was James Gray who, 'by his own account, became a voluntary exile and migrated to Hobart Town'.)[4] However, academic texts and reference books were generally read only in university circles, which in the 1950s and 1960s were still small. How much influence such texts had on general opinion is debatable.

The general public continued to believe that convicts were mostly trivial offenders. By now, wrote A.G.L. Shaw, it was a popular legend that 'most of the convicts were more sinned against than sinning, victims of a harsh criminal law, driven by want to some petty crimes in time of economic depression or social stress . . . the myth is now firmly embedded in the national ethos, where it will doubtless remain for generations.'[5] He was right.

This positive view of convicts was encouraged by a wave of novels set in the colonial era. They described convicts in the mass as dreadful, but individual convicts as ordinary people. In 1941 Eleanor Dark published *The Timeless Land*, the first and most popular book in a trilogy. It described Sydney's first decade, from three points of view: Aborigines (the main voice), white officials (secondary) and convicts (a distant third). Convicts as a whole are 'old, sick, idle, depraved, ignorant [and] treacherous', a 'shuffling, ill-smelling crowd' with few skills, made anti-social by brutal conditions in Britain. But the two major convict characters are enterprising and interesting, seizing chances as they appear. *The Timeless Land* was highly praised as a literary historical novel, and sold reasonably well.

More popular and with much higher sales was Edward Timms' twelve-book series which began in 1948 and centred on an immigrant English family's experience in Australia. By 1978 E.V. Timms' novels had run to many editions, with 850,000 copies sold. He had the Marcus Clarke view of penal stations, with their 'terrors and horrors . . . the unendurable torture of the chains and the blood-dripping lash', but such comments were few, for his books were pot-boiler romances in which convicts and their children lust after each other like everyone else. In *The Scarlet Frontier* (1953) the heroine is appalled when a tall dark stranger admits to her that he is the son of a convict; but since he is 'a splendid, deep-chested, muscled specimen of hard and virile manhood' she soon forgets this, and weds him with the possible problems of marrying into a convict family never discussed.[6]

The most widely read convict novel of the mid-century was *Sara Dane* (1954). The author, Catherine Gaskin, grew up in Sydney but left Australia in her late teens and became a best-selling international novelist. Inspired by the life of Mary Reibey, *Sara Dane* told of a young woman, of gentry stock falsely accused of theft, who is transported to Sydney in 1793. She marries an officer, proves herself a shrewd businesswoman, assists her husband to make a fortune, and aims to be accepted despite her convict past, so that her children will not be disadvantaged. *Sara Dane* shows convicts in the bulk as 'miserable-looking', dirty and slovenly (though not depraved), but even more than the other novels, individuals are exactly the same as other people, able to rise above their convict past. The novel graphically describes the problem confronting convicts; though by an 'unwritten law' the past is never spoken of, everyone knows it, and they can never really live it down. All except Sara, who marries into the French gentry; not a method available to many convicts.[7]

The heroes of nineteenth-century convict novels and narratives were often in chain gangs and penal settlements, not in the normal community, and were depicted as forever tainted by their convict experience. The convict characters created by mid-twentieth-century novelists are either assigned servants or have served their sentences, living in the community like everyone else. They are not inevitably tainted, but can overcome their past. Sara Dane might want to escape from other people looking down on her, but she knows, as the reader knows, that she is as good as they are.

Babette Smith describes how in New South Wales, the result of the dominant 'trivial offenders' theory, the novels, and the passage of time—over a century since the end of transportation—was that by the late 1960s some people were beginning to admit, even celebrate, their convict ancestry. The Fellowship of First Fleeters was founded in Sydney in 1968, exclusively for convict descendants; the 1788–1820 Pioneer Association was more restrained, but many of those pioneers were in fact convicts. In 1966 A.G.L. Shaw wrote that 'until recently', convicts' descendants had been 'unduly sensitive' about their past—indicating that in 1966 he thought they were not. As questions about the past multiplied, the Mitchell Library asked the Society of Genealogists to handle family history queries. 'We were inundated,' recalled the president of the day. But research was restricted: the researcher asked a question to which the staff member found an answer. People were not allowed to read the records themselves.[8]

Tasmania was slower to openly acknowledge its connection to the convict past, possibly because transportation had ended thirteen years later there, possibly because a small island would generally be later in taking up new ideas, or possibly because there had been so many more convicts per head of population. But convicts were written about. The main convict texts, West's *History* and the narratives of Martin Cash and Mark Jeffrey, were reprinted, though mostly on mainland Australia. *For the Term of His Natural Life* was never out of print and was widely read, even on the Tasmanian school syllabus, though schoolchildren of the time remember expurgated versions, with the homosexuality removed.

The main publication about Tasmania's convicts was neither an academic work nor a novel. Beverley Coultman Smith, born in Tasmania but not of convict descent, was a cadet journalist with the *Mercury*. In 1941 he wrote *Shadow over Tasmania*. 'For the first time the truth about the state's convict history', shouted the front cover. 'The very name "convict" calls up unpleasant associations,' wrote Smith. The public saw convicts as 'innocent men, women and youths torn from their cosy English firesides, herded like cattle into filthy transports, spewed upon the shores of Tasmania, insufficiently fed, weighted down with half a hundredweight of chains, flogged and kicked into inhuman labour, confined in small and insanitary cells, until they collapsed and died or became loathsome, savage animals.' No one was actually writing like this at the time; it was the *His Natural Life* story, and the tourist experience.

This picture was wrong, said Smith. Transportation was 'a far-sighted and, on the whole, successful colonisation system', planned by Britain to give felons a new start. Inhumane treatment was rare, and well-behaved convicts could prosper. Convicts' crimes might appear trivial, but 'the great majority were potential or habitual criminals'. Some stories Smith told had never been heard before or since, such as the description of sports days at Port Arthur, with convicts enjoying running races and feats of strength, and receiving 'luxuries' as prizes. The source for much of the book was Johnnis Danker, a Dane who migrated to Tasmania in 1885, aged 27. This 'quaint and likeable character' worked as a guide, builder and timber-splitter at Port Arthur. Old lags gave him such a different account of transportation from the usual story told at Port Arthur, which was based on *His Natural Life*, that Danker determined to reveal the truth and collected all the information he could. He probably gave it to Smith because he realised that otherwise it would not be published.

Though it said little new and some stories were of questionable accuracy (those sports!), *Shadow over Tasmania* was important. Convicts were still a topic to be wary of in Tasmania in 1941, and the book's publication created a stir. 'There was a bit of a fuss,' wrote Smith's son Craig. 'Being a born "stirrer" my father got great joy from flying in the face of the community stigma about the past—he would still grin about it whenever it was brought up in his later years.' *Shadow* presented transportation in a new light, as a system 'of which we should be proud, not ashamed—for it laid the foundations of Tasmania today'. No one had stated this, at least not publicly, since the days of the Tasmanian Union a century earlier. Sales were huge: new editions were regularly published, and by 1978 *Shadow over Tasmania* had sold almost 200,000 copies. It is still in print.[9]

So many sales meant the message must have made an impact, though this was not obvious in a survey I undertook in 2007–08 of 118 people

born in Tasmania before 1950. Mainly members of the University of the
Third Age and historical societies, the survey participants were likely to
have been interested in history, so figures are probably higher than for the
generation population, but they do show the relative popularity of such
books. *For the Term of His Natural Life* was by far the most widely read
convict book among those surveyed:

For the Term of His Natural Life	76 per cent
Martin Cash, the Bushranger of Van Diemen's Land	26 per cent
Shadow over Tasmania	20 per cent
The Broad Arrow	12 per cent

People were not asked about more modern convict novels like *Sara Dane*, but
any other convict book would find it hard to beat a 76 per cent readership.
(A majority of the 118 survey subjects, 70 per cent, were descended from
convicts, but only a tenth of them knew this when they were growing up.)

Shadow over Tasmania's message that the convict past was nothing to
be ashamed of had little impact on other writers. From 1940 to 1970 at
least two dozen Tasmanian books were set in the convict era, but rather
than a convict past their authors preferred the pioneer foundation story.
All were amateur, if experienced, historians, and their books were mostly
local histories, with a few family histories, biographies and memoirs. The
best-known was Karl von Stieglitz, descendant of a pioneer family. He
believed that free settlers had made Tasmania, and should be praised for
it. Even so, at least one upper-class Tasmanian, Sir William Crowther,
thought von Stieglitz wrote too much about the seamy side of Tasmania's
past—when in fact he hardly mentioned it.

Despite Sir William's opinion, these books avoided convicts. Most
referred to them only in passing, with no context, for example, mentioning a convict probation station at Cleveland. In the traditional way, the
only convicts identified were those with no descendants, who were interesting, enterprising or quaint: Irish political prisoners, bushrangers or old
lags. Otherwise, everyone was a free settler, with some perhaps deliberate
errors: von Stieglitz stated that migrants from Norfolk Island were free
settlers, mostly from the army and navy, when in fact they were almost all
former convicts.[10]

Three biographers of convict families were particularly evasive. In his book about the Reibey family, von Stieglitz described how Mary Reibey, a high-spirited girl in Yorkshire, rode the squire's horse without permission, was arrested for theft, and sent to Australia. On the ship she met Lieutenant Reibey, and they were married and lived happily ever after. The word 'convict' was not used. In his centenary history of Charles Davis Ltd, Basil Rait portrayed the founder of the firm as a free settler. A.D. Baker did not admit that his subject, Richard Dry, was the son of a convict, merely saying that Dry's parents had arrived with the earliest settlers. Baker and another author, Kate Dougharty, both said at the start of their books that there had been too much dwelling on the convict system instead of pioneers' achievements. Neither mentioned it again.[11]

In 1952 John Skemp published his reminiscences about growing up at Myrtle Bank. His book, which spoke frankly about local people including old lags, caused some upset. Skemp did not mention that he himself was descended from a convict, but described his mother's family as free settlers from Norfolk Island;[12] Norfolk Islanders were also of convict origin, but Skemp did not admit this, and might not have known it. His mother's family had been respectable landowners, and therefore could not be of convict background.

Some writers romanticised old lags, now so far in the past. Alfred Burbury recalled that most of the old lags on his family property at Oatlands said they had been transported for poaching, though Old Major admitted to having stolen a halter. When people sympathised with him for having been sent out for such a petty offence, he replied, with a twinkle in his eye, 'Aye, lad, but there was a horse on the end of it!' 'They were all lighthearted old fellows as a rule and we liked them very much,' said Alfred. He recalled fondly how they all used to go off on the spree after payday, and come back much the worse for wear.[13]

Karl von Stieglitz had much the same view:

A good many of us can still remember the last of the lags in Tasmania . . . They did not seem to bear any sort of grudge against the system that had sent them out here and were a cheerful lot of old rogues full of yarns . . . and not overkeen on too much soap and water . . .

Some people used to keep a supply of clay pipes and plug tobacco for them, and second-hand boots were always in great demand, with a little tea and sugar. Most of them . . . were tramps, who spent their time wandering in blessed freedom about the country. And woe betide any fowls or ducks that let them get too close in quiet spots, where their squarkings would not be heard too clearly up at the house where they belonged.[14]

Ann Stafford Bird, daughter of a prominent politician, was raised in the Huon, and wrote a sentimental history of the area. It began by describing brave early settlers, overcoming hardship. But as well,

We all know the meaning of the phrase 'Ticket-o'-leave'. It was a brand, but not an irradicable [sic] one. Old Father Time uses a good eraser, and this phrase no longer calls up painful memories in Tasmania. It has faded out.

It is a pity that it has to come into this tale of the Huon River, but it is necessary, as these folks certainly took a great part . . . Most were good workers when treated well, and I am glad to say that later, their trials over, many were able to own their homes and farms . . .

Whatever their reputation had been in by-gone days, the majority of them made good and their many descendants are worthy and good citizens . . . Many of these people had been sent out through no fault of their own, and many of the wrongs they had committed were chiefly the result of the hard conditions of their life in England . . .

We particularly liked to talk with one old grandmother; I think she was a great-grandmother. To us she seemed very, very old. She had been a beauty, and her black eyes could still flash, though her face was weather-beaten and furrowed. She knew the history of all her neighbours far and near, and finished many of these tales with a slow shake of the head and a wink, which always meant that the rest of the tale was not fit for us to hear. Needless to say, she never referred to her own history, and we never asked questions, though we longed to.[15]

To these authors, convicts might have started out unfortunately, but made good; they either worked hard and became respectable citizens, or were amusing and interesting, perhaps omitting to wash, perhaps nicking a chicken or two, but bearing no grudge, a twinkle in their eyes, a healthy part of the community.

There were few negative comments about the convict system, and even fewer about convicts. The most notable came in Peter Bolger's *Hobart Town* (1973), based on his Master of Arts thesis. Bolger claimed that transportation effectively chose the inadequate. Most convicts were idiots, weak or deformed, work-shy, chronically ill; down-at-heel, shambling inefficients, feckless and idle. But 'convict spawnings' were rare, so at least they left few traces. Bolger gave no primary, or indeed secondary, sources for this by now extremely unusual tirade.[16] No one else wrote in a similar vein, and Bolger seemed to make little impact on the 'trivial offences' theory, which most people took for granted by now.

Overall, books showed convicts in a positive light, as genial rather than feckless or amoral, let alone evil. In *Tasmania* (1966), Michael Sharland provided the strongest defence. Time had mellowed the convict taint 'until today there is no semblance of it'. The system had been a blessing for Tasmania, 'as it achieved its purpose, the colonization and development of the country'. Now that it was seen in its true light as a great colonisation enterprise, and with the knowledge that many prisoners became good settlers, 'Tasmanians have no wish to hush it up'. Since the stigma had disappeared, there was even an aura of romance about it.[17]

A governor of Tasmania agreed. In his autobiography, Lord Rowallan described a pleasant time in the free and easy atmosphere of Tasmania in the late 1950s. Only once did he refer to the past. 'Of course there were some ghastly stories since Tasmania was a penal colony. Young men and women were transported to Tasmania for stealing half a crown. But life is strange in the way that good grows out of bad . . . Certainly the transported ones suffered through having been taken from their families, but in Tasmania they found opportunities they could never have had at home.'[18] Presumably Rowallan was summing up what Tasmanians had told him, and it was a typical view of the time.

In the 1950s and 1960s, as we have seen, only a few Tasmanians knew they were descended from convicts. Born in 1943, Vicki Schofield grew up in Smithton, and in the 1950s often visited her grandparents in

Longford. The extended family would sit round the kitchen table, with the kettle boiling on the wood-fired stove, and reminisce. Vicki heard tales of her great-great-grandfather, convict John Stephens, a blacksmith transported for stealing a cow. Her great-grandmother, in her nineties, told tales of seeing old lags sitting in the village square. At Christmas and Easter her husband, a butcher, gave parcels of meat to them. There was neither pride nor shame in convict heritage, recalled Vicki—it was just what had happened, 'all very benign'. Her grandfather was proud of his Irish heritage, and told tales of how his convict grandfather helped the Irish patriot convicts escape, so the convict heritage was tinged with anti-British dissent.

Another Irish family were the McShanes, who farmed the large property of Stonehenge, near Oatlands. Bob McShane, born in 1936, remembered his father telling the children about the convict ancestor—'but we had a different spin on it, that the original McShane came out for stealing hay from the English landlord. He was released because of good behaviour and he liked it so much that he sent for his two sons to come out, and they came out as free settlers, so we had the best of both worlds.' The family were quite proud of their convict ancestry, said Bob: his father told them that it was the English who should have been locked up.

A handful of people were researching their family histories and finding convicts. Hardly anyone did this before the Second World War, but in the 1950s and 1960s there was a little more interest, partly because research was slightly easier. Convict records had been kept by the Chief Secretary's Department and then the Supreme Court, in no order, on the floor in a dusty vault. Determined researchers could consult them, but without indexes it was hard to find specific information. In 1951 the government set up the State Archives as part of the State Library, and it took over the convict records—but they were not for everyone to read. In 1961 a television program reported that an American scholar had arrived to study records about convicts. Questions were asked in parliament about the right of foreign scholars to read records about people whose descendants might still be living, and the Tasmanian Library Board restricted access. Researchers had to apply for permission to read the records, stating what they wanted to read and why, and they had to be bona fide students engaged in research of historical value (that is, not family historians).

In 1963 the Board decided that it would vet publications based on the records, after Lloyd Robson from the Australian National University asked to publish names in his thesis on the origins of convicts. Certainly not! said the Board.

In 1970 Peter Bolger was permitted to consult the convict records for his thesis about the history of Hobart. In 1972 he asked if he could include names of convicts in the published version. The Board refused, but by now it was losing ground. In 1971 it allowed the Genealogical Society of the Church of Jesus Christ of Latter-Day Saints (Mormons) to microfilm the records, as long as the Church did not use the information to cause embarrassment to any living person (an unenforceable restriction, since the Mormons were based in America) and gave the State Archives a copy of the microfilm. Now researchers could not harm the original records. The Archives staff compiled an index, and Peter Eldershaw, the State Archivist, wrote a guide. Research was now easier, and more comprehensive as more records were acquired. In 1976 seven members of the Archives staff petitioned to remove what they described as needless censorship, by lifting the restrictions. A year later the Board agreed. Finally the convict records were more accessible, though restrictions were lifted only gradually. In the early 1980s researchers had no direct access to the records; staff looked up items for them.

These restrictions were put in place partly to dampen the enthusiasm of family historians. Many archivists looked down on them, seeing them as amateurs poking about for their own amusement rather than 'proper' historians. Family history was not yet a common interest, but did exist, with genealogical societies founded in New South Wales as long before as 1932 and in Victoria ten years later. There was none in Tasmania, but people were allowed to undertake research if they were acceptable to those in charge: Peter Eldershaw, and Geoffrey Stilwell, librarian and archivist, who had a passion for Tasmanian history. They were well aware that some families had convict antecedents, said Jill Salmon, who worked in the Archives from 1961. 'Geoffrey used to say, "We know what we know, don't we, Jill?"' He was smug about it.' His friends remember occasional parties when, with much enjoyment, he would tell people of their convict ancestry.[19] Others were more circumspect: Kevin Green, who also worked in the Archives, recalled Peter Eldershaw worrying about whether to inform someone that the person he was asking about had been a convict. He decided that since this information had not been asked for, he should not divulge it—it was an extremely touchy topic, commented Kevin.[20]

Henry Allport, the bibliophile, without a drop of convict blood himself, was said to keep a list of people descended from convicts. He left his house and contents to be set up as the Allport Library and Museum of Fine Arts, but when his belongings were catalogued after his death in 1965, no such list was found. Present-day staff thought Allport's relatives would have destroyed it—'it would have been the first to go,' commented the Allport Librarian, Marian Jamieson.[21]

In 1960 Christopher Koch was given a temporary job in the Archives. 'Like many other Tasmanians, I was innocent of any serious knowledge of the history of my own island,' Koch wrote. 'That past—still so close to us—was full of curious gaps. It was a past which many Tasmanians still did not want to know about, in 1960, for fear of disturbing an ancestor in chains.'

> My mother led us to believe that her family tree contained no convicts—
> those ancestors whom Tasmanians most dreaded to discover. I asked her
> several times if she could be sure of this; after all, convict ancestors were
> to be found in a great many families that had settled here before 1850.
> Her eyes would widen, her lips would purse, and she would deny it with
> the same indignation she would have shown had I suggested she was a
> criminal herself. *No!* Her family was entirely respectable.
>   She probably believed it.

The family history Christopher was told concentrated on the aristocratic Devereux family, whose pedigree went back to a cousin of William the Conqueror.

Once working in the Archives, Koch looked up his own family history. 'I boasted to Geoffrey that my family contained no convicts; since then, my cousin Wendy has discovered Margaret Meara, an Irish maternal great-great-grandmother who was transported from Tipperary for theft at the age of twenty, in 1845. I feel sure Geoffrey knew about her, but was too polite to say so. When I confessed recently,' said Koch, writing in 1992, 'he merely said quietly: "I knew about the Youngs". This, I've found, is another branch containing a felon.'

Koch continued:

> The Hidden Convict has been until recently the ghost at the feast for many Tasmanians. He (or she) was hidden by our parents and grandparents with great cunning: and this made the giant convict registers in the [Archives] a source of scandalous fascination for me. Like a secret agent, while Geoffrey and Peter smiled knowingly, I pored over the records of transported felons whose contemporary descendants were business leaders in the town, or had been at school with me.

People who found convict ancestors were sometimes upset, recalled Koch. Once the staff and some distinguished visitors stayed behind in the Archives after it closed, enjoying a drink or two:

> The evening wore on. Geoffrey [Stilwell] appeared as sober as Geoffrey always does, drinking or no; but nobody else did. And Geoffrey confided to me that if Mr Justice Crisp looked somewhat bemused and preoccupied, it was because his Honour had made a fatal decision, about half an hour ago: he had decided to check the convict registers. His Honour had been entirely confident that the Crisp family was untainted by what used to be called the Stain, but he just wanted to make sure. This, Geoffrey was inclined to point out, was generally a big mistake, if you wanted to believe . . . that you were felon-free, and it proved to be so in this case. Mr Justice Crisp had discovered his convict forebear Samuel Crisp, transported for sheep-stealing.
>
> A little later, we noticed that the judge had disappeared. Nobody was very concerned except Geoffrey, who did not like the idea of this distinguished visitor wandering in the tunnels [of the Archives], perhaps lost, and so went in search of him. A short time later, Geoffrey hurriedly reappeared, looking very agitated, waving his hands, and delivering one of his most memorable lines. 'Quick! Quick! His Honour has collapsed among the Arthur papers!'[22]

Geoffrey Stilwell had already discovered that he was descended from a convict. Kevin Green, who was working in the Archives, recalled how one morning, Geoffrey silently laid the evidence before Peter Eldershaw. Peter read it, and said, 'To be transported for stealing a loaf of bread is one thing, but malicious slaying is going too far.' Geoffrey might have seen a convict ancestor as something of a joke, but Geoffrey's family did not. An aunt-by-marriage wrote to him in horror, alluding to her husband Tom (born in 1907) and son Tommy, Geoffrey's uncle and cousin:

Dear Geoff,

This is not an easy letter to write, it is also one that I feel must be written. We all appreciate that your overriding interest is delving into the past & presumably you have every right to do so, but why not consider the feelings of people living in the present & the future.

If, as one has been told, you have 'dug up' some rather unsavoury facts about Tom's grandfather, I think it was a very mistaken idea ever to tell Tommy—he may at the moment find it all rather amusing but when he marries & has a family he may look on it in a very different light.

He mentioned all this business the other night after he had seen you, & I think was rather shocked to find the effect it had on his father. For anyone like Tom who has devoted most of his life in the interests of his family & also taken a pride in his name, it was about the most rotten thing that could have happened. It has really hit him very hard. The harm has been done, but surely Geoff it would be possible for you to drop the whole affair—<u>at least I am asking you never to mention it to anyone again</u> & I hope Tommy has the sense not to either.

Tom has not seen this letter, & I rely on you to keep it to yourself.

I feel very bitterly about the matter because of the effect it has had on Tom,

Will not say any more,
Sincerely,
Mary[23]

So in 1964 this middle-aged couple considered discovering a convict in the family tree absolutely devastating, and wanted it never mentioned again, but their son found it amusing. Note that Mary never mentions the dreadful word, as nimbly as any nineteenth-century Tasmanian.

Others reacted in a similar way. In 1944 Alfred Burbury wrote the 62-page 'Burbury Chronicles', not for publication—but even so, Thomas Burbury, the founder of the dynasty, was given a new story. According to the Chronicles he was born in 1808 (1809 actually) into a yeoman family, and 'in 1832 he came with his wife Mary and infant daughter to V.D. Land on the ship Gulnare, 330 tons'. Not so—in reality Thomas arrived on the *York* as a convict in 1832, with Mary and the baby following on the *Gulmare* in 1833. Did Alfred know about his convict background? Mary Ramsay (née Burbury), from a later generation, thinks he did not; some family members did, some didn't, and these accepted the *Gulmare* myth as the truth.

In 1956 Wynifred Sinclair (née Burbury), living in Melbourne and therefore distant from the family reaction, started to write a biography of Thomas Burbury. 'Can't that woman be stopped?' demanded several older Burburys. They were devastated when she reported that Thomas had been a convict, and Mary Ramsay thinks they didn't want to know. Her mother told her that an acquaintance, Ian Gibson, used to imply that the Burburys had a shady past, 'and much to my joy we later found out that the Stanfields from whom he was descended and the Gibsons did too,' wrote Mary. At this period most people were extremely upset if convict ancestors were discovered.[24]

One day in 1959 Warwick Risby, aged twelve, was in the office of his family's prosperous timber firm in Hobart. Ancestors' portraits on the wall caught his eye: his grandfather, his great-grandfather and so on. He started to ask questions about family history and, when answers were insufficient, began his own research. He found convicts—the original Risby had arrived with the First Fleet. 'Dad listened, with apprehension,' he reported, 'and my grandmother Gladys Risby told me, "Don't start telling people that, we're a respectable family." It was only later we found that she too was descended from convicts.'

People researching family history, let alone admitting convict ancestry, were exceptions. Archivists only encouraged researchers acceptable to them: people they knew, educated people. Others were not helped nearly as much, for the uncultured could not be let loose with the records, which they did not know enough about to interpret. History was for the upper classes, the people it was written about. This was a widely held belief among the educated in the 1950s and 1960s, and archivists, keepers of the record, tended to be among the most conservative. In any case, few people were interested in family history. Even when convicts were not involved, other family members often had the reaction: 'Why are you bothering with that old stuff?' In one family, when one young member started research, the matriarch commented, 'Why does she want to find that out? What's interesting about that?'[25]

When I was growing up in Tasmania, convicts were seldom mentioned. I was born in Hobart in 1949, though both my parents came from New South Wales. My father's family, the Pillingers, had grown wheat at Lake Cargelligo in the north-west for several generations, and we didn't know much about his mother's family, except that they were called Newland and had a house in Sydney called Terra Nova, which Dad translated from Latin as 'new land'—so ingenious of them to call their house after their name. My mother's father had been a soldier settler near Cootamundra, until forced by drought and ill health from being gassed in the trenches to give up his property, and all we knew about that family was that they had been Anglo-Irish. My maternal grandmother was the one most interested in family history. Staggeringly snobbish—her most devastating comment was that someone was 'C.O.M.', short for 'common', a word it was thought common even to say—she was proud of being descended from squatters. Descended was the right word in that this was several generations back and the soldier-settler period had intervened, but you would have thought that she herself was the chatelaine of a huge grazing property. She told us that we were related to William Charles Wentworth (*not*, she stressed, through his convict mother) and several other notable pioneers, and had a family tree which went back to the 1200s, starting with Lords but rapidly descending to Misters.

My parents came to Tasmania in 1949 and Dad, a vet, joined the Tasmanian Department of Agriculture. Dad had no idea his father's family originally came from Tasmania, and when he was posted to Oatlands, he was astonished to find a large photograph of the Hon. Alfred Pillinger hanging in the Town Hall, and the name Pillinger well known. As outlined in Chapter 11, in the nineteenth century they had a large property at Woodbury, north of Oatlands, and Alfred had been the local member of parliament, rising to become Minister for Lands and Works. We met distant cousins, who told us that the original James Pillinger had arrived in the colony as a surgeon on board a ship.

But family history wasn't important. Hardly anyone was interested in it, and it was never discussed much, except by people like Granny, and Christopher Koch's great-uncle, who thought they had something aristocratic in the family tree. Nor were convicts, and I never heard that anyone was descended from convicts. We visited Port Arthur in much the same spirit as we might have visited Stonehenge: a relic of a distant past which had nothing to do with our lives.

There was little Australian history taught at school. The government curriculum for primary schools for 1951 shows that Grade 6 learnt about Tasmania's early history, with convicts and land settlement mentioned as topics. Material about convicts produced for schools gave a brutal picture of floggings and harsh treatment. Did the writer of the curriculum think this would grab children's interest? Yet people who were at school then do not remember learning much about Tasmania's history. My class learnt a few lessons about Bowen landing at Risdon with convicts, then a bit about Governor Arthur, and that seemed to be it. 'We had to colour in pictures, here's a convict, a lion, a tiger, it didn't mean anything,' commented Jenny Jacobs. 'The focus was on Port Arthur and it all seemed so remote,' recalled Lorraine Wootton. 'We never considered that some of our ancestors may have been convicts and we weren't made aware of the high percentage of early inhabitants who WERE convicts.' The small amount we learnt about convicts was ancient history, in the past, nothing to do with the present. 'You never even thought to ask if you had a convict in the family.'[26]

There might still have been some sense of shame connected with convicts, but as a child I certainly didn't notice it. What stopped them being discussed seemed to be lack of interest. We never thought about them. Tasmania was progressive, with increasing industrialisation made possible by hydro-electric development. Everything was improving—standards of living, literacy, health, average age of death. Wonderful new machines kept appearing, like washing machines and televisions. Newspapers were full of happy migrants loving their new life, of progress and prosperity in the

Long Boom of the 1950s and 1960s. Convicts had nothing at all to do with this.

Many people who arrived as migrants in this period have similar views. 'I didn't have a clue about anything about Australia,' said Mary May, who came from England as a bride. 'I was just following my husband.' Ivan Sauer came to Tasmania from New Zealand in 1952, to a job at the Hydro Electric Commission. He visited the Hobart museum and Port Arthur, and thought the brutal side of the convict past was emphasised, with 'leg-irons, broad arrow suits and a ducking-box . . . It all seemed to be part of a distant past.' A colleague hinted 'that it was not always wise to pursue the subject at a personal level with some locals'. Kitty Courtney commented: 'When we arrived we were told that the convicts were lucky to come out here, that 90 per cent of them were successful, with opportunities they'd never have had in Britain.' The same as Lord Rowallan's remark, and probably what a great many other newcomers were told—Tasmanians' general opinion.

A few people did know more of the convict past. Margaret Scott emigrated to Tasmania in 1959 and related in her memoirs, written in 2000, that she found Hobartians 'inwardly wracked by various manifestations of the cultural cringe and by terrible fears—especially fear of the wild . . . of the convict past, of tales of sadistic overseers and cannibal runaways, but again, still more of what might be discovered in the family tree'. I find this surprising, as I can't remember anyone being wracked by terrible fears, and we loved bushwalking in the wild, but it is of course one person's perception. Audrey Hudspeth, who moved to Tasmania as a post-war bride, said she knew about the convict past and felt that Van Diemen's Land had a sinister ring, and friends wrote to ask, 'What are you doing, all washed up among the convicts?' But in Tasmania, like most migrants, she did not sense the presence of convicts.[27] Anyone who did, like Margaret Scott, did not say anything about it at the time.

14

OUT IN THE OPEN

As I was growing up, our family had no idea that any of our ancestors had been convicts. In 1976 I became interested in family history, and I wrote up my research for Dad's Christmas present as a short book: 'The Pillinger family of Tasmania'. I repeated the family story that the original James Pillinger had come out as a ship's surgeon, and first settled on Norfolk Island. When I came across a list that put him in an ex-convict category, I assumed this was a mistake—I knew James had been a surgeon, not a convict. Nothing else I found about any of the ancestors suggested they had been convicts, for once people were freed their convict past was seldom mentioned, except in a code which I could not yet understand.

Meanwhile a distant cousin of Dad's, Herbert Collis, was researching the family history, and discovered that our mutual ancestor, Jane Hadden, had been a convict. Not just any old convict either, no stealing a loaf of bread or pair of stockings, but transported for assault and robbery, described as 'turbulent', and in the colony a bigamist and possible accomplice in murder. Herbert wrote this up in another privately printed book, 'No Tears for Jane'. It revealed not just that Dad's great-grandmother had been a convict, but the Pillingers had been too. It turned out that the original James Pillinger, a convict, married a convict's daughter, Elizabeth; their son James married a convict's daughter, Sophia; their son George married convict Jane's daughter Mary. George and Mary fled to New South Wales and never mentioned either the word 'convict' or even the word 'Tasmania'. Dad, their grandson, had no idea that his family came from Tasmania, no idea of the four convict ancestors.

By this time, the late 1970s, it was interesting, even fashionable, to have a convict ancestor. Dad was tickled pink. He wondered if he could count Elizabeth's stepfather, also a convict, among his ancestors, loved the fact that Jane had been turbulent, and drew up a coat of arms displaying all the items his ancestors had been transported for stealing—ten silver cups, a silver watch, a pair of stockings and so on. Everyone who came to the house was shown it. There was a reunion in New South Wales for Jane Hadden's descendants, with a great throng turning up. Dad loved it. You could not imagine, he said, a more respectable, law-abiding, well-behaved, polite and proper group of Australians, all gathered to commemorate their descent from a convict transported for hitting a customer's head with a bottle and stealing money. Then it turned out that Dad's mother's family, the Newlands, were also descended from convicts—there had been a good reason to assume the name, and Terra Nova for the house. Dad had few if any Australian antecedents who were not of convict stock.

Dad adored it all, but my maternal grandmother, so proud of her descent from squatters, was appalled. 'I can't think why your father's so interested in all this,' she said to me. 'He should just leave it alone! Never mind, dear, there's nothing like that on *our* side of the family.'

In 1982 she died. Shortly afterwards another historian in the family discovered that her side, too, was descended from convicts—well-known ones this time, Henry and Susannah Kable of the First Fleet, who had had goods stolen on the trip out and initiated a court case to reclaim them. They won, establishing that convicts were people in the eyes of the law. We were all proud of this, but Granny wouldn't have been. Dad was keen to tell her that she too had the convict taint. 'As soon as I get to Heaven I'm going to find your grandmother, and tell her about Henry and Susannah,' he said.

'Dad, if you die in that frame of mind, you'll be shouting it up from down below,' I'd reply.

So three of my four grandparents were descended from convicts, and we had known nothing at all about it. Dad didn't think his father or mother knew either, since there was never any hint of secrecy, and certainly my maternal grandmother had no idea. By this stage, the 1980s, many people saw nothing to be ashamed of in convict ancestry. I didn't—it didn't even cross my mind to be ashamed. Far more shameful as far as I was concerned were my maternal grandfather's Anglo-Irish forebears, oppressors of the struggling Irish.

Thousands of Australian families were in the same situation, finding out about convict ancestry with interest and pleasure, even pride. How had this change in attitude come about?

As already discussed, acceptance of convict ancestry had been slowly growing. By the 1980s it was well over a century since transportation ended, and convicts were mostly great-grandparents at least, satisfactorily distant. Still, in the 1960s few people had been willing to admit convict descent.

The major factor in changing wariness to enthusiasm was the dramatic mind shift of the 1960s and 1970s, which saw respectability—formerly praised—as dull, and rebellion and independence as exciting, challenging oppressive authority. Gough Whitlam's Labor government of 1972 fostered many new ideas—equality for women, more money for education, universal medical insurance, recognition of Aboriginal land rights, assistance to the arts, free university education, and generally an acceptance of change. Snobbery went by the board, with the enterprising working class seen as more heroic than the selfish capitalist middle class. In this environment, convicts were praised as people who showed initiative in stealing in the first place, rebels against the oppressive British authorities—the more turbulent the better. History was moving from narrating the exploits of the elite to including everyone; all people had lives worth remembering, everyone was part of the nation's story. As well, youth enjoyed shocking the older generation—and what more shocking for these fuddy-duddies than a convict ancestor?

Growing interest in family history was a world-wide phenomenon. Many Americans (and Australians) became interested in family history after reading the book *Roots* (1976), or seeing the television program made from it, telling of an African-American's forebears. Family research was now physically simpler, with archives making records and indexes available, often on microfilm which was easier to handle than the original volumes. A higher standard of education meant people were better equipped for the complex job of researching their families.

From the mid-1970s family history blossomed in popularity all over Australia. Many people researched on their own, but looking up the family tree can be complicated, and societies were founded to provide encouragement and support. As well as existing genealogical societies in Victoria and New South Wales, more were founded in South Australia (1973), Queensland (1978) and Western Australia (1979). Membership boomed: the New South Wales society grew from 629 members in 1972, to 10,000 in 1987. The Australian Institute of Genealogical Studies was founded in 1973. In Tasmania, in 1978 a group of people met under the Institute's umbrella, and two years later the Genealogical Society of Tasmania was formed in Hobart. Branches were soon established in Launceston, Burnie, Devonport and the Huon, with good membership figures. The Tasmanian Family History Society, as it is now called, is vibrant, with many publications and other activities. All these societies have played an important role in the family history boom, not only assisting but educating their members, stressing the need for absolute accuracy in family history research.

The growing interest in general family history came to include convicts. At first people were tentative. Once the Genealogical Society set up its library and welcomed researchers, people flocked in. 'The most common story was that their ancestors had been guards on a convict ship,' said Maurice Appleyard, one of the librarians. 'It would nearly always turn out that they'd been convicts on the convict ship. We used to joke that the ship had five convicts and 250 guards.' But once the first researchers broke the ice and told their stories of convict ancestry, it became clear that most of these were nothing to be ashamed of. The overwhelming majority of convict ancestors were transported for minor theft which in the 1970s would have brought them a reprimand or a small fine, and while they might have had later punishments for being drunk, missing Divine Service, more petty theft or being out after hours, these were hardly disgraceful. They could even be turned into amusing stories.

An example of the change in attitudes is the biography of Thomas Burbury, which had created such a stir in the family when Wynifred Sinclair began to research it in 1956. It was finally published in 1979, and the foreword ran: 'Not so long ago there was considerable reluctance to reveal convict ancestry; indeed, in some families there still is'; but now Thomas Burbury's descendants 'chronicle his achievements . . . with pride, and justifiably so'. A few Burbury descendants were still unhappy about it, and some older family members were upset or annoyed to be told about convict ancestors. When a friend of mine told his father about their convict ancestor, his father replied testily, 'Well, you might be descended from a convict, but I'm not!' Lloyd Robson commented that when the first volume of his *History of Tasmania* was published in 1983, some people were upset at the mention of convicts. As time went by, these older family members died and convicts became more and more acceptable, so the number shamed by the knowledge continually decreased—though a few remain.[1]

The reason why few of these stories contained anything really discreditable was that only a minority of convict records contained anything shameful, such as violence, and on the whole, only the better-behaved convicts had descendants. Women ancestors were by definition wives and mothers—or at least mothers—and therefore praiseworthy. Male ancestors were the successful convicts, attractive enough to gain one of the scarce women as a partner. Those who scraped a living as labourers, became shiftless tramps or continued to commit major crimes like violent assault, rape or murder were not attractive marriage partners and mostly did not have children. With the vast surplus of men, women could choose partners who had a skill and could earn more, who were prepared to support a family. Many men missed out, and they tended to be the rougher ones. The typical story related by a convict descendant was not about such people: it told of a convict couple who committed initial minor offences and perhaps a few more along the way, then married, settled down, and worked as farmers, publicans, artisans or housewives as they raised their family—decent, law-abiding citizens.

People did not just write family histories, they were active in many connected areas. They visited family graves and former homes, all around Australia and in Britain and Ireland. They met distant relatives. At Hobart Airport in January 2008 I was chatting to friends who were there to welcome their fifth cousin. They had met on the internet, all descended from one eighteenth-century forebear, and she was coming from England to visit them. One of the forebear's sons was transported to Van Diemen's

Land, another stayed in England. How had their stories compared? I asked. The Tasmanian family had done better for decades, but now both enjoyed about the same levels of prosperity.

So popular did family history become that it engulfed the majority of Australians. In 1999 a national survey asked how interested respondents were in their family history. The answers were:

Very interested	42.0%
Somewhat interested	46.5%
Not interested	11.5%[2]

Many people wrote family histories. Thousands of stories were told. They showed convicts in a new light, as people, family members. When people discover an ancestor a bond develops instinctively: this person is part of my family. Virtually everyone writing about family, convicts or not (even, I have noted, academic historians), tends to look on the bright side, finds reasons for anything discreditable, stresses achievements and good points, sees everything in the positive light in which people generally view their relations.

This produced a new situation. Before family historians came on the scene, history books had mostly seen convicts not as ordinary people but as criminals, with only a few upper-class or political prisoners depicted as individuals. Academic historians had written about convicts under sentence, at least partly because this was much easier to research. John Williams the convict has mentions in several convict records, all the information on his period in the penal system collected more or less together. John Williams the ex-convict is part of the general population, one of a number of John Williamses. Family historians were willing, even keen, to spend weeks laboriously tracking him through the maze of possible records, working out which one was their John Williams. They showed John Williams not just committing offences as a convict, but marrying, having children, living in the community. Such convicts were revealed as normal citizens like anyone else—the first time convicts had been depicted in this way.

A good example of the difference family historians made is the story of Maria Lawley, a tattooed teenage prostitute transported to Van Diemen's

Land in 1844 for seven years for stealing a cloak, shawl and scarf. She had been convicted of a previous crime, and her behaviour on the ship out was 'bad and troublesome'. After serving her probation, Maria worked as a servant for various families, but was sentenced to hard labour for being absent without leave, for 'leaving her masters child while she went away with a soldier to have connex[io]ns with him', and for being pregnant. She obtained her ticket of leave in 1849. A historian merely reading Maria's convict record would be justified in classing her as unpromising.

However, Maria settled down. She married ex-convict Edward Walker and they had thirteen children, with Maria's first illegitimate child brought up in the new family. Edward worked as a shoemaker, and Maria was the local midwife. She was occasionally in trouble for disturbing the peace and using obscene language in the local hotel, but after she died in 1905, aged 87, the *Examiner* printed a glowing obituary, describing her as 'highly respected throughout the district', and leaving fourteen children, 129 grandchildren and 43 great-grandchildren to mourn her loss. 'Highly respected throughout the district': the harsh words of the convict record show no potential for this praise.

A point to stress about family histories is their accuracy. Some academics, particularly sociologists, treat family historians as fanciful, making up not only their convict ancestors' story, but even the link, relying on 'spiritual kinship' rather than research. In 1988 an academic historian observed that family history 'belongs, with its adherents, in the realms of the "great unwashed" and has no significance for real history'. Such academics need to attend meetings of family history societies, to understand that family historians never imagine, never fabricate. The societies' whole existence is underpinned by the need for accurate research.[3] Many family histories prove to be just as accurate as academic history, and academics praise them for illuminating areas where their own history cannot reach, so this condescension is fast fading, at least in Tasmania; in 2008 historian Babette Smith, who researched her own convict ancestor's story in *A Cargo of Women*, told me this was not yet the case in New South Wales.

Meanwhile, academic historians too were writing about convicts, and coming to much the same conclusions as the family historians. There was some writing in the 1970s, particularly about female convicts, who were shown as downtrodden victims, 'the slaves of slaves', having to conform to one of two stereotypes—the convict whore or 'God's police', domestic angels.[4] There was much more about convicts in the next decade, particularly encouraged by the 1988 bicentenary of white settlement: more books, films and television. The best-selling book was art historian Robert Hughes' *The Fatal Shore* (1987), a description of the transportation system. Hughes wrote it, he said, because he knew nothing about transportation: he had learnt nothing about it at school and no one ever mentioned it, because they were embarrassed by it. His research showed him a brutal system: a brutal life in working-class Britain, and a brutal legal system which condemned convicts to a terrible life in Australia, with starvation, hard work, injustice, floggings and general misery. Hughes emphasised the penal colonies, the appalling treatment. Women were rough, drunken and immoral; homosexuality was rampant. Van Diemen's Land was the worst of the worst, the convicts' hell, 'a new abode of misery'. Hughes did comment that most convicts were 'ordinary sinners' rather than debased criminals.

Finally Hughes asked: had transportation achieved the four aims the British had for it? It did not remove the criminal class from Britain, or deter criminals there. But it did reform convicts, because assignment was the most successful penal rehabilitation system in the British Empire; and it did colonise Australia.[5] This description of assignment is contrary to what Hughes showed in the body of the book, especially for Van Diemen's Land; if readers missed this page, they would have an almost entirely negative view of the convict system. Hughes, however, was quite sympathetic to convicts themselves, those ordinary sinners (as long as they were male). The overriding picture the book gives is of petty thieves ground down by a brutal system.

The other best-selling book about Tasmanian convicts, possibly challenging *For the Term of His Natural Life* as the most popular novel ever written about the island, was Bryce Courtenay's *The Potato Factory* (1995). Like traditional convict novels, it tells the story of individuals who rise above the brutalities of the system. In contrast, some modern novels depict the convict system as tough but controlled, an avenue to advancement rather than brutal repression, for example Matthew Kneale's *English Passengers* (2000) and Richard Flanagan's *Wanting* (2008), and in New South Wales, Kate Grenville's *The Secret River* (2005).

Academic critics disapproved of *The Fatal Shore* and detested *The Potato Factory*, but they were both extremely popular—though in Tasmania at least, they had little impact on the way people felt about convicts. Nothing was going to dent the general belief in the 'trivial offences' theory, which Tasmanians had held for over a century. Academic historians were beginning to accept it as well. Mostly working in New South Wales, they depicted convicts as ordinary people convicted of minor offences, caught up in a system which could be tough, but allowed them to have some control over their lives. Babette Smith and Portia Robinson showed convict women as capable and independent, overcoming their convict pasts to become respectable wives and mothers; other authors showed Jewish and Irish convicts in a similar way—like family historians, depicting their own groups of convicts in the best possible light. Marjorie Tipping wrote a huge tome on convicts transported on the *Calcutta*, the first to land in Tasmania. She became very sympathetic to 'my convicts' and she too portrayed them as kindly as she could. Other authors showed convicts as ordinary people with valuable skills who formed an efficient colonial workforce; working-class Britain transforming itself into the foundation of Australian society. Hamish Maxwell-Stewart depicted even convicts at the penal station at Macquarie Harbour, traditionally seen as irreclaimable villains, as ordinary people to be viewed sympathetically.[6]

Many people celebrate convict ancestry. In about 2000 John Cameron started the convict brick trail in Campbell Town, whereby people pay to have a brick inscribed with their convict ancestor's details laid as part of a trail. John reported that convict descendants sponsoring bricks come from all over Australia, and from New Zealand, the United States, Canada, Britain, South Africa, Zimbabwe, Holland and Sweden. Convict descendants have even penetrated the nobility, and include a Scottish Baroness.

Women convicts in particular have evoked a positive reaction. Notably sympathetic is Christina Henri, a Hobart artist who conceived the project 'Roses from the Heart'. Participants make and embroider bonnets to commemorate individual female convicts, 'with empathy for convict women who endured much', and Henri aims to gather 25,000 bonnets, one for each woman transported to Australia. This has caught the imagination of thousands of people. In 2009, for example, Christina attended a Blessing of the Bonnets ceremony in Lesmurdie in Western Australia, where a group adopted a shipload of women and made a bonnet for each. 'A few of those sewing bonnets reported physical and emotional experiences of bonding with their convict woman, such as a sense of being watched, or a feeling of a gentle touch,' reported Henri. 'There was a general consensus within the group that the girls were guiding their progress.' No mention of prostitutes, degradation or anything negative: Henri's female convicts are all heroines, with even a hint of sainthood. By mid-2009 she had 14,500 bonnets, like John Cameron not only from English-speaking countries round the world but from places as far removed from Tasmania's convict heritage as Europe and Africa.[7]

The result of family history, academic work, novels and television is that convicts came into mainstream discussion about Australia's past, not just in universities but in the general population. With so many family histories being told, and so many convict couples having hundreds if not thousands of descendants, a huge number of Australians could read about convict ancestors portrayed positively as family members. Many people in high positions were acknowledged as descended from convicts, such as Australia's prime minister, Kevin Rudd. In Tasmania, three recent high-profile office-holders, governor William Cox, premier Paul Lennon and Hobart lord mayor Rob Valentine, were all descended from convicts.

As research grew exponentially, a far higher percentage of people realised they were of convict descent. In the 1950s the figure might have been 1 or 2 per cent. In 1997 I undertook a survey of university students in Hobart—not the most representative sample, but the only group I could survey for free. Of 127 respondents, 20 per cent knew they were descended from convicts, and over half of these, 56 per cent, only knew through recent research as the story had not been handed down through the family. Such a small and unrepresentative survey provides only an indication of the situation; in a 1999 national survey, 14 per cent of people in the convict states (Tasmania, New South Wales and Western Australia) acknowledged convict descent, though since Tasmania had a higher percentage of convicts than the other states, the 20 per cent figure is probably comparable.[8]

In 2006 I undertook a larger, more representative survey, with 451 respondents. Of these, 36 per cent knew they were descended from convicts, the majority, 61 per cent, only through recent research. In a decade, the percentage had nearly doubled, with many more having found out through research. Among those from outside Australia, 3 per cent were descended from convicts, born while Australian parents were overseas. Of those from mainland Australia, a quarter, 26 per cent, were descended from convicts. And of those born in Tasmania, almost half, 48 per cent, knew they were descended from convicts.

What has been the reaction to knowledge of convict ancestors? In 2008–09 I undertook a further, more detailed, survey, with 156 respondents. Half knew they were descended from convicts, and almost all of these, 85 per cent, knew through recent research. Most of this research, 80 per cent, was done after 1980. Nearly two-thirds of those who knew of a convict ancestor reacted positively to the news. Of these, 33 per cent were interested; 25 per cent were pleased, delighted or excited; 14 per cent were pleasantly surprised; and 7 per cent were proud. Fourteen per cent of reactions were negative, with people refusing to believe the news, shocked, horrified, or angry that they had not been told before. Nearly a quarter of those who had convict ancestors reported neutral or mixed reactions from different family members.

Comments varied. 'Some of the older generation were not pleased. I suspect some had known but had kept it secret. Other members of the family were pleased and interested,' ran one response. Another: 'Mum was horrified that her great-great-grandfather was caught for being drunk and disorderly.' 'Wonderful. A strange sort of pride!' 'I'm very proud to be descended from two convicts from Tasmania.' 'Surprise as the family denied any connection with convict ancestry.' 'Quite excited really. I think [my convict ancestors] were great.' 'Typical of THAT side of the family.' 'My mother . . . wasn't deeply upset but she wasn't thrilled either. They'd been vague about the family history.'

There was a clear-cut answer to how respondents perceived convicts. Seventy-five per cent believed they were ordinary people transported for trivial offences (rather than members of a criminal class, serious lawbreakers or urban layabouts who preferred theft to work). Even more, 94 per cent, believed that after their release convicts merged into the general population (rather than returning to crime or becoming shiftless tramps).

These surveys suggest that over a third of Tasmanians, and half those born there—about 180,000 people in total—know they are descended from convicts; and that few people see this as a reason for shame, but on the contrary are interested in, even proud of, their ancestors, whom they see as ordinary people who committed trivial offences.

The convict stain did not vanish overnight. Older family members in particular took some time to adjust to it, and it is still advisable to be careful when discussing this topic. In 2008 I attended a meeting of a Tasmanian local history society to talk about the convict stigma. The president and secretary were both of convict descent, and before the meeting, the secretary said to the president, 'Can't you find a convict in So-and-so's family? I don't want him sitting there looking superior.' I studied him while I was speaking; he was certainly not displeased to have no convict blood. Neither is my husband. Other people claim that there is still a feeling of superiority because of a lack of convicts in South Australia particularly. 'Proclamation Day celebrates South Australia being founded as a free colony. The freedom from convicts isn't stated, but it's understood.'[9]

On the other side of the ledger, some stories showed how despite the general secrecy, some families had kept convict stories alive. Archibald McDowell, a free settler, arrived in 1823 and took up land in the Bothwell district. In about 2003 one of his descendants was in the Bothwell cemetery, and noticed people putting flowers on his grave. She went over to say hello, and they told her that they were descended from a convict who had lived in the district. McDowell had been very good to him, helping him in many ways, for example assisting him to bring his family out from England. To honour this benefactor, the family was still putting flowers on his grave a century and a half later.[10]

The story of convicts coming out of the closet is much the same in New South Wales, as Babette Smith showed in her book *Australia's Birthstain*, but attitudes changed more slowly in Western Australia. There, wrote Bob Reece in 2006, convictism is still a dark secret; 'a kind of general amnesia has buried it from public view until now'. With the last convict arriving in 1868, later than the other colonies, there had not been enough time 'for romanticisation to replace embarrassment'. Convicts only gradually emerged in the open. In 1959 Alexandra Hasluck published a study of Western Australia's convicts, the first—and for many years the only—book on the topic, but few people acknowledged convict ancestors, and the 'best forgotten' tradition still ruled. Convict records were opened in 1975 (much the same time as Tasmania's), and in the 1980s more works about convicts appeared. Interest was slow to grow, though in recent years there have been more signs of openness, and in 2002 the premier, Geoff Gallop, spoke proudly of his own convict ancestor.[11]

With all the changes in recent decades, the cultural cringe towards Britain is virtually dead. At the Boxing Day test in Melbourne in 2006 England's cricket fans, the Barmy Army, began singing a chorus that ran, 'You all live in a convict colony.' This irritated the Australian crowd, but then some Australians began singing, 'You sent us to a sunny paradise.' There was a roar of cheering from the crowd.[12] I decided the convict cringe had finally disappeared when in 2007 Sheikh Taj Aldin Alhilali was widely quoted as claiming that Australian Muslims were more entitled to the country than those with convict heritage. Earlier, this would have resulted in howls of outrage, but in 2007 there was only amusement. As far away as Helsinki, the Sheep Thief Bar is decorated with a picture of a convict holding a sheep under one arm, a beer in his hand, welcoming patrons to come inside and be served by a genuine descendant of a convict.[13] When this is related in Australia, people laugh. No longer does 'Citizen' write to the newspaper expressing shock and horror.

An economist has calculated that in 2009, some 74 per cent of Tasmanians have convict ancestry, and that only sixteen babies born on the island in 2009 can claim to be purely of free settler descent.[14] Publication of this news will bring only interest, not shame. If convict blood did have any effect, Tasmania would be a different society—but clearly it does not. And as the economist wrote:

> the whole point of this exercise is pretty silly. International arrivals may well have convict ancestry, and the original settlers may have had as well. The concept that an individual is a convict, or possesses convict inheritance after seven generations, is ridiculous. We all have 128

ancestors at that level. If one of them stole a napkin, it is hardly worth losing sleep over.

But from the 1850s there have been claims that the convict past left Tasmania with a dark legacy. Visitors stated that Tasmania could not overcome its past, and many of those influenced by Marcus Clarke agreed that 'the shadow of the nameless wickedness and agony of those times' would never fade. In the 1920s, Graeme Thirkell thought that the 'brutal and brutalized past added a note of menace to the harsh and mysterious landscape'. Margaret Scott had similar feelings when she arrived in the 1950s, as described in the previous chapter. In the 1980s and 1990s there was more. The program to Richard Bladel's play *Transylvania* (1997) stated:

> Tasmania has been endowed as Australia's psychological sink, the country's instabilities somehow draining south, becoming more concentrated and noxious. Certainly many of Australia's ailments do seem more intense here . . . Have the spiritual wounds, so deeply inflicted here of convictism's brutal and deeply wounded masculinity ever healed? has our denied past had a devastating effect on our present?[15]

All through the play I was pondering this question, and that night saw the birth of this book. Plenty of people think there still is a dark stain. They can be divided into two groups: newcomers, who feel that the past was so dreadful that it must have an effect on the present, and novelists, poets and playwrights, like Bladel, Richard Flanagan, Christopher Koch, Peter Hay and Margaret Scott. Working in fiction, they're expected to give their imaginations free rein, though doubtless their opinions are genuine.

Growing up in Tasmania, I never felt any ill effect from the dark past; it was never suggested, and no one seemed to think of it at all. All people can do is state their beliefs, based on their own perceptions, for there is no concrete evidence either way. In education, crime, or any other measurement, Tasmania is much the same as elsewhere, and in any case it would be hard to isolate the convict past as a cause of current ills in a small, isolated and relatively impoverished community.

Many people in my surveys pointed out that if the past did leave a stain, it is more likely to be found in the British treatment of the

Aborigines rather than convicts. Distinct from all Europeans whether they were convicts or not, the Aboriginal people had lived in Tasmania for tens of thousands of years. While European settlements were small, Aborigines co-existed reasonably happily with the newcomers. They still had most of their hunting grounds and could continue their traditional way of life. But as British settlers moved into the midlands in the 1820s they took these hunting grounds for farming. When the Aborigines retaliated the Europeans attacked them—it was generally agreed at the time that the Aborigines were naturally a peaceful people and the Europeans were the first to use violence—and trouble escalated. By the late 1820s it was all-out war, with many Europeans determined to exterminate the Aborigines. Though the British government officially protected the Aborigines, there was little or no protection in fact, and when the remaining Aborigines were removed to Flinders Island in the early 1830s there were only a few hundred left of the 5000—or perhaps more—of 30 years earlier.

At the time and since, many people blamed convicts for their brutality towards Aborigines, but virtually the whole white society shared the same opinion about them, and the blame for their treatment ultimately lies with the British government, which allowed settlement in their land and made no real provision for their protection. The fate of the Aborigines is an enormously shameful legacy for the island.

In two surveys I asked respondents whether they thought the convict past had left a stain. People gave similar answers, whether born in Tasmania, the Australian mainland or overseas. In 2006, some 61 per cent of respondents believed that the convict system has had an effect on Tasmania today, but their answers focused on built heritage—Georgian stone buildings and so on—which was not what I had intended. Two years later I rephrased the question: 'Do you think the convict past has any effect on the Tasmanian psyche at present?' Just over half, 55 per cent, said Yes, but their descriptions of such an effect varied enormously. Their answers fell into 33 categories, the largest, in order, pride in the past; 'questioning authority'; 'it makes us different'; 'determination'; and 'low self-esteem'. From both surveys, I would conclude that over half of Tasmania's population think the convict past still affects the island, providing built heritage, pride in the past and different, interesting history. Few people mentioned any negative effect.

Some people are vehement that there is no stain, just like the people I surveyed who had been born in the 1920s and 1930s. In May 2008 I gave a course based on this book to a University of the Third Age class. I asked members whether they thought Tasmania's past had left a stain. Their answers were probably influenced by my scepticism, but of the sixteen who had migrated to Tasmania, fifteen said no, and one yes, though because of Aborigines not convicts. Of the twelve born and bred in Tasmania, none thought there was a stain—and several were adamant about it. 'There's no dark past. No more than elsewhere.' 'It's a manufactured thing.' 'It's subjective—it depends on the individual.' One class member described how she had taken her mother to visit Port Arthur. 'I was thinking, "Isn't this gorgeous", while she was saying, "Oh, I feel the pain and the tragedy!" It all depends on your own perception.'

What has the effect of convicts been on Tasmania? It has always had some: for a start, convicts and their descendants have always formed about three-quarters of the white population. This has little impact on the population generally: there is no discernible difference between those of convict descent and others. Its main consequence is on individuals, giving them an interest, perhaps a pride, occasionally still shame.

Tasmania was formed as a convict colony: without convicts we would not be here, or at least not in this form. Convicts formed much of the labour force in the transportation period and later, building those magnificent Georgian mansions and public edifices. Convicts were among those who killed Aborigines, though ultimate responsibility for this must rest with British government policy. Many convicts started businesses and farms which helped Tasmania to prosper.

Once transportation ended in 1853, and allowing a decade or so for many convicts to go to the mainland or settle down in Tasmania, convicts had almost no effect in practical terms. After they were pardoned most returned to the ordinary working-class habits of life they had before they were convicted, and were much the same as the working class in any British community, toiling to support themselves and their families, settled, socialised, perhaps committing a few offences but nothing major. Tasmania quickly became a quiet, law-abiding community, much the same as any other.

There was however the stigma of being a convict colony, which most colonists felt acutely. They did their best to negate it by ignoring it, by denying the convict past, by hiding the evidence of any living person's descent from convicts and by refusing to allow for a second that the convict past had any connection with the present. This policy worked amazingly well. By the 1920s, and perhaps earlier, people in Tasmania took little notice of convicts, and when they did, most showed sympathy and interest—as long as convicts were seen as in the past, nothing to do with the present. By the 1950s convicts were only a vague past presence, useful as a lure for tourists.

From the 1970s there was a new interest in convicts. Now that there was little shame involved, that the convict stigma had really gone, people were pleased to acknowledge them. Family historians were finding them in their family trees and talking about them with pride. Academics were studying them. Novelists were writing about them. Convict tourism thrives. Genealogical tourism is growing. Tasmania must be the only community in the entire world with such a large proportion of the population descended from criminals—and proud of it. Tasmania is now known for its convict past, and this heritage is viewed not with contempt, or as a cause for shame, but with great interest. The convict past gives Tasmania a unique identity.

APPENDIX 1

HOW MANY CONVICTS LEFT VAN DIEMEN'S LAND?

O fficial figures in *Statistics of Tasmania* show that 21,437 ex-convicts left Van Diemen's Land in the nine years from 1847 to 1855. Before 1824 the convict population was small, though some left the island. A conservative estimate: if an average of 300 a year left between 1824 (when convicts started to arrive in larger numbers) and 1837, then 1000 a year between 1838 (when Victoria was settled) and 1846, these figures plus 21,437 give a grand total of 34,637, or 48 per cent of all convicts, leaving the island. This is a minimum, for more convicts left illegally, especially once Victoria was settled.

At the end of 1853, when transportation to Van Diemen's Land ended, all 72,500 convicts had arrived, and 19,000 were still under sentence. This left 53,500 who had died in the system or been freed. If 10 per cent never left the system, 90 per cent had: approximately 48,000. Many would have died—those who arrived before 1820 would have been elderly by then—but since half the convicts had arrived in the previous decade, and about a quarter in the 1830s, most would still have been relatively young.

In 1853 Van Diemen's Land contained 22,000 free adults, both 'always free' and ex-convict. Of these, approximately 16,000 were ex-convicts. This means that 32,000 convicts (48,000 minus 16,000) had either died or left the island—60 per cent. Removing those who died in Van Diemen's Land before 1853 brings the total back to about half.

Both these tallies give an approximate figure of half of all convicts and ex-convicts leaving the island. More left after 1853, as more convicts were freed and Tasmania sank into depression, so perhaps 60 per cent in total left the island: Michael Roe, the doyen of Tasmanian historians, thinks the figure could be as high as 70 per cent.

APPENDIX 2
SELECTED PEOPLE MENTIONED
IN THE TEXT

For abbreviations, see 'Notes' (page 279)

Edward Abbott: *ADB,* supplementary volume, p. 1.
Francis Abbott: *ADB*, vol. 3, pp. 2–3.
John Adcock: CON 31/1/257.
Elizabeth Allen: CON 40/2/171.
Benjamin Allison: CON 31/3/881.
Mary Morton Allport: J. Richardson, 'A Hobart mistress and her convict servants', *THS*, vol. 10, 2005.
James Ames: CON 31/1/283.
Alice Anderson: CON 40/2/133.
Margaret Armstrong: CON 40/2/96.
Thomas Armstrong: CON 31/1/183.
Thomas Arnold: CON 31/1/311.
Jane Austen: CON 40/2/109.
Eliza Bailey: CON 40/2/619.
William and Mary Bailey: K. Edwards, 'The Reverend William Bailey: A wolf in shepherd's clothing?' *THRAPP*, vol. 47, no. 2, 2000.
Sarah Baker: CON 40/2/563.
J.D. Balfe: Anon [J.D. Balfe], *Letters of Dion*, Hobart, 1851, pp. v, vi, 4, 21, 22, 42.
William Barnes: P.L. Brown (ed.), *The Narrative of George Russell*, London: Oxford University Press, 1935.
George Barrett: CON 31/5/2237.

Nehemiah Bartley: N. Bartley, *Opals and Agates*, Brisbane, 1892, pp. 3, 7.

George Beard: CON 31/5/2102.

Charles Biffon: CON 18/4/2408.

William Bird: CON 31/5/2076.

Martha Bisgrove: CON 40/2/339.

Thomas Blacks: CON 18/22/1125.

Agnes Blair: CON 40/2/461.

John Blewitt: CON 31/3/2680.

Thomas Blimson: CON 31/1/887.

Elizabeth Bolton: CON 40/2/343.

William and Sarah Bond: 'The autobiography of Sarah Bond', chapters 1–3 (TAHO).

Sarah Bonner: CON 40/1/306.

William Bonnill: CON 31/3/2424.

Thomas Bonnor: CON 31/5/2319.

William Booth: CON 31/3/2971.

Percival Bosworth: CON 33/53/12406.

Peter Bourne: CON 31/3/2475.

John Bowen: A. Alexander, *Obliged to Submit*, Hobart, 1991, chapter 1.

Justice Bowles: CON 31/5/2062.

John Bowman: CON 33/108/25814.

John Bowtell: CON 31/5/1890.

Thomas Braid: CON 31/5/2162.

William Branton: CON 31/3/2432.

James Brown: CON 31/5/2240.

John Brown: CON 31/48/2266.

Mary Ann Brown: CON 41/6/726.

Thomas Brown: CON 31/1/495.

James Browning: CON 31/5/2187.

Thomas Bryan: CON 31/3/2578.

John Buck: CON 31/3/2533.

William Buck: CON 31/3/2789.

Thomas Burbury: W. Sinclair and E. Christensen, *Thomas Burbury: A pioneer of Van Diemen's Land*, Melbourne: W. Sinclair, 1979; CON 31/5/1779.

Samuel Burton: CON 31/3/2955.

James Butler: CON 31/5/2095.

Henry Button: H. Button, *Flotsam and Jetsam*, Launceston: A.W. Birchall, 1909.

Patrick Casey: CON 33/18/4306.

Martin Cash: M. Cash, *Martin Cash, the Bushranger of Van Diemen's Land*, Hobart: 'Mercury' Steam Press Office, 1870, 1880; J.D. Emberg and B.T. Emberg, *The Uncensored Story of Martin Cash (Australian Bushranger) as Told to James Lester Burke*, Launceston: Regal, 1991.

Esther Clark: CON 40/2/384.

John Clark: M. Tipping, *Convicts Unbound*, South Yarra: Viking O'Neil, 1988, p. 283.

David Collins: Alexander, *Obliged to Submit*, chapter 2.

Ellen Connor: T. Cowley, *A Drift of Derwent Ducks*, Hobart: Research Tasmania, 2005, pp. 294–7.

Isaiah Cook: CON 31/8/2354.

James Cooper: CON 31/6/506.

John Cronin/Glass: information from Lyndall Ryan; CON 33/100/23513; Departure Index (TAHO).

Sarah Cullen: CON 40/2/464.

John Davies: J.S. Levi and G.H.K. Bergman, *Australian Genesis*, Carlton South: Melbourne University Press, 2002; S. Petrow, 'Outsider in Politics: John Davies in parliament 1861–1872', *THRAPP*, vol. 50, no. 4, 2003; *HTA*, 15, 16, 17 April 1861; *Mercury*, 12, 14 June 1872.

Charles Davis: A. Alexander, *Charles Davis*, Melbourne: Charles Davis Ltd, 1998, chapters 1 and 2.

John Davis and family: P. MacFie, R. Morris-Nunn and J. Dudley, 'A Social History of Pontville', Brighton Council, 1995.

Rosina Davis: V. Maddock, 'A Lie Lived', in *Our Female Ancestors Discovered and Remembered*, Hobart: TFHS Inc. Hobart Branch Writers Group, 2008.

William Davis: CON 31/10/1019.

John Demer: CON 33/32/7633.

William Derrincourt: L. Becke (ed.), *Old Convict Days*, New York: New Amsterdam Book Company, 1899.

Thomas Dibble: CON 31/10/797.

Richard Dillingham: TAHO NS 157/1 6 November 1831, 28 December 1831, 10 February 1832, 29 September 1836, 4 October 1838, 27 November 1839; Victorian Births Deaths and Marriages no. 5446 (TFHS Library); CON 31/10/768.

Ann Dinham: M. Sprod (ed.), *The Whitehead Letters*, Hobart THRA, 1991, pp. 110, 242; CON 41/34/814.

Ann Dixon: CON 40/3/66.

John Dow: CON 31/9/393; *HTC*, 23 May, 5 September, 19 December 1834, 5 June 1835; K. Mackenzie, *Scandal in the Colonies*, Carlton, Vic.: Melbourne University Press, 2004, pp. 1–2.

William Dowling: M. Glover, The Dowling Letters, Hobart: THRA, 2005, pp. 51, 53.

Dunbabin family: T. Dunbabin, 'The Dunbabin Family' in *The Companion to Tasmanian History*, ed. A. Alexander, Hobart, 2005, p. 110; information from John May, Cynthia Alexander, Lindsay Whitham.

Henry Easy: H. Anderson, *Farewell to Judges and Juries*, Hotham Hill: Red Rooster, 2000, pp. 213–15.

John Eyres: CON 18/11/303.

William Farrier: CON 18/16/715.

John Pascoe Fawkner: 'Reminiscences of John Pascoe Fawkner', La Trobe Library Journal 1/3, pp. 5, 43; J.P. Fawkner *Reminiscences of Early Hobart Town 1804–1810*, Malvern: Banks Society, 2007.

Thomas Field: CON 31/14/797.

Flanagan family: M. Flanagan, *In Sunshine or in Shadow,* Sydney: Picador, 2002, pp. 55–6, 60–2.

Roderick Flannagan: CON 31/14/495.

Errol Flynn: Mireya Ranger, 'They were a roving lot: The YOUNGS of Sydney', *Australian Family Tree Connections,* 2009.

Ephraim Folley: CON 31/14/739.

William Franklin: CON 31/14/734.

James and Mary Freeman/Prince: L. Mickleborough, 'A "Freeman" or a "Prince"?' in *Pros and Cons of Transportation: A collection of convict stories,* Hobart: TFHS Inc. Hobart Branch Writers' Group, 2004.

John Frost: J. Frost, *The Horrors of Convict Life,* Hobart: Sullivan's Cove, 1973.

Alfred Gaby: Australian War Memorial records <www.awm.gov.au/research/people/honours_and_awards/person.asp?p=444883>; Pioneer Index (TAHO); V. Blair, 'Robert Whiteway', in *Pros and Cons,* TFHS Inc. Hobart Branch Writers Group, pp. 23–9; D. Elliott, 'Gaby, Alfred', in *ADB,* vol. 8, p. 607.

Hannah Gibb: CON 40/4/220.

David Gibson: *Lachlan Macquarie: Governor of New South Wales: Journals of his tours in New South Wales and Van Diemen's Land,* Sydney: Library of Australian History, 1979, pp. 181, 190–1; Tipping, *Convicts Unbound,* pp. 275–7.

John Goff: CON 31/16/1301.

Robert Gough: CON 33/7/1603.

Charlotte Graham: CON 41/5/381.

John Grant: CON 31/16/740.

William Grant: CON 33/16/3633.

James Gray: *CT,* 21 December 1852; *HTC,* 8, 11, 19 February, 1, 3 March 1853; *Mercury,* 22 January 1889.

Frances Gunn: Melville's *Almanac,* Hobart, 1833, p. iii.

William Gunn: information from Campbell Gunn; A. Alexander, 'Tasmania's unsung heroes', *THRAPP,* vol. 53, no. 2, 2006.

Jane Hadden: H. Collis, 'No Tears for Jane: A Hadden family history', Ashburton, Victoria, 1982; A. Alexander, 'A turbulent career, Jane Hadden', in *Pros and Cons,* Hobart: TFHS Inc. Hobart Branch Writers Group, pp. 60–1; CON 40/2/506.

James Halley: P. Macfie, R. Moris-Nunn and J. Dudley, 'A Social History of Pontville', Brighton Council, 1995.

Job Harris: CON 33/49/11556.

William Hartnell: CON 31/19/711.

Hayes family: <www.oldbaileyonline.org/browse.jsp?id=t18010415-145-defend1225&div=t18010415-145>; Alexander, *Obliged to Submit,* chapter 1; TAHO PRO 2732, 15 May 1801; PRO reel 87, p. 324; OBSP, V Sessions 1801, trial 486.

James Hevey: CON 18/17/2364; CON 31/21/1604.

Samuel Hivall: CON 31/19/884.

George Hobler: A.G.L. Shaw, *Convicts and the Colonies,* London: Faber & Faber, 1966, pp. 223–4.

Henry and Sarah Hopkins: A. Alexander, 'Henry Hopkins and George Clarke: Two Tasmanian Nonconformists', *THRAPP*, vol. 28, no. 3–4, 1981.

John Hornsby: CON 33/102/24162; Pioneer Index, TAHO; *Mercury*, 29, 3 April 1903.

Benjamin Hyrons: G. Squires, 'Benjamin Hyrons: shoemaker, convict, storekeeper, innkeeper and stage-coach proprietor', *THRAPP*, vol. 24, no. 2, 1977.

John Isaacs: Tipping, *Convicts Unbound*, p. 283.

William Jacobs: Tipping, *Convicts Unbound*, p. 262.

Arnoldus Jantjies: CON 31/24/550.

Mark Jeffrey: M. Jeffrey, *A Burglar's Life, or The Stirring Adventures of the Great English Burglar, Mark Jeffrey*, Sydney: Angus & Robertson, 1968.

Edward Jones: CON 31/23/407.

Charles and Ellen Kean: J.M.D. Hardwick (ed.), *Emigrant in Motley*, London: Rockliff, 1954.

Rosanna Keegan: Philip Tardif, *Notorious Strumpets and Dangerous Girls*, Sydney: Angus & Robertson, 1990, pp. 748–9.

Thomas Lafarelle: *HTA*, 14 March, 20 November 1846.

Alexander Laing: AOT NS 1332/12, pp. 1–2, 10, 44–5; NS 906 pp. 1, 3 (TAHO); CON 31/27/17.

William Langham: CON 18/16/909.

Maria Lawley: *Examiner*, 3 February 1905; CON 41/4/325L, CON 15/3 p. 325, CON 19/4.

Maria and Edward Lord: Alexander, *Obliged to Submit*, chapter 3; G.P.R. Harris, *Letters and Papers of G.P. Harris*, Sorrento: Arden Press, 1994, p. 30; D. Shelton: Arden Press, (ed.), *The Parramore Letters*, Epping, NSW: D. Shelton, 1993, p. 61.

James Lynch: CON 33/72/12846.

Michael Lyons: CON 33/69/16206.

Beatrice McBarnett: CON 40/2/545.

Thomas McBrian: CON 31/5/2289 (under B).

Stanley McDougall: Australian War Memorial records; *Mercury*, 2 February 2009; L. Robson, *A History of Tasmania*, vol. II, Melbourne: Oxford University Press, 1991, p. 335.

Matthew and Johanna McGann: information from Lesley McCoull.

Lewis McGee: Australian War Memorial records <www.awm.gov.au/research/people/honours_and_awards/person.asp?p=453165>; Pioneer Index (TAHO); Quentin Beresford, 'McGee, Lewis' in *ADB*, vol. 10, pp. 268–69.

James McHugh: *Advocate*, 14 November 1917.

McLachlan family: N. McLachlan, *Waiting for the Revolution*: Ringwood, Vic., Penguin, 1989, p. 6.

Bob McShane: interview with Bob McShane, 3 April 2009.

MacWilliams family: L. Frost, ' "Wished to get out to our mother": Convict transportation as family experience', *THRAPP*, vol. 53, no. 3, 2006; CON 40/9/74, 128, 129.

Leslie Maddock: information from Vee Maddock.

Worthy Mann: CON 31/30/858.

Maria: CON 40/7/81.

John Martin: *HTC,* 14 July 1854.

Emanuel Mellor: CON 31/32/1635.

William Millar: CON 31/32/2775.

James Miller: CON 31/30/906.

John Moody: CON 31/30/1132.

Christopher Moran: CON 31/32/2004.

Thomas Morgan: CON 31/31/1482.

Morrisby family: V. Adnum, 'A verbal history of Rokeby in the twentieth century', Clarence Council, no date, p. 246.

Julia Mullins: T. Cowley, 'Julia Mullins', in *Pros and Cons*, TFHS Inc. Hobart Branch Writers Group, pp. 30–4.

Harry Murray: G. Franki and C. Slater, *Mad Harry: Australia's most decorated soldier*, East Roseville: Kangaroo Press, 2003.

Charles Naish: CON 31/33/350.

John Naylor: CON 31/33/426.

Samuel Norster: CON 31/32/496; CON 31/33/384.

Mary Nye: J. Purtscher, 'Mary Nye: the whole truth and nothing but the truth, so help me . . .', in *Pros and Cons*, TFHS Inc. Hobart Branch Writers Group, pp. 79–81.

Mrs Thomas O'Donnell: Cowley, *Derwent Ducks*, p. 325.

William Parramore: D. Shelton (ed.), *The Parramore Letters*, Epping, NSW: D. Shelton, 1993.

Alexander Pearce: T.D. Sprod, *Alexander Pearce of Macquarie Harbour: Convict bushranger-cannibal*, Hobart: Blubber Head Press, 1977; K. McGoogan, *Lady Franklin's Revenge*, London: Bantam Press, 2006, p. 296.

Pillinger family: A. Alexander, 'The Pillinger family of Tasmania', 1976, unpublished manuscript; Collis, 'No Tears for Jane'; Robson, *History of Tasmania*, vol. II, p. 97; J.S. Weeding, *A History of the Lower Midlands of Tasmania,* Launceston: Regal Pubs, 1994, pp. 34–5; *ADB*, vol. 5, pp. 446–7.

Hannah and Matthew Power: Alexander, *Obliged to Submit*, chapter 2.

Augustus Prinsep: Mrs A. Prinsep (ed.), *The Journal of a Voyage from Calcutta to Van Diemen's Land*, London: Smith, Elder & Co, 1833, pp. 44, 105, 117.

William Quantrill: CON 31/34/24.

Janet Ranken: P. Clarke and D. Spender, *Life Lines: Australian women's letters and diaries*, Sydney: Allen & Unwin, 1992, p. 152.

Anne Reilly: CON 40/8/278.

Mary Ann Rennie: POL 16, 1 May 1848 (TAHO); A. McKinlay, 'Linking Families', in *Pros and Cons*, TFHS Inc. Hobart Branch Writers Group, p. 65.

Warwick Risby: information from Warwick Risby, 8 May 2008.

James Ross: James Ross, *Hobart Town Almanac*, 1836, p. 60.

Billy Rowe: James Fenton, *Bush Life in Tasmania*, London: Hazell, Watson & Viney, Ltd, 1891, pp. 48–51; CON 31/37/790.

Amy Rowntree: J. Ransley, 'Rowntree, Amy Casson' in *Companion to Tasmanian History*, ed. Alexander, p. 314.

Henry Savery: H. Savery, *Quintus Servinton*, Brisbane: Jacaranda Press, 1962, pp. 305, 332; H. Savery, *The Hermit of Van Diemen's Land*, St. Lucia: University of Queensland Press, 1964, pp. 35–7, 47–8, 191–217.

Jerome Savory: CON 31/40/2136.

Vicki Schofield: interview with Vicki Pearce née Schofield, 8 February 2009.

Ellen Scott: T. Cowley, 'Ellen Scott of the Flash Mob', in *Convict Lives*, Hobart: Research Tasmania, 2009.

Mary Scott: CON 31/38/160; Pioneer Index, marriages; Convict Index, Mary Scott.

Benjamin Shadbolt: M. King, *The Penguin History of New Zealand*, Auckland: Penguin, 2003, pp. 174–5.

William Shapton: CON 31/40/2094.

Joseph Shaw: CON 31/40/2325.

Thomas Sidney: P. MacFie et al., 'A Social History of Pontville'.

John Sinclair: CON 31/40/2192.

Mary Smallshaw: A. Alexander, *A Wealth of Women*, Sydney: Duffy & Snellgrove, 2000, p. 6.

Christopher Smith: CON 31/40/2331.

George Smith: CON 31/38/753.

John Spring: CON 33/45/96.

John Sturzaker: *Examiner*, 15 July 1843; information from Lesley McCoull.

Joseph Sutcliffe: CON 18/10/1083.

Edward Sweeney: CON 31/38/24986.

Alexsander Szurdurski: CON 18/4/2161.

Frederick Thomas: CON 31/44/1618.

Henry Tingley: M. Clark, *Select Documents in Australian History*, vol. 1, Sydney: Angus & Robertson, 1968, p. 131; Tasmanian Pioneer Index, TAHO, Tingley; CON 31/43/888.

Thomas Turner: CON 31/42/206.

James Undy: P. MacFie et al., 'A Social History of Brighton'.

Joseph Walters: CON 31/45/866.

'Old Watts': *Tasmanian Mail*, 7 February 1885.

James Webber: CON 31/45/756.

John West: P. Ratcliff, The *Usefulness of John West*, Launceston: The Albernian Press, 2003; *ADB*, vol. 2, pp. 590–2.

John White: CON 31/48/2266.

Thomas White: CON 31/45/860.

Andrew Whitehead: Tipping, *Convicts Unbound*, pp. 55, 321; Alexander, *Obliged to Submit*, chapter 1.

Eliza Williams: information from Meredith Hodgson, who is studying the Leake Papers, University of Tasmania Archives.

George Williams: CON 33/13/3138.

John Williams (convict): CON 31/48/2382.

John Williams (cook): J.G. Williams, *Adventures of a Seventeen-year-old Lad*, Boston: The Collins Press, 1894, p. 105.
George Wilson: CON 31/48/2593.
Withers family: V. Worthington, *Anastasia: Woman of Eureka*, Ballarat, 2006.
Lorraine Wootton: email from Lorraine Wootton, 9 October 2007.
James Youren: CON 31/47/96.

ACKNOWLEDGEMENTS

Thanks first of all to 'Founders & Survivors: Australian life courses in historical context 1803–1920', where I have been working as project manager for three years. Familiarity with convict records gained through the job has been of enormous assistance in writing this book, and analysis of material transcribed enabled me to reach conclusions in areas where this was previously impossible or very difficult. Thanks to the project investigators, particularly Professor Hamish Maxwell-Stewart and Professor Janet McCalman, who allowed me to use the material. In future years the project will release wonderful material and analysis: this book is only a start. Thanks also to the transcribers employed by the project for passing on interesting stories. For more information see the website <www.foundersandsurvivors.org>.

Thanks to the participants in the class I ran at the Hobart University of the Third Age on this book's topic, for their many interesting and useful suggestions, stories and comments. Thanks also to the members of the many historical and other societies I addressed: the Tasmanian Historical Research Association, Colonialism and its Aftermath, the Tasmanian Family History Society, the Female Factory Research Group, the Bothwell Historical Society, Lindisfarne School for Seniors, and the Order of Australia Association. The discussions after my talks were always helpful and inspiring.

Thanks to the University of Tasmania for allowing me to conduct two surveys among their students; the staff of the Archives Office of Tasmania, the Tasmania Library, and now the Tasmanian Archive and Heritage Office; and the University of Tasmania Archives. Thanks to all those hundreds of people who filled in my survey forms and made interesting and helpful comments, and to colleagues in the School of History and Classics, University of Tasmania.

Thanks to the staff of Allen & Unwin, the publishers: Elizabeth Weiss, Angela Handley, Katri Hilden and Karen Ward. They have all been wonderful colleagues.

A number of people read all or part of the book and made extremely useful comments: many thanks to Lucy Frost, Hamish Maxwell-Stewart, Michael Roe, Leone Scrivener, Dianne Snowden, Clive Tilsley, Chris Wilson and Ted, Cathy and Jude Alexander. Any errors are of course my responsibility.

For discussing ideas, alerting me to information, telling me their stories, lending photographs or providing general encouragement, thanks to all of the above as well as: Cynthia Alexander, Maurice Appleyard, Angus Bethune, Roma Blackwood, James, Lorinne and Peter Boyce, Nick Brodie, Frances Burgess, Bill Calver, John Cameron, Naomi Canning, Tim Causer, Eleanor Cave, Luke Clarke, Sue Collins, Henry Cosgrove, Craig Coultman-Smith, Kitty Courtney, Trudy Cowley, June Dallas, Margaret Davies, Fiona Duncan, Robyn Eastley, Caroline Evans, Lea Finlay, Martin Flanagan, John Fowler, Heather Gibson, Kevin Green, Campbell Gunn, Gwen Hardstaff, John and Barbara Hargrave, Tony Harrison, Christina Henri, Julie Hill, Rob Hill, Tim Hill, Meredith Hodgson, Caroline Homer, Brian Hortle, Audrey Hudspeth, Cheryl Hughes, Jenny Jacobs, Marian Jamieson, Andrew Jampoler, Marie Kays, Christopher Koch, Chris Leppard, Margaret Lindley, Lesley McCoull, Fiona MacFarlane, Peter MacFie, Beth and Lyndsay McLeod, Bob McShane, Vee Maddock, Rosalie Malham, Julia Mant, Tony Marshall, John and Mary May, Marian May, Jenna and Philip Mead, Eva Meidl, Leonie Mickleborough, Ian Morrison, Elizabeth Parkes, Jai Paterson, Bryan Pearce, Chris and Janet Pearce, Vicki Pearce, Stefan Petrow, Bernard Piggott, Joyce Purtscher, Cassandra Pybus, Mary Ramsay, Anthony Rayner, Eric Reece, Warren Reed, Henry Reynolds, Lyn Richards, Bev Richardson, Wendy Rimon, Maree Ring, Warwick Risby, Patricia Rubenach, Lyndall Ryan, Jill Salmon, Ivan Sauer, Pam Sharpe, Babette Smith, Tony Stagg, Grant Stebbings, Geoffrey

Stilwell, Sandra Taylor, Barbara Walker, Kate Warner, Jill Waters, Lindsay Whitham, Bob Wilson, Elisabeth Wilson, David Woodward, Richie Woolley and Lorraine Wootton.

Thanks especially to family members: to my father, mother and grandmother for their reaction to the convict past; to my aunt Jill for her memories of England in 1953; my niece Rebecca Aisbett for discussion about the situation in South Australia; my husband James for living uncomplainingly with convicts for years and providing many facts and figures; and my children Jude, Cathy and Ted for their enthusiastic support, wonderful editing and ruthless eradication of anything antiquated; and Ted for the mathematical calculations.

NOTES

Abbreviations used in the notes

ADB   *Australian Dictionary of Biography*
CC   *Cornwall Chronicle*
CT   *Colonial Times*
HRA   *Historical Records of Australia*
HTA   *Hobart Town Advertiser*
HTC   *Hobart Town Courier*
HTG   *Hobart Town Gazette*
TAHO   Tasmanian Archive and Heritage Office, State Library of Tasmania
          (also contains all CON records)
TFHS   Tasmanian Family History Society Inc.
THRA   Tasmanian Historical Research Association
THRAPP Tasmanian Historical Research Association *Papers & Proceedings*
THS   *Tasmanian Historical Studies*
TM   *Tasmanian Mail*
UTA   University of Tasmania Archives

1 Birth of a convict colony

1   W.C. Wentworth, *A Statistical, Historical, and Political Description of the Colonies of New South Wales and . . . Van Diemen's Land*, London: G. and W.B. Whittaker, 1819, pp. 120–5, 127, 129–32, 152–6.
2   W.H. Hudspeth, 'Experiences of a settler in the early days of VDL', Royal Society of Tasmania *Papers & Proceedings*, 1935, pp. 143–8, 151; John West, *The History of Tasmania*, vol. 1, Launceston: Henry Dowling, 1852, p. 81; James Backhouse, *A Narrative of a Visit to the Australian Colonies*, London: Hamilton, Adams, 1843, p. lxii.
3   Alex Castles, 'The Vandemonian spirit and the law', *THRAPP*, vol. 38, nos 3 & 4, 1991, pp. 110, 112, 118; *HTG,* 1 March 1817.

4   Robert Knopwood, *The Diary of the Reverend Robert Knopwood*, Hobart: THRA, 1977, pp. 180–2; *HRA*, vol. 3, no. 2, pp. 61, 65; *HRA*, vol. 3, no. 3, p. 337.

5   Samuel Guy, *A Van Diemen's Land Settler*, Sydney: St Mark's Press, 1991, pp. 7, 15–16; John Pascoe Fawkner, *Reminiscences of Early Hobart Town*, Malvern: Banks Society, 2007, pp. 69, 92.

6   Knopwood, *Diary*, pp. 85, 361, 447, and see 'Convicts' in Index, p. 700.

7   Knopwood, *Diary*, throughout, and see 'Groves, James' in Index, p. 708; Fawkner, *Reminiscences*, pp. 23, 25, 55, 78–80; James Boyce, *Van Diemen's Land*, Melbourne: Black Inc., 2008, p. 105.

8   Knopwood, *Diary*, p. 177.

9   Knopwood, *Diary*, p. 79; *HRA*, vol. 3, no. 3, p. 366.

10 Jane Roberts, *Two Years at Sea*, London: J.W. Parker, 1834, p. 125; James Holman, *A Voyage Round the World*, London: Smith, Elder, 1835, p. 395; Russel Ward, *The Australian Legend*, Melbourne: Oxford University Press, 1958, pp. 35–6; Knopwood, *Diary*, see 'Convicts' in Index, e.g. p. 55.

2 Convicts in Britain and on the high seas

1   John West, *The History of Tasmania*, vol. 2, Launceston: Henry Dowling, 1852, pp. 323–4.

2   J.F. Mortlock, *Experiences of a Convict*, Sydney: Sydney University Press, 1965, p. 68.

3   'Founders & Survivors: Australian life courses in historical context 1803–1920', for which I am project manager, gave me permission to use data transcribed, and I analysed 5048 convict records in CON 31/1 to CON 31/5 (male) and CON 40/1 to CON 40/2 (female), with the ratio of men to women the same as in the number of total convicts; Lloyd Robson, *The Convict Settlers of Australia*, Carlton, Vic: Melbourne University Press, 1965, chapter 3; Marian Quartly, 'Convicts', in *The Oxford Companion to Australian History*, Melbourne: Oxford University Press, 1998, p. 157.

4   Dianne Snowden, 'A white rag burning', *THRAPP*, vol. 56, no. 3, 2009.

5   Lloyd Evans and Paul Nicholls, *Convicts and Colonial Society*, South Melbourne: Macmillan, 1987, p. 108.

6   Analysis of 5048 convict records (see note 3). Robson, *Convict Settlers*, p. 67.

7   Quartly, 'Convicts', p. 157; James Moore, *The Convicts of Van Diemen's Land*, Hobart: Cat and Fiddle, 1976, pp. 91–3; Robson, *Convict Settlers*, pp. 76–8.

8   Founders and Survivors project, analysis of 5048 convicts from CON 31.

9   CON 31/3/2714; CON 31/7/2168; CON 31/3/3091.

10 Charles Bateson, *The Convict Ships*, Glasgow: Brown, Son and Ferguson, 1959, pp. 356–70, 381–94.

11 CON 31/40/2205; CON 31/5/2225; CON 31/2/725; CON 31/5/2224; CON 31/3/896.

12 Bateson, *Ships*, pp. 252–6, 283–7; Michael Roe, *An Imperial Disaster: The wreck of George the Third*, Hobart: THRA, 2006, p. 1.

13 Bateson, *Ships*, pp. 290–1.

14 Evans and Nicholls, *Convicts*, pp. 108–10; CON 31/3/2408; Surgeon's journal for the *Moffatt*, adm101–055–04, PA 290510.JPG (TAHO).

3 Convicts under assignment in Van Diemen's Land

1   George Arthur, *Observations Upon Secondary Punishments,* Hobart: James Ross, 1833, pp. 16, 23–5; John West, *The History of Tasmania*, vol. 2, Launceston: Henry Dowling, 1852, p. 326.

2   A.G.L. Shaw, *Convicts and the Colonies*, London: Faber & Faber, 1966, pp. 244–5.

3   Babette Smith, *Australia's Birthstain*, Sydney: Allen & Unwin, 2008, p. 198.

4   Hamish Maxwell-Stewart, 'Crime and health—an introductory view' in *Effecting a Cure: Aspects of health and medicine in Launceston*, ed. Paul Richards, Launceston: Myola House of Publishing, 2006, pp. 36, 44, 48.

5   Mrs A. Prinsep (ed.), *The Journal of a Voyage from Calcutta to Van Diemen's Land*, London: Smith, Elder, and Co., 1833, p. 111.

6   James Fenton, *Bush Life in Tasmania*, London: Hazell, Watson, & Viney Ltd., [1891], p. 48.

7   Shaw, *Convicts and the Colonies*, p. 226.

8   *HTC*, 3 May 1828.

9   Joan Dehle Emberg and Buck Thor Emberg, *The Uncensored Story of Martin Cash*, Launceston: Regal, 1991, pp. 73–4, 95, 109, 216, 218, 255; Peter MacFie, 'Dobbers and cobbers', *THRAPP*, vol. 35, no. 3, 1988, p. 112.

10 Founders and Survivors project, analysis of 5048 convicts; Lloyd Robson, *The Convict Settlers of Australia*, Carlton, Vic.: Melbourne University Press, 1965, p. 92.

11 John Mitchel, *Jail Journal*, Dublin 1854; this edition Dublin: M.H. Gill & Son, 1913, pp. 12, 218, 227.

12 Mitchel, *Jail Journal*, pp. 230–1, 242–5.

4 Convicts after sentence

1   Information from Hamish Maxwell-Stewart, Founders and Survivors project.

2   CON 33/11/2520; CON 33/37/9016; CON 33/49/11400; CON 33/23/5520; CON 33/22/5410; CON 33/21/5083; CON 31/1/1132; CON 33/55/13047; CON 41/31/1132; CON 33/82/19074; CON 33/17/3973; CON 33/78/18107.

3   CON 33/56/13156; 'The Vet' [J. Hornsby], *Old Time Echoes of Tasmania*, Hobart: [no publisher named], 1896, p. 15; John Frost, *The Horrors of Convict Life*, Hobart: Sullivan's Cove, 1973; June Starke (ed.), *Journal of a Rambler: The journal of John Boultbee*, Auckland: Oxford University Press, 1986, p. 12.

4   Hamish Maxwell-Stewart, *Closing Hell's Gates*, Sydney: Allen & Unwin, 2008, pp. 187–9: Frank Clune & P.R. Stephensen, *The Pirates of the Brig Cyprus*, New York: William Morrow and Company, 1963.

5   Charles Walch, *The Story of the Life of Charles Edward Walch*, Hobart: [no publisher named], 1908, p. xxxi; J.F. Mortlock, *Experiences of a Convict*, Sydney: Sydney University Press, 1965, pp. 99, 114–16.

6   Data collected by Founders and Survivors project; Lloyd Robson, *The Convict Settlers of Australia*, Carlton, Vic.: Melbourne University Press, 1965, p. 93.
7   Founders and Survivors project, analysis of 1 in 25 sample (7500 convict records).
8   James Backhouse, *A Narrative of a Visit to the Australian Colonies*, London: Hamilton, Adams, 1843, p. 495; J.C. Byrne, *Twelve Years' Wanderings in the British Colonies*, London: Richard Bentley, 1848, p. 64; Statistics of Tasmania, 1835–70, emigration figures, e.g. 1848, p. 5.
9   H. Butler Stoney, *A Residence in Tasmania,* London: Smith, Elder, 1856, p. 150.
10 Backhouse, *Narrative*, p. li.
11 James Fenton, *History of Tasmania*, Launceston, 1884; facsimile edition Hobart: Melanie Publications 1978, pp. 246–7.
12 Founders and Survivors project, analysis of 1 in 25 sample.
13 Alex Castles, 'The Vandemonian spirit and the law', *THRAPP*, vol. 38, nos 3 & 4, 1991, p. 110; Lloyd Robson, *A History of Tasmania, Volume II,* Melbourne: Oxford University Press, 1991, pp. 12–14.
14 Eustace FitzSymonds, *A Looking-glass for Tasmania*, Adelaide: Sullivan's Cove, 1980, pp. 172–3; P. MacFie, R. Morris-Nunn and J. Dudley, 'A social history of Pontville', Brighton Council, 1995, pp. 22–3; Ian Brand, *The Convict Probation System*, Sandy Bay: Blubber Head Press, 1990, p. 189; Robson, *History*, vol. 2, pp. 14–15; Edward Curr, *An Account of the Colony of Van Diemen's Land*, London: George Cowie, 1824, pp. 39–40; James Boyce, *Van Diemen's Land*, Melbourne: Black Inc, 2008, pp. 165–6, 222–4.
15 Boyce, *Van Diemen's Land*, pp. 181, 217–18.
16 A. Alexander, *The Eastern Shore: A history of Clarence*, Clarence: Clarence City Council, 2003, chapters 2–4; A. Alexander, *Brighton and Surrounds*, Brighton: Brighton Council, 2006, chapters 2–5.
17 *HRA,* vol. 3, no. 3, pp. 279, 365.
18 A. Russell, *A Tour through the Australian Colonies*, Glasgow: David Robertson, 1840, p. 7; Henry Widowson, *Present State of Van Diemen's Land*, London: S. Robinson, 1829, p. 64; Godfrey Mundy, *Our Antipodes*, ed. D. Baker, Canberra: Pandanus Books, 2006, p. 203–4, 213; Mortlock, *Experiences*, p. 88.
19 <www.ukonline.co.uk/thursday.handleigh/demography/life-death/life> [13 February 2008]; Rebecca Kippen, 'Death in Tasmania using civil death registers to measure nineteenth-century cause-specific mortality', PHD thesis, ANU, 2002, p. 64; Russel Ward, *The Australian Legend*, Melbourne: Oxford University Press, 1958, p. 34; Roderick Floud & Paul A. Johnson, *The Cambridge Economic History of Modern Britain*, vol. II; Cambridge: Cambridge University Press, 2004, p. 291.
20 <www.utas.edu.au/arts/conhealth/marriage.html> [9 May 2009]; Trudy Cowley, *A Drift of Derwent Ducks*, Hobart: Research Tasmania, 2005, p. 255.
21 Mrs A. Prinsep (ed.), *The Journal of a Voyage from Calcutta to Van Diemen's Land*, London: Smith, Elder and Co., 1833, pp. 112–13; H.P. Fry, 'Four letters from Hobart 1839–45', *THRAPP*, vol. 11, no. 1, 1964, p. 21; Louisa Ann Meredith, *My Home in Tasmania*, vol. 1, London: John Murray, 1852, p. 153; D.C. Shelton

(ed.), *The Parramore Letters*, Epping, NSW: D. Shelton, 1993, p. 23; William Stones, *My First Voyage*, London: Simpkin, Marshall, 1858, p. 156.

22 Cowley, *Derwent Ducks*, p. 294.

23 Jennifer Parrott, 'Agents of industry and civilisation: The British government emigration scheme for convicts' wives', *Tasmanian Historical Studies*, vol. 4, no. 2, 1994, pp. 25–30.

24 *HRA*, vol. 3, no. 3, p. 366; David Burn, *A Picture of Van Diemen's Land*, Hobart: Cat & Fiddle Press, 1973, p. 47.

25 Burn, *Picture*, p. 47; *The Times*, 3 April 1826; Mortlock, *Experiences*, p. 106.

26 Shelton, *Parramore Letters*, p. 45; *The Times*, 30 December 1823.

5 Convict and free

1 G.T. Lloyd, *Thirty-Three Years in Tasmania and Victoria*, London: Houlston and Wright, 1862, p. 3.

2 George Evans, *A Geographical, Historical, and Topographical Description of Van Diemen's Land*, London: John Souter, 1822, pp. 9, 26, 61, 79, 98, 121, 111, 122, vi; Charles Jeffreys, *Van Diemen's Land*, London: J.M. Richardson, 1820, pp. 3, 68, 121, 131, 135–6; James Dixon, *Narrative of a Voyage to New South Wales and Van Diemen's Land*, Edinburgh: John Anderson, 1822, p. 45.

3 James Boyce, *Van Diemen's Land*, Melbourne: Black Inc., 2008, p. 160; Hamilton Wallace to his father, 10 September 1825, *Fifteen Tasmanian Letters* (TAHO).

4 John Dixon, *The Condition and Capabilities of Van Diemen's Land*, London, 1839: Smith, Elder, p. 51.

5 Mrs A. Prinsep (ed.), *The Journal of a Voyage from Calcutta to Van Diemen's Land*, London: Smith, Elder, and Co., 1833, p. 45; *The Times*, 11 October 1824; George Russell, *The Narrative of George Russell*, London: Oxford University Press, 1935, pp. 50–2, 408; H.P. Fry, 'Four letters from Hobart 1839–45', *THRAPP*, vol. 11, no. 1, 1964, p. 21; T. Betts, *An Account of the Colony of Van Diemen's Land*, Calcutta: Baptist Mission Press, 1830, pp. 43, 47; A. Russell, *A Tour through the Australian Colonies*, Glasgow: David Robertson, 1840, p. 108; D.C. Shelton (ed.), *The Parramore Letters*, Epping, NSW: D. Shelton, 1993, p. 23; H. Butler Stoney, *A Residence in Tasmania*, London: Smith, Elder, 1856, p. 151; Henry Widowson, *Present State of Van Diemen's Land*, London: S. Robinson, 1829, p. vi.

6 Russell, *Narrative*, pp. 50, 408, 409; Charles Darwin, *Narrative of Surveying Voyages*, London: H. Colburn, 1839, p. 535; Prinsep, *Journal*, p. 52; Stephen Murray-Smith, *The Dictionary of Australian Quotations*, Richmond: Heinemann, 1984, p. 95.

7 Jane Roberts, *Two Years at Sea*, London: J.W. Parker, 1834, p. 127; June Starke (ed.), *Journal of a Rambler: The journal of John Boultbee*, Auckland: Oxford University Press, 1986, p. 11; *The Times*, 3 April 1826; David Burn, *A Picture of Van Diemen's Land*, Hobart: Cat & Fiddle Press, 1973, pp. 16–17; Lloyd, *Thirty-Three Years*, pp. 258–9; Widowson, *Present State*, p. 53; J, Syme, *Nine Years in Van Diemen's Land*, Dundee: the author, 1848, p. 133.

8   Prinsep, *Journal*, p. 63; W.H. Breton, *Excursions in New South Wales, West-ern Australia and Van Diemen's Land*, London: Richard Bentley, 1833, p. 462; Lloyd, *Thirty-Three Years*, p. 172; Boyce, *Van Diemen's Land*, p. 157; Louisa Ann Meredith, *My Home in Tasmania*, vol. 1, London: John Murray, 1852, p. 41; Widowson, *Present State*, p. vi.

9   Oliné Keese [Caroline Leakey], *The Broad Arrow*, North Ryde: Eden, 1988, pp. 80–5, 102–6, 300–1; in following paragraphs, pp. 88–9, 53, 28, 57, 78, 168.

10   Gillian Winter, ' "We speak that we do know" ', *THRAPP*, vol. 40, no. 4, 1993, p. 149; Keese, *Broad Arrow*, p. 88–9.

11   Boyce, *Van Diemen's Land*, p. 126.

12   James Calder, *Rambles on Betsy's Island, Tasman's Peninsula, and Forestier's Penin-sula*, Adelaide: Sullivan's Cove, 1985, pp. 11–13, 21–2, 26.

13   Alex Castles, 'The Vandemonian spirit and the law', *THRAPP*, vol. 38, nos 3 & 4, 1991, pp. 106–8; Lloyd Robson, 'Damnosa Haereditas?' in *The Flow of Culture: Tasmanian studies*, ed. Michael Roe, Canberra: Australian Academy of the Humanities, 1987, p. 96; Murray-Smith, *Dictionary*, p. 18; E. Daniel and Annette Potts (eds), *A Yankee Merchant in Gold Rush Australia*, Melbourne: William Heinemann, 1970, pp. 155, 69–70; Amanda Laugesen, *Convict Words*, South Melbourne: Oxford University Press, 2002, p. 203; Anthony Trollope, *Australia and New Zealand*, vol. II, Melbourne: Robertson, 1876, p. 128.

14   Castles, 'Vandemonian spirit', throughout.

15   Shelton, *Parramore Letters*, p. 67.

16   G. Boyes diary 17 July 1834 (UTA); Eustace FitzSymonds, *Mortmain*, Hobart: Sullivan's Cove, 1977, pp. 144–5.

17   *Examiner*, 2 November 1850; Boyce, *Van Diemen's Land*, p. 152.

18   G. Boyes diary, 8 May 1847 (UTA); E.M. Finlay, 'Making good in Van Diemen's Land: Robert Logan', *THRAPP*, vol. 40, no. 2, 1993, pp. 49, 70–1.

19   A. Alexander, *Blue, Black and White: The history of the Launceston Church Gram-mar School*, Launceston: the school, 1996, pp. 10, 13, 24; John Molony, *The Native-Born: The first white Australians*, Carlton South, Vic.: Melbourne University Press, 2000, p. 41; A. Alexander, *Obliged to Submit*, Hobart: Montpelier Press, 1999, pp. 49–51; A. Alexander, 'Independent schools in Tasmania', *THRAPP*, vol. 52, no. 1, 2005.

20   John West, *The History of Tasmania*, vol. 2, Launceston: Henry Dowling, 1852, p. 333.

21   *Examiner*, 10 May 1843, 19 November 1845; *HTA*, 11 April 1845.

22   *Statistics of Van Diemen's Land for 1847*, Hobart Town, 1848, pp. v, 10.

23   Marquis de Beauvoir, *A Voyage Round the World*, vol. I, London: Murray, 1870, p. 210.

24   *Guardian*, 13 November 1850.

25   J.F. Mortlock, *Experiences of a Convict*, Sydney: Sydney University Press, 1965, p. 92; Boyce, *Van Diemen's Land*, p. 159.

26   Alan Atkinson, *The Europeans in Australia: A history, Volume two: Democracy*, Melbourne: Oxford University Press, 2004, p. 72; *CC*, 26 May 1852.

27 Michael Sturma, *Vice in a Vicious Society: Crime and convicts in mid-nineteenth century New South Wales*, St Lucia: University of Queensland Press, 1983, p. 13; Brian Fletcher, *Landed Enterprise and Penal Society: A history of farming and grazing in New South Wales before 1821*, Sydney: Sydney University Press, 1976, p. 220.

28 Molony, *Native Born*, pp. 40–2, 54–9, 123–32, 178.

29 FitzSymonds, *Mortmain*, pp. 96–8.

6 The transportation debate

1 *HTA* 1844–1846, especially 2, 9 August, 11, 25 October, 6, 31 December 1844, 10, 24 January, 8, 11 April, 21 November 1845, 2 January, 3 March, 20 November, 22 December 1846; *Examiner*, 23 November, 18, 28 December 1844, 8 March, 7 June, 28 July, 1 October, 19, 26 November 1845, 3, 7, 14, 24, 31 January, 4 March, 3 October, 5 December 1846; A.G.L. Shaw, *Convicts and the Colonies*, London: Faber & Faber, 1966, pp. 298–9.

2 Michael Roe, 'Anti-transportation (of convicts)' in *Companion to Tasmanian History*, ed. A. Alexander, Hobart: Centre for Tasmanian Historical Studies, 2005, p. 19; Shaw, *Convicts*, pp. 302–3; James Boyce, *Van Diemen's Land*, Melbourne: Black Inc., 2008, p. 240.

3 *Examiner*, 1 July 1846, 14 August 1850; *CC*, 3 October 1846; *HTA*, 21 February, 29 July 1845.

4 *Examiner*, 23 March, 30 October, 16, 23 November 1844, 7 June, 19 November 1845.

5 Richard Davis, 'Denison, William Thomas' in *Companion*, ed. A. Alexander, pp. 102–3; *Examiner*, 10, 24 April, 8, 12 May 1847, 27 January 1849, 30 October 1850; *HTA*, 6 December 1844.

6 *HTA*, 6 February 1852; *CC*, 2 July 1851.

7 John Mitchel, *Jail Journal*, Dublin, 1854; this edition Dublin: M.H. Gill & Son, 1913, pp. 244–5, 286.

8 *CT*, 1 June, 20 July, 3 September 12 October, 2 November 1852; Babette Smith, *Australia's Birthstain*, Sydney: Allen & Unwin, 2008, p. 234.

9 *HTA*, 21 February 1845, 4, 11, 18 May 1847; *Examiner*, 12 May 1847; *Mercury*, 10 July 1878.

10 *Guardian*, 22 May, 7 August, 24 November 1847.

11 *Examiner*, 22 May, 25, 30 October, 3, 6, 24 November, 11 December 1847; *HTA*, 2 July 1847; *CC*, 16 October 1847; *HTA*, 5 November 1847.

12 John West, *The History of Tasmania*, vol. 1, Launceston: Henry Dowling, 1852, pp. 247–8, 270, 278; *Examiner*, 27 May 1848, 5 February, 19 April 1851.

13 *Examiner*, 28 October, 22, 25 November, 27 December 1848, 14 August, 7 September 1850; *HTA*, 3 November, 5 December 1848.

14 *Examiner*, 25 November 1848, 6, 27 January, 3 February 1849.

15 *Examiner*, 2, 12 January, 12 September 1850; West, *History*, vol. 1, p. 295; Shaw, *Convicts*, pp. 335–6, 342; *HTA*, 5 December 1848, 14 August 1849, 20 April, 19 October 1852, 11 August 1853; *CC*, 25 August 1849, 31 August 1850; Anon [J.D. Balfe], *Letters of Dion*, Hobart: *Advertiser*, 1851.

16 *CC, HTA* and *CT* were virtually silent; *HTC,* 2, 5, 9 April 1850; *Guardian,* 6 April 1850.
17 *Guardian,* 6 April 1850; *HTC,* 10 April 1850; *Examiner,* 10, 13 April 1850.
18 West, *History,* vol. 1, p. 297; *Examiner,* 28 October 1848; Michael Roe, 'The establishment of local self-government in Hobart and Launceston', *THRAPP,* vol. 14, no. 1, 1966, p. 37.
19 *Guardian,* 30 January 1850; *HTC,* 2, 6 February 1850; Michael Roe, *Quest for Authority in Eastern Australia,* Parkville: Melbourne University Press, 1965, p. 101.
20 *Guardian,* 2, 6, 9 February 1850; *Examiner,* 30 January, 9, 13 February 1850.
21 *Guardian,* 31 July, 7, 14, 23 September, 2 October, 6 November, 2, 4 December 1850, 1 January 1851, 9 October 1852.
22 *Examiner,* 14, 21, 31 August, 7, 11, 21 September 1850; *Guardian,* 28 September, 2, 9 October 1850.
23 *Mercury,* 22 January 1889; CON 33/48/11275; CSD 7/49/D1009 (TAHO); M. Glover, *The Dowling Letters,* Hobart: THRA, 2005, p. 63; West, *History,* vol. 1, p. 297; *Examiner,* 14 November 1850; *CT,* 19 November 1852.
24 *Guardian,* 12, 16, 23 October, 2 November 1850.
25 *HTC,* 30 October 1850; *Examiner,* 2, 14 November 1850.
26 Shaw, *Convicts,* p. 343; *Guardian,* 13, 27 November, 4 December 1850; *HTC,* 13 November 1850.
27 *Guardian,* 19 February, 26 March, 26 April, 24 May 1851.
28 *Examiner,* 14 August, 16, 30 October 1850, 8, 11, 15, 18 January 1851.
29 Godfrey Mundy, *Our Antipodes,* ed. D. Baker, Canberra: Pandanus Books, 2006, p. 240–2, 254.
30 *Examiner,* 5, 12 February, 15 March, 19 April, 15 March, 16 July 1851, and throughout during the rest of 1851; Shaw, *Convicts,* p. 345.
31 Roe, 'Self-government', p. 32; *Examiner,* 16 August, 8, 29 October, 10 December 1851.
32 *Examiner,* 29 October 1851; Smith, *Birthstain,* p. 252, and at a book launch in Hobart, 27 April 2008.
33 Mitchel, *Jail Journal,* pp. 264–5.
34 *Examiner,* 4 September 1852; William Howitt, *Land, Labour and Gold,* London: Longman, Brown, Green and Longmans, 1855, p. 443; *HTA,* 12 October 1852.
35 *Guardian,* 13, 20 November 1852; *CT,* 16 November 1852.
36 *HTA,* 20, 23 November 1852, 11 August 1853; *CT,* 19, 23 November 1852; *HTC,* 20, 22 November 1952; *Guardian,* 24 November 1852; *Examiner,* 27 October 1852.
37 *HTC,* 1 January 1853; *Guardian,* 8 January 1853; *CT,* 24 December 1852, 3 January 1853; Roe, 'Self-government', pp. 34–7; Stefan Petrow and Alison Alexander, *Growing with Strength: A history of the Hobart City Council,* Hobart: Hobart City Council, 2009, pp. 16–20.
38 *Examiner,* 3 March 1853, 13 August 1853; *HTA,* 10 August 1853.

39 *HTA*, 10, 11 August 1853; *HTC*, 11, 12 August 1853; *CT*, 11 August 1853; *Examiner*, 11 August 1853; Roe, 'Self-government', p. 37; Kirsty Reid, *Gender, Crime and Empire: Convicts, settlers and the state in early colonial Australia*, Manchester: Manchester University Press, 2008, p. 256.

40 *Guardian*, 6 April 1850; Sir William and Lady Denison, *Varieties of Vice-regal Life*, Hobart: THRA, 2004, p. 38.

7 The convict stigma

1 Conversation with Pam Sharpe.

2 Clive Emsley, *Crime and Society in England 1750–1900*, New York and London: Longman, 1987, pp. 60, 129–33; John Briggs et al., *Crime and Punishment in England*, London: UCL Press, 1996, pp. 18–19, 21, 126, 139, 165, 167, 188, 191; Barry Godfrey and Paul Lawrence, *Crime and Justice 1750–1950*, Devon: Willan Publishing, 2006, pp. 73, 111, 113–15; Eamonn Carrabine et al., *Criminology: A sociological introduction*, London: Routledge, 2004, pp. 31–2; Hamish Maxwell-Stewart, 'Crime and health—an introductory view' in *Effecting a Cure: Aspects of health and medicine in Launceston*, ed. Paul Richards, Launceston: Myola House of Publishing, 2006, p. 35; Michael Sturma, *Vice in a Vicious Society*, St Lucia: University of Queensland Press, 1983, p. 1.

3 David Philips, *Crime and Authority in Victorian England: The Black Country 1835–1860*, London: Croom Helm, 1977; Sturma, *Vice*, p. 2; James Boyce, *Van Diemen's Land*, Melbourne: Black Inc., 2008, p. 8.

4 John Mitchel, *Jail Journal*, Dublin: M.H. Gill & Son, 1913, p. 245; James Backhouse, *A Narrative of a Visit to the Australian Colonies*, London: Hamilton, Adams, 1843, pp. 20, 199.

5 Brian Fletcher, *Landed Enterprise and Penal Society*, Sydney: Sydney University Press, 1976, p. 88, 210–12; D.C. Shelton (ed.), *The Parramore Letters*, Epping, NSW: D. Shelton, 1993, p. 66; Charles Darwin, *Narrative of Surveying Voyages*, London: H. Colburn, 1839, p. 535; J.B. Hirst, *Convict Society and its Enemies: A history of early New South Wales*, Sydney: George Allen & Unwin, 1983.

6 Marian Quartly, 'Convicts' in *The Oxford Companion to Australian History*, Melbourne: Oxford University Press, 1998, pp. 156–7; Boyce, *Van Diemen's Land*, pp. 224–5.

7 Bob Reece, 'Writing about convicts in Western Australia' in *Building a Colony: The convict legacy*, eds Jacqui Sherriff and Anne Brake, Perth: Centre for Western Australian History, 2006, pp. 100–6.

8 Noel McLachlan, *Waiting for the Revolution*, Ringwood, Vic.: Penguin, 1989, pp. 14–17; Andrew Jampoler, email to the author 14 August 2008.

9 Hirst, *Convict Society and Its Enemies*, pp. 189–91.

10 McLachlan, *Waiting*, pp. 18–19, 62; Babette Smith, *Australia's Birthstain*, Sydney: Allen & Unwin, 2008, p. 205.

11 [Hordern Melville], *The Adventures of a Griffin*, London: Bell and Dalby, 1867, p. 48; H. Butler Stoney, *A Residence in Tasmania*, London: Smith, Elder, 1856,

p. v; Mrs Favell Lee Mortimer, *Far Off; or, Asia and Australia described*, London: T. Hatchard, 1856, p. 313.

12 Mitchel, *Jail Journal*, p. 177.

13 Cassandra Pybus and Hamish Maxwell-Stewart, *American Citizens, British Slaves: Yankee political prisoners in an Australian penal colony, 1839–1850*, Carlton South, Vic.: Melbourne University Press, 2002; Hugh Anderson, *Farewell to Judges and Juries: The broadside ballad and convict transportation to Australia*, Hotham Hill, Victoria: Red Rooster, 2000, 168–70, 173–5.

14 Anderson, *Farewell*, p. 489.

15 Richard Whatley, *Remarks on Transportation*, London: B. Fellowes, 1834.

16 W. Ullathorne, *The Catholic Mission in Australia*, Adelaide: Libraries Board of South Australia, 1963, pp. iv–v.

17 Ullathorne, *Catholic Mission*, pp. 15–18, 22–33, 49–55.

18 David Burn, *Vindication of Van Diemen's Land*, London: J.W. Southgate, 1840, p. 8.

19 Godfrey Mundy, *Our Antipodes*, ed. D. Baker: Pandanus Books, Canberra, 2006, pp. 3, 5. 10.

20 John West, *The History of Tasmania*, vol. 1, Launceston: Henry Dowling, 1852, p. 282; P.L. Brown (ed.), *Clyde Company Papers*, vol. VI, London: O.U.P., 1968, p. 262.

21 *Examiner*, 1 June 1844.

22 Kirsty Reid, *Gender, Crime and Empire: Convicts, settlers and the state in early colonial Australia*, Manchester: Manchester University Press, 2008, p. 206.

23 Sturma, *Vice*, p. 3.

24 *Examiner*, 12 March 1842, 11 December 1847, 10 September 1851; *CC*, 16 October 1847; *HTA*, 6 April 1847.

25 *Examiner*, 10 September 1851; *CC*, 21 November 1846.

26 *Examiner*, 22 December 1849, 16 August 1851.

27 Boyce, *Van Diemen's Land*, p. 240; Smith, *Australia's Birthstain*, chapter 8, Rodney Croome, 'Homosexuality' in *Companion to Tasmanian History*, ed. A. Alexander, Hobart: Centre for Tasmanian Historical Studies, 2005, p. 180.

28 *Guardian*, 29 May 1847; Kirsten McKenzie, *Scandal in the Colonies*, Carlton, Vic.: Melbourne University Press, 2004, pp. 12–13.

29 J.M.D. Hardwick, *Emigrant in Motley*, London: Rockliff, 1954, pp. 93, 104–10, 171; David Burn, *A Picture of Van Diemen's Land*, Hobart: Cat & Fiddle Press, 1973, p. 51.

30 Charles Dickens, *Great Expectations*, London: Geoffrey Cumberland, Oxford University Press, 1955, pp. 2–3, 344.

31 H. Maxwell-Stewart, 'World Heritage Serial Nomination for Australian Convict Sites Consultant's Report', unpublished article, Hobart, 2007.

32 Benson Bobrick, *East of the Sun: The conquest and settlement of Siberia*, London: Mandarin, 1992, pp. 270–300; W. Bruce Lincoln, *The Conquest of a Continent: Siberia and the Russians*, London: Jonathan Cape, 1994, pp. 162–7, 198–9, 202, 206; Peter Wilson Coldham, *Emigrants in Chains: A social history of forced*

emigration to the Americas 1607–1776, United Kingdom: Allen Sutton, 1992, pp. 7, 11, 115; A. Roger Ekirch, *Bound for America: The transportation of British convicts to the Colonies, 1718–1775*, Oxford: Clarendon Paperbacks, 1987, pp. 5, 48–58, 97, 177–79, 186–9.

33 Anton Chekhov, *The Island: A journey to Sakhalin*, New York: Washington Square Press, 1967, pp. 24–8, 37, 40, 46, 53, 231–2.

8 Initial efforts to defeat the convict stigma

1 Charles Walch, *The Story of the Life of Charles Edward Walch*, Hobart [no publisher named], 1908, p. lvii; R. Edmond Malone, *Three Years' Cruise in the Australasian Colonies*, London: Richard Bentley, 1854, p. 29.

2 Godfrey Mundy, *Our Antipodes*, ed. D. Baker, Canberra: Pandanus Books, 2006, pp. 111–12; John Molony, *The Native-born: The first white Australians*, Carlton South, Vic.: Melbourne University Press, 2000, p. 159.

3 Anthony Trollope, *Australia and New Zealand*, vol. II, Melbourne: Robertson, 1876, p. 133.

4 Charles Dilke, *Greater Britain*, London: MacMillan and Co., 1869, p. 354; Trollope, *Australia and New Zealand*, p. 128; *Mercury*, 24 February 1863.

5 John Martineau, *Letters from Australia*, London: Longmans, Green, 1869, pp. 62–3; James Fenton, *History of Tasmania*, Launceston, 1884; facsimile edition Hobart: Melanie Publications, 1978, p. 251.

6 Fenton, *History*, p. 249; *Mercury*, 21 September 1864, 21 July 1871; *HTC*, 10 November 1827, 11 December 1850; *Mercury*, 26 April, 3 June 1916, 16 March, 21 May, 12 June 1917.

7 L.V. Andel (ed.), *Clerk of the House: The reminiscences of Hugh Munro Hull*, Melbourne: L.V. Andel, 1984, p. 10; P. Walker, *All That We Inherit*, Hobart: J. Walch & Sons, 1965, p. 143; John Pascoe Fawkner, *Reminiscences of Early Hobart Town*, Malvern: Banks Society, 2007, p. 21, 28, 41, 65, 69.

8 *Mercury*, 26 January 1859; Brighton Council Minutes, 3 April 1873 (TAHO).

9 Martineau, *Letters*, pp. 62–3, 66; Walch, *Life*, p. xxxi.

10 John West, *The History of Tasmania*, vol. 2, Launceston: Henry Dowling, 1852, pp. 330, 327.

11 Michael Sturma, *Vice in a Vicious Society*, St Lucia: University of Queensland Press, 1983, p. 7; Kirsten McKenzie, *Scandal in the Colonies*, Carlton, Vic.: Melbourne University Press, 2004, pp. 1–12.

12 Clive Emsley, *Crime and Society in England 1750–1900*, New York and London: Longman, 1987, p. 60; Eamonn Carrabine et al., *Criminology: A sociological introduction*, London: Routledge, 2004, p. 36.

13 John Milner and Oswald Brierly, *Cruise of H.M.S. Galatea*, London: W.H. Allen, 1869, p. 323; Marquis de Beauvoir, *A Voyage Round the World*, vol. 1, London: Murray, 1870, p. 193; Henry Nesfield, *A Chequered Career*, London: Bentley, 1887, p. 216.

14 David Kennedy, *Kennedy's Colonial Travel*, Edinburgh: Edinburgh Publishing Co., 1876, p. 142; Nesfield, *Chequered*, p. 217.

15 Kennedy, *Colonial Travel*, p. 133, 124.

16 Frederick Jobson, *Australia*, London: Hamilton Adams, 1862, p. 122; Martineau, *Letters*, p. 86.

17 Daniel Puseley, *The Rise and Progress of Australia, Tasmania, and New Zealand*, London: Warren Hall & Co., 1858, p. 196; Dilke, *Greater Britain*, p. 354, 358–9; F.J. Cockburn, *Letters from the Southern Hemisphere*, Calcutta: F. Carbery, 1856, p. 124; Trollope, *Australia and New Zealand*, pp. 140, 143, 172; H. Butler Stoney, *A Residence in Tasmania*, London: Smith, Elder, 1856, p. 8; de Beauvoir, *Voyage*, p. 214; Kennedy, *Colonial Travel*, p. 147; E. Daniel and Annette Potts (eds), *A Yankee Merchant in Gold Rush Australia*, Melbourne: William Heinemann, 1970, p. 182.

18 Cockburn, *Letters*, p. 51.

19 A. Alexander, *The Eastern Shore: A history of Clarence*, Clarence: Clarence City Council, 2003, chapter 5; Emily Warner, 'Crime' in *Companion to Tasmanian History*, ed. A. Alexander, Hobart: Centre for Tasmanian Historical Studies, 2005, p. 91.

20 Milner and Brierly, *Cruise*, p. 349; Dilke, *Greater Britain*, pp. 354, 358; Martineau, *Letters*, pp. 66–7; de Beauvoir, *Voyage*, p. 216; Trollope, *Australia and New Zealand*, p. 130; *Statistics of Tasmania* 1869, p. viii.

21 Percy Clarke, *The 'New Chum' in Australia*, London: J.S. Virtue, 1886, p. 324; Stoney, *Residence*, p. 150; Sturma, *Vice*, p. 7; West, *History*, vol. 2, p. 334; Henry Reynolds, '"That hated stain": The aftermath of transportation in Tasmania', *Historical Studies*, vol. 14, no. 53, 1969, p. 26; Trollope, *Australia and New Zealand*, pp. 158–9.

22 *The Times*, 3 January 1870; Russel Ward, *The Australian Legend*, Melbourne: Oxford University Press, 1958, p. 60; James Boyce, *Van Diemen's Land*, Melbourne: Black Inc., 2008, p. 139; Michael Roe, 'The Burden of Tasmanian History' in *The Flow of Culture*, ed. M. Roe, Canberra: Australian Academy of the Humanities, 1987, p. 4.; David Burn, *A Picture of Van Diemen's Land*, Hobart: Cat & Fiddle Press, 1973, p. 50; Oliné Keese, *The Broad Arrow*, North Ryde: Eden, 1988, p. 93.

23 G. Boyes diary, 11 June 1846 RS 25/2(8) (UTA).

24 Walch, *Life*, p. 52.

25 *Information Regarding the Colony of Van Diemen's Land*, London: [no publisher named], 1853, pp. 9, 11, 16; H.M. Hull, *The Guide to Tasmania*, Hobart Town: J. Walch, 1858, throughout and pp. 16, 47–8.

26 Keese, *Broad Arrow*, p. 89; Roe, 'Burden', p. 10.

27 Trollope, *Australia and New Zealand*, p. 155; Robson, *History*, vol. 2, pp. 16–18.

28 Hugh Hull, *The Experiences of Forty Years in Tasmania*, London: Orger & Meryon, 1859, p. 9.

29 Jonathan Sweet, 'Colonial exhibition design: The Tasmanian timber tower at the London International Exhibition, 1862', *THRAPP*, vol. 44, no. 4, 1997.

30 Stefan Petrow, 'Claims of the colony: Tasmania's dispute with Britain over the Port Arthur penal establishment 1856–1877', *THRAPP*, vol. 44, no. 4, 1997, p. 227; *Mercury*, 12 March, 4 June 1867.

31 *Mercury*, 19, 20, 21, 23, 24 February, 11 March 1863.

32 *Mercury*, 21 September 1864, 19 April 1871.

33 Gillian Winter, '"We speak that we do know"', *THRAPP,* vol. 40, no. 4, 1993, pp. 148–50.

34 Reynolds, 'Hated stain', pp. 23, 27–9; Andrew Piper, 'What is to be done with the man? The role of invalids in the establishment of Launceston general hospital' in *Effecting a Cure: Aspects of health and medicine in Launceston,* ed. P. Richards, Launceston: Myola House of Publishing 2006, pp. 56–8; Joan Brown, *"Poverty is not a Crime": Social services in Tasmania 1803–1900,* Hobart: THRA, 1972.

35 *British Australasian,* 6 September 1894; 'The Vet' [J. Hornsby], *Old Time Echoes of Tasmania,* Hobart: [no publisher named], 1896, p. 70.

36 Scott Bennett and Barbara Bennett, *Biographical Register of the Tasmanian Parliament,* Canberra: Australian National University Press, 1980, pp. 50, 18, 34–5, 80, 122; Walch's Almanac 1865, pp. 39–45: NS 1332/12, p. 46 (TAHO); Alison Alexander, *Glenorchy 1804–1964,* Glenorchy: Glenorchy City Council, 1986; Alison Alexander, *The Eastern Shore: A history of Clarence,* Clarence: Clarence City Council, 2003; Alison Alexander, *Brighton and Surrounds*: Brighton: Brighton Council, 2006.

37 Memoirs of Grace Walch, unpublished, in the possession of Julia Johnson.

38 Charles Du Cane, *Tasmania: Past and Present,* Colchester: [no publisher named], 1877, pp. 14–15.

39 Gillian Winter, 'Portraying "That hated stain"; convict drama and convict audiences at the Theatre Royal, Hobart', *THRAPP,* vol. 48, no. 2, pp. 228–34; *Mercury,* 6 April 1864.

9 Forgetting the past

1 Kirsten McKenzie, *Scandal in the Colonies,* Melbourne: Melbourne University Press, 2004, p. 1.

2 Robyn Eastley, 'Using the records of the Tasmanian Convict Department', *THS* 9, 2004.

3 Christopher Koch, 'Archival days—an afterword' in *Tasmanian Insights,* ed. G. Winter, Hobart: State Library of Tasmania, 1992, p. 230.

4 Bob Reece, 'Writing about convicts in Western Australia' in *Building a Colony: The convict legacy,* eds Jacqui Sherriff and Anne Brake, Perth: Centre for Western Australian History, 2006, pp. 109–10.

5 Police Letter Books, Port Sorell Police District, 16 November 1868 (TAHO); Brighton Council Minutes 3 April 1873 (TAHO); AC 427/1/1, 1892, Police Charge Book (TAHO).

6 Information from Christine Walch, Angus Bethune, Lindsay Whitham, Roma Blackwood, Cynthia Alexander, Henry Cosgrove, Naomi Canning, Eric Reece, Heather Gibson, Sue Collins, Pamela Pillinger.

10 *For the Term of His Natural Life*

1 H. Thomas, *Guide for Excursionists from the Mainland to Tasmania,* Melbourne: H. Thomas, 1869, pp. 86–7, 154–60; H. Thomas, *Guide to Excursionists between Australia and Tasmania,* Melbourne: H. Thomas, 1873, pp. 42, [68], 154; Anon

[Louisa Anne Meredith], *Walch's Tasmanian Guide Book*, Hobart: J. Walch & Sons, 1871, pp. 21, 140–8; F. Algar, *A Handbook to the Colony of Tasmania*, London: F. Algar, 1863, p. 2; David Young, *Making Crime Pay*, Hobart: THRA, 1996, pp. 14–17.

2   Lurline Stuart (ed.), *Marcus Clarke: His natural life*, St Lucia: University of Queensland Press, 2001, pp. xix–xlviii.

3   Stuart, *Marcus Clarke*, p. 122.

4   Noel McLachlan, *Waiting for the Revolution: A history of Australian nationalism*, Ringwood, Vic.: Penguin, 1989, p. 113.

5   *Mercury*, 19, 29 April, 2 May 1871.

6   Young, *Crime*, p. 22; 'The Vet' [J. Hornsby], *Old Time Echoes of Tasmania*, Tasmania: [no publisher named], 1896, p. 220; *British Australasian*, 21 June 1894.

7   David Burn, *An Excursion to Port Arthur in 1842*, Hobart: Oldham, Beddome & Meredith, 1942, pp. 16–19; Young, *Crime*, p. 24; Martin Cash, *The Adventures of Martin Cash*, Hobart: 'Mercury' Steam Press Office, 1870, p. 49; F.J. Cockburn, *Letters from the Southern Hemisphere*, Calcutta: F. Carbery, 1856, p. 68; Anthony Trollope, *Australia and New Zealand*, vol. II, Melbourne: Robertson, 1876, pp. 140, 145–8, 152–3.

8   William Senior, *Travel and Trout in the Antipodes*, London: Chatto & Windus, 1880, pp. 71–4.

9   E. Reeves, *Homeward Bound after Thirty Years*, London: Swan Sonnenschein, 1892, pp. 55–8; Hume Nisbet, *A Colonial Tramp*, London: Ward & Downey, 1891, vol. 2, p. 271–2; R.C. Seaton, *Six Letters from the Colonies*, Hull: Wildridge & Co, 1886, p. 63; Percy Clarke, *The 'New Chum' in Australia*, London: J.S. Virtue, 1886, p. 322; Trollope, *Australia and New Zealand*, p. 134; Garnet Walch, *Guide to Tasmania*, Melbourne: [no publisher named], 1890, pp. 91–2.

10 Nisbet, *Tramp*, p. 271; Clarke, *New Chum*, p. 322; T.H. Grattan Esmond, *Round the World with the Irish Delegates*, Dublin: Sealy, Bryers and Walker, 1893, pp. 57–8; Reeves, *Homeward*, p. 55; Charles Du Cane, *Tasmania: Past and Present*, Colchester: [no publisher named], 1877, pp. 7–11; M. Davitt, *Life and Progress in Australasia*, London: Methuen & Co., 1898, pp. 332–4.

11 Walch, *Guide*, p. 91; Young, *Crime*, pp. 53–5, 65–6.

12 Young, *Crime*, pp. 44–5, 55–8.

13 *TM*, 8 January 1898; Young, *Crime*, pp. 47–8, 70–83.

14 Tasmanian Steam Navigation Company, *Guide for Visitors to Tasmania*, Hobart: [no publisher named], 1887, pp. 16, 46, 80; *Beautiful Tasmania*, Hobart: Tasmanian Tourist Association, 1912, pp. 60, 70; H. Haywood, *Through Tasmania*, Launceston: Launceston *Examiner*, 1885, pp. 32, 74–5; T.M. Hogan and Hal Gye, *The Tight Little Island: A trip through Tasmania*, Hobart: J. Walch & Sons, [1912], p. 70; H. Thomas, *Guide to Excursionists between Australia and Tasmania*, p. 41.

15 Young, *Crime*, pp. 50–1.

16 J.F. Mortlock, *Experiences of a Convict*, Sydney: Sydney University Press, 1965, pp. ix–xxvii; CON 31/31/1250; *Tasmanian Morning Herald*, 31 October, November–December 1866.

11 The One Forbidden Subject

1   *TM*, 9 March 1889.
2   *Cyclopedia of Tasmania*, vol. 1, Hobart: Maitland and Krone, 1900, pp. 38, 57, 58, 64, 318, 463.
3   *Cook's Railway Official Guide Book to Tasmania*, Melbourne: Thos. Cook & Son, 1894, p. 20; S.O. Lovell, *The Centenary of Tasmania*, Hobart: John Vail, Govt. Printer, 1903, pp. 17, 19, 29.
4   *Cyclopedia*, vol. 2, pp. 386–9; Critchley Parker, *Tasmania, the Jewel of the Commonwealth*, Melbourne: The Tasmanian Government, 1937, p. 6.
5   NS 2101/1/1 (TAHO); University of Tasmania calendars, 1902–11, reports on public examinations; Lovell, *Centenary*, pp, 16, 19, 28, 30; Alexander and George Sutherland, *The History of Australia and New Zealand*, London: Longmans, Green, 1913, pp. 159–62; AE 346/1/8, August 1908 (TAHO); Edward Arnold, *The Australian Commonwealth*, London: Edward Arnold, [1902].
6   University of Tasmania calendars 1910–20; Ernest Scott, *A Short History of Australia*, London: Oxford University Press, 1916, pp. 47, 53, 62, 56–7, 164; ED 248/1/1, Examination Papers for High Schools (TAHO).
7   *Mercury*, 22, 23, 24 February 1904; Michael Roe, *The State of Tasmania*, Hobart: THRA, 2001, pp. 237–41; *The Tasmanian Motorists' Comprehensive Road Guide*, Hobart: Tas. Government Tourist Dept., 1920, pp. 30, 34.
8   *Guide for Visitors to Tasmania*, Hobart, 1887, pp. 7, 16, 46; T.M. Hogan and Hal Gye, *The Tight Little Island: A trip through Tasmania*, Hobart: J. Walch & Sons, [1912], p. 39.
9   *Mercury*, 16 February 1889; Louis Becke (ed.), *Old Convict Days*, New York: New Amsterdam Book Company, 1899, pp. v–vi; Thomas R. Dewar, *A Ramble Round the Globe*, London: Chatto & Windus, 1894, p. 178; Garnet Walch, *Guide to Tasmania*, Melbourne: [no publisher named], 1890, p. 92; Hogan and Gye, *Tight*, p. 39, Lloyd Robson, 'Damnosa Haereditas?' in *The Flow of Culture: Tasmanian studies*, ed. Michael Roe, Canberra: Australian Academy of the Humanities, 1987, p. 93.
10 Roe, *State of Tasmania*, pp. 14–15; Josiah Hughes, *Australia Revisited*, London: Simpkin, Marshall, Hamilton, Kent & Co., 1891, p. 248.
11 J.R. Skemp, *Memories of Myrtle Bank*, Melbourne: Melbourne University Press, 1952, pp. 49–59, 60–2.
12 Brighton Historical Society, scrapbook 4, p. 93; Charles Furlong, *The Settler in Tasmania, 1873–1879*, Hobart: Sullivans Cove, 1982, p. 14; Scott Bennett (ed.), *A Home in the Colonies: Edward Braddon's letters to India*, Hobart: THRA, 1980, p. 86; Michael Sprod (ed.), *The Whitehead Letters*, Hobart: THRA, 1991, p. 112.
13 Babette Smith, *Australia's Birthstain*, Sydney: Allen & Unwin, 2008, p. 36; *TM*, 27 September 1879; David Young, *Making Crime Pay*, Hobart: THRA, 1996, p. 94; *British Australasian*, 29 November 1900; Robson, *History*, vol. 2, p. 288.
14 *Tasmanian News*, 5 June 1900.
15 *Clipper*, 4 December 1909, 5 March 1904, 4 October 1902, 8 August 1903.

16 R.C. Seaton, *Six Letters from the Colonies*, Hull: Wildridge & Co., 1886, p. 64; 'Petrel', *In Southern Seas*, Edinburgh: R. Grant, 1888, p. 49.

17 P.R. Stephenson, *The Foundations of Culture in Australia*, Sydney: W.J. Miles, 1936, pp. 63–6; Brian Fletcher, *Australian History in New South Wales*, Kensington, N.S.W.: NSW University Press, 1993, p. 154.

18 *TM*, 20 February 1904, p. 25; Roe, *State of Tasmania*, p. 231; G.B. Lancaster, *Pageant*, London: Allen & Unwin, 1933; Roy Bridges, *The League of the Lord*, Sydney: Australasian Publishing, 1950, and *That Yesterday was Home*, Sydney: Australasian Publishing, 1948; Leslie Norman, *Tasmania's Strange Story*, Hobart: Come to Tasmania Organisation, [1920s], p. 22.

19 Gwenda Sheridan, 'The Pioneer Memorial Highway' in *Companion to Tasmanian History*, ed. A. Alexander, Hobart, 2005, p. 277; Young, *Crime*, p. 108; *Mercury*, 29 May 1936; George Porter, *Wanderings in Tasmania*, London: Selwyn & Blount, 1934, pp. 106, 126, 148.

20 P.B. Walker, *Prelude to Federation*, Hobart: O.B.M. Publishing, 1976, pp. 50–6; *Statistics of Tasmania*, Hobart, 1887, p. 76; Roe, *State of Tasmania*, pp. 36–8, 194–203.

21 Letter from Minnie Clarke to Poppy Clarke, Summerhome, in possession of Julia Johnson; Margaret Glover, 'A colonial abroad—Mary Augusta Walker in England, 1889–1890', *THRAPP*, vol. 48, no. 3, 2001, pp. 155, 157, 158; Fiona MacFarlane, *Quirky Names in Tasmanian History*, Hobart: Fiona MacFarlane, 2006, pp. 48–9.

22 R.M. Johnson, *Tasmanian Official Record*, Hobart: Tasmanian Government, 1890, pp. 359, 361; 1892 p. 402; Henry Reynolds, '"That hated stain": The aftermath of transportation in Tasmania', *Historical Studies*, vol. 14, no. 53, 1969, pp. 22, 24.

23 *The Times*, 19 October 1881; Daniel Bandmann, *An Actor's Tour*, Boston: Cupples, Uphem, 1885, p. 75; Nundo Lall Doss, *Reminiscences, Europe and Australia*, Calcutta: M.C. Bhowmick, 1893, p. 145; Dewar, *Ramble*, pp. 174, 178; Hughes, *Australia*, pp. 248–9; James Duckworth, *A Trip Round the World*, Rochdale: J. Clegg, 1890, p. 50.

24 *TM*, 13 April 1878, 11 June 1892; A. Alexander, 'Couvreur, Jessie Catherine' in *Companion* ed. Alexander, p. 88.

25 Robson, 'Damnosa', p. 94; Roe, *State of Tasmania*, p. 236; *Mercury*, 2 September 1902.

26 Roe, *State of Tasmania*, pp. 235–6; *Mercury*, 4, 5, 6 September 1902; *Clipper*, 13 September 1902.

27 *Mercury*, 10 September 1902.

28 Roe, *State of Tasmania*, p. 207; *British Australasian*, 6 September 1894.

29 Noel McLachlan, *Waiting for the Revolution*, Ringwood, Vic.: Penguin, 1989, pp. 88, 112, 152; Roe, *State of Tasmania*, p. 38.

30 Fletcher, *Australian History*, p. 153; McLachlan, *Waiting*, p. 152; Smith, *Birthstain*, p. 311.

31 McLachlan, *Waiting*, pp. 132–8, 154, 234, 246; Fletcher, *Australian History*, p. 8.

32 Edith Emery, *A Twentieth Century Life*, Hobart: Artemis, no date, pp. 263, 269–70, 270.

33 *Mercury,* 27 July, 18, 21 August 1944.

34 Stephen Murray-Smith, *The Dictionary of Australian Quotations*, Richmond: Heinemann, 1984, p. 207.

35 Ludwig Salvator, *Hobart Town or Summer Holiday Resort in the Antipodes*, Prague, 1886, translated by Eva Meidl, chapter VIII.

36 Rupert Godfrey (ed.), *Letters from a Prince*, London: Warner Books, 1998, p. 355; Trudy Cowley, *A Drift of Derwent Ducks*, Hobart: Research Tasmania, 2005, p. 325.

37 Marie Bjelke Petersen, *The Captive Singer*, London: Hodder & Stoughton, 1917, p. 286, and *The Rainbow Lute*, London: Hutchinson, 1932, p. 154.

38 Information from Angus Bethune, Heather Gibson, Henry Cosgrove, Roma Blackwood, Cynthia Alexander, Sue Collins, Naomi Canning, Lindsay Whitham, Eric Reece, Pamela Pillinger.

39 *Collegiate School Magazine*, 1927, p. 40; J.R. Richardson, 'The Club at the Peninsula', *Tasmanian Tramp,* vol. 1, 1933, p. 23.

40 Fletcher, *Australian History*, pp. 160–1; Miles Franklin and Dymphna Cusack, *Pioneers on Parade*, Sydney: Angus & Robertson, 1939, pp. 202, 206, 208, 210, 239.

41 Hermione Ranfurly, *The Ugly One*, London: Michael Joseph, 1988, pp. 185–6.

12 'A thing of which we may well feel proud'

1 *Statistics of Tasmania* 1871, p. 4; Noel McLachlan, *Waiting for the Revolution*, Ringwood, Vic.: Penguin, 1989, p. 145; *Tasmanian News,* 5 June 1900.

2 James Fenton, *History of Tasmania*, Launceston, 1884: facsimile edition Hobart: Melanie Publications, 1978, chapter 11, pp. vii, 264.

3 *Mercury,* 25 June 1930; J.W. Beattie, *Port Arthur and Tasman Peninsula*, Hobart: Mercury Office, 1905; *Clipper,* 5 March 1904.

4 Michael Roe, *The State of Tasmania,* Hobart: THRA, 2001, pp. 229–30; Babette Smith, *Australia's Birthstain*, Sydney: Allen & Unwin, 2008, p. 35; Brian Fletcher, *Australian History in New South Wales*, Kensington, N.S.W.: NSW University Press, 1993, pp. 71–5, 154.

5 J.B. Walker to Mary Walker, 22 May, 1 Oct 1889 (UTA).

6 *TM,* 26 October 1889; J.B. Walker, *Early Tasmania*, Hobart: Government Printer, 1914; Roe, *State of Tasmania*, pp. 229–30.

7 David Kennedy, *Kennedy's Colonial Travel*, Edinburgh: Edinburgh Publishing Co., 1876, p. 133; R.C. Seaton, *Six Letters from the Colonies*, Hull Wildridge & Co., 1886, p. 64; Percy Clarke, *The 'New Chum' in Australia*, London: J.S. Virtue, 1886, p. 322; Mark Twain, *More Tramps Abroad*, London: Chatto & Windus, 1897, p. 70; Smith, *Birthstain*, pp. 9, 10, 257; Charles Du Cane, *Tasmania: Past and Present*, Colchester: [no publisher named], 1877, p. 14; Henry Button, *Flotsam and Jetsam*, Launceston: A.W. Birchall, 1909, p. 48; Barry Godfrey and Paul Lawrence, *Crime and Justice 1750–1950*, Devon: Willan Publishing, 2006, p. 112; Roe, *State of Tasmania*, pp. 234, 244.

8 James Fenton, *Bush Life in Tasmania*, London: Hazell, Watson & Viney, [1891], p. 47.

9 'The Vet' [J. Hornsby], *Old Time Echoes of Tasmania*, Tasmania: [no publisher named], 1896, Preface, p. 231; Roe, *State of Tasmania*, p. 228.

10 Fletcher, *Australian History*, pp. 154–5; David Roberts, '"More sinned against than sinning": George Arnold Wood and the noble convict' in *Making Australian History*, eds D. Gare and D. Ritter, Melbourne, 2007, p. 123.

11 G.A. Wood, 'Convicts', *RAHS Journal*, VIII/IV, 1922, pp. 177–200; Roberts, 'More sinned', pp. 124–6; W.K. Hancock, *Australia*, Brisbane: Jacaranda Press, 1961, p. 24; information from Angus Bethune.

12 Roberts, 'More sinned', p. 123; *The History of Tasmania, written specially for Truth*, Melbourne: Truth, 1915.

13 Information from Angus Bethune and Christopher Koch (friend of Warren Reid); P.B. Walker, *Prelude to Federation*, Hobart: O.B.M. Publishing, 1976, p. 63.

14 Martin Flanagan, *In Sunshine or in Shadow*, Sydney: Picador, 2002, p. 27.

15 *Mercury*, 25, 26, 27, 28, October 1886; Gillian Winter, 'Portraying "that hated stain": convict drama and convict audiences at the Theatre Royal, Hobart', *THRAPP*, vol. 48, no. 2, pp. 231–4.

16 *TM*, 9 March 1889; *Mercury*, 14, 15, 16, 18, 19 February 1889.

17 *Mercury*, 16 June 1891.

18 Andrew Pike and Ross Cooper, *Australian Film 1900–1977*, Melbourne: Oxford University Press, 1980, pp. 4–5, 10–12, 20, 26, 30–1, 33, 37, 39, 43, 51, 73, 87, 99, 101; *Mercury*, 7, 8, 9, 10, 12 September 1911; *Clipper*, 29 August, 14, 21 November, 5 December 1908, 30 January, 19 June, 17 July, 25 September, 4, 11 December 1909.

19 *ADB*, vol. 10, pp. 144–5; *Mercury*, 25, 26, 27, 30 July, 5 August 1926.

20 Michael Roe, 'The Filming of "His Natural Life"', *Journal of Australian Studies*, vol. 24, 1989, pp. 41–2.

21 *Mercury*, 30 July, 5 August 1926; *Examiner*, 29 July 1926.

22 *Weekly Courier*, 16 September 1926; Roe, 'Filming', pp. 43–5, 47.

23 *Mercury*, 30, 31 August, 1, 2, 3 September 1927.

24 *Examiner*, 6, 8 September 1927.

13 Paving the way

1 Martin Flanagan, *In Sunshine or in Shadow*, Sydney: Picador, 2002, p. 69.

2 Lloyd Robson, *The Convict Settlers of Australia*, Carlton, Vic.: Melbourne University Press, 1965; A.G.L. Shaw, *Convicts and the Colonies*, London: Faber & Faber, 1966, pp. 164–5; Humphrey McQueen, *A New Britannia*, Ringwood, Vic.: Penguin, 1975; C.M.H. Clark, *A History of Australia*, Melbourne: Melbourne University Press, vol. I, 1962; vol. II, 1968; vol. III, 1973; Noel McLachlan, *Waiting for the Revolution*, Ringwood, Vic.: Penguin, 1989, pp. 5, 157; Marian Quartly, 'Convicts' in *The Oxford Companion to Australian History*, Melbourne: Oxford University Press, 1998, p. 155.

3 Russel Ward, *The Australian Legend*, Melbourne: Oxford University Press, 1958, pp. 15, 29–34.

4 Babette Smith, *Australia's Birthstain*, Sydney: Allen & Unwin, 2008, p. 44; *ADB*, vol. 1, pp. 178, 328, 439, 470; vol. 2, p. 126, 582; vol. 4, p. 286; John Cobley, *The Crimes of the First Fleet Convicts*, Sydney: Angus & Robertson, 1970.

5 Shaw, *Convicts*, p. 146.

6 *ADB*, vol. 12, pp. 233–4; E.V. Timms, *The Pathway of the Sun*, Sydney: Angus & Robertson, 1978, back cover, and *The Scarlet Frontier*, Sydney: Angus & Robertson, 1953, pp. 42, 55, 58, 168.

7 Catherine Gaskin, *Sara Dane*, London: Sydney Collins, 1970, Author's Note, pp. 11, 13, 15, 25, 67, 98–9, 134, 162, 137, 189–90.

8 McLachlan, *Waiting*, p. 5; Smith, *Birthstain*, p. 41, 44; Shaw, *Convicts*, p. 149.

9 Bev Coultman Smith, *Shadow over Tasmania*, Hobart: J. Walch & Sons, 1976, pp. [5–6], 9–12, 15, 66, 150; 1978 edition, back cover; *Examiner* and *Mercury*, 31 October 1978; David Young, *Making Crime Pay*, Hobart: THRA, 1996, p. 112.

10 Karl von Stieglitz, *A Short History of Campbell Town*, Launceston: Telegraph, 1948, p. 53, and *A History of Bothwell*, Launceston: Telegraph, 1958, p. 67, and *Longford Past and Present*, Launceston: Telegraph, 1947, p. 6; National Trust of Australia (Tasmania) Historical Committee, *Campbell Town Tasmania*, Campbell Town: National Trust, 1966, p. 20; J.S. Weeding, *A History of the Lower Midlands*, Launceston: Mary Fisher Bookshop, 1973, p. 129.

11 Karl von Stieglitz, *Entally (1821) Pageant of a Pioneer Family*, Hobart: Scenery Preservation Board, 1950; A.D. Baker, *The Life and Times of Sir Richard Dry*, Hobart: Oldham, Beddome & Meredith, 1951, pp. x–xii; Kate Dougharty, *A Story of a Pioneer Family in Van Diemen's Land*, Launceston: [no publisher named], 1953, p. 5.

12 J.R. Skemp, *Memories of Myrtle Bank*, Melbourne: Melbourne University Press, 1952, p. 83; information from Grant Stebbings.

13 Karl von Stieglitz, *A History of Oatlands and Jericho*, Launceston: Telegraph, 1960, p. 70.

14 von Stieglitz, *Oatlands*, p. 92.

15 Mrs Arthur Garnsey, *The Romance of the Huon River*, Melbourne: Whitcombe & Tombs, n.d, pp. 26–8.

16 Peter Bolger, *Hobart Town*, Canberra: Australian National University Press, 1973, pp. 36, 99, 137.

17 Michael Sharland, *Tasmania*, Sydney: Nelson Doubleday, 1966, pp. 17–18.

18 Thomas Rowallan, *The Autobiography of Lord Rowallan*, Edinburgh: P. Harris, 1976, pp. 168–9, 172.

19 Information from Bryan Pearce and Jill Salmon.

20 Robyn Eastley, 'Using the records of the Tasmanian Convict Department', *THS* 9, 2004, pp. 139–42; Smith, *Birthstain*, p. 41; information from Dianne Snowden, Michael Roe and Kevin Green.

21 Information from Michael Roe, Marian Jamieson and Tony Marshall.

22 Christopher Koch, *The Many-Coloured Land: An Irish memoir*, North Sydney: Vintage Books, 2008, pp. 3–4, 5, 8; Christopher Koch, 'Archival days—an afterword', in *Tasmanian Insights*, ed. G. Winter, Hobart: State Library of Tasmania, 1992, pp. 229–31. Koch asked that 'Cork' in the original be changed to 'Tipperary'.

23 NS 1383/2 (TAHO).

24 Von Stieglitz, *Oatlands*, p. 68; Free Arrivals Index (TAHO); CON 31/5/1779; information from Mary Ramsay.

25 Information from Leone Scrivener.

26 Curriculum for primary schools, Hobart, 1951; 'The history of Tasmania', *Pictorial Social Studies*, vol. 24, no date (TAHO).

27 Margaret Scott, *Changing Countries*, Sydney: Australian Broadcasting Corporation, 2000, pp. 159–60; information from Audrey Hudspeth.

14 Out in the open

1 Wynifred Sinclair and Elizabeth Christensen, *Thomas Burbury*, Melbourne: W. Sinclair, 1979, p. xi; information from Peter MacFie; Lloyd Robson, 'Damnosa Haereditas?' in *The Flow of Culture: Tasmanian studies*, ed. Michael Roe, Canberra: Australian Academy of the Humanities, 1987, p. 95.

2 Ronald Lambert, 'Reclaiming the ancestral past: narrative, rhetoric and the "convict stain"', *Journal of Sociology*, vol. 38, no. 2, 2002, p. 112.

3 Babette Smith, *Australia's Birthstain*, Sydney: Allen & Unwin, 2008, p. 54; B.K. Tranter and J. Donoghue, 'Convict ancestry: a neglected aspect of Australian identity' in *Nations and Nationalism*, vol. 9, no. 4, 2008, pp. 555–7.

4 Miriam Dixson, *The Real Matilda*, Harmondsworth: Penguin, 1976; Anne Summers, *Damned Whores and God's Police*, Ringwood: Penguin, 1975.

5 Robert Hughes, *The Fatal Shore*, London: Harvill, 1987, pp. xi, 356, 358–9, 582–8.

6 Babette Smith, *A Cargo of Women*, Kensington: N.S.W.: NSW University Press, 1988; Portia Robinson, *The Women of Botany Bay*, Sydney: Macquarie Library, 1988; Patrick O'Farrell, *The Irish in Australia*, Sydney: New South Wales University Press, 1986; John Hirst, *Convict Society and its Enemies: A history of early New South Wales*, Sydney: George Allen & Unwin, 1983; Stephen Nicholas (ed.), *Convict Workers*, Cambridge: Cambridge University Press, 1988; Deborah Oxley, *Convict Maids*, Cambridge: Cambridge University Press, 1996; Hamish Maxwell-Stewart, *Closing Hell's Gates*, Sydney: Allen & Unwin, 2008; Alan Atkinson and Marian Quartly, *Australians 1838*, Sydney: Fairfax, Syme & Weldon Associates, 1987; Ian Duffield and James Bradley (eds), *Representing Convicts*, New York: Leicester University Press, 1997; M. Tipping, *Convicts Unbound*, South Yarra: Viking O'Neil, 1988.

7 *Mercury*, 20 July 2009; information from Christina Henri <www.christinahenri.com.au>.

8 Lambert, 'Reclaiming', p. 115.

9 Information from Brian Hortle and Rebecca Aisbett.

10 Information from John Fowler.

11 Bob Reece, 'Writing about convicts in Western Australia' in *Building a Colony: The convict legacy*, eds Jacqui Sherriff and Anne Brake, Perth: Centre for Western Australian History, 2006, pp. 98–104, 108–10; Smith, *Birthstain*, p. 39.

12 Information from Margaret Lindley.

13 *Mercury,* 12 January 2007; information from Margaret Lindley and Pam Sharpe.

14 Calculations from demographic figures from *Statistics of Tasmania* and *Tasmanian Year Books* 1850–2009 by Ted Alexander.

15 Program to Richard Bladel's play *Transylvania*, Peacock Theatre, Hobart, 23 July to 2 August 1997, Zootango Theatre, Tasmania.

SELECT BIBLIOGRAPHY

Backhouse, James, *A Narrative of a Visit to the Australian Colonies*, London: Hamilton, Adams, 1843

Boyce, James, *Van Diemen's Land*, Melbourne: Black Inc., 2008

Briggs, John, et al., *Crime and Punishment in England*, London: UCL Press, 1996

Burn, David, *Vindication of Van Diemen's Land*, London: J.W. Southgate, 1840

Carrabine, Eamonn et al., *Criminology: A sociological introduction*, London: Routledge, 2004

Cash, Martin, *The Adventures of Martin Cash*, Hobart Town: 'Mercury' Steam Press Office, 1870

Castles, Alex, 'The Vandemonian spirit and the law', *THRAPP,* 38/3 & 4, 1991.

Coultman Smith, Bev, *Shadow over Tasmania*, Hobart: J. Walch & Sons, 1976

Cowley, Trudy Mae, *A Drift of Derwent Ducks*, Hobart: Research Tasmania, 2005

Cyclopedia of Tasmania, Hobart: Maitland and Krone, 1900, vols I and II

Duffield, Ian and Bradley, James (eds), *Representing Convicts: New perspectives on convict forced labour migration*, New York: Leicester University Press, 1997

Eastley, Robyn, 'Using the records of the Tasmanian Convict Department', *THS*, vol. 9, 2004

Emsley, Clive, *Crime and Society in England*, New York and London: Longman, 1987

Fawkner, John Pascoe, *Reminiscences of early Hobart Town 1804–1810*, Malvern, Vic.: Banks Society, 2007

Fenton, James, *History of Tasmania*, Launceston, 1884; facsimile edition Hobart: Melanie Publications, 1978

—— *Bush Life in Tasmania*, London: Hazell, Watson & Viney, [1891]

Flanagan, Martin, *In Sunshine or in Shadow,* Sydney: Picador, 2002

Fletcher, Brian, *Landed Enterprise and Penal Society: A history of farming and grazing in New South Wales before 1821*, Sydney: Sydney University Press, 1976

—— *Australian History in New South Wales 1888–1938*, Kensington, N.S.W.: NSW University Press, 1993

Frost, Lucy, '"Wished to get out to our mother": convict transportation as family experience', *THRAPP*, vol. 53, no. 3, 2006

Godfrey, Barry and Lawrence, Paul, *Crime and Justice 1750–1950*, Cullompton, Devon: Willan Publishing, 2006

Hardwick, J.M.D. (ed.), *Emigrant in Motley*, London: Rockliff, 1954

Hirst, J.B., *Convict Society and its Enemies: A history of early New South Wales*, Sydney: George Allen & Unwin, 1983

Jeffrey, Mark, *A Burglar's Life; or, The stirring adventures of the great English burglar Mark Jeffrey*, eds W. and J.E. Hiener, Sydney: Angus & Robertson, 1968

Keese, Oliné [Caroline Leakey], *The Broad Arrow: Being the story of Maida Gwynnham, a 'Lifer' in Van Diemen's Land*, North Ryde: N.S.W.: Eden, 1988

Knopwood, Robert, *The Diary of the Reverend Robert Knopwood, 1803–1838: First chaplain of Van Diemen's Land*, Hobart: THRA, 1977

Koch, Christopher, 'Archival days—an afterword', in *Tasmanian Insights*, ed. G. Winter, Hobart: State Library of Tasmania, 1992

Lloyd, G.T., *Thirty-three Years in Tasmania and Victoria*, London: Houlston & Wright, 1862

Lyons, Lewis, *The History of Punishment*, London: Amber Books, 2003

McKenzie, Kirsten, *Scandal in the Colonies: Sydney and Cape Town, 1820–1850*, Carlton, Vic.: Melbourne University Press, 2004

McLachlan, Noel, *Waiting for the Revolution: A history of Australian nationalism*, Ringwood, Vic.: Penguin, 1989

McQueen, Humphrey, *A New Britannia: An argument concerning the social origins of Australian radicalism and nationalism*, Ringwood, Vic.: Penguin, 1975

Maxwell-Stewart, Hamish, 'Crime and health—an introductory view', in *Effecting a Cure: Aspects of health and medicine in Launceston*, ed. Paul Richards, Launceston: Myola House of Publishing, 2006

—— 'World Heritage Serial Nomination for Australian Convict Sites Consultant's Report', unpublished article, Hobart, 2007

—— *Closing Hell's Gates*, Sydney: Allen & Unwin, 2008

Mitchel, John, *Jail Journal*, Dublin, 1854; this edition Dublin: M.H. Gill & Son, 1913

Molesworth, William, *Report from the Select Committee of the House of Commons on Transportation*, London: Hooper, 1838

Molony, John, *The Native-born: The first white Australians*, Carlton South, Vic.: Melbourne University Press, 2000

Moore, James, *The Convicts of Van Diemen's Land, 1840–1853*, Hobart: Cat and Fiddle, 1976

Mortlock, J.F., *Experiences of a Convict*, Sydney: Sydney University Press, 1965

Mundy, Godfrey, *Our Antipodes*, ed. D.W.A. Baker, Canberra: Pandanus Books, 2006

Nicholas, Stephen (ed.), *Convict Workers: Reinterpreting Australia's past*, Cambridge: Cambridge University Press, 1988

Oxley, Deborah, *Convict Maids: The forced migration of women to Australia*, Cambridge: Cambridge University Press, 1996

Quartly, Marian, 'Convicts', in *The Oxford Companion to Australian History*, Melbourne: Oxford University Press, 1998

Reece, Bob, 'Writing about convicts in Western Australia' in *Building a Colony: The convict legacy*, eds Jacqui Sherriff and Anne Brake, Perth: Centre for Western Australian History, 2006

Reid, Kirsty, *Gender, Crime and Empire: Convicts, settlers and the state in early colonial Australia*, Manchester: Manchester University Press, 2008

Reynolds, Henry, '"That hated stain": the aftermath of transportation in Tasmania', *Historical Studies*, vol. 14, no. 53, 1969.

Robson, Lloyd, 'Male convicts transported to Van Diemen's Land, 1841–1853', *THRAPP*, vol. 9, no. 2, 1961

—— '*The Convict Settlers of Australia*, Carlton, Vic.: Melbourne University Press, 1965

—— *A History of Tasmania: Volume I, Van Diemen's Land from the earliest times to 1855*, Melbourne: Oxford University Press, 1983

—— 'Damnosa Haereditas? Tasmania's British inheritance in the later nineteenth century', in *The Flow of Culture: Tasmanian studies*, ed. Michael Roe, Canberra: Australian Academy of the Humanities, 1987

—— *A History of Tasmania: Volume II, Colony and state from 1856 to the 1980s*, Melbourne: Oxford University Press, 1991

Roe, Michael, 'The burden of Tasmanian history', in *The Flow of Culture: Tasmanian studies*, ed. M. Roe, Canberra: Australian Academy of the Humanities, 1987

—— 'The filming of "His Natural Life"', *Journal of Australian Studies*, vol. 24, 1989

—— *The State of Tasmania: Identity at federation time*, Hobart: THRA, 2001

Savery, Henry, *Quintus Servinton*, Brisbane: Jacaranda Press, 1962

—— *The Hermit in Van Diemen's Land*, St Lucia: University of Queensland Press, 1964

Shaw, A.G.L., *Convicts and the Colonies*, London: Faber & Faber, 1966

Shelton, D. (ed.), *The Parramore Letters: Letters from William Thomas Parramore*, Epping, N.S.W.: D. Shelton, 1993

Skemp, John Rowland, *Memories of Myrtle Bank: The bush-farming experiences of Rowland and Samuel Skemp*, Melbourne: Melbourne University Press, 1952

Smith, Babette, *A Cargo of Women: Susannah Watson and the convicts of the Princess Royal*, Kensington, N.S.W.: NSW University Press, 1988

—— *Australia's Birthstain: The startling legacy of the convict era*, Sydney: Allen & Unwin, 2008

Snowden, Dianne, 'A white rag burning: Irish women who committed arson in order to be transported to van Diemen's Land', *THRAPP*, vol. 56, no. 1, 2009

Stuart, Lurline (ed.), *Marcus Clarke: His natural life*, St Lucia: University of Queensland Press, 2001

Sturma, Michael, *Vice in a Vicious Society: Crime and convicts in mid-nineteenth century New South Wales*, St Lucia: University of Queensland Press, 1983

Tipping, Marjorie, *Convicts Unbound: The story of the* Calcutta *convicts and their settle-ment in Australia*, South Yarra: Viking O'Neil, 1988

Trollope, Anthony, *Australia and New Zealand*, vol. II, Melbourne: Robertson, 1876

Ullathorne, W., *The Catholic Mission in Australia*, London, 1837; this edition Adelaide: Libraries Board of South Australia, 1963

'The Vet' [J Hornsby], *Old Time Echoes of Tasmania*, Hobart: [no publisher named], 1895

Ward, Russel, *The Australian Legend*, Melbourne: Oxford University Press, 1966

West, John, *The History of Tasmania*, vols 1 and 2, Launceston: Henry Dowling, 1852

Whatley, Richard, *Remarks on Transportation, and on a Recent Defence of the System*, London: B. Fellowes, 1834

Winter, Gillian, ' "We speak that we do know, and testify that we have seen": Caroline Leakey's Tasmanian experiences and her novel *The Broad Arrow*', *THRAPP*, vol. 40, no. 4, 1993

Wood, G.A., 'Convicts' in *RAHS Journal*, VIII/IV, 1922

Young, David, *Making Crime Pay: The evolution of convict tourism in Tasmania*, Hobart: THRA, 1996

Surveys

In 1998 I published an article, 'The Legacy of the Convict System', in *Tasmanian Historical Studies*, vol. 6, no. 1, which comprised my initial work on this subject. In my research for this article I conducted a survey among 127 students at the University of Tasmania, where I was working part-time as a tutor, and I also interviewed nine elderly Tasmanians about their opinions on the convict stain: Cynthia Alexander, Angus Bethune, Roma Blackwood, Naomi Canning, Sue Collins, Heather Gibson, Pamela Pillinger, Eric Reece and Lindsay Whitham.

In 2006, when I decided to write this book, I conducted a longer survey among as many people as I could contact, eventually 451. They comprised 243 university students, and members of audiences I addressed: the Hobart University of the Third Age, the Bothwell Historical Society, the Tasmanian Historical Research Association, the Lindisfarne School for Seniors, the Tasmanian Family History Association (AGM and Hobart branch), and a Female Factory Research Group quiz night.

As further questions needed answering, in 2007–08 I conducted a smaller survey, qualitative rather than quantitative, with 156 respondents, mainly members of the Hobart University of the Third Age and several historical societies. (The 118 respondents mentioned in Chapter 13 were those from this group born before 1950.) I ran a class based on this book at the University of the Third Age, and many comments by class members are added in the text. Other people mentioned in the text, such as Bob McShane, Vicki Pearce, Pam Sharpe and Chris Wilson, provided stories, reminiscences, opinion and comment on an individual basis.

Convict records

Tasmania's convict records are housed in the Tasmanian Archive and Heritage Office (TAHO), State Library of Tasmania. The main groups I consulted for this book were

CON 31: conduct records of male convicts under assignment; CON 33: conduct records of male convicts under probation; CON 40: conduct records of female convicts under assignment; and CON 41: conduct records of female convicts under probation. More information about TAHO's convict records can be found at its website <www.statelibrary.tas.gov.au/tasmemory>.

INDEX